Themis Bar Review
Multistate Performance Test

ISBN 978-1-935445-89-0
1-935445-89-8

Table of Contents

How to Use This Book

Introduction to the Multistate Performance Test

Practice Multistate Performance Tests

HOW TO USE THIS BOOK

This book includes previously administered Multistate Performance Tests (MPTs), and is intended to be used in conjunction with the various components of the Themis MPT Workshop presented in the myThemis™ Learning Portal. Although you should feel free to practice as many of the Performance Tests in this volume as you are comfortable with, we encourage you to first view the MPT lecture series as assigned in your myTo-Do List for guidance as to how to prepare for this portion of the bar exam.

INTRODUCTION TO THE MULTISTATE PERFORMANCE TEST

Table of Contents

INTRODUCTION TO THE MULTISTATE PERFORMANCE TEST

I. INTRODUCTION

The Multistate Performance Test ("MPT") allows bar candidates an extremely short time in which to research and write a lawyer-like project. Here's the good news: you don't need to know *any* specific knowledge of the law to do well on the MPT. Everything you'll need to write a strong response is given to you by the National Conference of Bar Examiners—the issue to be addressed, the background of the issue, the facts on which the analysis will be based, and the legal authorities on which you will rely. As such, the MPT is commonly described, rightfully so, as an "open book" or "closed universe" examination. In law school parlance, the MPT may also resemble a "canned" memo project that you might have encountered during first-year legal writing, where it was your job to sift through pages and pages of factual and legal material—some relevant, some not so much—in an attempt to complete the writing assignment.

Be careful on the MPT, however. Even though you don't need to know any specific law, the MPT certainly isn't easy. On the MPT, you'll have to review and dissect more than a dozen densely filled pages of facts and legal authorities on your way to completing a polished legal document under stressful examination conditions. And you have only 90 minutes to do all of this!

But don't fret—you can easily conquer the MPT with practice. The following information is designed to help you understand the format of the MPT, to expose you to important considerations to keep in mind when preparing and outlining your response, and to give you advice and tips that you can use when you're ready to begin writing your response.

A. PURPOSE

The MPT is designed to test your ability to perform practical everyday tasks of a new lawyer, in the context of a specific problem involving a client. The MPT tests problem-solving skills through factual and legal analysis and the application of this analysis to the performance of the assigned task. Applicants perform tasks such as writing an objective memorandum or brief, a statement of the facts of a case, a witness cross-examination plan, and a closing argument, to identify just a few projects.

B. HISTORY

Having just celebrated its first decade as part of some states' bar examinations, the MPT has gained acceptance across the nation. Since it was first administered in 1997, at least 34 jurisdictions have included either one or two MPT questions in their bar examinations. In fact, 50 percent of all U.S. bar applicants take at least one MPT. If those testing in California and Pennsylvania—the two U.S. jurisdictions that develop their own performance tests—are included, more than two-thirds of all bar applicants take a performance test.

C. GRADING

The MPT is somewhat similar to traditional essay exams in that it asks for a written answer. There are some important differences, however. Because a full set of facts and a library of applicable law are provided in the testing materials, a mere recitation of the facts and the law alone won't count for much credit. Rather, examiners are looking for your ability to identify critical facts, complete a reasoned legal analysis, and organize and write an answer that reads clearly and concisely.

Moreover, the MPT tests a skill set that isn't otherwise tested on the bar examination—the ability to sort relevant and irrelevant facts, analyze the relevant law, and create a document similar to one that might be needed in practice. Because the question provides more time than a typical essay question, the MPT affords applicants with greater opportunity to show their ability to analyze and organize their answers in a compelling manner. As a result, many boards of law examiners have indicated that they find the MPT to be the most realistic test of what a new attorney might be asked to do.

MPT graders have reported that there isn't a great deal of disparity among the answers because the law is provided. Therefore, determining the relative quality of MPT answers is largely dependent on how well the applicants can apply the law to the facts and analyze the issues. The best MPT answers are typically those that most effectively use the facts.

Keep in mind that each jurisdiction determines the number of MPT's administered (either one or two) and how much weight is given to that portion of the exam in comparison to the other essays. Generally, the weight of each MPT is greater than a regular essay question, worth anywhere between 1.5 to 2.0 times a regular essay. While grading the MPT is the sole responsibility of the particular jurisdiction that adopted the MPT, the National Conference of Bar Examiners holds an MPT grading workshop for graders during the weekend following the bar examination and provides "Drafters' Point Sheets" to serve as helpful aids for jurisdictions in developing their own sample responses.

II.   SKILLS REQUIRED ON THE MULTISTATE PERFORMANCE TEST

According to the National Conference of Bar Examiners, the MPT requires applicants to: (1) sort detailed factual materials and separate relevant from irrelevant facts; (2) analyze statutory, case and administrative materials for relevant principles of law; (3) apply the relevant law to the relevant facts in a manner likely to resolve a client's problem; (4) identify and resolve ethical dilemmas, when present; (5) communicate effectively in writing; (6) complete a lawyering task within time constraints.

These skills are tested by requiring applicants to perform one of a variety of lawyering tasks. Although it isn't feasible to list all possibilities, examples of tasks applicants might be instructed to complete include drafting the following: a memorandum to a supervising attorney; a letter to a client; a persuasive memorandum or brief; a statement of facts; a contract provision; a will; a counseling plan; a proposal for settlement or agreement; a discovery plan; a witness examination plan; a closing argument. These, and other possible documents, are described below in Section V.C.

A.   TESTABLE AREAS

The National Conference of Bar Examiners has identified five testable areas on the MPT. Most questions will require you to tackle one or more of these skills.

1.   Factual Analysis

When testing on this area, the examiners will give you one of three possible tasks: (i) Draft an opening statement for trial; (ii) Draft a closing argument for trial; or (iii) Draft jury instructions.

2.   Fact Gathering

You will recognize this area because the examiners will present you with your client's case, and ask you what additional factual evidence you need to gather to improve your client's position.

3. **Legal Analysis and Reasoning**

You should demonstrate the ability to analyze statutory, case and administrative materials for relevant principles of law and apply them to specific factual situations. Think back to first-year legal research and writing. Legal analysis and reasoning includes the ability to: identify and formulate legal issues; identify relevant legal rules within a given set of legal materials; formulate relevant legal theories; elaborate legal theories; evaluate legal theories; and criticize and synthesize legal argumentation.

4. **Problem Solving**

You will recognize this area because it is the only MPT problem that asks you to go beyond the legal solutions to your client's problem by considering non-legal solutions.

You should demonstrate the ability to develop and evaluate strategies for solving a problem or accomplishing the objectives of your client. The problem-solving process includes the ability to identify and diagnose the problem, generate alternative solutions and strategies, and recommend a solution.

5. **Recognition and Resolution of Ethical Dilemmas**

You will recognize this area because when testing on ethical dilemmas, the examiners must include in the problem the code of ethics for lawyers in the relevant jurisdiction.

Keep in mind that not all MPTs will require you to identify and resolve ethical dilemmas. Because the MPT is considered a "closed universe" examination, if your test materials don't contain any legal authorities defining the appropriate ethical standards that exist in the jurisdiction, then you'll unlikely have to address any ethical concerns. If, on the other hand, your materials do contain applicable rules of professional conduct, whether excerpted from the relevant statute or hidden in case law, then it's a good bet that the examiners are looking for you to discuss these concerns.

B. OTHER SKILLS

In addition to the expressly identified skills noted above, the following skills are also necessary for any strong MPT response.

1. **Time Management**

Although it's not necessarily the most important substantive skill, applicants generally identify the issue of time management as one of their most problematic areas on the MPT. This shouldn't be too much of a surprise. The MPT is, for the most part, unfamiliar territory for many applicants, as they aren't exposed to examinations of this type during law school. On the MPT, you have only 90 minutes in which to read and analyze an assortment of unfamiliar materials, usually comprised of 12-25 pages of both facts and law, and to compose a sometimes similarly unfamiliar assignment.

Time management requires focus, discipline, and most importantly, the ability to separate the important from the unimportant—or, in legal terms, the relevant from the irrelevant. The MPT requires the applicant to discard certain facts and law in order to solve a problem. Compare that to law school essay examinations, where they typically contain only relevant facts, notwithstanding the occasional red herring.

2. Ability to Follow Directions

You must be able to follow directions. It sounds so simple, but it's often ignored in the haste to begin writing. The MPT is a task-specific assignment: you must perform the task identified to receive credit. If you are instructed to write a letter to a client in which you evaluate various courses of action and instead write a persuasive brief, you will have done nothing but demonstrate to the examiners your inability to read and follow simple directions.

3. Writing for the Proper Audience, With the Proper Style

Before writing your answer, you must identify who your audience is, and whether or not you are expected to be objective or subjective in your argument.

a. Audience

There are two possibilities for audience: (i) lay people (The jury or your client), or (ii) lawyers (partners in your firm, opposing counsel, or judges). When writing for lay people, do not use legal terminology. You may be asked to explain complex legal principles to lay people, but you must do it in a way that someone who does not have a legal education would understand.

b. Objective or persuasive

On every MPT, you will be required to determine if your answer is to objective or persuasive. Obviously, your emphasis will be quite different depending on which determination you make. If you are asked to write something that will go to the court (motions, trial briefs, etc.), you should always be persuasive. If, on the other hand, you are asked to draft a memo to the senior partner of your firm, laying out the strengths and weaknesses of your case, you should write objectively.

In both persuasive and objective answers, you must discuss not only the strengths of your case, but also the weaknesses. When are writing persuasively, it is acceptable to emphasize the strengths, and explain away the weaknesses.

4. Grammar, Punctuation, and Spelling

There is an old saying: "The devil is in the details." In and of itself, writing a document with grammatical errors and poor punctuation or spelling doesn't mean you're incompetent, and it probably won't be enough to fail the MPT in the absence of other problems. But poor grammar, punctuation, and spelling can certainly leave a bad impression on the examiners about your thoroughness and meticulousness in serving your client. Remember—the examiners, by administering the MPT, are gauging your abilities to be a lawyer. Not paying attention to the rules of English probably won't serve you—or your future clients—well.

III. COMPONENTS OF THE MULTISTATE PERFORMANCE TEST

Each MPT question typically contains two parts: the File and the Library. Usually, these two sections will be separated by a cover sheet, making the determination of which is the File and which is the Library quite easy. (The File is usually the first section, and the Library the second.) Occasionally, the information that might have been separately contained in the File and Library are combined in a single File section. If this is the case, look for any legal authorities in the File. Together, the information in the File and Library should total between 12 and 24 pages.

A. FILE

1. Task Memorandum

The first document in the File is the Task Memorandum (sometimes referred to as the Call Memorandum because it contains, of course, the call of the question). This is the most important item in the MPT materials because it tells you what you're supposed to do. As it will be discussed more fully below, you must carefully review the Task Memorandum and make sure you address the specific question or questions asked, format your response exactly as required, and follow all of the directions as closely as possible. Think of the Task Memorandum, which is usually from a supervising attorney, as your work assignment or project sheet.

2. Other Information

In addition to the Task Memorandum, the File consists of source documents containing all the facts of your case. The File might include, for example, transcripts of interviews, depositions, hearings or trials, pleadings, correspondence, client documents, contracts, newspaper articles, medical records, police reports, hospital records, and lawyer's notes. Relevant as well as irrelevant facts are included. Facts are sometimes ambiguous, incomplete, or even conflicting. As in practice, a client's or supervising attorney's version of events may be incomplete or unreliable.

B. LIBRARY

The Library consists of cases, statutes, regulations, and rules, some of which may not be relevant to the assigned lawyering task. MPT's are commonly set in the fictitious state of Franklin in the fictitious Fifteenth U.S. Circuit. The legal authorities listed above are written by the examiners specifically for the test question. They follow the common tiered system for courts: the trial court is the District Court; the intermediate appellate court is the Court of Appeal; and the highest court is the Supreme Court. The states of Columbia and Olympia are also fictitious states in the Fifteenth U.S. Circuit and are occasionally used in lieu of the state of Franklin.

In some instances, the Library will also include cases, statutes, and code from real jurisdictions. Don't be thrown off by these cases and statutes from, for example, the United States Supreme Court or the U.S. Code. You are still writing a document in the fictitious state of Franklin in the fictitious Fifteenth U.S. Circuit.

When reviewing the Library, you are expected to extract the legal principles necessary to analyze the problem and perform the task. Remember: the MPT isn't a test of substantive law, and problems may arise in a variety of fields. Library materials provide the necessary substantive information to complete the task. Don't fall into the trap of relying on law that you have learned elsewhere. The general instructions to the MPT state: "What you have learned in law school and elsewhere provides the general background for analyzing the problem, the information in the File and Library provide the specific materials with which you must work." This means that you are not allowed to discuss or apply any law that is outside of what is contained in the library.

IV. OVERVIEW OF STRATEGY—*RED ROW*

Although there are no restrictions on how you apportion your time, you should be sure to allocate ample time to reading and digesting the materials and organizing your answer before you begin writing it. A good rule of thumb is to divide your time equally—45 minutes reading and organizing (which includes outlining) and 45 minutes writing your response. Below is a skeleton of the recommended strategy for approaching the MPT. Think of the mnemonic device *RED ROW.*

> ➤ **R**ead the Instructions, Task Memorandum, and Instruction Sheet
>
> ➤ **E**valuate task
>
> ➤ **D**etermine format
>
> ➤ **R**ead Library and File
>
> ➤ **O**utline response
>
> ➤ **W**rite your document

V.   PUTTING *RED ROW* INTO PRACTICE

A.   READ INSTRUCTIONS AND TASK MEMORANDUM

Before diving into the MPT question, you should quickly review the general instructions even though you'll likely be familiar with them as a result of all of your preparation. After all, the examiners can change the directions at any time, and your familiarity with the instructions on past MPT examinations will help you quickly identify any new or amended directions, if any, that you need to pay attention to.

After reviewing the instructions, carefully examine the Task Memorandum. This is the single most important page (sometimes two pages) in the File because it contains your directions, introduces your problem, and identifies your task. After reading the Task Memorandum, you'll know whether you're to write an objective memorandum, a persuasive brief, a client letter, or any one of a number of other possibilities. The information contained in the Task Memorandum provides the foundation and guidance for the rest of your time and effort on the MPT.

You should read the Task Memorandum at least twice to be certain you have identified your task and the issue or issues to be resolved. So that you don't lose sight of the issue that needs addressing, you should write the issue on the top of the Task Memorandum or on a scratch piece of paper (if your jurisdiction provides it) to remind yourself of the question that's posed as you work your way through the facts and law.

B.   EVALUATE TASK

When examining the Task Memorandum, you must read it pro-actively, with a critical eye toward solving a specific problem. You must read carefully and quickly while, at the same time, anticipating the information that may be contained in the File and Library that could help address the particular issue you have been asked to resolve. Look for key words in the question. Are you asked to *discuss, explain, describe, argue, prove, dispute, disprove, justify, analyze*? Each of these terms denotes a different approach to the question and will mean a different approach when you write your document.

Also, make sure you follow the directions contained in the Task Memorandum. While the directions may ask you to draft an objective memorandum, the Task Memorandum may give you specific instructions on how to format the document or information on what include (and not include) in the document. For instance, the Task Memorandum, even when asking you to draft an objective memorandum, may ask you to identify additional facts that would strengthen a party's position, state the most persuasive arguments that can be made to support a given position, or identify likely outcomes. Failure to address all of the questions posed to you by the Task Memorandum raises a red flag that you might not be addressing a client's concerns or objectives fully.

The Task Memorandum will indicate the document you'll have to draft. As a result of law school, you're most likely familiar with the format and structure of common legal documents.

C.   DETERMINE FORMAT

Sometimes, however, you might be asked to create a document that you might not have ever drafted or—*even worse*—ever seen. For instance, you might be asked to draft jury instructions, commentary to legislation, a premarital property agreement, or even a last will and testament. Usually, if you're asked to draft a document that examiners think would be unfamiliar to those with only three years of classroom training, they will include a separate Instruction Sheet which explains how to set out the document and gives an example of how the document should look. Even so, you should familiarize yourself with the common documents, the structure or form of the documents, the minimum components of the documents, and the legal standard (if any) to be used.

The following are some common documents that applicants have been asked to draft:

1.   Memorandum of Law

A memorandum of law is an *objective*, even-handed document in which the attorney presents all of the arguments that either side could make, assessing the relative strength of each. Attorneys and their clients rely on solid, objective memoranda of law in making key strategy decisions. Because a memorandum of law is written for those familiar with the law (usually a supervising attorney, an associate attorney or a judge), it is important that it be straightforward and even-handed. Although it's appropriate to use legal terminology in a memorandum of law, you should fully discuss or define legal terms that aren't commonly used.

2.   Pleadings

The first essential of good pleading is to be clear. The next is to be brief.

a. Complaint

A complaint sets out the basic facts and legal reasons that a plaintiff believes are sufficient to support a claim against a defendant. You may be asked to draft either a civil or a criminal complaint. A complaint is *persuasive*.

b. Answer

Like a complaint, an answer is *persuasive*. An answer is the defendant's response to the plaintiff's complaint in which the defendant may deny any of plaintiff's allegations, offer any defenses, and make any counterclaims against the plaintiff, cross-claims against other defendants, or third-party claims against third parties otherwise not involved in the lawsuit.

3.   Motions

A motion is a written application asking the judge to make a ruling or order on a legal issue. Motions to dismiss and motions for summary judgment are two common pretrial motions.

a. Motion to dismiss

By filing a motion to dismiss, the defendant requests the court to dismiss the lawsuit because the plaintiff isn't entitled to any legal relief. This is a *persuasive* document.

b. Motion for summary judgment

By making a motion for summary judgment, the moving party claims that all necessary factual issues are resolved or need not be tried because they are so one-sided. Like motions to dismiss, the motion must *persuade* the judge to act.

c. Motion in limine

This is *persuasive* pretrial motion that requests the court to issue an interlocutory order that prevents an opposing party from introducing or referring to potentially irrelevant, prejudicial, redundant, or otherwise inadmissible evidence until the court has ruled on its admissibility.

4. Writings to Parties

If ask to draft a correspondence, you will likely either address your client or opposing counsel.

a. Letters to client

The purpose of a client or opinion letter is to inform and advise the client about the case. The letter may respond to a particular concern raised by the client, or it may be a more general assessment of the situation. Either way, the letter is always *objective*. In addition to assessing the strengths and weaknesses of your client's legal position on a given matter, the letter may suggest strategy or request further information.

b. Letters to opposing counsel

Letters to opposing counsel include demand and negotiation letters. They are always *persuasive* documents. Writing to an opposing attorney isn't easy. You must weigh your words as carefully as any professional writer might in writing an article or essay. Your job isn't just to win court cases, it is to maintain relationships and sell your settlements so that you never even get to court. Your tone should be less formal than if you were writing to a judge, but avoid the stodgy, arrogant, or overbearing writing style.

5. Other Documents

a. Persuasive briefs

Persuasive briefs may be either trial or appellate briefs, and as the name suggests, they're *persuasive* in tone and analysis. A trial brief is designed to convince the trial judge to adopt a legal standard or to rule a certain way at trial. An appellate brief is a document submitted to an appeals court. It contains all the legal arguments as to why your client should win the case. Its purpose is to persuade the judges to rule In your client's favor.

b. Position papers

A position paper is an essay that presents an opinion about an issue. Position papers range from the simplest format of a letter to the editor through to the most complex in the form of an academic position paper (think law review article). Because position papers are most useful in contexts where detailed comprehension of one's views is important, in an attempt to cause change, they represent a *persuasive* document.

c. Statement of facts

A statement of facts is a legal document that sets forward factual information without argument. The goal of a statement of facts is to present factual information in a clear, easy to understand way. Remember to include only the legally significant facts in your statement of facts as the File will likely include information that might not be relevant to the issue. Also, make sure you include legally significant facts that both favor and hurt your client's position, although of course, you'll want to focus the statement of facts so that the positive facts are highlighted. While statements of fact are generally *objective*, they may become slightly *persuasive* by highlighting favorable facts and de-emphasizing damaging information.

d. Discovery requests

Sometimes, the examiners will ask you to draft certain discovery requests: interrogatories, requests for admissions, written deposition questions, etc. If this is the case, the examiners will likely provide an instruction sheet with examples.

e. Opening statements and closing arguments

Both opening statements and closing arguments are *persuasive* pieces while not being argumentative. An opening statement starts the trial, and it's generally the first time that the judge or jury hears from you. The opening statement is generally constructed to serve as a "road map," giving the judge or jury a preview of things to come. A closing argument is your concluding statement at trial, which reiterates the important arguments for the judge or jury. It may not contain any new information and may only use evidence introduced during trial. To draft effective and persuasive opening statements and closing arguments, you need to be a zealous advocate for your client—the more persuasive you are, the more likely you'll be forwarding your client's interests. Emphasize the strengths of your case, and don't concede weak positions.

D. READ LIBRARY AND FILE

Generally, reading the Library before you read the File is the suggested approach to attacking the testing materials. By reading the law in the Library first, your subsequent reading of the File will be formed by your knowledge of the controlling statutes and cases. If you read the File first, it may prove difficult to distinguish the relevant from the irrelevant information. You may not be able to distinguish which facts are relevant and important until you know the law and how the cases in your jurisdiction have interpreted that law. The one exception is when confronted with a problem-solving task. In that case, the file should be read first, followed by the library.

Also, keep in mind that some File and Library materials may be irrelevant; after all, one skill tested by the National Conference of Bar Examiners is your ability to sort out the irrelevancies. Keep the following considerations in mind.

1. Considerations When Reading the Library

a. Read carefully

Recall that all of the legal authorities you need are contained in the Library. Therefore, it is important that you spend an adequate amount of time reading the information in it. Some applicants make the fatal mistake of breezing through statutes or cases that contain legal rules with which they feel comfortable in law school. Remember that the examiners may have rewritten statutes and cases in whole or in part or may have created new legal authorities altogether. So, the elements of adverse possession that you learned in law school might not be the same as that followed by the Franklin courts. Thus, if you examine the issue using elements of common law adverse possession, you'll most likely fail to establish adverse possession in Franklin.

b. Note the jurisdiction and dates of the cases

Knowing the jurisdiction and dates of the cases appearing in the Library is important in jurisdictions that follow common law like Franklin. A recent decision in Franklin will be given great weight. Next in descending order would be recent precedent in jurisdictions whose law is the same as Franklin law. Least weight would be given to precedent that stems from dissimilar circumstances, older cases that have since been contradicted, or cases in jurisdictions that have dissimilar law. Don't assume that the cases in the Library are all controlling cases from the Franklin Supreme Court. They're not.

c. Cross-reference the cases

It's important to examine the cases in relation to each other. For instance, one case might be cited by another case. Recognize the significance of the referencing of one legal authority in other legal authority. Usually, a case that cites to another case in the Library will elaborate on a particular rule of law put forward in that earlier case, develop an exception to that earlier rule, or furnish you with a factual distinction from your problem. You should read cases in the Library in the order they were decided, beginning with the earliest.

d. Pay attention to footnotes

Examiners use footnotes in hopes that you will overlook the important information contained in them. After all, footnotes are in smaller print and located at the very bottom of the page. Don't fall for this trick.

e. Dissect block quotations

A block quotation, also known as a long quotation, is a quotation in a written document, usually a case, set off from the main text as a distinct paragraph or block. A block quotation is often distinguished visually using indentation on both the left and right sides. Examiners sometimes use block quotations because they want to make sure there is no ambiguity or uncertainty as to how the specific language is written. When examiners use block quotations, you'll usually incorporate some of that language in your own document because it contains elements or factors of a rule.

f. Look for commentary

Pay close attention to any "official comments" or other commentary in a statute or code provision. Examiners oftentimes include such commentary to highlight an issue, draw your attention to counterarguments, or signal a legal distinction. In the absence of any cases addressing the statute or code provision, the commentary provides an alternative mechanism on how to interpret the legislation.

g. Address all of the library materials

It should be apparent by now that not all of the legal authorities in the Library will be relevant. But that doesn't mean that you can simply ignore the case, statute or code provision. Even if the particular legal authority has no place in your document, you should still include the irrelevant authority and quickly explain why it doesn't apply to your particular situation. You don't want to spend too much time doing so—a short sentence or two will be sufficient to show the examiners that you did examine all of the library materials and you understood that it didn't apply to the situation at hand.

2. Considerations When Reading the File

One of your biggest challenges will be to identify the relevant facts from the irrelevant ones. Don't be surprised if you find yourself reading a fair amount of material that you believe will be irrelevant to your actual analysis of the problem. Following the tips below will help you find, keep and discard the appropriate facts.

a. Identify the parties

While it's self-evident to identify the parties in the File materials, it's also important to recognize their legal relationships to each other as well as to your client. By understanding how the parties are connected to one another, you'll be more aware of the legal significance of the facts contained in the File materials.

b. Stay on the issue

As noted above, you should write the issue on the top of the Task Memorandum or on a scratch piece of paper to remind yourself of the question that's posed as you work your way through the facts and law. By reading the File with the issue at the forefront of your mind, you can more easily identify the legally relevant facts from the avalanche of information given to you.

c. Attack the shorter documents first

It's not uncommon for the File materials to contain several documents of different lengths. For instance, you might have a one-page police report, a two-page interview, and a six-page deposition transcript. You should read the shorter documents first as these are likely to contain important nuggets of information that might give you a more informed reading of the longer documents.

d. Read the facts with a critical eye

As you read through the File documents, you should pay just as much attention to the information that's not included in the File as you do to the information that's included in it. Ask yourself whether additional facts would have made the issue easier to address and, further, why the examiners intentionally left out that piece of information. Knowing what's in and not in the File should help you focus your response to the issue at hand.

E. OUTLINE RESPONSE

Recall that the instructions state that the MPT "will be graded on your responsiveness to instructions regarding the task you are to complete, which are given to you in the first memorandum in the File, and on the content, thoroughness and organization of your response." You are graded on the "thoroughness and organization" of your response. Outlining your answer in advance is the key to being "thorough" and to good "organization."

Write a brief scratch-paper outline—phrases, words, ideas—that's not too long, but enough to give you a path through the document and make you feel like you know what you will do. In the outline, make sure you include the elements of the rules and the facts you'll be using to establish those elements.

F. WRITE YOUR DOCUMENT

Once you've finished your reading of the Library and File, you're ready to begin the task of writing your document. At this point, you should have half of your time remaining, or 45 minutes. Double-check the Task Memorandum once again to verify your task. Rely on your outline that you just constructed to make sure you address all of the points and included all of the legally significant facts in your document. Under the stress of exam conditions, even the most conscientious of students sometimes inadvertently miss an important argument or fact.

1. Considerations When Writing Your Document

a. Pay attention to format

Remember: the Task Memorandum will help you structure your document. If the Task Memorandum asks you to draft a client letter, then begin your document with a mock letterhead. Don't forget, also, to include the salutation (*e.g.*, "Dear Ms. Smith:"). If the Task Memorandum requires you to write a trial brief, don't forget to include the appropriate case caption. If the Task Memorandum doesn't provide you with an organizational approach, organize your document issue by issue if it is *objective*, or argument-by-argument if it is *persuasive*.

b. Pay close attention to the question asked

Once of the worse things you can do is to spend 45 minutes writing a polished document that doesn't address the issue presented to you. Not only will have you wasted half of your time, the examiners won't have known the amount of work you put into reading, analyzing and outlining the materials in the File and Library. So always verify that you're addressing the specific question or questions asked of you in the Task Memorandum.

c. **Don't add or invent facts (unless asked to do so)**

Again, the MPT is a "closed universe" examination. That means all of the information you need to develop your arguments and complete your document is contained in the testing materials. Therefore, you need not add facts to the File. There is one noteworthy exception, however. Sometimes, the directions on the MPT may ask you to identify additional facts that would strengthen or, alternatively, weaken a party's position. If you are to explore the effect or impact of additional "hypothetical" facts, the Task Memorandum will likely expressly indicate so.

d. **Use headings**

Headings guide the examiner through your document. You should use headings to make your arguments stand out to the reader. You can also use them to help you clarify and develop your analyses. For instance, if you have headings with very little discussion underneath, consider either expanding your analysis a bit more or combining the headings so that you discuss additional arguments under a broader topic heading.

e. **Budget your time carefully**

Forty-five minutes should be sufficient time for you to complete your document regardless of the particular assignment you're asked to draft. This assumption, however, is predicated on the fact that you've satisfactorily completed the earlier steps of RED ROW within the suggested time limits, including outlining your response. Developing a good outline on the front end will make the final 45 minutes for the writing process much easier.

f. **Remember: grammar, spelling and punctuation counts**

Again, the examiners are testing your ability to communicate well, both verbally and in a written format. The writing part means spelling, grammar, punctuation, capitalization and vocabulary. Even if all you want to do is spend your time in a courtroom, you'll still, at least sometimes, have to file motions and briefs that you'll end up writing or editing. Show the examiners that you'll be able to "sound" like a lawyer when you're communicating with clients or other attorneys.

g. **Know your audience**

Does the Task Memorandum ask you to draft a *persuasive* or *objective* document? Make sure you're clear as to the tone of your document. It will usually be guided by the party who will be reading your document in your factual situation. The goal of persuasive legal writing seems obvious enough. For instance, you might want the court—whether at the trial or appellate level—to adopt your client's position, no more, no less. The goal of objective legal writing is to provide a balanced assessment of the situation. You should make sure you examine both the strengths and weaknesses of not only your client but also the opposing party.

h. **Don't forget IRAC**

Good legal writing is good legal writing. What you learned in first-year legal writing is also applicable on the MPT (and the rest of the essays on the bar examination, for that matter).

i. Assume that the reader hasn't read the file or library

Your job after 90 minutes is to have produced a lawyer-like task. The fruits of your labor will be a memorandum of law, a trial brief, a set of interrogatories, or a number of other possibilities. Your final work-product should be able to stand up by itself. In other words, an outside reader—in this case, the examiner—should be able to read your document and understand the background of the case at hand, the materially significant facts involved, and the basis of the legal authorities you've used to make an argument and reach a conclusion. By assuming that the reader hasn't read the file or library, you should be more alert and aware of incorporating more facts and law into your document.

j. Citations

Although citations aren't necessary, applicants should use them when writing for an audience of lawyers or judges. After all, it's a good idea to show the examiner from where you obtained the information. This applies to materials you're referencing from both the File and Library.

k. Use common sense

Although all of the information is provided to you in the File and Library, you should let your experience of the world and your common sense guide you in interpreting these materials. Common sense is essential to solving real-world problems, and it's just as important to rely on commonsensical principles of interpretation and construction when analyzing facts and law.

l. Reach a conclusion

Lawyers are expected to reach conclusions based on a reasoned analysis. For example, either plaintiff wins or defendant wins. You're expected to reach conclusions in your document as well.

m. Practice, practice, practice

The key to success on the MPT is practice, practice, and more practice. You need to be able to put all of the above strategies to the test, and the only way to do so is to sit down and take several past MPT questions. Your goal during practice sessions is to spend the time acquainting yourself with the format of the examination and reacquainting yourself with the mechanics of legal writing and the persuasiveness and objectivity that goes along with the documents.

VI. CONCLUSION

Keep these tips in mind as you're taking the MPT:

➢ Budget your time.

➢ Focus on the call of the question.

➢ Be organized.

➢ Write clearly and concisely.

➢ Use the appropriate format and tone for the assigned document.

➢ Remember that the MPT is a test of fundamental lawyering skills rather than substantive knowledge.

Practice Multistate Performance Tests

THE MPT®

MULTISTATE PERFORMANCE TEST

In re Field Hogs, Inc.

In re Field Hogs, Inc.

In re Field Hogs, Inc.

FILE

LIBRARY

POINT SHEET

Instructions

The back cover of each test form contains the following instructions:

You will have 90 minutes to complete this session of the examination. This performance test is designed to evaluate your ability to handle a select number of legal authorities in the context of a factual problem involving a client.

The problem is set in the fictitious state of Franklin, in the fictitious Fifteenth Circuit of the United States. Columbia and Olympia are also fictitious states in the Fifteenth Circuit. In Franklin, the trial court of general jurisdiction is the District Court, the intermediate appellate court is the Court of Appeal, and the highest court is the Supreme Court.

You will have two kinds of materials with which to work: a File and a Library. The first document in the File is a memorandum containing the instructions for the task you are to complete. The other documents in the File contain factual information about your case and may include some facts that are not relevant.

The Library contains the legal authorities needed to complete the task and may also include some authorities that are not relevant. Any cases may be real, modified, or written solely for the purpose of this examination. If the cases appear familiar to you, do not assume that they are precisely the same as you have read before. Read them thoroughly, as if they all were new to you. You should assume that the cases were decided in the jurisdictions and on the dates shown. In citing cases from the Library, you may use abbreviations and omit page references.

Your response must be written in the answer book provided. If you are taking the examination on a laptop computer, your jurisdiction will provide you with specific instructions. In answering this performance test, you should concentrate on the materials in the File and Library. What you have learned in law school and elsewhere provides the general background for analyzing the problem; the File and Library provide the specific materials with which you must work.

Although there are no restrictions on how you apportion your time, you should be sure to allocate ample time (about 45 minutes) to reading and digesting the materials and to organizing your answer before you begin writing it. You may make notes anywhere in the test materials; blank pages are provided at the end of the booklet. You may not tear pages from the question booklet.

This performance test will be graded on your responsiveness to the instructions regarding the task you are to complete, which are given to you in the first memorandum in the File, and on the content, thoroughness, and organization of your response.

In re Field Hogs, Inc.

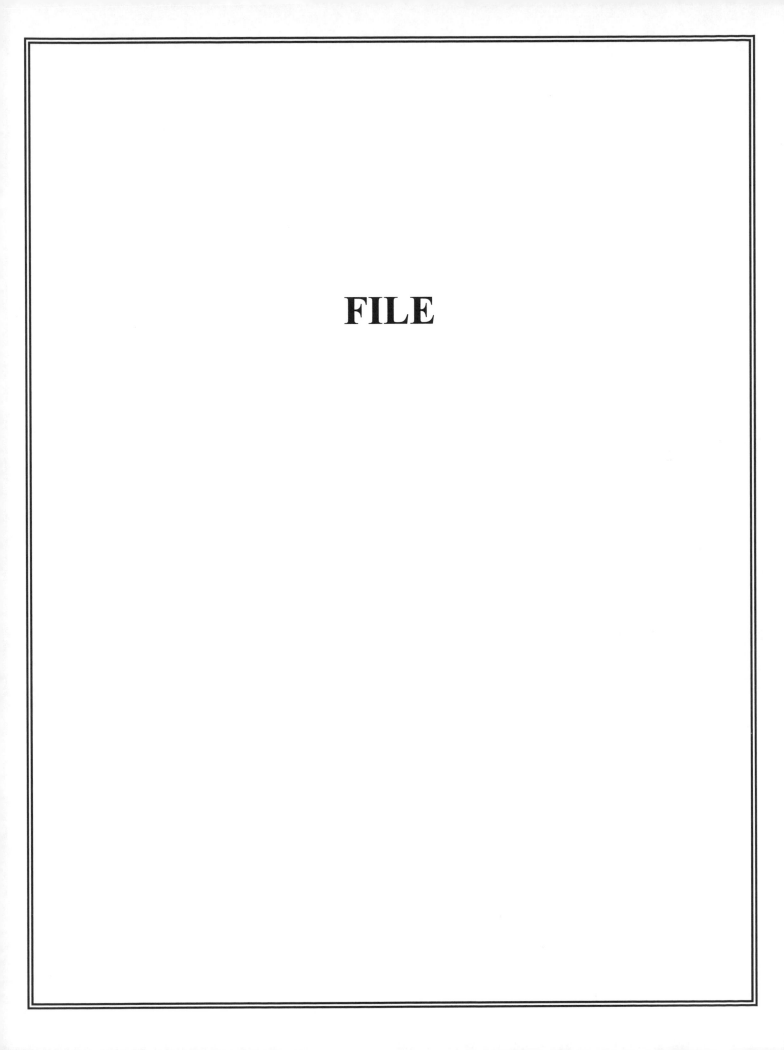

FILE

In re Field Hogs, Inc.

Delmore, DeFranco, and Whitfield, LLC
Attorneys at Law
1800 Hinman Avenue
Windsor, Franklin 33732

TO: Examinee
FROM: Carlotta DeFranco
DATE: July 26, 2011
RE: Arbitration Clause for Field Hogs, Inc.

Our firm has represented Field Hogs, Inc., for over seven years. Field Hogs manufactures heavy lawn equipment for the consumer market. We have represented Field Hogs in four lawsuits in Franklin. The last case received a lot of negative publicity, and the company is concerned about reducing the costs of litigation and avoiding negative publicity for any future claims.

Accordingly, Field Hogs has asked us to draft an arbitration clause to insert into its consumer sales contracts. I attach a copy of the firm's standard commercial arbitration clause, which has not been used in consumer transactions.

The client may be able to avoid litigation through arbitration, but also may face extra costs with arbitration. Please draft a memorandum for me in which you address the following:

(1)(a) Would the firm's clause cover arbitration of all potential claims by consumers against Field Hogs under Franklin law? Why or why not? Be sure to explain how your conclusion is supported by the applicable law.

(b) Would the firm's clause's allocation of arbitration costs be enforceable against consumers under Franklin law? Why or why not? Be sure to explain how your conclusion is supported by the applicable law.

(2)   Draft an arbitration clause for Field Hogs's consumer sales contracts that will be enforceable under Franklin law, and briefly explain how your draft language addresses the client's priorities, as described in the attached client meeting summary.

Do not concern yourself with the Federal Arbitration Act; focus solely on Franklin state law issues.

Delmore, DeFranco, and Whitfield, LLC

OFFICE MEMORANDUM

TO: File
FROM: Carlotta DeFranco
DATE: July 19, 2011
RE: Client Meeting Summary: Bradley Hewlett, Field Hogs COO

Today, I met with Bradley Hewlett, chief operating officer of Field Hogs since its founding in 1998. Hewlett is well versed in Field Hogs's business and has the authority to make decisions concerning any litigation involving the company.

Field Hogs designs and manufactures heavy lawn, garden, and field maintenance equipment, which it markets to consumers. Its product lines include heavy-duty lawn mowers (the Lawn Hog line), medium-duty walk-behind brush mowers (the Brush Hog line), and heavy- duty walk-behind field-clearing equipment (the Field Boar line). Lawn Hogs mow large acreages that require frequent mowing, Brush Hogs clear fields of tall grass and saplings one inch or less in diameter, and Field Boars take down saplings up to three inches in diameter.

Field Hogs sells only in Franklin. Its products sell best in semirural areas surrounding major metropolitan areas—the right combination of income and demand.

Hewlett explained that because Field Hogs markets to consumers, it makes product safety a centerpiece of its research and marketing. It holds patents on several devices that prevent its machines from moving or cutting when the operator does not have a grip on the machine. All of Field Hogs's equipment can do real damage if not used properly, so the company invests enormous effort in making its safety features work well and durably, and in writing clear operating instructions.

Hewlett stated that Field Hogs made some mistakes in its product manuals a few years back that cost the company a lot of money. In fact, Hewlett stated, "While we've gotten very careful about what we do, we're also realistic. We know we can't keep everybody from misusing our products. Still, if we can avoid some costs on the really frivolous tort cases, that would greatly reduce our litigation expenses."

The *James* case, and the publicity surrounding it, was a wake-up call for the company. Hewlett stated:

> That was the case where a Field Boar basically ran over the customer. It was terrible. We wanted to settle the case, even though we knew that the customer had misused the machine. But as you know, the customer wouldn't hear of it. The litigation costs and fees drew down our reserves, and until the verdict, we had trouble with potential lenders because of the bad publicity. We were very satisfied with the verdict in our favor, but as you told us, it could have gone either way, and a large judgment could have ruined us. We realized that you can't control what will happen with juries, and win or lose, the expenses of litigation can really get out of hand.

Hewlett added that the company is "very interested in arbitration, even though we know that it, too, can be very expensive." He went on to add that he hopes that arbitration will be less public, yield lower awards, and be less expensive than traditional litigation. Hewlett also anticipates that professional arbitrators will be more predictable than juries. With respect to the costs of arbitration, Hewlett stated, "We know that we'll have to pay for the arbitrator's time and that it's not cheap. But when we've arbitrated contract disputes with our suppliers, we've basically split costs down the middle, so we want to do that here, too."

Hewlett stated that Field Hogs definitely doesn't want to spend a lot of time litigating the validity of the arbitration clause. Hewlett is aware that Field Hogs's sales contracts already say that Franklin law applies, and he wants to know what Franklin law says about arbitration in such consumer transactions.

Hewlett closed our meeting by saying, "It's especially important to know exactly what we can expect as our products get into the hands of more and more people, but avoiding jury trials is the most important thing to me."

I told Hewlett that we would do some research on the points raised in our meeting and get back to him.

Delmore, DeFranco, and Whitfield, LLC

OFFICE MEMORANDUM

TO: File
FROM: Carlotta DeFranco
DATE: January 20, 2011
RE: Summary of Tort Litigation Against Field Hogs, Inc.

Majeski v. Field Hogs, Inc. (Franklin Dist. Ct. 2004): Plaintiff buyer sued for foot injuries resulting from improper use of safety handle on a Brush Hog. Plaintiff claimed inadequate warnings and defects in design and manufacture under negligence, warranty, and strict liability theories. During discovery, plaintiff conceded that his use of the machine did not comply with instructions printed in manual. RESULT: summary judgment for Field Hogs.

Johan v. Field Hogs, Inc. (Franklin Dist. Ct. 2005): Plaintiff buyer sued for serious leg injuries resulting from improper use of Brush Hog on a slope. Plaintiff's claims identical to those in *Majeski*. The company's manual was ambiguous about the maximum slope for recommended use. Trial court denied Field Hogs's motion for summary judgment. RESULT: verdict for plaintiff for $1.5 million.

Saunders v. Field Hogs, Inc. (Franklin Dist. Ct. 2008): Plaintiff buyer sued for knee injuries incurred while standing in front of a Lawn Hog during operation by another. Plaintiff conceded operation of mower by her 10-year-old son; the company's manual did not clearly warn against use of mower by minor children. RESULT: verdict for plaintiff for $400,000.

James v. Field Hogs, Inc. (Franklin Dist. Ct. 2010): Plaintiff buyer sued for permanent disfigurement in an accident involving a Field Boar, relying on defective design and manufacture theories. Discovery revealed factual conflict regarding plaintiff's compliance with instructions during operation of machine. The *Franklin Journal* published a three-part article about the case, focusing on the "Costs of

Justice" for plaintiffs. RESULT: verdict for Field Hogs.

Delmore, DeFranco, and Whitfield, LLC
Standard Commercial Arbitration Clause

Any claim or controversy arising out of or relating to this contract or the breach thereof shall be settled by arbitration. Arbitration shall occur in accordance with the rules and procedures for arbitration promulgated by the National Arbitration Organization.

National Arbitration Organization:
Procedures for Consumer-Related Disputes

Payment of Arbitrator's Fees

If all claims and counterclaims are less than $75,000, then the consumer is responsible for one-half of the arbitrator's fees up to a maximum of $750. The consumer must pay this amount as a deposit. It is refunded if not used.

If all claims and counterclaims equal or exceed $75,000, then the consumer is responsible for one-half of the arbitrator's fees. The consumer must deposit one-half of the arbitrator's estimated compensation in advance. It is refunded if not used.

The business must pay for all arbitrator compensation beyond the amounts that are the responsibility of the consumer. The business must deposit in advance the arbitrator's estimated compensation, less any amounts required as deposits from the consumer. These deposits are refunded if not used.

Administrative Fees

In addition to the arbitrator's fees, the consumer must pay a one-time $2,000 administrative fee.

Arbitrator's Fees

Arbitrators receive $1,000/day for each day of hearing plus an additional $200/hour for time spent on pre- and post-hearing matters.

LIBRARY

LeBlanc v. Sani-John Corporation

Franklin Court of Appeal (2003)

In 1998, Jacques LeBlanc began servicing and cleaning Sani-John's portable toilets in Franklin City under a service contract. The service contract, drafted by Sani-John, contained a provision requiring arbitration in Franklin of "any controversy or claim arising out of or relating to this agreement, or the breach thereof."

Pursuant to this contract, Sani-John supplied LeBlanc with all chemicals required to clean and service the toilets. After several months, LeBlanc allegedly suffered injury from exposure to these chemicals. LeBlanc filed a complaint against Sani-John, alleging in tort that Sani-John had failed to warn him of the dangerous and toxic nature of these chemicals and had also failed to provide him with adequate instructions for their safe use.

Sani-John sought to compel arbitration pursuant to the contract. The district court found that LeBlanc's claims "arose out of or related to . . . his contract with defendant Sani-John; they were for personal injuries LeBlanc received while performing on that contract." The court granted Sani-John's motion to compel arbitration.

LeBlanc appeals, arguing that the arbitration clause in his contract with Sani-John does not subject him to arbitration over his tort claims against Sani-John. The arbitration clause here provided:

> Any controversy or claim arising out of or relating to this agreement, or the breach thereof, shall be settled by arbitration.

Franklin courts generally favor arbitration as a mode of resolution and have adopted broad statements of public policy to that end. In *New Home Builders, Inc. v. Lake St. Clair Recreation Association* (Fr. Ct. App. 1999), we held that all disputes between contracting parties should be arbitrated according to the arbitration clause in the contract unless it can be said with positive assurance that the arbitration clause does not cover the dispute. As we said then and reaffirm here, only *the most forceful evidence* of purpose to exclude a claim from arbitration can prevail over a broad contractual arbitration clause. *Id.*

Arbitration promotes efficiency in time and money when a dispute between parties is

contractual in nature. However, when a dispute is not contractual but arises in tort, our courts have been reluctant to compel arbitration. Some courts have limited arbitration clauses where tort claims are concerned. In *Norway Farms v. Dairy and Drovers Union* (Fr. Ct. App. 2001), for example, the court of appeal opined that "absent a clear explicit statement in a contract directing an arbitrator to hear tort claims by one party against another, it must be assumed that the parties did not intend to withdraw such disputes from judicial authority."

This approach suggests that unless the parties have explicitly included tort actions within the scope of an arbitration clause, they must not have intended such claims to be subject to arbitration.

Cases in other jurisdictions suggest that, even where the arbitration clause explicitly covers tort claims, public policy may bar compelling arbitration of such claims. For example, in *Willis v. Redibuilt Mobile Home, Inc.* (Olympia Ct. App. 1995), the Olympia Court of Appeal reversed a trial court's order compelling arbitration of a products liability claim. The relevant arbitration clause provided:

> Any claim, dispute, or controversy (whether in contract, tort, or otherwise) arising from or related to the sale of the Mobile Home shall be subject to binding arbitration in accordance with the rules of the Olympia Arbitration Association.

The Olympia court reasoned that the plaintiffs' products liability claims "did not require an examination of the parties' respective obligations and performance under the contract." *Id.* Further, the court suggested that "[t]he tort claims are independent of the sale. Plaintiffs could maintain such claims against defendants regardless of the warranty and the sale transaction." *Id.*

In the case at hand, the arbitration clause contains no explicit reference to tort claims but requires arbitration only of those disputes "arising out of or relating to this agreement, or the breach thereof." In our view, for the dispute to "arise out of or relate to" the contract, the dispute must raise some issue the resolution of which requires construction of the contract itself. The relationship between the dispute and the contract does not exist simply because the dispute would not have arisen absent the existence of a contract between the parties.

If such a connection to the contract is not present, the parties could not have intended tort claims to be subject to arbitration under a clause covering only claims "arising out of or relating to" the contract. If the duty allegedly breached is one that law and public policy impose, and one that the defendant owes generally to others beyond the contracting parties, then a dispute over the breach of that duty does not arise from the contract. Instead, it sounds in tort. An arbitration clause that covers only contract-related claims (like the clause at issue here) would not apply.

We do not reach the question of how to interpret an arbitration clause that explicitly includes tort claims within its scope. We are troubled by the Olympia court's view that parties may never agree to arbitrate future tort claims. We see no reason to go so far. We note only that parties should clearly and explicitly express an intent to require the arbitration of claims sounding in tort. In turn, courts should strictly construe any clause that purports to compel arbitration of tort claims.

The contract in this case does not clearly and explicitly express the requisite intent. Therefore, the judgment of the trial court is reversed, and the matter is remanded for reinstatement of LeBlanc's complaint.

Reversed and remanded.

Howard v. Omega Funding Corporation

Franklin Supreme Court (2004)

Defendant Omega Funding Corp. (Omega) extends loans to consumer borrowers. In December 1999, Omega entered into an automobile loan contract with plaintiff Angela Howard, a 72-year-old woman with only a grade-school education and little financial sophistication. The $18,700 loan was secured with a security interest in the car purchased by Howard and bore an annual interest rate of 17 percent.

The loan contract contains an arbitration agreement that allows either party to elect binding arbitration as the forum to resolve covered claims. Regarding costs, the agreement provides as follows:

> At the conclusion of the arbitration, the arbitrator will decide who will ultimately be responsible for paying the filing, administrative, and/or hearing fees in connection with the arbitration.

The agreement also contains a severability clause, which states that

> [i]f any portion of this Agreement is deemed invalid or unenforceable, it shall not invalidate the remaining portions of this Agreement, each of which shall be enforceable regardless of such invalidity.

Howard, whose only source of income was Social Security benefits, was eventually unable to make the loan payments. Omega repossessed the automobile and later sold it at auction, leaving a deficiency of $16,763.00. Howard then sued Omega in Franklin District Court, alleging violations of the Franklin Consumer Fraud Act. Thereafter, Omega filed a motion to compel arbitration pursuant to the contract and a motion to dismiss. Howard opposed the motions, arguing that the arbitration clause was itself unconscionable. The district court granted Omega's motion to compel arbitration and dismissed Howard's complaint. The court of appeal affirmed, and we granted review.

When a party to arbitration argues that the arbitration agreement is unconscionable and unenforceable, that claim is decided based on the same state law principles that apply to contracts generally. Franklin law expresses a liberal policy favoring arbitration agreements. Our law, however, permits courts to refuse to enforce an arbitration agreement to the extent that grounds exist at law or in equity for the revocation of any contract. Generally recognized contract defenses, such as duress, fraud, and unconscionability, can justify judicial refusal to enforce an arbitration agreement.

Unconscionability sufficient to invalidate a contractual clause under Franklin law requires both procedural unconscionability — in that the less powerful party lacked a reasonable opportunity to negotiate more favorable terms and in that the process of signing the contract failed to fairly inform the less powerful party of its terms—*and* substantive unconscionability—in that the terms of the contract were oppressive and one-sided. Here, Omega has conceded procedural unconscionability. That leaves us with Howard's contention that the provisions relating to costs are substantively unconscionable.

Our lower courts have had difficulty in reviewing arbitration clauses that allocate costs. To some extent, this difficulty arises from the variety of cost-allocation measures under review. In *Georges v. Forestdale Bank* (Fr. Ct. App. 1993), the court of appeal reviewed a provision requiring the consumer to pay a small initial fee to the arbitrator and requiring the seller to cover all remaining costs. The court confirmed that "the cost of arbitration is a matter of substantive, not procedural, unconscionability" but concluded that the relatively minimal cost of the initial fee did not render the clause substantively unenforceable.

In *Ready Cash Loan, Inc. v. Morton* (Fr. Ct. App. 1998), the court of appeal reviewed an arbitration provision in a consumer loan agreement that divided the costs of arbitration. The clause limited the borrower/consumer to paying 25 percent of the total costs of arbitration and required the lender to pay 75 percent, regardless of who initiated the arbitration. Despite the unequal division, the court of appeal invalidated the clause, reasoning that "the clause . . . does not relieve the chilling effect on the borrower, given the potential expansion of costs involved in disputing substantial claims." *Id.*

In *Athens v. Franklin Tribune* (Fr. Ct. App. 2000), the court of appeal invalidated an arbitration clause in an employment contract that permitted the arbitrator to award costs. In *Athens*, the costs of arbitration included a filing fee of $3,250, a case service fee of $1,500, and a daily rate for the arbitration panel of $1,200 per arbitrator.[1] The court of appeal noted that "the provision at issue in *Ready Cash* allocated a portion of the costs to the consumer. The provision in this case potentially allocates all the costs to the consumer, serving as a greater deterrent to potential disputants."

Finally, in *Scotburg v. A-1 Auto Sales and Service, Inc.* (Fr. Ct. App. 2003), the court of appeal reviewed an arbitration clause that

---

[1] In a typical arbitration clause, parties select a private arbitration service, such as the National Arbitration Organization. In so doing, parties typically adopt that service's rules and procedures.

was completely silent on the allocation of costs. The defendant argued that the court should adopt the reasoning of a line of Columbia cases which held that absent a showing by the plaintiff of prohibitive cost, such arbitration clauses were enforceable. The *Scotburg* court rejected that argument and, relying solely on Franklin law, concluded that "the potential chilling effect of unknown and potentially prohibitive costs renders this clause unenforceable as a matter of substantive unconscionability."

These cases provide no clear framework within which to analyze the arbitration clause in the present case. The clause here leaves the allocation of costs to the discretion of the arbitrator. If Howard did not prevail in arbitration, then she could be forced to bear the entire cost of the arbitration. This prospect could discourage Howard and similarly situated consumers from pursuing their claims through arbitration.

We remand for a factual determination of the costs that the plaintiff might bear in the absence of the original cost and fee clause. If those costs exceed those that a litigant would bear in pursuing identical claims through litigation, we direct the trial court to reinstate Howard's claim and to deny Omega's motion to compel arbitration.

Vacated and remanded.

POINT SHEET

In re Field Hogs, Inc.
DRAFTERS' POINT SHEET

In this performance test, examinees are associates in a small law firm that represents Field Hogs, Inc. Field Hogs manufactures heavy lawn and field equipment. Field Hogs has been sued four times on various products liability and tort theories; the firm successfully defended two of these cases, but in two others juries awarded $1.5 million and $400,000 to the plaintiffs. Field Hogs wants to limit its costs and any unwanted publicity in future litigation. The law firm has been asked to draft an arbitration clause for Field Hogs's consumer sales contracts. Examinees have been given a copy of the firm's standard commercial arbitration clause and have been asked to address two questions and complete one drafting task:

(1)(a) Would this clause cover arbitration of all potential claims by consumers against Field Hogs under Franklin law? Why or why not? The examinee should explain how his or her conclusion is supported by the applicable law.

(b) Would this clause's allocation of arbitration costs be enforceable against consumers under Franklin law? Why or why not? The examinee should explain how his or her conclusion is supported by the applicable law.

(2) Draft an arbitration clause for the sales contracts that will be enforceable under Franklin law, and briefly explain how that draft language addresses the client's priorities, as described in the attached client meeting summary.

The following discussion covers all the points the drafters intended to raise in the problem. Examinees need not cover them all to receive passing or even excellent grades.

I. OVERVIEW

The File includes the task memorandum from the senior partner, a summary of an interview with Bradley Hewlett, Chief Operating Officer of Field Hogs, and a memorandum summarizing the four tort/products liability litigations against Field Hogs. These last two documents provide information about Field Hogs's litigation history and why it wants to use arbitration. In addition, the File contains excerpts from the National Arbitration Organization rules, which are incorporated by reference into the law firm's standard commercial arbitration clause.

The material in the client interview regarding Field Hogs's priorities helps to inform the legal discussion and provides a basis to assess how particular drafts might meet those priorities. Examinees should note that Field Hogs would prefer a clause that will compel arbitration, and that Field Hogs does not want to add to its costs by having to litigate the enforceability of the arbitration clause in court. Thus, examinees should focus not only on whether Field Hogs may ultimately win such litigation, but also on whether the clause will minimize the risk of such litigation.

A good answer will reference at least the following facts:

- Field Hogs manufactures a product that can be dangerous if not used properly. Thus, Field Hogs has exposure to tort claims (likely on a products liability theory).

- Field Hogs has defended multiple tort litigations and has incurred costs (including jury verdicts) that have affected its overall business planning.

- The law firm's standard commercial arbitration clause does not explicitly reference arbitration of tort claims or the shifting of costs of arbitration, but it explicitly incorporates by reference the rules of the National Arbitration Organization.

- The National Arbitration Organization has rules governing the allocation of costs of arbitration between "consumers" and "businesses."

- These rules create a two-tiered system for cost allocation, with different provisions governing claims under $75,000 and claims of $75,000 or more. Regardless of the amount of the claim, consumers must pay a minimum $2,000 administrative fee.

  - Under $75,000: consumers' share of fees is capped at $2,750 ($2,000 administrative fee plus maximum of $750 for arbitrator's fees).

  - $75,000 or over: no cap on fees ($2,000 administrative fee plus one-half the arbitrator's fees, with no upper limit).

II. RELEVANT LAW

The Library contains two Franklin cases:

In *LeBlanc v. Sani-John Corp.* (Fr. Ct. App. 2003), the plaintiff brought a tort claim against the defendant for injuries caused by the chemicals used to clean the defendant's portable toilets. The court addressed the question of whether a clause with general language requiring arbitration of all claims "arising out of or relating to" a contract should be interpreted to require arbitration of a tort claim. The court reviewed three answers to the question: 1) the general language does include tort claims (*New Home Builders, Inc.*); 2) the general language does not include tort claims, but a clause explicitly requiring arbitration of tort claims might do so (*Norway Farms*); and 3) even clauses that explicitly require arbitration of tort claims should be held unenforceable as a matter of public policy (*Willis*, an Olympia case). The *LeBlanc* court adopted the second approach (*Norway Farms*).

LeBlanc is significant in the following ways: 1) it establishes that the firm's existing clause (which uses the phrase "arising out of or relating to this contract") is inadequate to compel arbitration of tort claims under Franklin law; 2) it advises courts to construe any such clause strictly; 3) in the same vein, it requires that drafters of such clauses "should clearly and explicitly express an intent to require the arbitration of" tort claims; and 4) in its quote of the *Willis* language, the court provides alternative language that an examinee might discuss for the Field Hogs clause ("[a]ny claim, dispute, or controversy (whether in contract, tort, or otherwise) arising from or related to" the contract).

Howard v. Omega Funding Corp. (Fr. Sup. Ct. 2004) discusses whether an arbitration clause that permits the arbitrator to shift costs and fees at the end of the arbitration is "substantively unconscionable" and therefore unenforceable. (The defendant in *Howard* conceded that the arbitration clause was procedurally unconscionable.)

The opinion discusses at least four different ways that arbitration clauses might allocate costs and fees, including

- A provision requiring the consumer to pay a small amount toward arbitration costs up front, with the business to pay the balance (*Georges*). The *Georges* court found the clause enforceable.

- A clause that requires consumer and business to pay unequal percentages of the costs (25 and 75 percent, respectively), with no clear upper limit on the amount consumers might be required to pay (*Ready Cash Loan, Inc.*). The *Ready Cash* court found the clause unenforceable.

- A clause that permits the arbitrator to divide costs and fees at the end of the arbitration (*Athens*). The *Athens* court found the clause unenforceable. The *Howard* court explicitly disapproves of a similar clause in its holding, resting its opinion in part on the fact that a plaintiff asserting identical statutory claims in litigation (as opposed to asserting such claims in arbitration) would be entitled to request costs and fees as the prevailing party; the clause at hand would in theory permit the arbitrator to award costs to the defendant in a way not contemplated by prevailing law.

- A clause that is silent on the allocation of costs (*Scotburg*). The *Scotburg* court used state substantive unconscionability law to find a "silent" clause unenforceable.

Howard offers examinees several important points: 1) it confirms the need to assess cost-allocation questions as a matter of substantive unconscionability, 2) it provides several different examples of cost-shifting devices for examinees to assess, 3) it suggests that examinees should compare the rights that plaintiffs have to obtain costs in arbitration with the rights that they would have in litigation, 4) it makes those comparisons in a case that raises statutory claims (under the Franklin Consumer Fraud Act) in which a claimant likely would have been able to obtain costs through litigation, and 5) it invalidates three out of the four relevant types of clauses.

III. ANALYSIS

The task memo suggests that examinees organize their answers into three separate sections. Good answers should distinguish between the "coverage" question (technically speaking, the "arbitrability" of tort claims) on the one hand and the "fairness" question (cost shifting) on the other. In addition, the task memo asks examinees to draft a clause that will be enforceable under Franklin law, and to assess briefly how that draft addresses the client's priorities. Good answers should assess the different types of arbitration clauses discussed in the cases, should assess how enforceable they may be, and could plausibly use language approved in the relevant cases as the basis for drafting a possible clause.[2]

No particular significance should attach to the sequence in which examinees answer the questions; good answers might take the three sections in any order. Examinees could choose to discuss both aspects of the firm's existing clause (coverage and cost shifting) before presenting a complete draft, or they could analyze each issue and follow it with drafted language embodying their analysis. The discussion below adopts the latter approach.

It should be noted that *Howard* identifies and discusses two different kinds of unconscionability: procedural and substantive. The case holding rests solely on a "substantive unconscionability" discussion—that is, on whether it is fundamentally unfair to shift the costs of

---

[2] The task memo specifically instructs examinees not to concern themselves with issues that may arise under the Federal Arbitration Act. Any such discussion is beyond the scope of the task memo.

arbitration. Nonetheless, examinees may discuss whether including the clause in a standard sales agreement adequately puts consumers on notice of their rights, and whether alternate procedures for highlighting or signing the clause might be required. As stated in *Howard*, procedural unconscionability occurs when "the less powerful party lacked a reasonable opportunity to negotiate more favorable terms and . . . the process of signing the contract failed to fairly inform the less powerful party of its terms." Thus, limited discussion of procedural unconscionability may be appropriate.

Some examinees may also note that a "silent" arbitration clause (one that does not specify how costs might be awarded or whether the clause might apply to tort claims) poses both procedural *and* substantive problems. Points may be awarded to examinees who frame and discuss the question of whether the firm's clause is truly "silent" (given its incorporation by reference of the N.A.O. rules) as to coverage and cost/fee shifting and, if so, whether it fairly puts consumers on notice of their rights under the clause. None of the cases develop this point extensively, so extended discussion of the point is not warranted, but the point is arguably implicit in the *Scotburg* (state common law) discussion of "silent" clauses.

1. *Would the firm's standard commercial arbitration clause cover arbitration of all potential claims by consumers against Field Hogs?*

In light of the statement of the law as set forth in *LeBlanc*, examinees should recognize and discuss the following points:

- The law firm's existing clause indicates that it covers "[a]ny claim or controversy arising out of or relating to [the] contract."

- Under *LeBlanc*, the clause is ambiguous as to whether it covers all disputes between the parties to the original transaction, including tort disputes, or only covers disputes which require construction of the contract, excluding later tort disputes.

- *LeBlanc* holds that the "arising out of" language, without more, covers only disputes which require construction of the contract and does not cover later tort claims between the parties, even if the tort claim would not have occurred if the parties had not signed the contract.

- Examinees should conclude (a) that the law firm's existing clause covers arbitration of contractual disputes but does *not* require arbitration of tort claims, (b) that Franklin law permits the arbitration of tort claims between parties to a consumer contract, but

(c) that any contract that seeks to cover such tort claims should state the parties' intention to do so explicitly and will be subject to strict construction by the court.

Draft Language: Examinees should not simply repeat the language of the law firm's standard arbitration clause. Instead, they should revise the language to make clear the parties' intention to cover any tort claims that might arise because of the use of the product purchased by the consumer from Field Hogs. The following language suggests one possible approach to this task, incorporating language suggested in *LeBlanc*:

"Any claim, dispute, or controversy (whether in contract, tort, or otherwise) arising out of or related to this contract or the breach thereof shall be settled by arbitration."

The task memo asks for a brief explanation of how the draft language addresses the client's priorities. As to this portion of the draft language, Field Hogs has asked the law firm to draft an arbitration clause that would render future tort claims involving its products arbitrable under the clause. To the extent this clause assures the arbitrability of tort claims under Franklin law, no ambiguity exists as to whether this clause meets the client's expressed wishes. An examinee might briefly state that according to Bradley Hewlett, Field Hogs prefers arbitration on the assumption that handling consumer claims in that manner will be "less public, yield lower awards, and be less expensive than traditional litigation . . . [and] professional arbitrators will be more predictable than juries."

2.   *Would the law firm's existing clause's allocation of arbitration costs be enforceable against consumers under Franklin law?*

Examinees should recognize and discuss the following points:

- The firm's existing clause (standing alone) is silent on the handling of costs; however, it incorporates the National Arbitration Organization's provisions by reference.

- The N.A.O.'s provisions create a two-tier system for cost allocation. For claims under $75,000, the consumer can be held to pay up to a maximum amount in costs of $2,750. For claims of $75,000 or over, the consumer pays a minimum amount of $2,000 but has no upward limit in costs.

- As to the existing clause, examinees should thus assess whether either a "silent" clause or one that permits an open-ended allocation of costs to the consumer complies with state law. Examinees should conclude that only one kind of provision appears to have been approved by a Franklin court: one that allocates a minimal initial cost to the consumer, with the business bearing the balance of the cost. *Georges v. Forest-dale Bank* (Fr. Ct. App. 1993).

- In *Howard*, the Franklin court uses the "unconscionability" doctrine to review allocations of the cost of arbitration. Each of the different cost-allocation provisions discussed in *Howard* represents a different possible way to allocate costs. Several of them match portions of the firm's clause and the N.A.O. rules:

    - Consumer pays a small initial cost; business bears the entire balance: The *Georges* case approved this approach. The portion of the N.A.O. rules which sets maximum fees for the consumer is thus arguably acceptable. However, a question remains as to whether the size of the initial cost presents an unreasonable barrier; examinees might note that the *Athens* case (discussed in *Howard*) involved total costs of arbitration that were comparable to, if somewhat greater than, those the N.A.O. rules require the consumer to bear. This case bears on that portion of the N.A.O. rules that impose an upper limit on the costs to be borne by a consumer (for cases under $75,000).

    - Consumer pays a fixed percentage of the overall costs: the *Ready Cash Loan* case disapproved of this approach because of the "potential expansion of costs involved in disputing substantial claims." The portion of the N.A.O. rules that allocates costs based on a fixed percentage would conflict with this holding, even more so because the consumer's potential share under the N.A.O. rules (50 percent) is larger than in *Ready Cash Loan* (25 percent). The case bears on that portion of the N.A.O. rules that imposes a percentage share of costs on the consumer (for cases of $75,000 or more).

    - Arbitrator decides on cost allocation at the end of the arbitration: The *Athens* court disapproved of this approach, noting that the arbitrator could require the consumer to pay all the fees, not just a share as in *Ready Cash*, thus posing arguably a greater deterrent to potential disputants. Neither the existing clause nor the N.A.O. rules provide for after-the-fact allocation by the arbitrator; an examinee would discuss this only as one among many options. The case does not bear on any aspect of the firm's existing clause or the N.A.O. rules.

    - "Silence" as to costs: The *Scotburg* court rejected the reasoning of a line of Columbia court decisions (which permitted clauses that were silent as to cost allocation except in those cases where the plaintiff could show that costs were prohibitive) and held that the fact that the arbitration clause made no provision for cost allocation had a "potential chilling effect of unknown and potentially prohibitive costs." Examinees might note that even if Field Hogs chose not to use the N.A.O. rules, the firm's existing clause is silent as to cost allocation and would thus face problems under *Scotburg*.

- As to the law firm's standard commercial arbitration clause, examinees should conclude that neither a "silent" clause nor a clause imposing an open-ended obligation on consumers is likely to satisfy Franklin law.

A better examinee may conclude that (a) Field Hogs faces the greatest risk of litigation over enforceability with a "silent" clause, an "arbitrator decides" clause, or a "no upper limit" clause; (b) Field Hogs would face a lower risk of litigation in using a "fixed consumer cost" clause; and (c) even a "fixed cost" clause faces possible litigation if the amount of the cost is too great. [In addition, a perceptive examinee may observe that in *Howard*, the loan contract at issue contained a severability clause ("If any portion of the Agreement is deemed invalid or unenforceable, it shall not invalidate the remaining portions of this Agreement. . ."), and recommend that Field Hogs include such a clause in its contracts.]

Draft Language: The drafting assignment in the task memo asks examinees to draft an enforceable arbitration clause and "briefly explain how your draft language addresses the client's priorities." In the client meeting memorandum, Bradley Hewlett indicates a desire to split the costs of arbitration down the middle, but he doesn't want to spend a lot of time (or money) litigating the validity of the arbitration clause. Hewlett also states that "avoiding jury trials is the most important thing."

As a drafting matter, an examinee might take one or both of two different approaches:

- First, an examinee might draft a clause that states a fixed maximum cost that the consumer will bear in connection with any arbitration. The case law provides relatively minimal guidance at best on what the amount of this maximum should be. The *Georges* case, discussed in *Howard*, approves what it describes only as a "small initial fee." The *Athens* case, also discussed in *Howard*, disapproves fixed initial costs and a daily rate that are comparable to those stated in the National Arbitration Organization procedures, but the problem in that case was the open-endedness of the potential allocation. Finally, the *Howard* case itself states a relatively open-ended comparative standard for these fixed costs: these should not "exceed those that a litigant would bear in pursuing identical claims through litigation." Given this ambiguity, the best answers will provide a structure for the cost-allocation clause but may leave the specific amount of the maximum blank, subject to further research. Such a clause might read: "Arbitration shall occur in accordance with the rules and procedures for arbitration promulgated by the National Arbitration Organization. The purchaser under this contract shall pay no more than $_____ of the costs of arbitration; Field Hogs will bear all other costs of arbitration as set forth under those rules."

- Second, an examinee might allocate the entire cost of arbitration to Field Hogs. Such a clause might read: "Arbitration shall occur in accordance with the rules and procedures for arbitration promulgated by the National Arbitration Organization, except that Field Hogs will bear the entire cost of all arbitration services under those rules."

The task memo asks for a brief explanation of how the draft language addresses the client's priorities. As to this portion of the draft language, Field Hogs has provided conflicting guidance. On the one hand, Hewlett indicates that he would prefer the cost-sharing arrangements Field Hogs has had in arbitrations with their commercial suppliers, where it has "split costs down the middle." On the other hand, Hewlett has made clear that he wants "to know exactly what [he] can expect" from arbitration, "avoiding jury trials is the most important thing," and finally, he does not want to litigate the validity of the clause itself.

The first draft clause attempts to balance these priorities by asking the consumer to share the costs of arbitration to the extent possible under Franklin law. In so doing, however, it may leave a small but distinct zone of risk that a Franklin court may find the cost allocation unconscionable. The second draft clause eliminates this zone of risk by allocating all costs to Field Hogs. In so doing, however, it overrides Field Hogs's desire for cost sharing, in favor of Hewlett's express concern for certainty of expectation and "avoiding jury trials." Either answer addresses the client's priorities.

In re Social Networking Inquiry

FILE

LIBRARY

POINT SHEET

Instructions

The back cover of each test form contains the following instructions:

You will have 90 minutes to complete this session of the examination. This performance test is designed to evaluate your ability to handle a select number of legal authorities in the context of a factual problem involving a client.

The problem is set in the fictitious state of Franklin, in the fictitious Fifteenth Circuit of the United States. Columbia and Olympia are also fictitious states in the Fifteenth Circuit. In Franklin, the trial court of general jurisdiction is the District Court, the intermediate appellate court is the Court of Appeal, and the highest court is the Supreme Court.

You will have two kinds of materials with which to work: a File and a Library. The first document in the File is a memorandum containing the instructions for the task you are to complete. The other documents in the File contain factual information about your case and may include some facts that are not relevant.

The Library contains the legal authorities needed to complete the task and may also include some authorities that are not relevant. Any cases may be real, modified, or written solely for the purpose of this examination. If the cases appear familiar to you, do not assume that they are precisely the same as you have read before. Read them thoroughly, as if they all were new to you. You should assume that the cases were decided in the jurisdictions and on the dates shown. In citing cases from the Library, you may use abbreviations and omit page references.

Your response must be written in the answer book provided. If you are taking the examination on a laptop computer, your jurisdiction will provide you with specific instructions. In answering this performance test, you should concentrate on the materials in the File and Library. What you have learned in law school and elsewhere provides the general background for analyzing the problem; the File and Library provide the specific materials with which you must work.

Although there are no restrictions on how you apportion your time, you should be sure to allocate ample time (about 45 minutes) to reading and digesting the materials and to organizing your answer before you begin writing it. You may make notes anywhere in the test materials; blank pages are provided at the end of the booklet. You may not tear pages from the question booklet.

This performance test will be graded on your responsiveness to the instructions regarding the task you are to complete, which are given to you in the first memorandum in the File, and on the content, thoroughness, and organization of your response.

FILE

MEMORANDUM

TO: Examinee
FROM: Bert H. Ballentine
DATE: July 26, 2011
RE: Social Networking Inquiry

I serve as chairman of the five-member Franklin State Bar Association Professional Guidance Committee. The committee issues advisory opinions in response to inquiries from Franklin attorneys concerning the ethical propriety of contemplated actions under the Franklin Rules of Professional Conduct. (These opinions are advisory only and are not binding upon the Attorney Disciplinary Board of the Franklin Supreme Court.)

We have received the attached inquiry, and we briefly discussed it at yesterday's meeting of the committee. Three of my colleagues on the committee thought that the course of conduct proposed by the inquiry would pose no problem, one was undecided, and my view was that the proposed conduct would violate the Rules. We agreed to look into the applicable law and then consider the matter in greater detail and come to a resolution at our meeting next week.

Those committee members who think the proposed conduct does not run afoul of the Rules will draft and circulate a memorandum setting forth their position. I, too, will circulate a memorandum setting forth my position that the proposed conduct would violate the Rules.

Please prepare a memorandum that I can circulate to the other committee members to persuade them that the proposed conduct would indeed violate the Rules. Your draft should also respond to any arguments you anticipate will be made to the contrary. Do not draft a separate statement of facts, but be sure to incorporate the relevant facts into your analysis. Also, do not concern yourself with any Rules other than those referred to in the attached materials.

In addition to the inquiry, I am attaching my notes of yesterday's brief discussion by the committee and the applicable Rules of Professional Conduct. As this is a case of first impression under Franklin's Rules, I am attaching case law from neighboring jurisdictions, which might be   relevant. (These Rules are identical for the states of Franklin, Columbia, and Olympia.) From reading these materials, I have learned that there are three approaches to resolving this issue. I believe that the proposed course of conduct would violate the Rules under all three of the approaches.

Allen, Coleman & Nelson, Attorneys-at-Law
3 Adams Plaza
Youcee, Franklin 33098

July 1, 2011

Franklin State Bar Association – Professional Guidance Committee
2 Emerald Square
Franklin City, Franklin 33033

Dear Committee Members:

I write to inquire as to the ethical propriety of a proposed course of action in a negligence lawsuit involving a trip-and-fall injury in a restaurant in which I am involved as counsel of record for the restaurant.

I deposed a nonparty witness who is not represented by counsel. Her testimony is helpful to the party adverse to my client and may be crucial to the other side's case—she testified that neither she nor the plaintiff had been drinking alcohol that evening. During the course of the deposition, the witness revealed that she has accounts on several social networking Internet sites (such as Facebook and MySpace), which allow users to create personal "pages" on which the user may post information on any topic, sometimes including highly personal information. Access to these pages is limited to individuals who obtain the user's permission by asking for it online (those granted permission are referred to as the user's "friends"). The user may grant such access while having almost no information about the person making the request, or may ask for detailed information about that person before making the decision to grant access.

I believe that the witness's pages may contain information which is relevant to the subject of her deposition and which could impeach her at trial—specifically, that she and the plaintiff had been drinking on the evening in question. I did not ask her to reveal the contents of the pages or to allow me access to them in the deposition. I did visit the witness's various social networking accounts after deposing her, and I found that access to them requires her permission. The witness disclosed during the deposition that she grants access to just about anyone who asks for it. However, given the hostility that the witness displayed toward me when I questioned her credibility, I doubt that she would allow me access if I asked her directly.

I propose to ask one of my assistants (not an attorney), whose name the witness will not recognize, to go to these social networking sites and seek to "friend" the witness and thereby gain access to the information on her pages. My assistant would state only truthful information (including his or her name) but would not reveal any affiliation with me or the purpose for which he or she is seeking access (i.e., to provide information for my evaluation and possible use to impeach the witness).

I ask for the Committee's view as to whether this proposed course of conduct is permissible under the Franklin Rules of Professional Conduct.

Very truly yours,

Melinda Nelson

Melinda Nelson

NOTES OF MEETING OF FRANKLIN STATE BAR ASSOCIATION
PROFESSIONAL GUIDANCE COMMITTEE

RE: MELINDA NELSON'S INQUIRY

Chairman Ballentine asks committee members for initial reactions to Ms. Nelson's inquiry, noting that this appears to be an open question under Franklin law, although different approaches have been followed in Olympia, Columbia, and elsewhere.

Ms. Piel comments that Ms. Nelson's proposed course of action seems harmless enough because social networking pages are open to the public.

Mr. Hamm agrees and states that it is worthwhile to expose a lying witness.

Chairman Ballentine asks if this matter involves a crucial misrepresentation.

Ms. Piel thinks the committee should allow harmless misrepresentations in the pursuit of justice.

Chairman Ballentine questions the impact on the integrity of the legal profession and asks for further discussion.

Mr. Haig favors the "no harm, no foul" approach and is not sure that there is any harm in the instant case.

Chairman Ballentine notes that the witness's testimony may be critical to the case.

Ms. Rossi is undecided and concerned that the committee has not yet referred to the specific Rules that would be involved, let alone any court's interpretation of them. Needs more information on the law.

Chairman Ballentine concludes that the matter should be reopened at the next meeting, with each committee member to look into the question and the law in the meantime.

All agree.

LIBRARY

EXCERPTS FROM FRANKLIN RULES OF PROFESSIONAL CONDUCT*

Rule 4.1 Truthfulness in Statements to Others

In the course of representing a client a lawyer shall not knowingly:

(a)   make a false statement of material fact or law to a third person;

. . .

Comment:

Misrepresentation

[1] A lawyer is required to be truthful when dealing with others on a client's behalf, but generally has no affirmative duty to inform an opposing party of relevant facts. A misrepresentation can occur if the lawyer incorporates or affirms a statement of another person that the lawyer knows is false. Misrepresentations can also occur by partially true but misleading statements or omissions that are the equivalent of affirmative false statements. For dishonest conduct that does not amount to a false statement or for misrepresentations by a lawyer other than in the course of representing a client, see Rule 8.4.

*   *   *

Rule 8.4 Misconduct

It is professional misconduct for a lawyer to:

(a)   violate or attempt to violate the Rules of Professional Conduct, knowingly assist or induce another to do so, or do so through the acts of another;

…

(c)   engage in conduct involving dishonesty, fraud, deceit or misrepresentation;

…

* These rules are identical to the American Bar Association Model Rules of Professional Conduct and have been adopted by the states of Franklin, Columbia, and Olympia.

Comment:

[1] Lawyers are subject to discipline when they violate or attempt to violate the Rules of Professional Conduct, or when they knowingly assist or induce another to do so or do so through the acts of another, as when they request or instruct an agent to do so on the lawyer's behalf. Paragraph (a), however, does not prohibit a lawyer from advising a client of action the client is lawfully entitled to take.

[2] Many kinds of illegal conduct reflect adversely on fitness to practice law, such as offenses involving fraud and the offense of willful failure to file an income tax return. However, some kinds of offenses carry no such implication. . . . [A] lawyer should be professionally answerable only for offenses that indicate lack of those characteristics relevant to law practice. Offenses involving violence, dishonesty, breach of trust, or serious interference with the administration of justice are in that category.

In the Matter of Devonia Rose, Attorney-Respondent

Olympia Supreme Court (2004)

In this proceeding, we affirm that members of our profession must adhere to the highest moral and ethical standards, which apply regardless of motive. We therefore affirm the hearing board's finding that the district attorney in this case violated the Olympia Rules of Professional Conduct.

On March 15, 2002, Chief Deputy District Attorney Devonia Rose arrived at a crime scene where three persons lay murdered. She learned that the killer was Neal Patrick, who had apparently abducted and brutally murdered the three victims. She also learned that Patrick was holding two hostages in an apartment at the scene, and that he was in touch by telephone with the police who surrounded the apartment (the conversations were taped). Rose heard Patrick describe his crimes in explicit detail to the police lieutenant in charge, who urged him to surrender peacefully. At one point, Patrick said that he would not surrender without legal representation and asked that a lawyer he knew be contacted. Attempts to reach the lawyer were unsuccessful (it later was learned that the lawyer had retired and was no longer in practice). Patrick then asked for a public de-fender, but no attempt to contact the public defender's office was made. Law enforcement officials later testified that, notwithstanding their efforts to contact the lawyer Patrick had named, they would not have allowed any defense attorney to speak with Patrick, because they believed that no defense attorney would have allowed Patrick to continue to speak with law enforcement, and they needed their conversation with Patrick to continue until they could capture him.

Instead, Rose offered to impersonate a public defender, and the police lieutenant on the scene agreed. The lieutenant introduced Rose to Patrick on the telephone under an assumed name. Patrick told Rose that he would surrender if given three guarantees: 1) that he be isolated from other detainees; 2) that he be given cigarettes; and 3) that "his lawyer" be present, to which Rose responded, "Right, I'll be there." In later conversations, it was clear that Patrick believed that Rose (under her pseudonym) represented him. Patrick then surrendered to law enforcement without incident and without harm to his two hostages. He asked if his attorney was present, and although Rose did not speak with him, she had the police lieutenant say that she was. Rose made no subsequent effort to correct the misrepresentations. The public defender who was subsequently assigned to the case found out about the misrepresentations two weeks later, upon listening to the taped conversations and speaking with her client. Shortly thereafter, Patrick dismissed the public defender, represented himself pro se (with advisory counsel appointed by the court), was tried, was convicted, and received the death penalty. The parties dispute whether he dismissed the public defender out of the mistrust precipitated by Rose's earlier deception.

The State's Attorney Regulation Counsel charged Rose with violating Olympia Rule of Professional Conduct 8.4(c), which provides, "It is professional misconduct for a lawyer to . . . (c) engage in conduct involving dishonesty, fraud, deceit or misrepresentation." The Rule and its commentary are devoid of any exceptions.

Rose asserts that her deception was "justified" under the circumstances. But, we believe, even a noble motive does not warrant departure from the Rules. District attorneys in Olympia owe a very high duty to the public because they are governmental officials. Their responsibility to enforce the laws does not grant them license to ignore those laws or the Rules of Professional Conduct.

Rose asks that an exception to the Rules be crafted for cases involving the possibility of "imminent public harm." But we are not convinced that such was the case here. Although law enforcement officials testified that they were certain that Patrick would have harmed the two hostages had he not been convinced to surrender, Rose had options other than acting deceptively. For example, Patrick could have been told that a public defender would be provided as soon as he surrendered, but no attempt to pursue such an option was made.

The level of ethical standards to which our profession holds all attorneys, especially prosecutors, leaves no room for deception. Rose cannot compromise her integrity, and that of our profession, regardless of the cause.

In mitigation, we credit Rose's commendable reputation in the legal community, her lack of prior misconduct, and her full cooperation in these proceedings. In addition, we believe Rose's motivation to deceive Patrick was in no way selfish or self-serving—she sincerely believed she was protecting the public. Hence, we affirm the hearing board's sanction of one month's suspension of license.

1

In re Hartson Brant, Attorney

Columbia Supreme Court (2007)

This is an appeal from the decision of the Columbia State Bar Disciplinary Committee, holding that Attorney Hartson Brant violated Columbia's Rules of Professional Conduct. For the reasons stated below, we reverse.

BACKGROUND

Brant is General Counsel of the Columbia Fair Housing Association, a private-sector not-for-profit association dedicated to eliminating unlawful housing discrimination in our state. The association received numerous complaints that the owner of the Taft Houses, a luxury condominium development on Columbia's seacoast, was discriminating against members of minority groups in the sale of its condominiums.

To determine whether the allegations were correct, and, if so, to collect evidence which would support the State Housing Commission in a lawsuit for violation of Columbia's fair housing statutes, the association, through Brant, undertook a "sting" operation: He instructed two legal assistants working for the association, neither of whom was an attorney and both of whom came from minority groups, to pose as a married couple. They were to seek information about purchasing a condominium in the development. Brant created false background stories concerning their supposed employment, finances, and references, all of which would depict them as qualified and highly desirable buyers.

At Brant's direction, the legal assistants first telephoned the development's sales office, explained their interest in purchasing a condominium, and discussed their "credentials" with the sales agent, who explicitly offered to sell them one of the 13 units still available. But when they visited the sales office and the same sales agent met them in person—and so became aware of their minority status—he told them that no units were available and that they must have misunderstood him. The couple lawfully recorded both the telephone and the in-person conversations, and it is clear from the recordings that there was no possible "misunderstanding."

This chain of events formed the crucial evidence which led to an action by the Columbia State Housing Commission against the owner of the Taft Houses for housing discrimination. That litigation was settled—the owner confessed to violation of the law, paid a substantial fine, and agreed to a consent judgment precluding such discrimination in the future.

However, after learning through discovery in that action of Brant's role in the ruse, the owner of the Taft Houses filed a complaint against Brant with the State Bar, alleging violation of the Rules of Professional Conduct. After a hearing, the Disciplinary Committee found Brant in violation of Rules 4.1(a) and 8.4(c) and ordered his suspension from practice for six months.

ANALYSIS

First, the fact that non-attorneys, and not Brant, actually carried out the ruse does not exempt Brant from liability for violation of the Rules. Rule 5.3(c)(1) states that "[w]ith respect to a nonlawyer employed or retained by or associated with a lawyer: . . . (c) a lawyer shall be responsible for conduct of such a person that would be a violation of the Rules of Professional Conduct if engaged in by a lawyer if: (1) the lawyer orders or, with the knowledge of the specific conduct, ratifies the conduct involved . . . ."

Here, Brant himself created the ruse and told the legal assistants what to do.

We may deal with the alleged violations of Rules 4.1(a) and 8.4(c) together, as they go to the same point. Rule 4.1(a) provides: "In the course of representing a client a lawyer shall not knowingly: (a) make a false statement of material fact or law to a third person." Here, on its face, Brant (through the legal assistants' statements) made a false statement of material fact to the sales agent while representing the association. Rule 8.4(c) provides: "It is professional misconduct for a lawyer to . . . (c) engage in conduct involving dishonesty, fraud, deceit or misrepresentation." Here, also on its face, Brant did (through the legal assistants' statements) engage in misrepresentation.

Some state courts strictly apply the plain language of the Rules and deem any misrepresentation, no matter the motivation, improper. *See, e.g., In the Matter of Devonia Rose* (Olympia Sup. Ct. 2004).

But we believe the Rules are not so rigid as to preclude the sort of activities at issue here, even though those activities are facially contrary to the Rules. Indeed, the commentary to Rule 8.4 states:

Many kinds of illegal conduct reflect adversely on fitness to practice law, such as offenses involving fraud and the offense of willful failure to file an income tax return. However, some kinds of offenses carry no such implication. . . . [A] lawyer should be professionally answerable only for offenses that indicate lack of those characteristics relevant to law practice. Offenses involving violence, dishonesty, breach of trust, or serious interference with the administration of justice are in that category.

Thus, we believe the test under the Rules is whether the conduct goes to the core of the integrity of the profession and adversely reflects on the fitness to practice law.

Some commentators have suggested the use of a conduct-based analysis of attorney behavior in cases involving dishonesty, misrepresentation, or deception. The analysis, which is not specific to any particular Rule but is applied across all relevant Rules in a unitary fashion, requires assessment of four factors: (1) the directness of the lawyer's involvement in the deception, (2) the significance and depth of the deception, (3) the necessity of the deception and the existence of alternative means to discover the evidence, and (4) the relationship with any other of the Rules of Professional Conduct, that is, whether the conduct is otherwise illegal or unethical. *See* Goldring & Bass*, Undercover Investigation and the Rules of Professional Conduct*, 95 FRANKLIN L. REV. 224 (2006).

For example, with respect to factor (2) in a contract dispute, an attorney who, without disclosing that he is acting on a client's behalf, visits an appliance dealership to verify the product lines being sold, has made a minor deception, which poses little, if any, harm to the deceived party (*cf. Devonia Rose*, wherein the deception went to the heart of the attorney-client relationship). As to factor (3), an attorney's misrepresentation or deception to obtain information which could be obtained through standard discovery tools, such as a subpoena, is more likely to constitute an ethical violation. Thus, the conduct-based analysis emphasizes the actual conduct of the attorney.

We see substantial merit in this approach as a general matter, but we think this case can be resolved on narrower grounds. Rather than strictly applying the language of the Rules or following a conduct-based analysis, we choose a third approach: a status-based analysis focusing on the importance and nature of the role that the attorney plays in advancing the interests of justice. The fact is that in the absence of this type of evidence-gathering, it would be virtually impossible to collect evidence of unfair housing practices. No property owner who engages in discrimination does so by explicitly stating, "We don't sell to minorities." The spirit of the Rules is to see that justice is done, without compromising the integrity of the profession. The type of misrepresentation at issue here—one that would be common to a great many cases which seek to root out violations of civil rights—is not one that goes to the core of the integrity of the profession and adversely reflects on the fitness to practice law.

Indeed, we can envision two other instances when similar misrepresentations would be vital to the proper administration of justice and would neither jeopardize the integrity of the profession nor reflect on the fitness to practice law. One would be when a prosecutor must mislead an alleged perpetrator of a crime in the interests of preventing imminent danger to public safety or of rooting out corruption or organized crime. Another such instance would be when an attorney is inves-

tigating the violation of intellectual property rights such as in cases of trademark counterfeiting.

We recognize that such a status-based test differentiates among attorneys, allowing some to engage in activities that would, if undertaken by others, violate the Rules. (Thus, a prosecutor's misrepresentation might be justified, but a defense attorney's might not.) In such cases, we believe that the misrepresentation (to prevent harm to the public or gather evidence of illegal acts) is necessary to achieve justice and does not reflect on the lawyer's fitness to practice.

Accordingly, we hold that misrepresentations that do not go to the core of the integrity of the profession, and that are necessary to ensure justice in cases of civil rights violations, intellectual property infringement, or crime prevention as indicated above, do not violate Columbia's Rules of Professional Conduct. We emphasize that we limit our reading of permissible actions of this sort only to these circumstances and extend it to no others.

Reversed.

POINT SHEET

In re Social Networking Inquiry
DRAFTERS' POINT SHEET

In this performance test item, examinees' senior partner is the chairman of the five-member Franklin State Bar Association Professional Guidance Committee. The committee issues advisory opinions in response to inquiries from Franklin attorneys concerning the ethical propriety of contemplated actions under the Franklin Rules of Professional Conduct. The committee has received an inquiry from Franklin attorney Melinda Nelson concerning the propriety of an investigation she wishes to undertake using the social networking pages of a nonparty, unrepresented witness. The inquiry raises an issue of first impression in Franklin. The senior partner has raised the inquiry with the committee at its most recent meeting.

After a cursory discussion, three of the committee members tentatively expressed the opinion that the proposed course of conduct would not violate the Rules, one was unsure, and the committee chair thought the Rules would be violated. The committee members agreed that each would consider the matter on his or her own, after researching the question, and they would further consider and fashion a response to the inquiry at their next meeting.

The committee chair has looked at relevant materials, which have reinforced his belief that his view is correct—that the proposed course of conduct would violate the Rules.

Examinees are asked to draft a memorandum analyzing the issue so as to persuade the other committee members that the chair's view is correct. Examinees need not restate the facts but must explain the basis for their analysis and conclusion that the proposed conduct would violate the Rules and also answer any arguments that might be made to the contrary.

The File contains 1) the instructional memorandum, 2) the letter from the Franklin attorney making the inquiry and setting forth the background and facts which give rise to it, and 3) notes of the committee meeting. The Library contains 1) the applicable Rules of Professional Conduct in force in Franklin and its two sister states, Olympia and Columbia (including commentary on the Rules), and 2) two cases—one from Olympia and one from Columbia—bearing on the legal issues posed by the inquiry.

The following discussion covers all the points the drafters intended to raise in the problem. Examinees need not cover them all to receive satisfactory or even excellent grades.

I. OVERVIEW

Examinees must, first, master the relatively simple facts at issue; second, master the somewhat more complex excerpted set of Franklin's Rules of Professional Conduct; third, as the question is one of first impression in the State of Franklin, discern the relevance of, and guidance to be derived from, the three differing applications of those Rules in other states, as set forth in the Olympia and Columbia cases, to situations which may in some ways be analogous to that posed by the inquiry; fourth, synthesize those differing approaches; and fifth, set forth the resulting analysis in the form of a memorandum which will persuade the members of the committee that the proposed course of conduct would violate the Rules, and refute any arguments to the contrary.

Examinees should address the following provisions of the Rules:

1) Rule 8.4, dealing with attorney misconduct: Is the proposed conduct of the attorney's assistant such that it constitutes "dishonesty, fraud, deceit or misrepresentation"?

2) Rule 4.1, dealing with truthfulness of statements to others: Does the proposed conduct of the assistant "make a false statement of material fact" to a third person?

3) Rule 5.3 (identical in Franklin), holding that an attorney is responsible for a nonattorney's conduct.

Examinees will be expected to analyze the applicability of each of these Rules. In doing so, as the question is one of first impression for Franklin, examinees should explain their conclusions as to the applicability of the three approaches used elsewhere, as set forth in the Olympia and Columbia cases. Thus, examinees should persuasively analyze application of the Rules to this fact situation using 1) the plain language of the Rules, 2) a status-based test, and 3) a conduct-based test. Examinees should then conclude that the proposed conduct is not within the Rules under any of the three tests.

II. DISCUSSION

A. Facts

Although examinees are instructed not to restate the facts, they must master those facts properly to apply the Rules. Melinda Nelson, the inquiring attorney, represents a defendant restaurant that is being sued for negligence in a "trip-and-fall" case. She has deposed a nonparty witness who is unrepresented by counsel and whose testimony is adverse to Nelson's client. In the course of that deposition, Nelson learned that the witness maintains several accounts with social networking Internet sites (such as Facebook and MySpace) and that the pages on these accounts may contain relevant information which would impeach the witness at trial. Specifically, the witness testified that neither she nor the plaintiff had been drinking alcohol on the evening in question. Nelson believes that information on the witness's social networking sites will show that the witness and the plaintiff had, in fact, been drinking.

As a general rule, as set forth in Nelson's inquiry, access to these accounts and the information on them is only by permission of the account holder or user, but that permission may be granted either with no inquiry or with detailed inquiry about the person seeking access, as the user wishes. Such persons granted access are called "friends." During the deposition, Nelson determined that the witness allows access to her social networking accounts to virtually anyone. However, Nelson does not wish to seek access herself, for the witness, who was very hostile to her at the deposition, would likely recognize her name and role in the litigation, and deny access.

Rather, Nelson proposes to instruct an assistant who is not an attorney to seek to "friend" the witness and so gain access to the pages on the accounts that may contain the suspected information. That assistant would not make any false statement (e.g., would use his or her real name), but would not reveal that he or she was acting at the direction of Nelson, nor reveal the purpose of the request to "friend" the witness. Attorney Nelson asks if this proposed course of action violates Franklin's Rules of Professional Conduct.

B. Analysis

1. Attorney Responsibility for Acts of an Agent

As an initial point, examinees should note that the proposed conduct of Nelson's assistant is attributable to Nelson as an attorney. As reported in *In re Hartson Brant*, an attorney in that case instructed two legal assistants to undertake a misrepresentation to ferret out housing discrimination. The Columbia Supreme Court applied Columbia's Rule 5.3, which is identical to

Franklin's, holding the attorney responsible for the legal assistants' conduct, noting that the attorney himself created the ruse and told the legal assistants what to do. In addition, Rule 8.4(a) proscribes violation of the Rules even when done "through the acts of another."

Here, as in the Columbia case, Nelson is determining the conduct and instructing the non-lawyer to undertake it. Hence, examinees should initially note that Nelson is responsible for the nonlawyer's conduct and, should it violate the Rules, would be responsible for that violation.

2. Rule 8.4

Rule 8.4 applies to actions that constitute professional misconduct. First, generally, any violation of the Rules constitutes professional misconduct. Rule 8.4(a). More specifically, Rule 8.4(c) proscribes "conduct involving dishonesty, fraud, deceit or misrepresentation." In the facts presented, it is more than likely that a deception is involved—the nonlawyer is not revealing that he or she is acting for the inquiring attorney. But does that deception amount to a violation of the Rule? As the Olympia decision in *In the Matter of Devonia Rose* and the Columbia decision in *In re Hartson Brant* reveal, there are three different approaches to the application of this Rule.

a. Strict Interpretation

Some courts have adopted the *Rose* approach—that there is an absolute bar to using deception. In *Rose,* the suspect, a confessed murderer, was holding two hostages while surrounded by police and in contact with them by telephone. The suspect said that he would surrender, without harming the hostages, on certain conditions, one of which was that his lawyer be present. The lawyer he requested was unavailable, and so he asked for a public defender. In that situation, law enforcement authorities would not allow any defense attorney to speak with the suspect, for a defense attorney would surely advise him to refrain from speaking with the police, and the communication link was vital if the murderer was to be apprehended without further loss of life. Rose, a deputy district attorney on the scene, with the agreement of law enforcement, posed as a public defender and engaged in telephone negotiations with the suspect, who eventually surrendered without further incident. It is worth noting that even after his surrender, the deputy district attorney did not reveal the ruse—it was only discovered by the actual public defender who took on the case two weeks later.

The Olympia State Attorney Regulation Counsel charged Rose with violation of Rule 8.4(c) of the Rules of Professional Conduct. The Olympia Supreme Court upheld a finding of violation. The court said that, no matter what the motive, the Rule against deceit must be absolute to uphold the integrity of the legal profession. The court noted that there were other avenues which could have been pursued without deception to induce the murderer to surrender. The court rejected Rose's request to craft limited exceptions to the Rule.

Thus, strict application of the plain language of Rule 8.4 would proscribe the proposed conduct. Examinees should note that the language of Franklin's Rule 8.4 is identical to the language of Olympia's Rule as applied by the *Rose* court, and so strict application of the plain language would be warranted for the reasons given by the *Rose* court. Further, the issue in the case at hand is negligence, not the far more momentous question of potential imminent criminal harm to the public found in *Rose*. If deceptive conduct to prevent harm to the public in *Rose* was not exempt, why then would deceptive conduct in the far less significant issue of negligence be found exempt? Perceptive examinees will note that, as the Olympia court remarked, even the best intentions and a sincere belief that the misrepresentation was preventing danger to the public do not justify a misrepresentation which harms the integrity of the profession.

b. Status-based Test

Other courts, however, have found that, notwithstanding the absolute language of the Rule, there should be limited exceptions to its absolute application, based on the status of the investigating attorney. Examinees should note, as *Brant* remarks, that such exceptions based on the attorney's status could be criticized because they do not treat all attorneys alike for engaging in similar conduct.

Brant, a Columbia decision, is an example of a status-based exception to Rule 8.4. There, an attorney for a private-sector, not-for-profit association dedicated to fair housing received complaints of discrimination by the owner of a condominium development for sale. Brant instructed two minority-group legal assistants to pose as a married couple and seek to buy a

condominium to determine whether such discrimination existed. Brant furnished them with a fictitious backstory. When the legal assistants telephoned the sales agent and recounted their fictitious credentials, the agent offered to sell them a condominium unit; but when they appeared in person (and their minority status became apparent), the sales agent said no units were for sale. This provided the necessary evidence for the Columbia State Housing Commission's successful (through settlement) lawsuit for housing discrimination.

The Columbia court acknowledged that the attorney (through the legal assistants) did make a misrepresentation. However, the court noted the Commentary to Rule 8.4, which indicates that the type of misrepresentation to be proscribed is that which "reflect[s] adversely on fitness to practice law" and concluded that this situation did not fit that standard. Rather, the court said, in some cases misrepresentation is necessary to achieve justice, for it is the only way to gather evidence, and thus is not contrary to the Rules. The court specified three situations in which an exception would apply—where the misrepresentation was by a prosecutor to prevent crime, or by attorneys to prove civil rights or intellectual property rights violations. The court was explicit that the exception it had crafted applied only to those three situations.

Examinees should argue that here, even those status-based exceptions established in the Columbia *Brant* case would not apply to Nelson's proposed conduct. A deception would be occurring: the nonlawyer seeking access to the witness's account pages would be omitting a highly material fact—that is, that the purpose of the request for access was to obtain information to impeach the witness's testimony in a lawsuit. None of the specific exceptions allowed by the Columbia court in *Brant* are applicable here—this case involves negligence, not criminal conduct or violations of civil rights or intellectual property rights. Thus, the use of the deception would be to gain an advantage in litigation which would not be possible without the deception. That purpose *does* adversely reflect on the fitness to practice law—Nelson is pursuing this ruse because she is sure the witness would not otherwise allow her access. That the witness seemingly allows all who request access to have it does not excuse the deception. Further, there could have been other means of gaining this evidence: Nelson presumably could have asked the witness about the evidence during the deposition. Hence, examinees should conclude that, even if a status-based exception were applied, the proposed conduct would violate Rule 8.4.

c. Conduct-based Test

Brant notes that the third approach, a conduct-based test, should not be analyzed with reference to a particular Rule, but rather across all Rules; that analysis is set forth separately below (see section 4). Nevertheless, it is possible that examinees will analyze the conduct-based test in the context of each individual Rule. They should not lose credit for doing so.

3. Rule 4.1

Rule 4.1(a) proscribes knowingly "mak[ing] a false statement of material fact or law to a third person." Again, Nelson is responsible if she knows that the person she instructed is making such a statement. Rules 5.3(c) and 8.4(a).

Here, the nonlawyer seeking access to the witness's account pages is not making a directly false statement of material fact to the witness—as Nelson's letter of inquiry indicates, the nonlawyer will only give truthful information (such as his or her name). But, as Nelson's letter also indicates, the nonlawyer will not reveal his or her association with Nelson or the reason for the request for access to the witness's account pages.

The Commentary to Rule 4.1 states: "Misrepresentations can also occur by partially true but misleading statements or omissions that are the equivalent of affirmative false statements." Examinees should point out that omitting the nonlawyer's association with Nelson and the reason for the request for access would be the equivalent of an affirmative false statement.

a. Strict Interpretation

Nelson believes that if the witness knew she was seeking access, the witness would not grant it. As the nonlawyer is, in essence, standing in the shoes of the lawyer, the same could be said for the nonlawyer—the witness would not grant access to the nonlawyer for the same reasons that she would not grant access to Nelson. The only way Nelson would gain access is by an affirmative false statement—i.e., using a fake name. For all intents and purposes, this is what she would be doing by having a nonlawyer to use the nonlawyer's name to gain access. That is the equivalent of an affirmative false statement and is contrary to the plain meaning of the Rule.

b. Status-based Test

Although the Columbia court, in *Brant*, excused false statements of this sort under Rule 4.1, it again limited that exception to situations not applicable here, based on the status of the attorney. Nelson is not a prosecutor seeking to prevent crime, nor is the subject matter of the litigation a civil rights or intellectual property rights violation. Thus, again, even if Franklin were to adopt the status-based exceptions set forth in *Brant*, those exceptions would not apply here. Nelson's proposed course of conduct would violate Rule 4.1(a) as well.

4. Conduct-based Test

Examinees should also consider that Franklin might adopt neither Olympia's strict interpretation set forth in *Rose* nor Columbia's status-based test set forth in *Brant*, and instead use a conduct-based test as referenced in *Brant*, which would be applicable across all the relevant Rules. Applying the factors proposed for that test, examinees should make the following points:

1) *The directness of the lawyer's involvement in the deception:* Here, Nelson's involvement would be direct, as she would instruct the nonlawyer to undertake the deception.

2) *The significance and depth of the deception:* The depth of the deception is minor, but its significance is major. It may result in impeachment of the witness's testimony, which would not have occurred without the deception.

3) *The necessity of the deception and the existence of alternative means to discover the evidence:* Whether the deception is necessary is questionable—one might ask why Nelson did not ask the witness at deposition what the content of the pages was and whether she would be allowed access to them. Nelson may have had and may still have other means—all untested—to discover the evidence. She could have asked the witness what her social networking pages said regarding the night in question. She could simply ask for "friend" access or could have asked about getting "friend" access in the deposition. She could have and still can subpoena the social networking site pages.

4) *The relationship with any other of the Rules of Professional Conduct:* Here, there is an interaction between Rules 8.4 and 4.1, both of which lead to a conclusion that the Rules bar the proposed course of conduct.

5. Response to Arguments that the Conduct Would be Permitted Under the Rules

In their preliminary discussion, some board members thought the conduct would be permissible because it was "harmless enough," worthwhile to expose a lying witness, and only accessed information that was already available to the public.

With regard to the notion that the deception is minor and thus within the Rules, examinees might concede that, while the deception is minor, it nonetheless could have significant consequences for the case outcome and for the witness's credibility. If the witness knew the assistant's relationship to the case or her motive in friending the witness—to get impeaching evidence—the witness would not grant access.

Rose and *Brant,* representing two possible approaches a Franklin court might take, make it clear that exposing a lying witness does not justify the use of deception. The *Rose* court refused to make an exception even where lives were in danger. *Brant* did carve out an exception for such a situation and extended it to situations that involve exposing discrimination or protecting intellectual property rights.

Finally, the argument that the information is already publicly available conflates the notion of publicly accessible websites with the accessibility of the information posted on an individual's pages. Even if the witness here is indiscriminate about allowing access to her personal information, someone trying to gain access to it must first seek her permission. And, as discussed earlier, the witness would not grant access to Nelson or her associate if she were informed of the associate's relationship with Nelson.

C. Conclusion

Attorney Nelson should be advised that the proposed course of conduct is not permissible under Franklin's Rules of Professional Conduct.

THE MPT

MULTISTATE PERFORMANCE TEST

Butler v. Hill

FILE

LIBRARY

POINT SHEET

Instructions

The back cover of each test form contains the following instructions:

You will have 90 minutes to complete this session of the examination. This performance test is designed to evaluate your ability to handle a select number of legal authorities in the context of a factual problem involving a client.

The problem is set in the fictitious state of Franklin, in the fictitious Fifteenth Circuit of the United States. Columbia and Olympia are also fictitious states in the Fifteenth Circuit. In Franklin, the trial court of general jurisdiction is the District Court, the intermediate appellate court is the Court of Appeal, and the highest court is the Supreme Court.

You will have two kinds of materials with which to work: a File and a Library. The first document in the File is a memorandum containing the instructions for the task you are to complete. The other documents in the File contain factual information about your case and may include some facts that are not relevant.

The Library contains the legal authorities needed to complete the task and may also include some authorities that are not relevant. Any cases may be real, modified, or written solely for the purpose of this examination. If the cases appear familiar to you, do not assume that they are precisely the same as you have read before. Read them thoroughly, as if they all were new to you. You should assume that the cases were decided in the jurisdictions and on the dates shown. In citing cases from the Library, you may use abbreviations and omit page references.

Your response must be written in the answer book provided. If you are taking the examination on a laptop computer, your jurisdiction will provide you with specific instructions. In answering this performance test, you should concentrate on the materials in the File and Library. What you have learned in law school and elsewhere provides the general background for analyzing the problem; the File and Library provide the specific materials with which you must work.

Although there are no restrictions on how you apportion your time, you should be sure to allocate ample time (about 45 minutes) to reading and digesting the materials and to organizing your answer before you begin writing it. You may make notes anywhere in the test materials; blank pages are provided at the end of the booklet. You may not tear pages from the question booklet.

This performance test will be graded on your responsiveness to the instructions regarding the task you are to complete, which are given to you in the first memorandum in the File, and on the content, thoroughness, and organization of your response.

FILE

Wiggins, Crawford & Samuelson
Attorneys at Law
322 Crescent Road
Ocean City, Franklin 33447

TO:	Examinee
FROM:	Sophia Wiggins
DATE:	February 22, 2011
RE:	Jennifer Butler v. Robert Hill

We represent Jennifer Butler in a suit against Robert Hill seeking a divorce and property distribution. Jennifer and Robert have two children; temporary custody and child support orders are in place that are not currently at issue. Robert has challenged the validity of the parties' underlying marriage. If there is no valid marriage, Jennifer cannot pursue a claim for divorce or a share of marital property. Even if the marriage is valid, Robert claims that the home that Jennifer and the children are living in is not marital property but instead is his individual property.

I have attached the relevant material from Jennifer's file. I will meet with her later this week in anticipation of trial. Please help me with the following two tasks:

First, draft a *short* memo which I may use to prepare for my meeting with Jennifer. In the memo, explain whether Jennifer and Robert's September 1, 2003, ceremonial marriage had any legal effect under Franklin Family Code § 301 *et seq.* Do not write a separate statement of facts, but be sure to incorporate the law and the relevant facts and reach a reasoned conclusion.

Second, draft a closing argument based on the evidence we expect to present at trial to convince the court that (1) there is a valid marriage and (2) the home is marital property and Jennifer is entitled to more than 50 percent of its value. Structure the closing argument as follows:

(1) A *brief* introduction of the case;

(2) Argument; and

(3) Relief sought.

Our closing argument should tell a persuasive story about why Jennifer should prevail, highlighting the evidence that we intend to bring out at trial to support the factors enumerated in the relevant statutes and case law. Be sure to address Robert's position by showing how the evidence fails to support his case and, in fact, supports Jennifer's.

MEMORANDUM

To: Jennifer Butler File
From: Sophia Wiggins
Re: Client Interview Notes

August 2, 2010

Today I met with client Jennifer Butler in regard to a family law matter. Jennifer related her story to me as follows.

In 2003, Jennifer Butler was 17 years old and pregnant with her first child when Robert Hill, the child's father, convinced her to marry him against the wishes of her parents. Robert told her he was single. In fact, unbeknownst to Jennifer at the time, Robert, age 22, was already married and had not yet been legally divorced. Jennifer's parents objected to the marriage and would not consent to it. Caught in a difficult situation, Jennifer married Robert in a civil ceremony with a forged parental consent that Robert had signed, and then she moved in with him.

From the date of the marriage ceremony, September 1, 2003, Jennifer and Robert lived together in Franklin. The parties had two children: Christina Hill, born November 14, 2003, and William Hill, born February 22, 2007. Jennifer never changed her surname. Shortly after the ceremony, Robert began verbally abusing Jennifer. Nevertheless, Jennifer stayed with Robert, living with him, taking care of their two young children, contributing financially to the support of the family, and putting up with Robert's emotional abuse. Both Jennifer and Robert were employed and contributed financially to the household; Robert consistently earned about twice as much as Jennifer. They had a joint checking account, but Jennifer also kept a separate savings account. Jennifer has a life insurance policy naming the children as beneficiaries.

In the summer of 2008, the couple was offered the opportunity to purchase the home that they had rented and had lived in for nearly five years. They put their joint income tax refund toward the down payment and purchased the home on August 12, 2008. Jennifer was not at the closing and has not seen the documents. We need to check the deed.

Butler v. Hill

Four months ago, Jennifer learned that Robert had been having an affair with a coworker and had lent the woman $10,000. Jennifer immediately decided to end the marriage. She and the children stayed in the home, and Robert moved to his mother's house one week later.

While Robert was moving out, Jennifer found in Robert's dresser drawer a copy of a divorce decree that granted Serena Hill a divorce from Robert. Jennifer had never heard of Serena before and had no prior knowledge that Robert had been previously married. When she confronted Robert, he claimed he had not bothered to tell her because he had thought he was divorced from Serena before he married Jennifer and only learned that he wasn't when he was served with the court papers.

Supplemental notes: February 15, 2011

Robert has recently requested that Jennifer and the children move out so that he can sell "his" house. He has told her he expects that she will move by the end of March, at which time he intends to change the locks and place the house on the market to sell.

Excerpt of Transcript of Telephone Interview with Louisa Milligan
(January 28, 2011)

Attorney Wiggins: Louisa, how well do you know Jennifer?

Milligan: We've been close friends for the past five years. I live just down the block from her. We have kids who are the same ages.

Attorney: Do you have reason to believe that Jennifer and Robert are married?

Milligan: Yes, we've been to many social gatherings together, including a celebration of their wedding anniversary.

Attorney: When was this?

Milligan: September of 2009. All of their family and friends came. We had a barbecue in their backyard.

Attorney: Did they specifically refer to themselves as husband and wife?

Milligan: Yes, always. And, in fact, at the anniversary party, Robert gave a toast saying that marrying Jennifer was the smartest thing he'd ever done.

Attorney: Did you ever have any reason to believe that they were not married?

Milligan: No, not until Jennifer called me recently and told me that Robert had apparently been married before and might not have been divorced when they married. She told me that she found a copy of a divorce order in Robert's dresser drawer when they separated last spring. She had not known that Robert was ever married before.

Attorney: Louisa, thank you very much for offering to testify to help Jennifer. We will be calling you again before the trial. Please call me if you have any questions or concerns.

Certificate of Marriage
State of Franklin
Ocean City Municipality
License Number 199330

I Hereby Certify that on the <u>1st</u> day of <u>September 2003</u>, the following persons were by me united in marriage at the Ocean City Courthouse in accordance with the License of the Clerk of the Court in the jurisdiction shown above.

Groom's name: <u>Robert Hill</u>   **Age**: <u>22</u>   **Birthplace**: <u>Columbia</u>

Residence: <u>6226 Berkeley Blvd., Ocean City</u>   **Marital Status**: <u>Single</u>

Bride's name: <u>Jennifer Butler</u>   **Age**: <u>17</u>   **Birthplace**: <u>Franklin</u>

Residence: <u>80 Octavia Street, Ocean City</u>   **Marital Status**: <u>Single</u>

Relationship to Groom if any: <u>None</u>

Consent of Parent of Underage Party (if applicable): <u>Yes, signed consent form presented at time of application for license.</u>

Monica St. George
_____
Signature of Authorized Officer

District Court Judge
_____
Title and Office

Ocean City Municipal Building
_____
Address of Authorized Officer

August 30, 2003
_____
License Date

STATE OF COLUMBIA
CIRCUIT COURT FOR BROOKFIELD COUNTY

Serena Hill, Plaintiff,	)))	
v.	))	Case Number D-445-2008
Robert Hill, Defendant	))))	

JUDGMENT OF DIVORCE

The Complaint for Divorce was heard before the Magistrate on this 15th day of April, 2008, in the Circuit Court for Brookfield County, Columbia. It is hereby

ORDERED that the Plaintiff, SERENA HILL, is granted a Divorce from the Defendant, RO-BERT HILL; and it is further

ORDERED that the Plaintiff is hereby restored to the use of her former name of SERENA JORDAN; and it is further

ORDERED that this judgment of divorce shall become final after 30 days.

Dated: 4/15/2008

Richard Mc Bain

Hon. Richard McBain

Magistrate Judge

DEED

THIS DEED, made on the **12th** day of **August, 2008**, by and between **Martin and Ruth Griffith, a married couple, Joint Owners in fee simple** ("Sellers") and **Robert Hill, a single individual, Sole Owner in fee simple** ("Buyer")

WITNESS that in consideration of the sum of $150,000, the Sellers hereby convey to the Buyer, in fee simple, that parcel of land, together with the improvements, rights, privileges, and appurtenances belonging to the same, situated in the State of Franklin, described as follows, to wit:

Lot 560, Square 6442, also known as 123 Newton Street, Ocean City, Franklin 33455.

And the Sellers covenant that they will warrant specifically the property hereby conveyed.

Martin Griffith
By: Martin Griffith

Ruth Griffith
By: Ruth Griffith

State of Franklin

I, Prudence Best, a notary public in and for the said State of Franklin, do hereby certify that Martin Griffith and Ruth Griffith are the persons who executed the foregoing Deed and did personally appear before me in said jurisdiction.

Prudence Best
Prudence Best, Notary Public

File Number: 07-23-1800

Return after Recording to
Robert Hill
123 Newton Street
Ocean City, Franklin 33455

You are cordially invited to help us celebrate

the

6th Wedding Anniversary

of

Jennifer and Robert

September 1, 2009, at 6 p.m.

123 Newton Street

Drinks, Dinner, Dessert

RSVP: 555-9080   No gifts please

LIBRARY

Butler v. Hill

FRANKLIN FAMILY CODE

§ 301. Marriage of a Minor; Parental Consent; Pregnancy

Marriage of Individual 16 or 17 Years Old

(a) An individual 16 or 17 years old may not marry unless

(1) the individual has the consent of a parent or guardian and the parent or guardian swears that the individual is at least 16 years old; or

(2) if the individual does not have the consent of a parent or guardian, either party to be married gives the clerk a certificate from a licensed physician stating that the physician has examined the woman to be married and has found that she is pregnant or has given birth to a child.

(b) A marriage by an underage person without valid consent as required by this section, though voidable at the time it is entered into, may be ratified and become completely valid and binding when the underage party reaches the age of consent. Validation of a marriage of an underage person by ratification is established by some unequivocal and voluntary act, statement, or course of conduct after reaching the age of consent. Ratification includes, but is not limited to, continued cohabitation as husband and wife after reaching the age of consent.

*   *   *   *

§ 309. Common Law Marriage—Age Restrictions

(1) A common law marriage entered into on or after January 1, 1990, shall not be recognized as a valid marriage in this state unless, at the time the common law marriage is entered into,

(a) each party is 18 years of age or older, and

(b) the marriage is not prohibited as provided in § 310.

§ 310. Prohibited Marriages

(1) The following marriages are prohibited:

(a) A marriage entered into prior to the dissolution of an earlier marriage of one of the parties;

(b) A marriage between an ancestor and a descendant, or between a brother and a sister, whether the relationship is by the half or whole blood;

(c) …

(2) Children born of a prohibited marriage are legitimate.

*   *   *   *

§ 410. Assignment of Separate Property and Equitable Distribution of Marital Property

Upon entry of a final decree of legal separation, annulment, or divorce, in the absence of a valid antenuptial or postnuptial agreement resolving all issues related to the property of the parties, the court shall

(a) assign to each party his or her sole and separate property acquired prior to the marriage, and his or her sole and separate property acquired during the marriage by gift, bequest, devise, or descent, and

(b) distribute all other property and debt accumulated during the marriage, regardless of whether title is held individually or by the parties in a form of joint tenancy or tenancy by the entireties, in a manner that is equitable, just, and reasonable, after considering relevant factors including, but not limited to,

> (1) the duration of the marriage;
> (2) the age, health, occupation, employability, sources of income, and needs of each of the parties;
> (3) each party's contribution as a homemaker or otherwise to the family unit;
> (4) – (11) …
> (12) the circumstances which contributed to the estrangement of the parties.

Hager v. Hager

Franklin Court of Appeal (1996)

This is an appeal from a decree of divorce. The trial court ruled that the parties' marriage was valid and granted a judgment of divorce to the Petitioner, Shirley Hager. Respondent Landon Hager has appealed, contending that the trial court erred in upholding the validity of the marriage. We agree and reverse.

In her petition, Shirley Hager alleged that she and Landon participated in a marriage ceremony on July 20, 1968. At that time, however, Landon had not secured a final decree of divorce from his first wife. He subsequently obtained that decree on March 2, 1969. Shirley's petition alleged that she was unaware that Landon was married to another woman at the time of their marriage and that Landon told her he was divorced. The dispositive issue on appeal is whether there was a valid marriage.

Shirley argues that the marriage was valid. But a bigamous marriage is void *ab initio*. All marriages which are prohibited by law because one of the parties has a spouse then living are absolutely void. A void marriage is one that has no effect. Notwithstanding Franklin Fam. Code § 301, it cannot be ratified. Indeed, persons who engage in such a marriage may be subject to criminal prosecution.

As a result, the marriage ceremony on July 20, 1968, could confer no legal rights. It was as if no marriage had been performed. The parties' marriage is void and cannot support an action for divorce.

The trial court held that the parties' 1968 marriage was merely voidable and that, since Landon had presented himself as Shirley's husband in all respects, he had ratified the marriage. But, as we have said, the marriage was prohibited, therefore void *ab initio,* and thus not subject to ratification.

We conclude, therefore, that the trial court's ruling that the marriage was valid was error and reverse the judgment.

Owen v. Watts

Franklin Court of Appeal (2003)

Thomas Owen appeals from an order granting summary judgment in favor of Cora Watts, decedent Ruby McCall's surviving sister and personal representative, in her action for possession of McCall's home at 316 Forest Avenue. Owen refused to leave the home after McCall's death, claiming that he was McCall's common law husband and that he was therefore entitled to a possessory dower interest in the property. The trial court held that Owen and McCall had never entered into a common law marriage. The court further held that Owen could not claim an interest in the property. Owen appeals.

The record before the trial court on the motion for summary judgment reveals that Owen moved into McCall's home some time after her husband's death in 1981 but before his own divorce in 1986. Owen testified on deposition that following his divorce, he asked McCall to marry him, but that McCall refused because marriage would jeopardize her continued entitlement to a benefit check which she was receiving as a result of her late husband's death. Owen testified that, over the years, he repeatedly asked McCall to marry him but that she refused these requests for the same reason. Owen claimed that McCall finally agreed in 2000 to marry him in 2001, but that she died before the marriage could take place. Cora Watts, McCall's sister, stated in an affidavit that McCall had told her that she had no intention of ever marrying Owen.

Owen represented that he and McCall cohabited and maintained joint bank accounts. He also produced affidavits from two members of the community who regarded him and McCall as husband and wife. Owen offered no evidence, however, which could persuade a rational and impartial trier of fact that, after his divorce, he and McCall had ever manifested an agreement that they were married, as opposed to a belief that they would become married at a later date.

Owen testified that, at the time he moved in with McCall, "she said, 'I want you to come and live with me. I want that we will be as man and wife.'" He claimed that he "said okay" and moved in with her. He further related that he moved in "because she asked me to come and live with her and make our home together as long as we both shall live, until death do us part."

These words, however, were evidently spoken at a time when Owen was already married and not yet divorced, and therefore could not legally agree to marry McCall. Owen was not divorced until October 22, 1986.

Under Franklin law, a common law marriage requires agreement by parties legally capable of entering into a valid marriage that they have a marriage relationship. Cohabitation continued after the removal of a legal impediment cannot ripen into a common law marriage unless it was pursuant to a mutual consent or agreement to be married made after the removal of the barrier.

Owen and McCall conducted their business affairs as single persons rather than as a married couple. McCall referred to herself as single, or as a widow who had not remarried, in deeds and other documents relating to property transactions, as well as in her tax returns. Similarly, in her will, McCall referred to Owen as a "friend" and left him a bequest in that capacity.

The question before the trial court was whether any impartial trier of fact could reasonably find by a preponderance of the evidence that Owen was McCall's common law husband. We agree with the trial court that no reasonable judge or jury could so find.

Franklin has long recognized common law marriages, the elements of which are a manifestation of mutual agreement, by parties able to enter into a valid marriage, that they are presently married, followed by cohabitation, including holding themselves out to the community as being husband and wife. *East v. East* (Fr. Ct. App. 1931).

Since ceremonial marriage is readily available and provides unequivocal proof that the parties are husband and wife, claims of common law marriage should be closely scrutinized, especially where one of the purported spouses is deceased and the survivor is asserting such a claim to promote his financial interest. The burden is on the proponent to prove, by a preponderance of the evidence, all of the essential elements of a common law marriage.

Owen's testimony established at most that he and McCall had, by the end of her life, agreed to be married at an unspecified future time. This is insufficient to establish the existence of a common law marriage under Franklin law.

For the foregoing reasons, the judgment of the trial court is hereby AFFIRMED.

Charles v. Charles

Franklin Court of Appeal (2005)

Teresa Charles appeals from the district court's judgment dissolving her marriage to Larry Charles. Teresa Charles contends that the district court erred in awarding her only 40 percent of the marital property.

The district court found that an equal division of the marital property was "not equitable under the facts of this case due to the conduct of Teresa Charles." The evidence established that Teresa was having an extramarital affair near the end of the marriage.

"The division of marital property need not be equal, but must only be fair and equitable given the circumstances of the case." *Shepard v. Shepard* (Fr. Ct. App. 2003). Generally, "the division of marital property should be substantially equal unless one or more statutory factors causes such a division to be unjust." *Id*. Pursuant to Franklin Fam. Code § 410, the district court is to distribute property upon consideration of any relevant factors supported by the evidence.

The district court, when dividing the marital property, is directed to consider the conduct of the parties during the marriage. However, it cannot use a disproportionate division of the marital property to punish a spouse for misconduct. "It is only when misconduct of one spouse changes the balance so that the other must assume a greater share of the partnership load that it is appropriate that such misconduct affect the property distribution." *Nelson v. Nelson* (Fr. Ct. App. 2002) (trial court properly based its marital property distribution on evidence of husband's extramarital affairs and use of marital funds to pay gambling debts). "The added burden placed on a spouse sufficient to justify a disproportionate division of marital property does not have to be a financial one." *Ballard v. Ballard* (Fr. Ct. App. 2004).

An extramarital affair can be an added burden sufficient to justify a disproportionate division of marital property provided that the evidence establishes the specific added burdens that the non-offending spouse suffered as a result of such misconduct.

The record establishes that Teresa's extramarital affair placed an added burden on Larry during the marriage justifying a disproportionate division of marital property favoring him. Larry testified:

> Well, she continued the relationship even after I confronted her about the affair and I told her I knew everything. She continued living under the same roof, still went on about her affair, lingerie hanging in the laundry room, kind of an in-your-face type of thing. I was still paying all the bills.

She was still not contributing anything, but she was spending our—or should I say my—income that would normally go toward the household for her so-called partying and her rendezvous with her boyfriend. And it's pretty hard to live under the same roof with somebody that you know has been sleeping with somebody else, but she's also still spending your money and eating your food, and you're just supposed to act like nothing happened. This went on like this for more than a year.

The district court properly considered the evidence of Teresa's misconduct during the marriage in distributing the marital property and awarding her only 40 percent of the marital property.

Affirmed.

POINT SHEET

DRAFTERS' POINT SHEET

In this performance test, examinees' firm represents Jennifer Butler in a divorce proceeding against Robert Hill. Examinees must perform two tasks. First, they must write a short objective memorandum for the senior partner to use to prepare for a meeting with Jennifer analyzing the validity of the parties' ceremonial marriage. Examinees should state the reasons and cite the authorities for their conclusions. Next, examinees must draft a closing argument to prepare the partner for a trial in the divorce and property distribution case.

The File contains the task memorandum, the partner's client interview notes, a transcript of a telephone interview with Louisa Milligan, Jennifer and Robert's marriage certificate, the judgment of divorce obtained by Serena Hill against Robert Hill, the deed for the parties' residence, and an invitation to Jennifer and Robert's anniversary party. The Library contains sections of the Franklin Family Code and three cases bearing on the subject.

The following discussion covers all the points the drafters intended to raise in the problem. Examinees need not cover them all to receive passing or even excellent grades. Grading is within the discretion of the user jurisdictions.

I. FORMAT AND OVERVIEW

Task One: Memo: Examinees' first work product should resemble a memorandum from one attorney to another and will be used by the partner to advise Jennifer as to the validity of her 2003 ceremonial marriage. Examinees should use the relevant facts along with the legal authorities and reach a reasoned conclusion as to the validity of the ceremonial marriage. Examinees are instructed *not* to write a separate statement of facts.

Task Two: Closing Argument: Examinees must draft the closing argument in the upcoming divorce trial to convince the court that (1) there is a valid marriage and (2) the home is marital property and Jennifer is entitled to more than 50 percent of its value. Their work product should resemble a well-developed draft, following the structure set forth in the call memorandum (introduction, argument, relief sought), and should be persuasive. In addition to setting forth the most persuasive story about the client's claims, examinees should anticipate the arguments that will be raised by Robert and must craft arguments, citing the applicable rules and case law, that will persuade the trial court that it should find that Jennifer has a valid common law marriage, is entitled to a divorce, and has an enforceable right to arguably more than 50 percent of the value of the house at 123 Newton Street because it is marital property.

II. DETAILED ANALYSIS

Task One: Is the couple's ceremonial marriage valid? Memo to Sophia Wiggins

Summary Response: No, the ceremonial marriage is not valid. Examinees must analyze the issue correctly. That Jennifer was underage at the time of the marriage without proper parental consent or doctor's certification would not render the marriage void because Jennifer could have ratified the marriage upon turning 18. However, the fact of Robert's prior marriage without a divorce created an absolute impediment to the validity of the ceremonial marriage. Thus the initial ceremonial marriage is invalid and void *ab initio* (*Hager v. Hager*).

Analysis:

- Robert has challenged the validity of the underlying marriage to protect his interest in the house. The property deed lists Robert as the sole owner in fee simple. If there is no valid marriage, Jennifer has no right to claim that the house on Newton Street is marital property, nor does she have the right to seek a divorce.

- Key facts: At the time of the ceremony in 2003, Jennifer was only 17 years old and was pregnant with their first child. Robert was 22, and, unbeknownst to Jennifer at the time, he was already married to Serena Hill and had not yet been legally divorced. Jennifer's parents objected to the marriage and would not give their consent to it.

- Under Franklin Family Code § 301(a), because Jennifer was only 17 years old, the parties were required to have either Jennifer's parents' consent or a doctor's certificate stating that she was pregnant. Jennifer and Robert had neither. Despite the fact that Jennifer was pregnant, they did not get a doctor's certificate attesting to this fact. Instead, Robert forged the parental consent form, which did not satisfy the statute's parental consent requirement and therefore is the equivalent of having no consent.

- Underage issue: Under Franklin law, the fact that Jennifer was underage at the time of the marriage ceremony does not render the marriage completely void. Franklin statute § 301(b) states that such a marriage is voidable at the time it is entered into; however, if it is ratified when the underage party reaches the age of consent (i.e., 18 years of age), then the marriage becomes completely valid and binding.

- Jennifer and Robert continued to live together for the next six-plus years and had two children. If Jennifer's age were the only problem with the ceremonial marriage, the marriage would have been ratified by the parties' continuing cohabitation as husband and wife after Jennifer was 18, and thus the initial marriage would be valid despite the lack of consent or doctor's certification. Franklin Fam. Code § 301(b).

- Prior existing marriage: Jennifer did not know that Robert was already married to Serena and was not yet divorced when he married Jennifer. Examinees should conclude that this is a serious defect and, in fact, renders the September 1, 2003, ceremonial marriage absolutely invalid and void. *See Hager v. Hager* (Franklin Ct. App. 1996). According to *Hager*, parties in a bigamous marriage cannot overcome the impediment to marriage. Any marriage under these circumstances is void *ab initio*, not merely voidable. A bigamous ceremonial marriage cannot be ratified; nor does it become effective once the prior marriage is legally dissolved. *Hager*.

- **Ultimate analysis:** The ceremonial marriage was not effective when entered into and did not become valid after Jennifer turned 18 or after Robert's divorce became final.

Task Two: Closing Argument, Part One: The parties have a valid common law

marriage.

- Franklin is one of the minority jurisdictions that recognize the validity of common law marriages. Franklin Fam. Code § 309. Under § 309, a party who is 18 years or older and not subject to a legal impediment as set forth in § 310 (i.e., if prior undissolved marriage exists or if relationship between the parties would be incestuous) can enter into a valid common law marriage. §§ 309 & 310.

- *Owen v. Watts* (Franklin Ct. App. 2003) sets forth the elements of a common law marriage in Franklin: a mutual agreement to be married in the present tense by parties able to enter into a valid marriage, followed by cohabitation and holding themselves out to the community as being husband and wife. *East v. East* (Franklin Ct. App. 1931) (cited in *Owen v. Watts*).

- *Owen* involved the personal representative (Cora Watts) of the woman who was allegedly the common law wife (Ruby McCall) and the man alleging to be her common law husband (Thomas Owen) in a dispute over rights to McCall's home.

- Owen alleged that he and McCall had a common law marriage. He moved into McCall's home after her husband died but before Owen's divorce had become final. After his divorce became final, Owen repeatedly asked McCall to marry him; however, she refused because she did not want to jeopardize her benefits as a widow. Finally, after many years of cohabitation, she agreed to marry him the next year, but she died before the marriage could take place.

  - Owen also alleged other facts that he claimed proved that he and McCall had a common law marriage: McCall's statements evincing her intent to be married to him when he moved in with her, joint bank accounts, and two affidavits of community members saying that they thought he and McCall were married.

  - McCall's sister testified that McCall had told her that she had no intention of marrying Owen; they filed separate income tax returns as single individuals and maintained separate business affairs. In McCall's will, she referred to Owen as a "friend" and left him a bequest in that capacity.

- The *Owen* court held that there was no common law marriage because the parties did not have a present agreement to be married when Owen was legally capable of entering into a marriage relationship.

- The burden of proof is on the proponent of a common law marriage to prove all elements by a preponderance of the evidence.

The following evidence favors a common law marriage between Jennifer and Robert:

- Robert's first wife, Serena, obtained a divorce judgment from Robert in Columbia on April 15, 2008. The order became final in 30 days, on May 15, 2008.

- Once Robert divorced, a common law marriage between him and Jennifer became possible. A preponderance of the evidence establishes that they had a valid common law marriage.

  - Mutual intent: Jennifer initially expressed her intent to marry Robert by participating in the ceremonial marriage. She had no idea that Robert had been married, let alone still was married. So in her mind, she and Robert were validly married. There is no evidence that Jennifer ever changed this intent while they cohabited. Robert claims that he thought his first wife had already finalized a divorce before his marriage ceremony with Jennifer. He went ahead with the ceremony and held himself out as being married to Jennifer. After the divorce was final, he continued to live with Jennifer and hold himself out as her husband, and he also stated at a public forum (i.e., their wedding anniversary party) how smart he had been to marry Jennifer.

  - Cohabitation: The parties continued to cohabit as husband and wife after the divorce became final. They continued to raise their two children together. They shared household expenses and bought a house. They had a joint bank account and filed at least one joint income tax return.

Until Robert moved out in 2010, Jennifer had no idea that there was a serious legal impediment to their marriage and in fact thought they were married. This is strong evidence demonstrating that both Jennifer and Robert had a present intent to be married at a time when a common law marriage could have been formed.

- Community reputation: Robert and Jennifer both held themselves out to the community as being married. Despite the fact that Jennifer had never adopted Robert's surname, neighbors believed that they were married.

- Louisa Milligan, a neighbor and friend, said that Robert and Jennifer always referred to themselves as married. Robert told everyone that marrying Jennifer was the smartest thing he had ever done. This evidence should establish that Robert also had a present intent to be married to Jennifer. The divorce had become final in May 2008 and the party occurred well thereafter, so this statement was made at a time when a common law marriage was possible.

Task Two: Closing Argument, Part Two: Jennifer is entitled to more than 50% of the value of the Newton Street house.

Because the legal impediment to a common law marriage (i.e., Robert's prior marriage) was removed by the April 15, 2008, Columbia divorce order (final on May 15, 2008), it is likely that the court will find that Robert and Jennifer had a valid common law marriage when the house on Newton Street was purchased on August 12, 2008. If so, then the house is marital property even though the deed is in Robert's name alone. Under Franklin Family Code § 410(b), the court has the power to distribute all property accumulated during the marriage, regardless of whether title is held individually or by the parties as joint tenants. Thus Robert's attempt to make

the house his individual property by putting his name alone on the deed was ineffective to prevent the house from becoming marital property.

Under Franklin law, the court is authorized to divide the marital property in a manner that is equitable, just, and reasonable. Franklin is not a community property state; instead it uses principles of equitable distribution. The court is directed to look at all relevant factors, including the circumstances that contributed to the marriage's breakup. Here the factors weigh heavily against Robert, and the court is likely to find that Jennifer is entitled to at least 50 percent, if not more, of the value of the house. It is highly unlikely that the court will order Jennifer to vacate the house. *Charles v. Charles* (Fr. Ct. App. 2005) supports Jennifer's position that Robert's adultery, his $10,000 loan, and his other behavior placed a greater burden on Jennifer. Thus, the court should award her more than 50 percent of the property. In *Charles*, the innocent spouse was awarded 60 percent of the marital property. Jennifer should be awarded at least that much.

Analysis:

- Robert and Jennifer had rented the house at 123 Newton Street for several years before they purchased it on August 12, 2008, three months after Robert's divorce became final on May 15, 2008. Therefore, it is highly probable that a common law marriage existed between Robert and Jennifer on the date of purchase.

- If the parties were married at the time of purchase, then the property is marital property, subject to equitable distribution at divorce, despite the fact that the house is titled solely in Robert's name.

- Jennifer contributed financially to the down payment, just as Robert did.

- Robert is attempting to deny Jennifer her rights to the marital property, first by putting the house in his name alone and later by telling Jennifer that she and the children must move out because the house is his sole property. This behavior is likely to demonstrate his lack of good faith in his dealings with Jennifer about the property.

- Robert has been deceitful with Jennifer throughout the marriage. He misrepresented his marital status. He convinced Jennifer to marry him and presented a forged parental consent form to accomplish this. The File memorandum notes that he was verbally and emotionally abusive to Jennifer. He also had an affair with a coworker while he and Jennifer were still together, and he loaned his paramour $10,000. Finally, Robert demanded that Jennifer and the children move out of "his" house.

- In *Charles*, the court held that the wife's extramarital affair could place an added burden on her husband sufficient to justify disproportionate division of marital property provided that the evidence established the specific added burdens that he suffered as a result of the misconduct. Jennifer should be able to argue that the factors above placed additional emotional and financial burdens on her.

- Examinees might cite the other factors in Franklin Fam. Code § 410(b)(1)–(12) that the court may consider in dividing property at divorce in support of their arguments that Jennifer is entitled to more than 50% of the value of the home.

In re Magnolia County

In re Magnolia County

FILE

LIBRARY

POINT SHEET

Instructions

The back cover of each test form contains the following instructions:

You will have 90 minutes to complete this session of the examination. This performance test is designed to evaluate your ability to handle a select number of legal authorities in the context of a factual problem involving a client.

The problem is set in the fictitious state of Franklin, in the fictitious Fifteenth Circuit of the United States. Columbia and Olympia are also fictitious states in the Fifteenth Circuit. In Franklin, the trial court of general jurisdiction is the District Court, the intermediate appellate court is the Court of Appeal, and the highest court is the Supreme Court.

You will have two kinds of materials with which to work: a File and a Library. The first document in the File is a memorandum containing the instructions for the task you are to complete. The other documents in the File contain factual information about your case and may include some facts that are not relevant.

The Library contains the legal authorities needed to complete the task and may also include some authorities that are not relevant. Any cases may be real, modified, or written solely for the purpose of this examination. If the cases appear familiar to you, do not assume that they are precisely the same as you have read before. Read them thoroughly, as if they all were new to you. You should assume that the cases were decided in the jurisdictions and on the dates shown. In citing cases from the Library, you may use abbreviations and omit page references.

Your response must be written in the answer book provided. If you are taking the examination on a laptop computer, your jurisdiction will provide you with specific instructions. In answering this performance test, you should concentrate on the materials in the File and Library. What you have learned in law school and elsewhere provides the general background for analyzing the problem; the File and Library provide the specific materials with which you must work.

Although there are no restrictions on how you apportion your time, you should be sure to allocate ample time (about 45 minutes) to reading and digesting the materials and to organizing your answer before you begin writing it. You may make notes anywhere in the test materials; blank pages are provided at the end of the booklet. You may not tear pages from the question booklet.

This performance test will be graded on your responsiveness to the instructions regarding the task you are to complete, which are given to you in the first memorandum in the File, and on the content, thoroughness, and organization of your response.

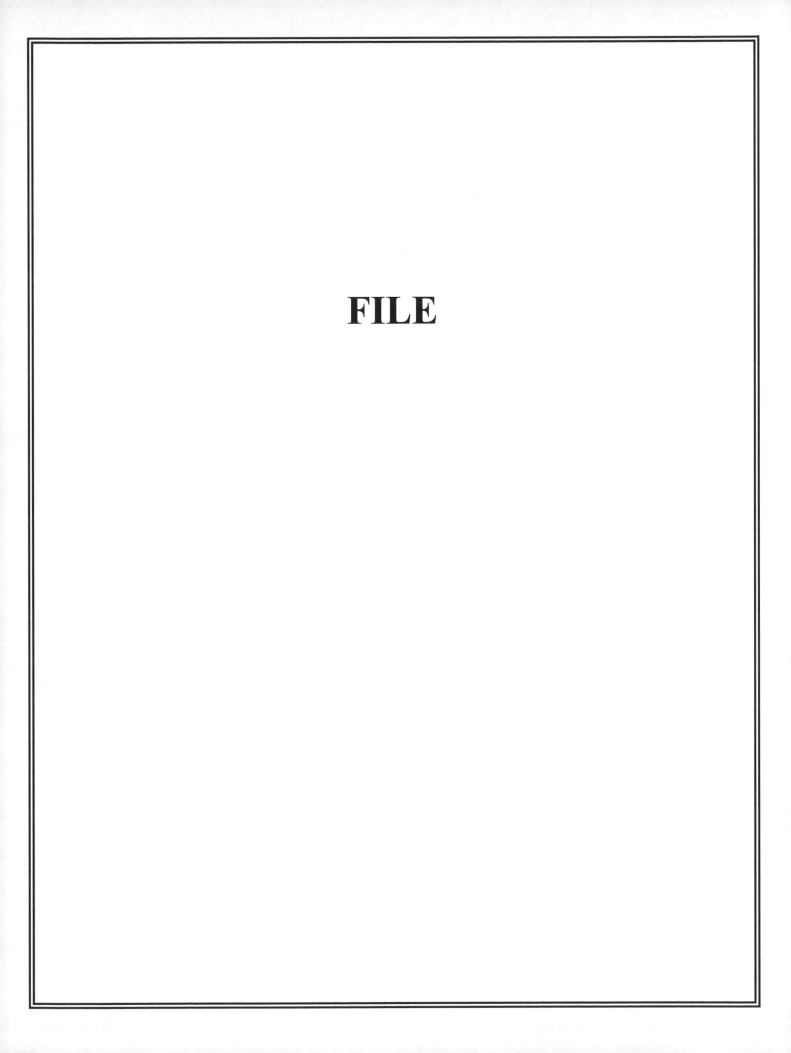

FILE

MEMORANDUM

To: Examinee
From: Lily Byron, Deputy County Counsel
Date: February 22, 2011
Re: Proposed Condemnation Action

The County is considering building a four-lane road connecting State Highway 44 (SH44) to State Highway 50 (SH50) to ease the demands on the County's transportation system. SH44 and SH50 run parallel to each other and are about five miles apart.

I have spoken with the County's Road and Bridge Department about the plans. (See attached notes.) To build the connector road, we will need to obtain easements and rights-of-way from various landowners giving us permission to construct the road. The one potential holdout is Plymouth Railroad, which owns and operates railroad facilities on a portion of the land between SH44 and SH50.

Before we can construct the connector road, we will need to obtain a 60-foot-wide easement from Plymouth over a portion of its railroad track. Our only option is to construct the connector road at ground level and have the road directly cross the railroad track. This is known as an "at-grade crossing," and it will require the installation of warning lights, railroad crossing arms, and other equipment designed to prevent cars and pedestrians from attempting to cross the railroad track while it is being used by a train.

Last week, I had a preliminary meeting with representatives of Plymouth. (See attached summary.) If we cannot reach an agreement with Plymouth, then the County will need to exercise its eminent domain powers under state law and file a condemnation action here in Magnolia County District Court to acquire the easement.

If we do so, Plymouth's representatives have told us that the railroad will claim that our condemnation action is preempted by federal law pursuant to the Interstate Commerce Commission Termination Act (ICCTA), a federal statute that governs railroad operations.

Please draft a memorandum analyzing whether a condemnation action to acquire the easement for the at-grade crossing of Plymouth's railroad track would be preempted under the ICCTA. Do not prepare a separate statement of facts, but be sure that your memorandum weaves together the law and the facts and reaches a reasoned conclusion.

COUNTY COUNSEL'S OFFICE
MAGNOLIA COUNTY

Notes of 1/18/11 meeting with James Wesson, Senior Engineer, County Road & Bridge Dept.

- SH44 and SH50 are north-south roads that run parallel to each other. SH44 is about five miles east of SH50. Presently, SH44 is the primary means for suburban County residents who live north of the City of Harley to commute into and out of the City.

- Currently, most commuters who live northeast of the City and work northwest of the City (in the Harley Business Park) drive several miles out of their way south on SH44 into the City and then out again north on SH50 to get to the Business Park in what amounts to a big U-turn. Building a connector road between SH44 and SH50 north of the City will create a shortcut to the Business Park, and thus will ease traffic congestion.

- The connector road will also provide access to a large residential subdivision, Red Bluff, which is proposed for development adjacent to the connector road. The total size of the development will be 1,300 acres, and it will include retail, office, institutional (church, medical, etc.), multi-family residential, and single-family residential buildings, as well as recreational and greenbelt spaces. The connector road will be the only means of access to the Red Bluff development.

- The connector road will be a four-lane boulevard, with two lanes going in each direction. It will be designated as a major thoroughfare by Magnolia County and, as such, will be an integral part of the regional mobility system for the area.

- A railroad track owned and operated by Plymouth Railroad Inc. runs parallel to and in between SH44 and SH50. The proposed connector road will have to cross the track. We have investigated the feasibility of building an overpass over the railroad track or an underpass under it, but both of those are cost-prohibitive. After extensive and detailed engineering analysis, the only viable and cost-effective option is an at-grade crossing.

- The proposed at-grade crossing will traverse the existing single-track segment of Plymouth's rail line. The segment does not include a passing track and is not used to stage trains for loading and unloading or to park railcars.

- Traffic safety and control devices for at-grade crossings include a range of passive and active devices designed to warn of the existence of a railroad track and prevent automobile and pedestrian access to the track immediately before, during, and after the time that the track is in use by a train. Passive devices include warning signs, warning pavement markings, crossing (also known as "crossbuck" or "X") signs, and number-of-track signs. Active devices include flashing-light signals (post-mounted), automatic gates, and overhead flashing-light signals. Typically, train speed must be reduced to between 5 and 15 miles per hour while the train passes an at-grade crossing, and the train's crew is required to sound the train's horn when approaching the crossing.

- However, the proposed at-grade crossing may qualify for designation as a "Quiet Zone" if enhanced safety features are installed, such as "constant warning" technology and quadruple gate systems that block vehicle traffic and prevent cars from driving around or between crossing arms into the path of an oncoming train. If so, train speed might need to be reduced by only a few miles per hour in the area of the crossing, and the train's crew would not have to sound the train's horn at the crossing. The County's budget for the connector road project includes sufficient funds to cover the cost of implementing a Quiet Zone.

- Because of the large number of significant variables to be considered, no single standard system of traffic safety and control devices is universally applicable for all at-grade crossings. The appropriate traffic control system to be used at an at-grade crossing should be determined by an engineering study involving both the government agency that is constructing the road and the railroad company.

COUNTY COUNSEL'S OFFICE
MAGNOLIA COUNTY

MEMORANDUM

To: File
From: Lily Byron, Deputy County Counsel
Date: February 16, 2011
Re: Meeting with Plymouth Railroad representatives

Yesterday, I met with Clark DeWitt, Assistant Director of Operations, and Monica Leo, Government Liaison for Plymouth, to discuss the County's proposed connector road between SH44 and SH50. I described the proposed location of the connector road, its purpose, and the benefits to County residents. I told the Plymouth representatives that the County wants to work with Plymouth to minimize any impact during construction of the crossing.

The Plymouth representatives expressed concern about the potential impact of the at-grade crossing on the company's railroad operations, citing problems they have encountered with at-grade crossings in other areas of the state. They declined to mention any specifics but told me that, based on Plymouth's past experience, any track crossing would increase track maintenance costs and interfere with the company's rail operations.

The Plymouth representatives also discussed the anticipated heavy use of the connector road by commuters and the potential safety risks to vehicles at the proposed crossing. They stated that the track between SH44 and SH50 is an active track that extends between Franklin and Columbia. The track is used by as many as 20 trains per day, most being heavy freight trains. They said that it takes more than half a mile to stop a heavy freight train even when emergency braking is used, and they expressed concerns about the railroad's potential liability in the event that a car or pedestrian were to be struck by a train. They also said that Plymouth would not consider granting an easement unless the County agreed to indemnify Plymouth for any harm that might result to persons or vehicles as a result of the at-grade crossing.

When I mentioned the possibility of the County instituting condemnation proceedings if Plymouth refuses to grant the easement, the Plymouth representatives stated that any condemnation action would be preempted under the Interstate Commerce Commission Termination Act.

LIBRARY

Butte County v. 105,000 Square Feet of Land
Franklin Court of Appeal (2005)

Butte County appeals from the trial court's dismissal of the County's condemnation action. Butte County sought to condemn 105,000 square feet of land owned by the defendant railroad SRX in Butte County.[1] The County wanted the property for a pedestrian and bicycle trail. SRX filed a motion for summary judgment contending that the condemnation action was preempted by the Interstate Commerce Commission Termination Act (ICCTA), 49 U.S.C. § 10101 *et seq.* The County maintained that the ICCTA does not necessarily preempt its eminent domain authority when dealing with railroads.

The preemption doctrine is rooted in the Supremacy Clause of the Constitution and stands for the general proposition that state laws that interfere with, or are contrary to, federal law must be invalidated. Application of the preemption doctrine requires the court to examine congressional intent, whether it be express or implied. The purpose of Congress is the ultimate touchstone in the preemption analysis.

In 1995, Congress passed the ICCTA, which reinforced the federal government's continued goals "to promote a safe and efficient rail transportation system" and to "ensure development and continuation of a sound rail transportation system with effective competition among rail carriers." 49 U.S.C. § 10101(3), (4). The ICCTA provides that "[e]xcept as otherwise provided in this part, the remedies provided under this part with respect to the regulation of rail transportation are exclusive and preempt the remedies provided under Federal or State law." *Id.* § 10501(b)(2). By enacting the ICCTA, Congress sought to ensure that states would not regulate rail transportation in a way that would conflict with or undermine the provisions of the ICCTA.

The preemption inquiry focuses on the degree to which the challenged state action burdens rail transportation. It is well settled that state and local regulation is permissible where it does not interfere with interstate rail operations. Rather, routine, nonconflicting uses, such as nonexclusive

---

[1] Condemnation (also called eminent domain) is the power of federal, state, or local government to take private property for "public use" so long as the government pays "just compensation," which is typically the fair market value of the property as of a certain date. The government can exercise its power of eminent domain even if a property owner does not want to sell the property. Examples of public uses for which a government might exercise its power of eminent domain include public utilities, roads, schools, libraries, police stations, and other similar public uses. Eminent domain may involve taking ownership of the property or a lesser property interest, such as an easement.

easements for at-grade road crossings, wire crossings such as overhead electric power lines, and underground sewer crossings, are not preempted so long as they do not impede rail operations or pose undue safety risks.

Thus, here, the inquiry is twofold: (1) whether the County's intended use of SRX's property would prevent or unreasonably interfere with railroad operations, and (2) whether the County's intended use would pose undue safety risks.

With regard to the first inquiry, SRX contends that a bicycle and pedestrian trail would interfere with railroad operations because the trail would impede its access to its signal boxes and prevent railroad maintenance. The County argues that SRX could access its signal equipment from the southern side of its property and could maintain its railroad track. Because SRX would still have vehicular access to its signal equipment and would have general access for the purpose of railroad maintenance, the Court concludes that the proposed easement would not impede railroad operations. *See Morgan City v. Metro Railroad* (Fr. Ct. App. 1998) (action to condemn part of train yard for city revitalization project preempted as it would leave insufficient room for loading and unloading of railcars).

This brings the Court to the next inquiry: whether the County's intended use would pose an undue safety risk. SRX contends that when an active railroad track is in close proximity to a pedestrian and bicycle trail, SRX's policy is to have its property line a minimum of 50 feet from the centerline of the railroad track. SRX argues that the proposed easement would reduce this distance to 25 feet and create a safety risk without the appropriate setback distance, fencing, and other safety precautions. The County responds that only a parking lot for the bike trail would be within 25 feet of the active rail and that the trail itself would maintain the 50-foot setback distance. In addition, the County intends to provide security fencing between any trail facility and active rail.

While a safety risk is always present whenever an active railroad track is involved, the Court agrees with the County that its maintenance of the 50-foot setback distance from the active railroad track along with fencing to prevent access to the active rail would prevent any undue safety risk. Therefore, because the use of SRX's property would not interfere with railroad operations and the County's implementation of proper safety precautions would prevent any undue risk, the County's condemnation action is not preempted by the ICCTA.

Reversed.

City of Elk Grove v. B&R Railroad

Franklin Court of Appeal (2007)

Defendant B&R Railroad appeals from a denial of its motion for summary judgment to dismiss the City of Elk Grove's condemnation action. B&R claimed that condemnation of its property would prevent or unduly interfere with railroad operations and interstate commerce and that, as a result, the condemnation action is preempted by 49 U.S.C. § 10501(b), the Interstate Commerce Commission Termination Act (ICCTA).

In its condemnation complaint, the City claimed it was entitled to obtain an easement across B&R's property to construct, install, operate, and maintain an underground storm sewer. The City alleges that before filing the condemnation action, it asked B&R to grant an easement allowing the City to move forward with construction and installation of the storm sewer. By letter, B&R advised the City that it would grant an easement only if the City agreed to indemnify B&R against any liability related to the existence and construction of the storm sewer on its property. The letter did not mention any concern that railroad service would be disrupted by the storm sewer project.

The City and B&R entered into negotiations for the storm sewer easement but were unable to reach an agreement regarding the terms of the easement. Among other things, the parties disputed whether the City should be required to "replace" rather than "restore" any railroad track that might be removed or disturbed by the storm sewer project and whether the project must be completed within B&R's specified timetable rather than the 120 calendar days proposed by the City. The City also refused to agree to B&R's proposed indemnification provisions, which would have required the City to contractually indemnify B&R for any environmental contamination resulting from the storm sewer construction and any property damage or bodily injury claims related directly or indirectly to the sewer line construction. After negotiations broke down, the City filed the instant condemnation action.

In its summary judgment motion, B&R claimed that the City's proposed storm sewer project would interfere with B&R's railroad operations and that therefore the project is subject to the ICCTA. The City conceded that construction of the storm sewer project would cause B&R's spur track (which is used for loading and unloading railcars) to be out of service for about one week (and possibly less with careful planning), but that railcar loads received by B&R could be unloaded from the main track during this brief period of time. The City further asserted that B&R's railcar volume on the track is low (approximately only 50 cars a year) and that construction of the storm sewer would not burden B&R's rail service. Finally, the City indicated that it would work with B&R in designing and constructing the storm sewer in order to minimize any interference with B&R's railroad operations caused by the construction and existence of the storm sewer.

As the party seeking summary judgment, B&R bore the burden of proving that condemnation of an underground easement on B&R's property for the storm sewer project would impede rail operations or pose an undue safety risk. It failed to meet its burden. The arguments raised over the terms of insurance coverage and written indemnification provisions involve allocation of risk, not the regulation of rail transportation.

Moreover, B&R has not explained how the distinction between "replacing" and "restoring" its track following construction of the storm sewer would affect its continued use of the track for rail transport. Though B&R contends that the City must comply with its timetable for completion and should hire only subcontractors experienced in working with railroad beds and tracks, it is questionable whether these issues are really in dispute, and the possible impact of the project's timing and the subcontractors' experience level with rail transportation is too speculative to justify preemption.

Affirmed.

Conroe County v. Atlantic Railroad Co.

Franklin Court of Appeal (2009)

Atlantic Railroad Co. appeals the judgment in condemnation granting Conroe County an easement for an at-grade crossing. We hold that the condemnation action is preempted under the Interstate Commerce Commission Termination Act (ICCTA) and reverse.

Atlantic operates an interstate rail network; its railroad facilities here include a regular railroad track and a passing track. A passing track is an integral component in the operation of a single-track line, as it enables multiple trains to use one main track by allowing trains on the same track heading in opposite directions to pass each other. One train switches to the passing track to allow the other train heading in the opposite direction to continue on the single main track. A passing track, like a main track, is "transportation" as defined by the ICCTA.

Here, Atlantic uses the passing track to stage meets and passes of trains for its rail operations, to load and unload trains, and to park coal trains. The County condemned a strip of Atlantic's land containing a segment of the passing track and proposes to make it a public crossing with a four-lane boulevard, which will access a planned residential development. This proposed crossing would cut the passing track into two pieces, each being approximately 4,900 feet long. There is another crossing available to access the proposed development at one end of the passing track. The existing crossing does not bisect the passing track.

In support of its position that there is no preemption, the County relies on *Butte County v. 105,000 Square Feet of Land* (Fr. Ct. App. 2005). *Butte* holds that routine crossings with nonconflicting uses are not preempted. However, if such crossings impede rail operations or pose undue safety risks, they are preempted by the ICCTA. *Id.*

Whether a state action is preempted by the ICCTA is determined on a case-by-case basis. It is a fact-specific inquiry. Here we are not considering a routine crossing with a nonconflicting use. The record shows that the proposed crossing would cut through Atlantic's passing track—a track used to meet and pass trains, to park 8,500-foot-long coal trains, and as a staging area for loading and unloading trains within a 30-mile area. In order to recover what it had prior to the taking—a 1.86-mile (9,820-foot) uncut passing track necessary to its railroad operations—Atlantic must move part of the passing track or the crossing must be removed.

Preemption cannot be avoided by simply invoking the convenient excuse of a state government entity's condemnation power. The County cannot do anything to Atlantic's property that would directly burden or impede the interstate traffic of the company or impair the usefulness of its facilities for such traffic. The record contains ample evidence establishing that placing the public crossing over the regular and passing tracks would interfere with railroad operations and cause safety hazards.

As to the impact of the crossing on rail operations, Atlantic has presented affidavits and testimony detailing the interference that would be caused by the crossing. Atlantic has demonstrated, among other things, that the passing track is the only uncut passing track within 30 miles and that the proposed crossing would affect the entire line.

Atlantic has also shown that it parks coal trains on the passing track approximately four days a week and that Atlantic is paid a fee based on the number of trains it is able to park on the passing track. These parked trains would block the crossing for extended periods of time. Atlantic's evidence further demonstrates that (i) by law, any train that blocks a public crossing for more than 10 minutes must be "broken" (divided into segments); (ii) when trains are broken, there is a delay of approximately 45 minutes for the reconnection; and (iii) if the train sits broken for longer than 4 hours, a federal law is triggered specifying that an air-brake test must be done before moving the train, which delays the train approximately 90 minutes. Atlantic has stated that when the track is used to pass trains, other trains may have to be broken and the same time added to their connection, causing scheduling problems and time delays throughout the line, not just at the passing track.

As to the issue of undue safety risk, Atlantic has presented evidence that citizens worry about emergency vehicles being able to proceed through the blocked crossing. Atlantic has also produced evidence of citizens' complaints that broken trains sitting approximately 140 feet from the crossing create a visual hazard and that, therefore, the trains need to be parked at least 250 feet from each side of the crossing so that drivers can see past both tracks. To park the trains farther from the crossing would take away the use of an additional 220 aggregate feet of the passing track.

Atlantic does not argue, and we do not hold, that the entire field of eminent domain law is preempted. However, when state eminent domain law amounts to a regulation of the railroad, it is expressly preempted. A state law may not impose operating limitations on a railroad's economic decisions, such as those pertaining to train length, speed, or scheduling. Moreover, when a law has the *effect* of requiring the railroad to undergo substantial capital improvements, it is preempted by the ICCTA. Here, the County chose to sever the passing track instead of expanding the existing crossing at the end of the track. It is hard to understand why the

County insists on pursuing a crossing over two *active* railway lines that will interfere with railroad operations when other viable entrances to the proposed residential development are physically available.

According to the evidence presented, the condemnation has the effect of regulating Atlantic now and in the future by affecting the speed and length of its trains, interfering with current railroad operations, and causing more federally mandated air-brake tests and, as a result, has a negative economic effect on the railroad.

The County's proposed crossing, which would bisect Atlantic's passing track with a four-lane boulevard, would impermissibly interfere with railroad operations. Moreover, as discussed above, the proposed crossing would create traffic hazards and therefore would pose an undue safety risk. Accordingly, we hold that the County's proposed action is preempted. We reverse and direct the trial court to dismiss the action.

POINT SHEET

In re Magnolia County
DRAFTERS' POINT SHEET

In this performance test item, examinees are employed by the Magnolia County Counsel's Office. The County is considering connecting State Highway 44 (SH44) to State Highway 50 (SH50) in order to ease the demands on the County's transportation system due to population growth. SH44 and SH50 run parallel to each other and are about five miles apart. Building a connecting road between these two highways will reduce traffic congestion into and out of the City of Harley caused by suburban commuters traveling to the Harley Business Park. It will also provide access to Red Bluff, a residential subdivision that is proposed for development midway between SH44 and SH50. Before the County can construct the connector road, it must obtain a 60-foot-wide easement from Plymouth Railroad Company over a portion of Plymouth's railroad track and install an at-grade crossing of the track.[2] If Plymouth refuses to grant the easement, then the County will need to exercise its eminent domain powers under state law and file a condemnation action in state court to force Plymouth to grant the easement. Plymouth is digging in its heels and contending that a condemnation action would be preempted by the Interstate Commerce Commission Termination Act (ICCTA), a federal statute that governs railroad operations. Examinees' task is to draft an objective memorandum analyzing whether a condemnation action to acquire the easement for the at-grade crossing of Plymouth's railroad track would be preempted under the ICCTA.

The File consists of the instructional memo from the supervising attorney, notes from a meeting between the supervising attorney and the senior engineer of the County's Road & Bridge Department, and a memo summarizing the preliminary meeting between the supervising attorney and Plymouth representatives. The Library contains three Franklin cases bearing on the subject.

The following discussion covers all the points the drafters intended to raise in the problem. Examinees need not cover all of them to receive passing or even excellent grades. Grading

---

[2] An at-grade crossing occurs when a road directly crosses a railroad track, rather than going over the railroad track by way of an overpass or going under the railroad track by way of an underpass. Typically, an at-grade crossing requires the installation of warning lights, crossing arms, and other equipment designed to prevent cars and pedestrians from attempting to cross a railroad track that is being used by a train.

is within the discretion of the user jurisdictions.

I.   Overview

The task is to write an objective memorandum analyzing whether the ICCTA would preempt a condemnation action by the County against Plymouth. No specific formatting guidelines are provided, except that examinees are instructed not to prepare a separate statement of facts. Instead, they are instructed to "weave[] together the law and the facts and reach[] a reasoned conclusion."

II.   Legal Authority

The following points, which examinees should extract and use in formulating their analyses, emerge from the cases in the Library:

- The preemption doctrine is rooted in the Supremacy Clause of the Constitution and stands for the general proposition that courts implement Congress's intent for a federal law to trump, and therefore supersede the enforceability of, a state law. The purpose of Congress is the ultimate touchstone in the preemption analysis. *Butte County v. 105,000 Square Feet of Land* (Franklin Ct. App. 2005).

- The ICCTA provides that "[e]xcept as otherwise provided in this part, the remedies provided under this part with respect to the regulation of rail transportation are exclusive and preempt the remedies provided under Federal or State law." *Butte County* (quoting 49 U.S.C. § 10501(b)(2)).

- By enacting the ICCTA, Congress ensured that states would not impose regulations on the railroads that conflict with or undermine those set forth in the ICCTA. *Butte County*.

- However, state and local regulation is permissible where it does not interfere with interstate rail operations. *Id.*

- Routine, nonconflicting uses, such as nonexclusive easements for at-grade road crossings, wire crossings such as overhead electric power lines, and underground sewer crossings, are not preempted so long as they do not impede rail operations or pose undue safety risks. *Id.*

- Where there is no impediment or undue safety risk involved, the ICCTA does not preempt a city's local condemnation proceeding to install subsurface utilities under the main line of an active railroad track. *City of Elk Grove v. B&R Railroad* (Franklin Ct. App. 2007).

- Under the two-prong preemption test articulated in *Butte County*, acquisition of an easement by eminent domain to permit a crossing of a railroad track in connection with construction of a new public road would not implicate 49 U.S.C. § 10501(b)'s preemption unless the road would (i) "prevent or unreasonably interfere with railroad operations" or (ii) "pose undue safety risks."

- On the other hand, proposed uses that prevent or unreasonably interfere with railroad operations or otherwise impose operating limitations on a railroad's economic decisions (such as those pertaining to train length, speed, or scheduling) will likely be preempted under the ICCTA. *Conroe County v. Atlantic Railroad Co.* (Franklin Ct. App. 2009).

  - Moreover, when a law has the *effect* of requiring a railroad to undergo substantial capital improvements, it is preempted by the ICCTA. *Id.*

III. Analysis

A. The ICCTA Is Implicated by the Proposed At-Grade Crossing and Any Related Eminent Domain Action.

As a preliminary matter, examinees should conclude that the ICCTA is implicated by the County's proposed connector road and at-grade crossing.

- Plymouth owns and operates railcars, tracks, and other equipment related to rail transportation, and the rail track in question is used by heavy freight trains.

- The situation here involves interstate railroad transportation, thus falling within the parameters of the statute.

  - Plymouth's track extends from Magnolia County, Franklin, into the neighboring state of Columbia. (*See* Memo to file.)

- By enacting the ICCTA, Congress sought to ensure that states would not regulate rail transportation in a way that would conflict with or undermine the provisions of the ICCTA. *Butte County*.

- Preemption analysis requires a factual assessment of the degree to which the challenged state action burdens rail transportation.

- It is a fact-specific inquiry determined on a case-by-case basis. *See Conroe County*.

B. A County Eminent Domain Action Would Not Be Preempted under the ICCTA Because the Crossing Would Not "Prevent or Unreasonably Interfere with Railroad Operations" or "Pose Undue Safety Risks."

At the meeting with the supervising attorney, the Plymouth representatives raised a number of concerns and issues about the proposed at-grade crossing. However, careful evaluation of Plymouth's claims and a thorough analysis of the cases in the Library should lead examinees to conclude that the proposed crossing would not prevent or unreasonably interfere with railroad operations or pose undue safety risks. A well-reasoned analysis should include the following points:

- With regard to the potential for interruption of Plymouth's rail operations, the memo summarizing the meeting with Plymouth representatives references the railroad's assertions that increased maintenance costs and other unspecified problems may result if the connector road and at-grade crossing are installed, based on its experiences in other areas of the state.

- In *City of Elk Grove*, the Court rejected generalized concerns about the potential impact of an underground storm sewer, concluding that the possible impact of the timetable for completing installation of the storm sewer and the subcontractors' experience level with rail transportation were "too speculative" to justify ICCTA preemption.

  - Here, Plymouth's concerns are even more amorphous and thus all the more speculative.

  - Even if the installation of the crossing increases track maintenance expenses, as mentioned by the Plymouth representatives, in order for there to be preemption based on the effect on rail operations, the state action must *prevent or unreasonably interfere with* railroad operations.

- It is unlikely that an unquantified increased maintenance expense for the railroad rises to that standard.

- This is in contrast to *Morgan City v. Metro Railroad* (Franklin Ct. App. 1988, cited in *Butte County*), in which the court held that the plaintiff city was preempted from condemning part of a train yard for a city revitalization project because it left too little land for the railroad to load and unload cars.

- There is no allegation that the connector road would prevent or unreasonably interfere with Plymouth's operations. The proposed site has no passing track or yard for loading or parking railcars.

- Also, like the municipality in *City of Elk Grove*, here the County is offering to work with Plymouth to minimize any impact that construction of the connector road and at-grade crossing might have on Plymouth's operations.

  - This is not a situation like the one in *Conroe County*, where the proposed crossing would have bisected a railroad company's passing track[3] and was of questionable necessity given the existence of another crossing that provided access to the proposed subdivision without interfering with the railroad company's operations.

  - Examinees may note that if the crossing qualifies as a Quiet Zone (and the County has already budgeted for such a designation), then train speeds at the crossing will be reduced by only a few miles per hour. (*See* Notes of meeting with James Wesson.)

- Plymouth's stated concerns about the potential safety risks to vehicles as a result of anticipated heavy use of the connector road can be addressed through the installation of appropriate safety measures, including passive devices (e.g., warning signs, warning pavement markings, crossing signs, and number-of-track signs) and active devices

---

[3] A passing track is an integral component in the operation of a single-track line in that it enables multiple trains to use one main track by allowing trains on the same track heading in opposite directions to pass each other. One train switches to the passing track to allow the other train heading in the opposite direction to continue on the single main track. A passing track is "transportation" as defined by the ICCTA. *Conroe County*.

(e.g., post-mounted flashing-light signals, automatic gates, and overhead flashing-light signals). *Id.*

- Installation of warning lights, railroad crossing arms, and other equipment would effectively prevent cars and pedestrians from attempting to cross the railroad track while it is being used by a train.

- Moreover, if the County is able to obtain Quiet Zone designation for the crossing, the additional safety features required (such as quadruple gates and "constant warning" technology) further reduce the risk of harm to any persons or vehicles at the crossing.

- Perceptive examinees may cite to *Butte County* for the proposition that while safety risk is "always present" whenever an active railroad track is involved, the proper inquiry is not whether there is *any* safety risk involved, but rather whether the proposed government action poses an *undue* risk.

  - The inability to eliminate any risk altogether is not a ground, standing alone, for preventing a government entity from exercising its eminent domain power under state law. *See Butte County.*

  - Indeed, in *Butte County*, the Court allowed a county to proceed with a state court action to condemn portions of a railroad's land for use as a bike and pedestrian trail.

  - Here, arguably, the proposed condemnation would serve more compelling public purposes, namely the construction of a much-needed connector road between two state highways that will not only alleviate traffic congestion but also provide the only means of access to the proposed Red Bluff development.

- Like the railroad in *City of Elk Grove*, Plymouth seems more concerned about protecting itself from liability than it does about genuine safety or operational issues. In both instances, the railroad is demanding that it be indemnified by the government agency against harms that may arise from the challenged governmental action (in *City of Elk Grove*, the storm sewer; here, the at-grade crossing). However, as the court noted in *City of Elk Grove*, any dispute over the terms of insurance coverage or written indemnification provisions "involve[s] allocation of risk, not the regulation of rail transportation." Thus, Plymouth's concern about indemnification cannot serve as a basis for ICCTA preemption.

- The *Conroe County* case is factually distinguishable on several grounds:
  - That case involved a passing track that was used to meet and pass trains, load and unload trains, and park 8,500-foot-long coal trains. The proposed crossing would have had significant, documented impacts on railroad operations, including loss of revenue due to the inability to continue parking coal trains along the crossing and delaying trains by up to 90 minutes to allow federal brake tests to be performed.
    - Here, as in *Butte County,* the proposed at-grade crossing would not impede Plymouth's access to its equipment or its railroad track; nor would the crossing affect any special-purpose railroad track (such as a passing track or a track used for parking trains).
    - It does not appear that the crossing would cause scheduling problems and delays, or any significant loss of capacity to the railroad's operations. At least the Plymouth representatives have not stated these problems specifically.
    - But note that, according to Plymouth, as many as 20 trains per day travel on this railway, and most are heavy freight trains. Conceivably, if 20 long trains have to slow down while passing through the crossing, there could be some impact on the railroad's schedule. However, there is nothing in the facts to indicate other possible schedule disruptions, such as the long delays in *Conroe County* required to comply with federal air-brake test regulations.
    - Nor does it appear that the crossing would directly burden or impede the interstate traffic of the railroad or the usefulness of the railroad's facilities for such traffic.
  - While not the focus of the preemption inquiry, the *Conroe County* court questioned why in that case the county chose to locate its crossing over a passing

track when other non-passing-track sites for the crossing were available. Here, there does not appear to be an alternative site that would have less impact on Plymouth's rail operations and yet would still serve the planned subdivision of Red Bluff and link SH50 and SH44. Examinees may note this when distinguishing Magnolia County's situation.

- Also, in *Conroe County,* there were citizen complaints about a potential "visual hazard" to vehicle drivers and blockage of emergency vehicles due to the railroad's use of the passing track for parking trains.

  - Here, per the supervising attorney's notes, the track is not used for parking trains, and thus there should not be any reduced visibility to motorists or blockage of emergency vehicles.

IV. Conclusion

Condemnation is a form of state regulation. State and local regulation is permissible where it does not prevent or unreasonably interfere with railroad operations or pose undue safety risks. However, such state action may be preempted by the ICCTA when it amounts to regulation of rail transportation.

For the reasons set forth above, it is likely that the County's proposed at-grade crossing of Plymouth's railroad track would be considered "routine" and "nonconflicting" and thus not preempted by the ICCTA.

In re Hammond

In re Hammond

In re Hammond

FILE

LIBRARY

POINT SHEET

In re Hammond

Instructions

The back cover of each test form contains the following instructions:

> You will have 90 minutes to complete this session of the examination. This performance test is designed to evaluate your ability to handle a select number of legal authorities in the context of a factual problem involving a client.

> The problem is set in the fictitious state of Franklin, in the fictitious Fifteenth Circuit of the United States. Columbia and Olympia are also fictitious states in the Fifteenth Circuit. In Franklin, the trial court of general jurisdiction is the District Court, the intermediate appellate court is the Court of Appeal, and the highest court is the Supreme Court.

> You will have two kinds of materials with which to work: a File and a Library. The first document in the File is a memorandum containing the instructions for the task you are to complete. The other documents in the File contain factual information about your case and may include some facts that are not relevant.

> The Library contains the legal authorities needed to complete the task and may also include some authorities that are not relevant. Any cases may be real, modified, or written solely for the purpose of this examination. If the cases appear familiar to you, do not assume that they are precisely the same as you have read before. Read them thoroughly, as if they all were new to you. You should assume that the cases were decided in the jurisdictions and on the dates shown. In citing cases from the Library, you may use abbreviations and omit page references.

> Your response must be written in the answer book provided. If you are taking the examination on a laptop computer, your jurisdiction will provide you with specific instructions. In answering this performance test, you should concentrate on the materials in the File and Library. What you have learned in law school and elsewhere provides the general background for analyzing the problem; the File and Library provide the specific materials with which you must work.

> Although there are no restrictions on how you apportion your time, you should be sure to allocate ample time (about 45 minutes) to reading and digesting the materials and to organizing your answer before you begin writing it. You may make notes anywhere in the test materials; blank pages are provided at the end of the booklet. You may not tear pages from the question booklet.

> This performance test will be graded on your responsiveness to the instructions regarding the task you are to complete, which are given to you in the first memorandum in the File, and on the content, thoroughness, and organization of your response.

In re Hammond

FILE

In re Hammond

Spencer & Takahashi S.C.
Attorneys at Law
77 Fulton Street
Gordon, Franklin 33112

DATE: July 27, 2010
FROM: Jane Spencer
TO: Applicant
SUBJECT: In re Hammond—Carol Walker Consultation

We have been retained by Carol Walker, a local attorney, in connection with her representation of William Hammond, a local businessman. Hammond owned the Hammond Container Company and the building which housed it; the building was destroyed by a suspicious fire on May 10, 2010.

Walker has been served with a subpoena duces tecum by the Gordon County District Attorney, compelling her to appear before a grand jury convened to investigate the circumstances of the fire and to testify and produce materials relating to her communications with Hammond. She does not want to have to appear before the grand jury and divulge anything related to the case. Based on my preliminary research, I believe we can successfully move to quash the subpoena. I have prepared a draft of our Motion to Quash, which I would like to file as soon as possible.

Please draft only the "Body of the Argument" for our Motion to Quash arguing that Walker may not be compelled to give the testimony or produce the materials in question, on the grounds that 1) under the Franklin Rules of Professional Conduct, she is prohibited from disclosing client communications, and 2) she has the privilege under the Franklin Rules of Evidence not to disclose confidential communications.

In drafting the body of the argument, follow our firm's briefing guidelines and be sure to remain faithful to our obligation to preserve client confidences under the Professional Rules.

Spencer & Takahashi S.C.
Attorneys at Law

MEMORANDUM   August 15, 2003

To:	All Lawyers
From:	Litigation Supervisor
Subject:	Persuasive Briefs

All persuasive briefs shall conform to the following guidelines:

[Statement of the Case]

[Statement of Facts]

Body of the Argument

The body of each argument should analyze applicable legal authority and persuasively argue how both the facts and the law support our client=s position. Supporting authority should be emphasized, but contrary authority also should generally be cited, addressed in the argument, and explained or distinguished. Do not reserve arguments for reply or supplemental briefing.

The firm follows the practice of breaking the argument into its major components and writing carefully crafted subject headings that illustrate the arguments they cover. Avoid writing a brief that contains only a single broad argument heading. The argument headings should succinctly summarize the reasons the tribunal should take the position you are advocating. A heading should be a specific application of a rule of law to the facts of the case and not a bare legal or factual conclusion or a statement of an abstract principle. For example, <u>improper</u>: IT IS NOT IN THE CHILD=S BEST INTERESTS TO BE PLACED IN THE MOTHER=S CUSTODY. <u>Proper</u>: EVIDENCE THAT THE MOTHER HAS BEEN CONVICTED OF CHILD ABUSE IS SUFFICIENT TO ESTABLISH THAT IT IS NOT IN THE CHILD=S BEST INTERESTS TO BE PLACED IN THE MOTHER=S CUSTODY.

The lawyer need not prepare a table of contents, a table of cases, a summary of argument, or an index. These will be prepared, when required, after the draft is approved.

4

In re Hammond

July 26, 2010

Ms. Jane Spencer
Spencer & Takahashi S.C.
77 Fulton Street
Gordon, Franklin 33112

Dear Jane:

Thank you for agreeing to represent me. A number of difficult issues have arisen in connection with the representation of one of my clients. I am writing in response to your request that I outline the facts.

I represent William Hammond, who established the Hammond Container Company about 10 years ago. Up until May 10 of this year, the company, located on South Main Street in a building owned by Hammond, manufactured disposable food containers for restaurants. On May 10, the company was put out of business when a fire destroyed the building. Hammond requested my advice as to whether he has any criminal exposure and whether he could file an insurance claim.

Thursday, I was served with a subpoena duces tecum by the District Attorney directing me to appear before a grand jury investigating the fire. Of course, I do not want to appear, and Hammond does not want me to reveal any of our communications. I would like your advice on whether I can move to quash the subpoena so that I do not have to appear. If there are grounds for a motion to quash, I would like you to draft the motion and supporting brief.

For your review, I have enclosed (1) the subpoena duces tecum; (2) a file memo summarizing my initial interview with Hammond; (3) a file memo summarizing a telephone conversation with Ray Gomez, Hammond's friend; and (4) a police incident report provided by the District Attorney.

Thank you for your attention to this matter. I look forward to meeting with you soon.

Very truly yours,

Carol Walker

Carol Walker

enc.

Walker & Walker, S.C.
Attorneys at Law
112 Stanton Street
Gordon, Franklin 33111

Date: May 12, 2010
From: Carol Walker
Memo to file of WILLIAM HAMMOND/HAMMOND CONTAINER COMPANY FIRE

Today I had a confidential meeting with William Hammond and agreed to represent him. On May 10, a fire destroyed a building he owned, housing the Hammond Container Company. He wanted advice as to whether he had any criminal exposure and whether he could file an insurance claim.

Hammond estimated the total value of the building as approximately $500,000, although it was encumbered by a mortgage with an outstanding balance of $425,000. The building was a total loss. It was insured in the amount of $500,000 under a policy issued by Mutual Insurance Company. Hammond claimed he was up-to-date on his premiums and said he had called Mutual for information about his coverage and the requirements for filing a claim.

Hammond said that he had been having financial difficulties in the past six months. He had lost two big accounts and did not have sufficient cash on hand to make the next payroll or mortgage payment. He said that a police officer contacted him on May 11, that he was too upset to talk at the time, and that the officer said he would contact him again soon. Hammond asked if he had to speak with the police—it seemed clear he wanted to avoid doing so—and I told him that he did not and that he should refer any questions to me. I also told him that if he was involved in any way in the fire, he could not collect on the insurance policy and could face criminal charges. I told him to contact me again within the week to allow me time to investigate the matter further.

Hammond appeared nervous during the meeting. He did not explicitly admit or deny involvement in the fire, nor did I explicitly ask about any involvement on his part. He did say that on the date of the fire he was with a friend, Ray Gomez, fishing at Coho Lake, about 60 miles from Gordon.

6

Walker & Walker, S.C.
Attorneys at Law
112 Stanton Street
Gordon, Franklin 33111

Date: May 17, 2010
From: Carol Walker
Memo to file of WILLIAM HAMMOND/HAMMOND CONTAINER COMPANY FIRE

Today I received a telephone call from a man who identified himself as Ray Gomez. He said he had been a friend of William Hammond for several years and was calling me at Hammond's request. He said he wanted to help but didn't know what he could do. Hammond had called him on May 13 and asked him to say that the two of them were together on May 10 fishing at Coho Lake. Gomez said he was surprised at the request given that they hadn't been together that day. The police called Gomez on May 14 and asked if he was with Hammond on May 10, and he replied that he wasn't. He didn't tell the police that Hammond had called him earlier. He said he knew nothing about the fire and wanted to help Hammond, but he didn't want to get into trouble himself. When I pressed him, he said he was afraid and probably should seek legal advice. I informed him that I represented Hammond and could not represent him as well. He said he knew that and had already set up an appointment with another attorney.

7

Date of Report: 5/16/2010   **Case No. 2010-57**

OFFENSE(S):	Suspected arson of building, 5/10/2010
ADDRESS OF INCIDENT:	20 South Main Street, Gordon
REPORTING OFFICER:	Detective Frank O'Brien
SUSPECT:	William Hammond, W/M, D.O.B. 11/5/1959

On 5/10/2010, a fire destroyed the building housing the Hammond Container Company.

On 5/11/2010, I contacted the owner, William Hammond, at his home at 815 Coco Lane, Gordon, at approximately 9:30 a.m. He identified himself and confirmed that he was the owner of the building destroyed in the fire. He stated he was too upset to talk, but did say he had been out of town the day of the fire with a friend and did not return to Gordon until late in the evening at which time he learned of the fire. He confirmed that the building was insured through Mutual Insurance Company but declined to talk further. I left my card and said I would re-contact him.

On 5/12/2010, I confirmed that Hammond was insured by Mutual Insurance Company for $500,000. Claim Manager Betty Anderson said that Hammond had requested claim forms and information but had not yet filed anything. She agreed to let me know when she had further contact with Hammond.

On 5/13/2010, I contacted Bob Thomas, manager of Gordon Savings & Loan, who said that six weeks ago Hammond had sought a business loan. The loan committee denied the loan after reviewing Hammond Container Company's financial condition.

On 5/14/2010, I again contacted Hammond. He identified Ray Gomez as the friend he claimed to have been with on 5/10/2010, but he referred all other questions to Attorney Carol Walker, claiming that she had advised him to do so.

Also on 5/14/2010, I contacted Gomez. He acknowledged that he knew Hammond but denied spending time with him on 5/10/2010.

On 5/15/2010, the Fire Marshal released a report finding no specific evidence of a cause but classifying the fire as suspicious and referring it to us for further investigation of arson. At this time, Hammond is a possible suspect.

cc: Gordon County District Attorney

In re Hammond

STATE OF FRANKLIN
GORDON COUNTY DISTRICT COURT

In re Grand Jury Proceeding 11-10,
Hammond Container Company

SUBPOENA DUCES TECUM

TO: Carol Walker
                 Walker & Walker, S.C.
                 112 Stanton Street
                 Gordon, Franklin 33111

YOU ARE COMMANDED to appear in the Gordon County District Court, State of Franklin, at 9:00 a.m. on August 3, 2010, before the Grand Jury convened in that Court to investigate the circumstances of the fire on May 10, 2010, that destroyed the building that housed the Hammond Container Company, located at 20 South Main Street, Gordon, Franklin, and to testify regarding your communications with William Hammond concerning the fire, and to produce all materials constituting or reflecting such communications.

This subpoena duces tecum shall remain in effect until you are granted leave to depart by order of the Court.

Dated this __22__ day of July, 2010.

Shirley S. Grant
Shirley S. Grant
Gordon County District Attorney

9

DRAFT

In re Grand Jury Proceeding 11-10, **Hammond Container Company**	**MOTION TO QUASH SUBPOENA** **DUCES TECUM**

Carol Walker, by and through her attorney, Jane Spencer, moves to quash the subpoena served on her in this matter. In support of this motion, Attorney Walker states the following:

1. Attorney Carol Walker has been subpoenaed to testify regarding her communications with William Hammond, her current client, concerning the fire that occurred at the Hammond Container Company and to produce all materials constituting or reflecting such communications.

2. To the extent that the State seeks to compel the testimony of Attorney Walker and the production of any materials regarding her communications with her client, Mr. Hammond, Attorney Walker asserts that she may not be compelled to appear or produce materials under the Franklin Rule of Professional Conduct 1.6.

3. To the extent that the State seeks to compel the testimony of Attorney Walker and the production of any materials regarding her communications with her client, Mr. Hammond, Attorney Walker asserts that she may not be compelled to appear or produce materials under the Franklin Rules of Evidence.

4. Attorney Walker thus refuses to testify or to produce materials in accordance with the subpoena.

WHEREFORE, Attorney Walker asks this Court to quash the subpoena that seeks to compel her to testify and produce materials in this matter, and for any and all other relief appropriate.

Signed: _____
　　　　　　　Jane Spencer
　　　　　　　Attorney for Carol Walker
Date:

LIBRARY

Rule 1.6 Confidentiality of Information

(a) A lawyer shall not reveal information relating to representation of a client unless the client gives informed consent, the disclosure is impliedly authorized in order to carry out the representation, or the disclosure is permitted by paragraph (b).

(b) A lawyer may reveal information relating to the representation of a client to the extent the lawyer reasonably believes necessary:

(1) to prevent reasonably certain death or substantial bodily harm;

(2) . . . ;

(3) to prevent, mitigate or rectify substantial injury to the financial interest or property of another that is reasonably certain to result or has resulted from the client's commission of a crime or fraud in furtherance of which the client has used the lawyer's services;

. . .

FRANKLIN RULES OF EVIDENCE

Rule 513 Lawyer-Client Privilege

…

(b) General rule of privilege. A client has a privilege to refuse to disclose and to prevent any other person from disclosing a confidential communication made for the purpose of facilitating the rendition of professional legal services to the client . . . .

…

> (3) Who may claim the privilege. The privilege may be claimed by the client . . . . The person who was the lawyer . . . at the time of the communication is presumed to have authority to claim the privilege but only on behalf of the client.

…

(d) Exceptions. There is no privilege under this rule:

> (1) Furtherance of crime or fraud. If the services of the lawyer were sought or obtained to enable or aid anyone to commit or plan to commit what the client knew or reasonably should have known to be a crime or fraud.
>
> . . .

Official Advisory Committee Comments

. . .

[3] A communication made in confidence between a client and a lawyer is presumed to be privileged. A party claiming that such a communication is not privileged bears the burden of proof by a preponderance of the evidence. The party claiming that such a communication is privileged must nevertheless disclose the communication to the court to determine the communication's status if the party claiming that the communication is *not* privileged presents evidence sufficient to raise a substantial question about the communication's status.

Franklin courts have not yet determined whether, to be sufficient, the evidence presented must establish probable cause to believe that the communication in question is not privileged, *see, e.g., State v. Sawyer* (Columbia Sup. Ct. 2002), or whether there must be "some evidence" to that effect, *see, e.g., United States v. Robb* (15th Cir. 1999).

§ 3.01 Arson of Building

Whoever, by means of fire, intentionally damages any building of another without the other's consent may, upon conviction, be imprisoned for not more than 15 years, or fined not more than $50,000, or both.

§ 3.02 Arson of Building with Intent to Defraud an Insurer

Whoever, by means of fire, intentionally damages any building with intent to defraud an insurer of that building may, upon conviction, be imprisoned for not more than 10 years, or fined not more than $10,000, or both.

. . .

§ 5.50 Fraudulent Claims

Whoever knowingly presents or causes to be presented any fraudulent claim for the payment of a loss or injury, including payment of a loss or injury under a contract of insurance, may, upon conviction, be imprisoned for not more than 5 years, or fined not more than $10,000, or both.

1

United States v. Robb

United States Court of Appeals (15th Cir. 1999)

John Robb appeals his conviction for mail fraud in the sale of stock of Coronado Gold Mines, Inc. The indictment alleged that Robb caused Coronado's stock to be sold on misrepresentations that the company was producing gold and earning money, that the price of the stock on the New York Mining Exchange was manipulated through such misrepresentations, and that the mails were used to facilitate the scheme.

Robb acquired a gold mine in Idaho that did not produce any ore that could be mined at a profit. The ore extracted contained only an average of $2.00 to $2.50 of gold per ton, with a cost of mining of at least $7 per ton. Robb claimed through advertisements and stockholder reports that the mine was yielding "ore averaging $40 of gold per ton." Robb caused Coronado's stock to be distributed to the public by high-pressure salesmanship, at prices that netted a $158,000 profit.

The sole error alleged on appeal is the district court's decision to admit the testimony of Ralph Griffin, a former attorney for Robb. At trial, Griffin's testimony for the Government showed that Robb controlled all mining operations and that Robb knew that the public information disseminated was false. Robb claims that allowing such testi-mony violated the attorney-client privilege. We disagree and affirm the conviction.

We have long recognized the attorney-client privilege as the oldest of the privileges for confidential communications known to the common law. It encourages full and frank communication between attorneys and clients. But because the privilege has the effect of withholding information from the fact finder, it should apply only where ne-cessary.

The purpose of the crime-fraud exception to the attorney-client privilege is to lift the veil of secrecy from lawyer-client communications where such commu-nications are made for the purpose of seek-ing or obtaining the lawyer's services to facilitate a crime or fraud.

To release an attorney from the attorney-client privilege based on the crime-fraud ex-ception, the party seeking to overcome the privilege must do more than merely assert that the client retained the attorney to facili-tate a crime or fraud. Rather, there must be some evidence supporting an inference that the client retained the attorney for such a purpose.

Once such evidence is presented, the district court must review, *in camera* (in chambers, without the parties being present), the attorney-client communications in question to determine their status. The court may properly admit the disputed communications into evidence if it finds by a preponderance of evidence that the allegedly privileged communications fall within the crime-fraud exception.

Contrary to Robb's claim, the Government satisfied the "some evidence" standard here, thereby triggering *in camera* review of the attorney-client communications and ultimately resulting in a decision that the communications were within the crime-fraud exception. The Government's evidence raised an inference that Robb retained Griffin in the midst of a fraudulent scheme; that during this time, Griffin was the primary source of legal advice to Robb, had access to all of Coronado's information, and had regular contact with Robb; and that records of the actual mining results demonstrated misrepresentations in the publicly disseminated information.

Subsequently, Robb had an opportunity to present evidence that he retained Griffin for proper purposes, but he failed to do so. Instead, the Government presented further evidence which was sufficient to enable it to carry its burden to prove by a preponderance of the evidence that Robb retained Griffin for *improper* purposes. As a result, the district court properly ruled that the communications between Robb and Griffin were not privileged.

We understand that the modest nature of the "some evidence" standard could lead to infringement of confidentiality between attorney and client. At the same time, a higher standard could improperly cloak fraudulent or criminal activities. On balance, we are confident that the "some evidence" standard achieves an appropriate balance between the competing interests and that the district courts may be relied upon to keep the balance true.

Affirmed.

State v. Sawyer

Columbia Supreme Court (2002)

Mark Sawyer appeals his conviction after a jury trial for bribery of a public official. Sawyer claims that the trial court erred in excluding the testimony of Attorney Anthony Novak regarding Novak's conversations with his client Connor Krause, the alderman whom Sawyer was convicted of bribing. The court of appeals affirmed Sawyer's conviction. We agree with the court of appeals that the trial court properly excluded the testimony.

Sawyer owned an automobile dealership in the City of Lena, Columbia, which was located on property to which the city had taken title in order to widen the street. As first proposed, the plan required razing Sawyer's business. The plan was later changed so that Sawyer's business would be untouched. A corruption investigation of the City Council led to charges against Sawyer for bribing Krause to use his influence to change the plan.

Before trial, Sawyer subpoenaed Krause's attorney, Novak, to testify. When Novak refused to testify, Sawyer moved the court to compel him to do so, claiming that (i) Krause was currently in prison having been convicted of taking bribes while he was an alderman; (ii) Krause initially told police that Sawyer had not bribed him; (iii) Krause retained and met with Novak, his attorney;

and (iv) Krause later agreed to testify against Sawyer in exchange for a reduced prison sentence. On those facts, Sawyer argues that Krause planned to testify falsely to obtain a personal benefit; that he retained Novak to facilitate his plan; and that, as a result, Krause's communications with Novak were not privileged.

Although the attorney-client privilege has never prevented disclosing communications made to seek or obtain the attorney's services in furtherance of a crime or fraud, in Columbia the mere assertion of a crime or fraud is insufficient to overcome the presumption that such communications are privileged. Rather, the moving party must present evidence establishing probable cause to believe that the client sought or obtained the attorney's services to further a crime or fraud.

Upon presentation of such evidence, the party seeking to establish the attorney-client privilege must disclose the allegedly privileged communications to the judge for a determination of whether they fall within the crime-fraud exception. The judge's review of the communications is conducted *in camera* to determine if the moving party has established that the communications fall within the crime-fraud exception.

Some courts have required disclosure of the disputed communications to the court upon the presentation merely of "some evidence" supporting an inference that the client sought or obtained the attorney's services to further a crime or fraud. *See, e.g., United States v. Robb* (15th Cir. 1999). We believe Columbia's "probable cause" standard strikes a more appropriate balance than the "some evidence" test because it protects attorney-client communications unless there is a strong factual basis for the inference that the client retained the attorney for improper purposes.

Applying the "probable cause" standard here, the trial court concluded that Sawyer failed to present evidence establishing probable cause to believe that Krause sought or obtained Novak's services to facilitate any plan to commit perjury. We agree. While the evidence would indeed support an inference that Krause retained Novak to facilitate perjury, it supports an equally strong inference that Krause retained him to ensure that his choices were informed—and that he failed to cooperate earlier because he was afraid he might expose himself to prosecution with no countervailing benefit. A greater showing of the client's intent to retain the attorney to facilitate a crime or fraud is needed prior to invading attorney-client confidences.

Affirmed.

POINT SHEET

In re Hammond

In re Hammond
DRAFTERS' POINT SHEET

In this performance test item, applicants work for a law firm. A partner in the firm, Jane Spencer, has received a request for guidance from another attorney, Carol Walker, who represents William Hammond, who, as a result of a suspicious fire, suffered the loss of a building that he owned and that housed his business. Hammond has sought Walker's advice about whether he has any criminal exposure and whether he may file an insurance claim for the loss of the building. Walker has suspicions that Hammond may have been involved in the fire, but Hammond has not explicitly admitted nor denied involvement and Walker has not explicitly asked.

Walker seeks advice from the applicants' firm on whether she can successfully move to quash a subpoena duces tecum issued by the District Attorney compelling her to appear before a grand jury convened to investigate the fire and to testify and produce materials relating to her communications with Hammond about the fire. Walker desires not to appear, and Hammond desires that she not disclose any of their communications.

Applicants' task is to prepare a brief in support of a motion to quash the subpoena on the grounds that under the Franklin Rules of Professional Conduct and the Franklin Rules of Evidence, Walker may not be compelled to give the testimony or produce the materials in question.

The File contains a memorandum describing the task, a memorandum on persuasive briefs, a letter from Walker to Spencer, a memorandum to file by Walker summarizing a meeting with Hammond, another memorandum to file by Walker summarizing a telephone conversation with Ray Gomez (a friend of Hammond), a police incident report, the subpoena duces tecum, and a draft of the motion to quash the subpoena.

The Library contains a provision of the Franklin Rules of Professional Conduct relating to the ethical duty of confidentiality, a provision of the Franklin Rules of Evidence relating to the attorney-client privilege and the crime-fraud exception, and provisions of the Franklin Criminal Code relating to arson. The Library also contains two decisions from jurisdictions outside Franklin bearing on a question, unresolved in Franklin, involving the attorney-client privilege and the crime-fraud exception.

I. Detailed Analysis

The following discussion covers all the points the drafters intended to raise in the problem. Applicants need not cover them all to receive passing or even excellent grades. Grading decisions are left to the discretion of the user jurisdictions.

In arguing the motion to quash the subpoena duces tecum, applicants must address two separate questions: First, may Walker be compelled to appear before the grand jury to disclose her communications with Hammond about the fire, whether by testimony or by production of materials, under the Franklin Rules of Professional Conduct? Second, may she be compelled to do so under the Franklin Rules of Evidence? As will appear, applicants should give a negative answer to each question.

In the call memo, applicants are urged to remain faithful to the Franklin Rules of Professional Conduct and observe client confidences. This requires applicants to distinguish carefully between those facts that are not protected by ethical and evidentiary rules and those that are protected, including any communications between Walker and Gomez and any suspicions Walker may have about Hammond's involvement in the fire.

- Applicants should include in their arguments only those facts that are *not* protected, as the task memorandum underscores the importance of maintaining client confidences.

A.   Whether Walker May Be Compelled to Appear before the Grand Jury to Disclose Her Communications with Hammond under the Franklin Rules of Professional Conduct

The first question for applicants to address is whether Walker may be compelled to appear before the grand jury to disclose her communications with Hammond about the fire, whether by testimony or by production of materials, under the Franklin Rules of Professional Conduct.

Under Rule 1.6 of the Franklin Rules of Professional Conduct—which is identical to Rule 1.6 of the American Bar Association's Model Rules of Professional Conduct, the source of many jurisdictions' analogous rules—a lawyer may not, as a general matter, reveal information relating to the representation of a client, whether or not that information consists of a communication between lawyer and client, and whether or not it is confidential.

- It is plain that the communications between Walker and Hammond about the fire fall within the general rule of confidentiality.

- On their face, they contain information relating to the representation and are confidential communications between lawyer and client.
- There are, however, three exceptions to Rule 1.6. The lawyer may make a disclosure
  - (a) if the client gives informed consent,
  - (b) if the disclosure is impliedly authorized in order to carry out the representation, and
  - (c) if any one of certain circumstances is found to exist—here, specifically, "to prevent, mitigate or rectify substantial injury to the financial interest or property of another that is reasonably certain to result or has resulted from the client's commission of a crime or fraud in furtherance of which the client has used the lawyer's services."

The exceptions to Rule 1.6 do not apply to Walker/Hammond communications

- The first exception, client consent, is not present. Hammond has not given Walker consent, informed or otherwise, to disclose their communications about the fire to the grand jury.
  - Indeed, he specifically requested that she not do so.
- Neither is the second exception present. Disclosure of the communications between Walker and Hammond about the fire to the grand jury or otherwise is not impliedly authorized in order to carry out Walker's representation of Hammond.
  - Again, Hammond has specifically requested that she make no such disclosure.
- Finally, the specified circumstance (the third exception) is apparently inapplicable at the threshold. That circumstance would be applicable only if Walker were to reasonably believe that disclosure of her communications with Hammond about the fire was necessary to "prevent, mitigate or rectify substantial injury to the financial interest or property of another that is reasonably certain to result or has resulted from" Hammond's "commission of a crime or fraud in furtherance of which" he "has used" her "services."
  - The very fact that Walker is seeking to quash the subpoena reveals that she has no such belief—and certainly has no such belief that disclosure *to the grand jury* is necessary.
  - In any event, it appears that "substantial injury to the financial interest or property of another" could result only if Hammond filed a fraudulent insurance claim.

- That Hammond will do so is not "reasonably certain."

- Walker has advised Hammond that if he was involved in any way in the fire, he cannot collect insurance and may face criminal charges.

- At the present time, without knowing the cause of the fire or whether Hammond will file an insurance claim, it is unreasonable, indeed speculative, to conclude that financial injury to a third party (i.e., the insurer) will occur.

- Thus, there is little basis for concluding that Walker has an obligation to reveal any client confidences.

- Further, the language of Rule 1.6(b) is permissive (e.g., "a lawyer *may* reveal information…") not mandatory, so even if an exception applied, the rules would not require Walker to disclose the communications.

In light of the foregoing, applicants should argue that Walker may not be compelled to appear before the grand jury to disclose her communications with Hammond about the fire, whether by testimony or by production of materials, under the Franklin Rules of Professional Conduct.

B. Whether Walker May Be Compelled to Appear before the Grand Jury to Disclose Her Communications with Hammond under the Franklin Rules of Evidence

The second question for applicants to address is whether Walker may be compelled to appear before the grand jury to disclose her communications with Hammond about the fire, whether by testimony or by production of materials, under the Franklin Rules of Evidence.

Summary of the applicable law

Under Rule 513 of the Franklin Rules of Evidence (which is similar to the lawyer-client evidentiary privilege in many jurisdictions), a client "has a privilege to refuse to disclose and to prevent any other person from disclosing a confidential communication made for the purpose of facilitating the rendition of" a lawyer's services. There is no privilege, however, if the client sought or obtained a lawyer's services in furtherance of a crime or fraud.

A confidential communication between a client and a lawyer is presumed to be privileged. To rebut the presumption, a party claiming otherwise must carry the burden of proof by a preponderance of the evidence. A party claiming that a confidential communication is privileged must nevertheless disclose the communication to the court to determine the communication's status if a party claiming that the communication is *not* privileged presents evidence sufficient to raise a substantial question about the communication's status. Franklin courts have not yet determined whether, to be sufficient, the evidence presented must establish probable cause to believe that the communication is not privileged, *see, e.g., State v. Sawyer* (Columbia Sup. Ct. 2002), or whether there must merely be "some evidence" to that effect, *see, e.g., United States v. Robb* (15th Cir. 1999).

- The Walker/Hammond communications are presumed to be privileged.

- From all that appears, all communications between Hammond and Walker about the fire were confidential and all were made for the purpose of facilitating the rendition of Walker's services as a lawyer to Hammond as a client.

- Therefore, all the communications in question are *presumed* privileged because they were confidential and are *in fact* privileged because they were not only confidential but were also made with a view toward the rendering of legal services.

- Hammond has impliedly (if not expressly) authorized, and instructed, Walker to claim the privilege on his behalf and to refuse to disclose any of the communications to the grand jury through his expressed desire that Walker not disclose *any* communications.

- As things stand, the Gordon County District Attorney cannot carry her burden of proof by a preponderance of the evidence that any of the communications between Hammond and Walker about the fire were not privileged by virtue of the crime-fraud exception.

- The District Attorney's evidence establishes the following:
    - the building housing the Hammond Container Company was destroyed by fire;
    - Hammond owned the business and the building;
    - Hammond had insured the building;
    - Hammond has made inquiries about filing an insurance claim, but has not filed such a claim;
    - Hammond sought a bank loan prior to the fire, and was turned down because of his company's financial condition;
    - the Fire Marshal classified the fire as suspicious in origin;
    - Hammond has not been willing to fully cooperate with the police;

- there is a discrepancy between what Hammond and his friend Gomez said they were doing the day of the fire; and

- Hammond retained Walker two days after the fire.

- To be sure, this evidence supports an inference that Hammond may have committed arson with the intent to defraud the insurer of his building and may intend to carry through by filing a fraudulent insurance claim.

  - Even if he caused the fire, Hammond has not violated Fr. Criminal Code § 3.01, Arson of Building, because that makes it a crime to damage with fire the building of another, not one's own building.

- But the evidence does not support an inference that Hammond *sought or obtained* Walker's services to further any such crime or fraud. True, the evidence allows conjecture about Hammond's purpose in retaining Walker, but it does not point to an improper purpose—to further a crime or fraud—rather than a proper one—to defend against an accusation of a crime or fraud.

- Whether the Gordon County District Attorney has sufficient evidence to require Walker to disclose her communications with Hammond about the fire for the court to determine their status (*in camera*) as privileged or nonprivileged depends upon whether the District Attorney has evidence sufficient to raise a substantial question about their status.

  - Whether the District Attorney has such evidence may depend in turn on whether the court would apply the stricter "probable cause" standard or the looser "some evidence" standard. Applicants should argue that the stricter standard applies.

  - If the court should apply the "probable cause" standard, the Gordon County District Attorney's evidence would be insufficient to require Walker to disclose her communications with Hammond about the fire for the court to determine their status as privileged or nonprivileged.

    - As explained, although the evidence supports an inference that Hammond may have committed arson with the intent to defraud the insurer of his building and may intend to carry through by filing a fraudulent insurance claim, it does not support an inference that Hammond sought or obtained Walker's services to further any such crime or fraud.

      - Hammond requested claim forms and information from Mutual Insurance before he hired Walker (*see* Police Report). Thus, it is unlikely that he sought advice from Walker about how to submit an insurance claim—he had already obtained such information.

- Moreover, the nature of the potential crime in this instance—insurance fraud—is not comparable to the complex financial fraud perpetrated by the defendant in *Robb*. In short, it is not the type of crime for which one would necessarily need legal advice to commit.

- There is evidence that Hammond had a motive to commit insurance fraud, but the police report notes only that the bank denied Hammond's application for a business loan. The more damaging information—Hammond's statements to Walker that he had been having financial problems and could not make his next payroll or mortgage payment—is found only in the privileged attorney-client communications at issue. Thus those statements are not available to the district attorney at this stage in the proceedings.

  - Applicants who divulge what Hammond told Walker regarding his dire financial straits may receive less credit for their discussion, as they will have violated client confidentiality.

- If the court should apply the "some evidence" standard, the Gordon County District Attorney's evidence would arguably remain insufficient to require Walker to disclose her communications with Hammond about the fire for the court to determine their status as privileged or nonprivileged.

  - It is true that the "some evidence" standard may apparently be satisfied by a client's retention of a lawyer "in the midst of a fraudulent scheme." *United States v. Robb* (15th Cir. 1999).

  - But whether Hammond is indeed involved in a "fraudulent scheme" is the very question to be resolved. To assume that he *is* involved simply begs the question. As stated, he sought advice about *whether* he could file an insurance claim, not *how* he could do so.

    - The Fire Marshal's report failed to find specific evidence of the cause of the fire, but classified it as suspicious. At this point in time, there is no determination that the fire was intentionally set. [Contrast with *Robb*, in which there was clear evidence of manipulation of the price of the mining stock.]

    - Just burning down his own building is not arson. Frank. Crim. Code § 3.01.

- By contrast, in *Robb*, there was evidence available to the government that the defendant had employed his lawyer in the midst of his fraudulent mining scheme, and the actual mining records revealed the misrepresentations in the publicly disseminated information. Accordingly, the government met the "some evidence" standard required to trigger *in camera* review of the attorney-client communications.

- The Walker/Hammond relationship appears much closer to that in *State v. Sawyer* (Columbia Sup. Ct. 2002): "While the evidence would indeed support an inference that Krause retained Novak to facilitate perjury, it supports an equally strong inference that Krause retained him to ensure that his choices were informed—and that he failed to cooperate earlier because he was afraid he might expose himself to prosecution with no countervailing benefit."

- There is an equally strong inference that Hammond, realizing that his financial situation made him a prime suspect in an arson investigation, retained Walker to ensure that he had sound legal advice in responding to police inquiries.

- Finally, it can be argued that the same public policy underlying the existence of the attorney/client privilege—encouraging clients to fully and frankly disclose matters to their attorneys—also supports the Franklin courts adopting a probable cause standard.

  - "[T]he attorney-client privilege [is] the oldest of the privileges for confidential communications known to the common law. It encourages full and frank communication between attorneys and clients…." *Robb*.

  - *Robb* recognized that the low "some evidence" standard had the potential to lead to infringement of confidentiality between attorney and client. But the *Robb* court reasoned that because of the risk that a higher standard could "improperly cloak fraudulent or criminal activities," the "some evidence" standard was appropriate. *Id.*

  - It could be argued that the *Robb* standard encourages fishing expeditions into privileged communications and that it could have a chilling effect on the attorney-client relationship. *Sawyer* is the better approach. Franklin should join Columbia in requiring a "strong factual basis for the inference" that the crime-fraud exception applies and the privileged communications should be submitted to the court for *in camera* review.

  - Opting for the probable-cause standard, as in *Sawyer*, will better protect the importance of maintaining the confidentiality of attorney-client communications and yet is not an insurmountable bar to those parties who believe that there is a substantial question regarding whether such communications are entitled to the privilege.

- In any event, no matter which standard the court might apply, and even if the court might end up requiring Walker to disclose her communications with Hammond about the fire so as to determine their status as privileged or nonprivileged, the result would likely be the same: The court would likely conclude that the communications were in fact privileged inasmuch as they are presumed to be such in light of their confidential character and the presumption is not rebutted by a preponderance of evidence proving the crime-fraud exception.

In light of the foregoing, applicants should argue that Walker may not be compelled to appear before the grand jury to disclose her communications with Hammond, whether by testimony or by production of materials, under the Franklin Rules of Evidence.

City of Ontario

City of Ontario

LIBRARY

POINT SHEET

Instructions

The back cover of each test form contains the following instructions:

You will have 90 minutes to complete this session of the examination. This performance test is designed to evaluate your ability to handle a select number of legal authorities in the context of a factual problem involving a client.

The problem is set in the fictitious state of Franklin, in the fictitious Fifteenth Circuit of the United States. Columbia and Olympia are also fictitious states in the Fifteenth Circuit. In Franklin, the trial court of general jurisdiction is the District Court, the intermediate appellate court is the Court of Appeal, and the highest court is the Supreme Court.

You will have two kinds of materials with which to work: a File and a Library. The first document in the File is a memorandum containing the instructions for the task you are to complete. The other documents in the File contain factual information about your case and may include some facts that are not relevant.

The Library contains the legal authorities needed to complete the task and may also include some authorities that are not relevant. Any cases may be real, modified, or written solely for the purpose of this examination. If the cases appear familiar to you, do not assume that they are precisely the same as you have read before. Read them thoroughly, as if they all were new to you. You should assume that the cases were decided in the jurisdictions and on the dates shown. In citing cases from the Library, you may use abbreviations and omit page references.

Your response must be written in the answer book provided. If you are taking the examination on a laptop computer, your jurisdiction will provide you with specific instructions. In answering this performance test, you should concentrate on the materials in the File and Library. What you have learned in law school and elsewhere provides the general background for analyzing the problem; the File and Library provide the specific materials with which you must work.

Although there are no restrictions on how you apportion your time, you should be sure to allocate ample time (about 45 minutes) to reading and digesting the materials and to organizing your answer before you begin writing it. You may make notes anywhere in the test materials; blank pages are provided at the end of the booklet. You may not tear pages from the question booklet.

This performance test will be graded on your responsiveness to the instructions regarding the task you are to complete, which are given to you in the first memorandum in the File, and on the content, thoroughness, and organization of your response.

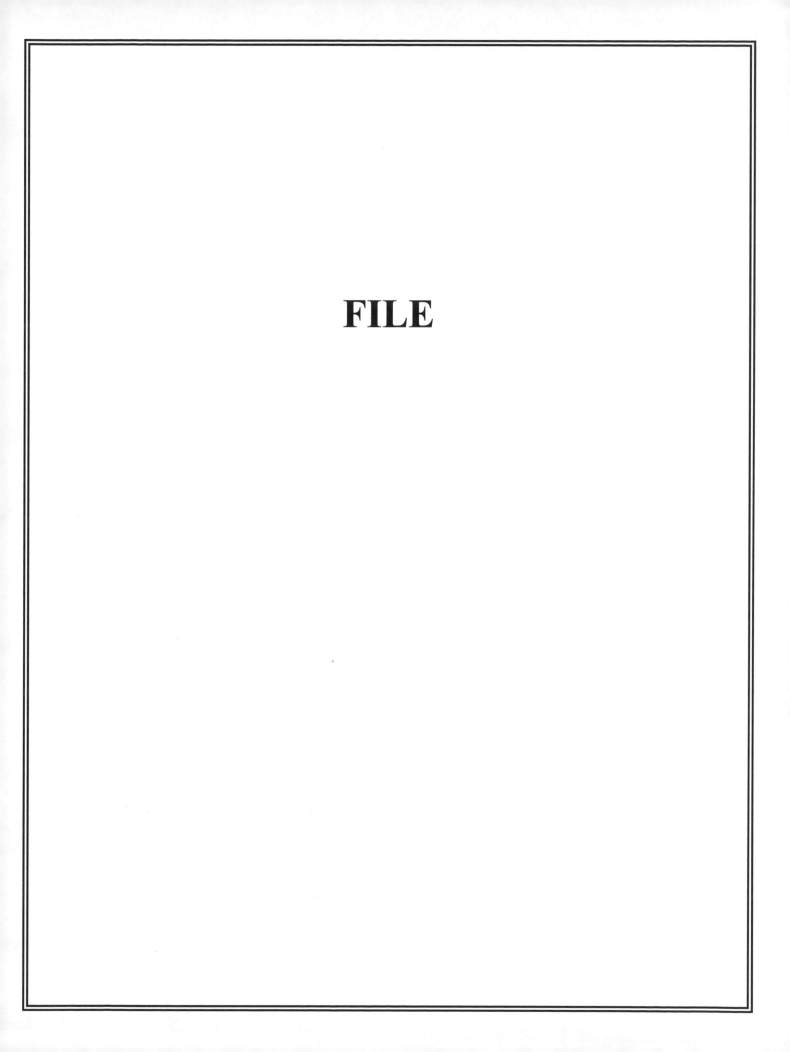

FILE

CITY OF ONTARIO
City Hall
131 West Fifth Street
Ontario, Franklin 33875

MEMORANDUM

To:	Applicant
From:	Lawrence Barnes, City Attorney
Date:	July 27, 2010
Re:	Liquor Control Commission Procedures

Since becoming City Attorney, I have been reviewing city ordinances for the Liquor Control Commission ("the Commission"). Any establishment in the city that sells or serves alcohol must hold a liquor license, which is issued by the Commission. When a licensee faces charges that could result in a fine or the loss of a license, the licensee is entitled to a hearing before the Commission. The Mayor and City Council believe that the present procedures for such hearings are cost-effective and expeditious. However, I want to ensure that Commission decisions reached following these procedures will be given preclusive effect and so cannot be relitigated in state and federal courts.

I have attached the applicable city ordinances, outlining the Commission's authority and hearing procedures. The only standardized form used in Commission proceedings is the attached "Notice of Liquor Control Violation."

Please prepare a memorandum analyzing whether, under the applicable legal authority, courts would extend preclusive effect to decisions rendered under the procedures set forth in the city ordinances. Your memorandum should:

- Identify which city procedures already comply with the requirements for preclusion;
- Identify which city procedures do **not** comply with the requirements for preclusion, and describe how those procedures should be changed for preclusive effect; and
- Explain how the changes you recommend would affect the city's goals of cost and time-effectiveness.

You need not draft the language of any of your proposed changes; I will draft any changes that may be needed.

23

Chapter Two: LIQUOR CONTROL ORDINANCES

2-1. **Liquor Control Commission.** The Mayor and the City Council shall constitute the Liquor Control Commission for the City of Ontario. The Commission is charged with the administration of the Franklin Liquor Control Act and the City Liquor Control Ordinances in the City of Ontario. The Mayor, acting on behalf of the Commission, shall have the following powers and duties:

> 1. To receive applications, investigate applicants, and grant, renew, or deny liquor licenses;
>
> 2. To enter or authorize any law enforcement officer to enter, at any time, any premises licensed under these Ordinances in order to enforce the ordinances of this City;
>
> 3. To maintain and update records relating to the granting or denial of liquor licenses;
>
> 4. To receive liquor license fees;
>
> 5. To conduct hearings and render decisions; and
>
> 6. To impose penalties, including fines and loss of license as provided in Section 2-5 of this Ordinance, and to receive any fines.

2-2. **Notice; Hearings.** If any licensee is charged with violation of any applicable law or ordinance, the Mayor shall issue written notice of the charge or charges against the licensee. Except under the emergency procedures in Section 2-6 of this Ordinance, no licensee shall be fined and no license shall be suspended or revoked prior to a hearing pursuant to this Section. Any licensee wishing to contest the charges must request a hearing concerning the charges within 10 business days of the notice. The Mayor shall conduct the hearing, which shall be held no later than five business days after the request.

2-3.   **Conduct of Hearings.** The Mayor shall have the power to issue subpoenas for witnesses. The Mayor shall have the power to place witnesses under oath, rule on objections, dismiss charges, conduct the evidentiary hearing in an efficient manner, and issue a fine and/or suspend or revoke a license as provided in this Chapter. The Mayor shall secure a court reporter for the hearing, costs of the reporter to be borne by the City.

2-4.   **Burden of Proof; Evidence.** The City shall have the burden of proving by a preponderance of the evidence the charges alleged against the licensee. Without the need for live testimony or other foundation, the Mayor will admit into evidence any report by the police or other investigative authority relevant to the charges. The City may also present evidence through other means. The licensee may cross-examine the witnesses presented by the City and may present evidence in its defense. The City may cross-examine the witnesses presented by the licensee and may present rebuttal evidence. The hearing shall be informal and the Franklin Rules of Evidence shall not apply.

2-5.   **Penalties for Violation. ******

2-6.   **Emergency Procedures. ******

[remaining provisions omitted]

CITY OF ONTARIO

City Hall

131 West Fifth Street

Ontario, Franklin 33875

NOTICE OF LIQUOR CONTROL VIOLATION

Notice to_____(name of licensee)_____

You are hereby notified that you have been charged with violating Section(s) _____ of the State of Franklin Liquor Control Act and/or the City of Ontario Liquor Control Ordinances. As a result of these violations, you will be penalized as provided in Section 2-5 of the City of Ontario Ordinances, including but not limited to fines, suspension of your liquor license, or revocation of your liquor license.

If you seek to contest the charge(s), you may contact the Office of the Mayor of the City of Ontario. Upon contacting the Office of the Mayor, you will receive further instructions about the procedures to be followed in connection with your claim. For further information concerning this process, please see the Ordinances of the City of Ontario, which you may also obtain by contacting the Office of the Mayor.

If you fail to contact the Office of the Mayor, it will be assumed that you do not dispute the charges against you and the penalties being imposed.

_____

(date & signature)

Mayor

City of Ontario, Franklin

LIBRARY

Thompson v. Franklin State Technical University

Franklin Supreme Court (1986)

The issue is whether the unreviewed decision of a state administrative hearing officer has preclusive effect.

Sarah Thompson filed a grievance against her former employer, Franklin State Technical University ("the University"), alleging that her discharge was the result of sex discrimination. In accordance with University grievance rules, an official from another University department was appointed as the hearing officer to hear the grievance.

At the hearing on Thompson's grievance, the University and Thompson together presented over 20 witnesses and 70 exhibits. Following the hearing, the hearing officer determined that the University had not engaged in sex discrimination but had valid, non-discriminatory grounds to discharge Thompson. The University Chancellor upheld the decision, and it became the University's final decision. Thompson did not seek judicial review of the University's final decision.

Thompson thereafter sued the University for damages in state court, claiming that the University engaged in sex discrimination when it fired her. The trial court granted the University's motion for summary judgment on the basis that the hearing officer's decision precluded Thompson from relitigating the issue in state court. Thompson appealed, arguing that the administrative decision should not have preclusive effect. The court of appeal affirmed. We granted review of this case of first impression.

The doctrine of preclusion gives finality to matters already decided where there has been an opportunity to litigate them. Courts have long applied the doctrine of preclusion to judicial determinations (claims or issues) in the interest of finality. For the same reason, we here apply the doctrine of preclusion to a determination made by an administrative agency.

The United States Supreme Court has created federal common law rules of preclusion, which we now adopt. Only where an administrative agency has the authority to adjudicate disputes and where the agency, in fact, does decide the disputed issues properly before it does the doctrine of preclusion apply. The doctrine of preclusion does not apply where the administrative agency acts "legislatively" in adopting rules, or "ministerially" in implementing action without discretion. The doctrine of preclusion can apply only when the parties had an opportunity to litigate the claim or issue before the agency; thus, the agency procedures must comport with the minimal requirements of due process.

While due process does not require all the procedural protections available in a court, the more an administrative agency acts like a court, the more sound the reasons for giving preclusive effect to its decisions. An agency acts like a court when it provides the opportunity for representation by counsel and follows basic rules of procedure and evidence.

Courts are more willing to preclude review where the parties litigated after some pre-hearing disclosure. Aggrieved parties must have the opportunity to present evidence through witnesses and exhibits and to challenge the evidence presented by the other parties through cross-examination and objections. It is critical that adjudicators, whether they be hearing officers, administrative law judges, or persons acting in a quasi-judicial capacity within an agency, be independent of those prosecuting the matter.

In cases where the above indicia of due process are present, the administrative agency's determinations should be accorded the same finality that is accorded the judgment of a court. Bringing a legal controversy to conclusion is no less important when the tribunal is an administrative one than when it is a court.

While the hiring and firing of employees are generally managerial matters, when the Uni-versity, pursuant to statutory authority, holds a hearing to decide a disputed employment matter, the University acts in a quasi-judicial capacity. In this case, pursuant to University rules, the hearing officer, appointed from another, unrelated University department, was charged to make a decision based on the evidence presented at the hearing. He heard disputed evidence from each party addressing the issue of sex discrimination. He made specific findings of fact and conclusions of law concerning the dispute. These actions are quasi-judicial in nature.

Thompson does not challenge the due process protections she was accorded. Moreover, Thompson had every motivation to litigate fully her allegations before the University. Both her job and her reputation were at stake. She used that opportunity to the
fullest.

Giving preclusive effect to an agency decision serves important public policies of adjudicating disputes once, bringing disputes to an end, and conserving judicial resources. Further, this practice encourages the parties to use local administrative procedures with adjudicators who have the greatest expertise in the subject of the dispute.

Thus, the University has met the requirements necessary for the court to apply the doctrine of preclusion.

Affirmed.

Lui v. Polk County Housing Board

Franklin Court of Appeal (2007)

Joe Lui appeals his eviction by the Polk County Housing Board ("the Board"), claiming that his right to due process was violated. After receiving a notice of eviction, Lui was given a hearing before the Board, which upheld the eviction. Lui then challenged the hearing process in Franklin state district court, which granted the Board's motion for summary judgment.

The heart of due process is notice and an opportunity to be heard. Lui argues that the notice of eviction failed to specify dates and times of the offenses charged. Lui concedes that he received a letter from the Board. The letter read:

> You are hereby notified that you have violated Paragraphs 12 and 14 of the lease between you and the Board, in that during June, July, and August, 2006, you failed to pay the rent on time, and on several occasions during the months of July and August of 2006, you failed to keep your dog on a leash when it was outside your home.

While due process requires that the accused know the charges against him in order to respond to them, notice is sufficient if it apprises the accused of the claims against him and gives him sufficient information to defend himself. It need not have the formality or completeness of an indictment. The notice here informed the accused of the specific paragraphs of the lease he was accused of violating. It also described which of his actions allegedly violated the lease and when those actions occurred in sufficient specificity that he could defend against the charges. For these reasons, the Board's notice satisfies the requirements of due process.

Lui next argues that he did not have a fair and independent tribunal. Lui claims that the Board acted as the investigator, prosecutor, and adjudicator, thus violating the requirements of fairness and independence. The Board owns and manages the homes, maintains records concerning the tenants, investigates complaints about tenants, brings complaints about tenants, and conducts hearings into those complaints. The hearing officer is a Board employee.

The due process requirement that there be a fair hearing before an impartial tribunal applies to administrative agencies as well as to courts.[1] Many potential risks to impartiality exist within administrative agencies. For example, impartiality may be impossible when there is a commingling of the investigatory,

---

[1] We treat city and county administrative agencies as we would state agencies. Because cities and counties are creatures of the state, their agencies are state agencies.

prosecutorial, and adjudicative functions. Similarly, where the adjudicator has personal or institutional financial interests in the outcome, impartiality is at risk. Likewise, where the adjudicator is under institutional pressure to reach a particular result, the danger of partiality is severe.

Administrative agencies serve many functions, and they need not maintain the same degree of separation of these functions as courts are required to do. Nevertheless, where these various functions, especially that of prosecutor or investigator, are mixed with that of the adjudicator within the same agency, the court must inquire whether these functions, as they are actually performed, are adequately separated so that there is no actual prejudice.

Our courts have struck down a procedure in which the adjudicator had access to the investigator's files outside the hearing. They also struck a procedure in which the agency's legal counsel both prosecuted the case on behalf of the agency and advised the agency's hearing officer on the law. However, in *Barber v. Piedmont Housing Authority* (Fr. Sup. Ct. 2004), another case involving public housing, our supreme court ruled that the manager of a public housing building was not so "management oriented" as to be disqualified from presiding over a hearing involving a tenant in a building across the city. In that case, the two managers had no contact other than at occasional management meetings and neither manager was in a position to influence the other. Further, the hearing officer testified that she had received no information about the eviction other than that presented at the hearing.

The Board argues that a requirement to hire independent hearing officers would bankrupt the Board because the Board issues about 1,000 evictions yearly. Due process does not require perfect hearings, but it does require hearings that meet the basic standard of fairness. The parties must be assured that the hearing officers are sufficiently independent that they will issue decisions based on the evidence and not on preconceived notions or institutional pressure. We are aware of instances in which agencies have financed the costs associated with fair hearings (i.e., hiring independent hearing officers, providing a right to counsel and prehearing discovery) from filing fees or from the fees issued for the license being regulated.

However, we need not reach the issue of whether the Board must employ independent hearing officers. In the case before us, the record is not clear as to the relationship between the hearing officer who conducted the hearing involving Lui and the manager who, on behalf of the Board, brought the charges against Lui. Thus, we cannot determine at this time whether the Board's policy of using its managers as hearing officers comports with due process.

We remand to the trial court to determine if the various functions outlined above, as actually practiced, were adequately separated so that there was no actual prejudice to Lui's rights.

Reversed and remanded.

1

Trenton Nursing Home v. Franklin Department of Public Health

Franklin Court of Appeal (2008)

Trenton Nursing Home ("Trenton") seeks a preliminary injunction to enjoin the Franklin Department of Public Health ("the Department") from proceeding with a hearing to revoke Trenton's skilled care facility license. Trenton complains that the Department hearing procedures violate due process by permitting hearing officers to deviate from the Franklin Rules of Evidence. Specifically, the Department rules permit hearing officers to receive hearsay evidence if it "is probative and if it reveals sufficient assurance of its truthfulness."

Due process requires that parties be given the opportunity to be heard. Ordinarily, witnesses will testify under oath and be subject to cross-examination. However, due process does not demand such formality. Due process requires only that the person aggrieved be given a chance to defend against the charges. A party may defend the charges by challenging the evidence presented against him, by his own presentation of evidence, or by both means.

In earlier cases dealing with hearing procedures of other Franklin agencies, our courts have ruled that the admission of hearsay evidence alone is insufficient grounds for finding that the protections of due process were violated. Rather, the evidence as a whole must be evaluated. Thus, applicants seeking disability or injury determinations before the Franklin Workers' Compensation Commission are permitted to submit medical reports even though such reports would be inadmissible in court as hearsay under the Franklin Rules of Evidence. *See Glover v. Workers' Compensation Comm'n* (Fr. Ct. App. 1998). Typically, in such a case, the agency has the right to have the party examined by a doctor of its choice. In *Glover*, the court made clear that the agency could challenge the testimony of the applicant's physician by producing its own doctors through a report or live testimony. Similarly, in *Franklin Department of Revenue v. Barnes* (Fr. Ct. App. 2003), the agency offered into evidence an agency-prepared summary of the records of a motor vehicle dealer to demonstrate that he violated tax regulations. Because the dealer possessed the records from which the summary was made, the court found that he was in a position to challenge the evidence, and therefore there was no due process violation.

Further, we note that the Rules of Evidence are designed in part to protect juries from hearing evidence that might unfairly prejudice them. Presumably, hearing officers are sufficiently independent as to not be unduly biased by evidence of a suspect nature.

On the other hand, we have struck down agency decisions that were based on "third-hand accounts" from "unnamed sources," the "accuracy of which" we could not evaluate. *See Lynbrook v. Franklin Dep't of Natural Resources* (Fr. Ct. App. 2007) (agency record comprised in large part of anonymous complaints of dumping hazardous materials could not support agency determination that regulatory violations had occurred).

There is no per se rule that the use of hearsay evidence violates due process. In fact, due process analysis does not demand that courts "check off," as with a laundry list, each of the requirements normally associated with due process. Thus, in *Kord v. New Lennox Hospital* (Fr. Sup. Ct. 1999), the Franklin Supreme Court rejected a due process challenge to the agency's decision even though the plaintiff did not have counsel or the right to prehearing discovery. The court explained that the rights to counsel and prehearing discovery were some, but not all, of the factors to be considered in determining whether the aggrieved party had a full and fair opportunity to be heard.

Because the hearing before the Franklin Department of Public Health has not yet occurred, we are unable to determine whether the hearsay evidence the agency plans to proffer, if any, meets the criteria of "suffi-cient assurance of its truthfulness" to satisfy the demands of due process.

As a guide to that hearing, we can say that due process does not require strict adherence to the Franklin Rules of Evidence.

The trial court's denial of the preliminary injunction was proper.

Affirmed.

POINT SHEET

City of Ontario
DRAFTERS' POINT SHEET

In this performance test, applicants work for the City Attorney's Office for the City of Ontario. Their task is to prepare an objective memorandum analyzing whether courts are likely to grant preclusive effect to decisions reached by an administrative agency, the City of Ontario Liquor Control Commission ("the Commission"). City ordinances provide that the mayor and city council constitute the Commission. The mayor, on behalf of the Commission, has the authority to grant and suspend licenses and to conduct hearings when a licensee objects to a Commission decision. The hearing procedures are set forth in the ordinances. The City Attorney wants to avoid litigating matters twice and wants Commission decisions to be given preclusive effect by the courts, while maintaining cost-effective and expeditious procedures.

The File contains the instructional memorandum from the supervising attorney, excerpts from the City of Ontario Liquor Control Ordinances ("LCO"), and the Notice of Liquor Control Violation form used by the City. The Library includes three cases.

The following discussion covers all the points the authors of the item intended to incorporate, but applicants may receive passing and even excellent grades without covering them all. Grading decisions are entirely within the discretion of the user jurisdictions.

I.   Overview

In preparing their objective memoranda, applicants should extract the requirements of preclusion from the cases and assess the City's hearing procedures in light of those requirements. Applicants are instructed not to draft the proposed changes. No particular format is given for the memorandum, but the call memo instructs applicants to identify what procedures currently comply with the requirements for preclusion, to identify those procedures that do not comply with preclusion requirements, and to describe what changes are necessary to conform to those requirements. Applicants must also discuss the effect of their recommended changes on the City's goals of having cost-effective and expeditious procedures for handling LCO violations.

Applicants may organize their answers as set forth in the task memorandum (which procedures comply, which do not, necessary changes, and time/cost implications), by LCO number or title (i.e., Notice, Conduct of Hearings, etc.) or by the due process requirements themselves and whether each LCO aspect comports with due process or does not, what changes are needed, and the time/cost implications thereof.

Summary of the Law of Preclusion

Thompson v. Franklin State Technical University (Fr. Sup. Ct. 1986) sets out the federal common law of preclusion, which the Franklin Supreme Court has adopted. Courts will grant preclusive effect to decisions of administrative agencies if

(1) the agency had the authority to adjudicate,

(2) the agency acted in an adjudicative manner (as opposed to a legislative or ministerial manner) and decided issues in dispute properly before it, and

(3) the agency adheres to procedures that offer some level of due process.

While it is more likely that a court will extend preclusive effect when the proceedings at the agency level have included more due process, the doctrine does not require that agency proceedings provide the full complement of procedural protections found in courts.

In determining whether agency proceedings afford sufficient due process, the first inquiry is the notice given to the party whose rights are affected. The notice must be sufficient to apprise an accused of the charges and provide sufficient information to defend against them. *Lui v. Polk County Housing Bd.* (Fr. Ct. App. 2007). The second requirement is that the party against whom the doctrine of preclusion is being applied must have had a full and fair opportunity to litigate or to be heard before the agency. A key component of a fair hearing is a fair and independent tribunal. Agency hearings where the investigative, prosecutorial, and judicial functions are commingled in the same person do not comport with the impartiality requirement. *Id.* The standard does not require the same degree of separation as is required of a court, but agencies must show that the functions of investigator, prosecutor, and adjudicator, as they are actually performed, are separated adequately so that there is no actual prejudice to the accused. *Id.*

Other aspects of due process include the right to counsel, the right to prehearing discovery or disclosure, and the right to present evidence and challenge evidence presented. *Thompson*. Not all of these rights must be afforded to satisfy due process. Courts look at the procedures as a whole to determine whether the party whose rights are affected had the opportunity to be heard. *Kord v. New Lennox Hospital* (Fr. Sup. Ct. 1999) (cited in *Trenton Nursing Home v. Franklin Dept. of Public Health* (Fr. Ct. App. 2008)). Due process requires only a fair hearing, not a perfect one. *Lui.*

The issue of cost- and time-efficiency may be addressed as part of the due process analysis. While more costly and elaborate processes might provide greater due process, they may not be necessary if the Commission provides the basic elements of fairness as specified above.

II.   Detailed Analysis

1. The agency must have the authority to adjudicate and must, in fact, adjudicate.[1]

- The Commission's authority to adjudicate alleged violations of the Liquor Control Act and related City ordinances is set forth in § 2-1.

- An agency adjudicates when it holds hearings, takes evidence, makes findings of fact and conclusions of law, and renders a decision. *Thompson.* The Commission acts in a quasi-judicial capacity when it holds a hearing under the procedures set forth in the Liquor Control Ordinances. The procedures provide for notice (§ 2-2), set out the burden of proof (§ 2-4), set out a procedure for evidence (§ 2-4), and provide for issuance of fines or suspension (§ 2-5). Applicants should conclude that the Commission acts in an adjudicative capacity when it follows these procedures.

- It could be argued that the hearings conducted under the current ordinances so violate due process as to raise a question whether the City is in fact adjudicating, but it is unlikely that a court would so conclude.

2. The agency's procedures must meet the requirements of due process.

a. Notice

- Applicants might note that the fact that the City affords a hearing (§ 2-2) before imposing sanctions on a licensee is a factor that weighs in favor of due process compliance. But the key is recognizing whether the hearing itself gives licensees a full and fair opportunity to litigate. *See Trenton.*

- Notice must be sufficient to apprise the accused of the charges and give the accused sufficient information to defend him- or herself. *Lui.*

- Section 2-2 of the ordinances simply provides that the mayor issue written notice of the charge(s) against the licensee. However, the ordinances do not meet the threshold for adequate notice because they do not require the identification of the law or ordinance allegedly being violated, the actions that constitute the violation, or when those acts were committed.

- The City's current Notice of Liquor Control Violation form demonstrates that the City's procedures do not provide sufficient notice. The form has a blank

---

[1] Note that a decision by a local government agency such as a county or city is treated the same as a state agency decision. *See Lui.*

for listing the section(s) of the Liquor Control Act or Ordinances that have been violated. However, the notice fails to identify what behavior by the accused is at issue or when that behavior allegedly occurred. Although more formal than the letter at issue in *Lui*, the City's notice does not give the accused sufficient information to adequately defend against the charges. Thus, the City's procedures will fail for lack of notice.

- The City must change its notice procedures to identify the behavior(s) that allegedly constitutes a violation of the Liquor Control Act or Ordinances and the approximate times when the accused engaged in that behavior.

- Astute applicants might suggest training City personnel who complete the notice form to include more, rather than less, specificity about violations.

- Making the notice more complete should have only a minor effect on the time- and cost-effectiveness of the procedures. Also, some time and expense will be necessary to properly train City staff who fill out the notice.

b. The right to a full and fair opportunity to litigate

An independent tribunal—the hearing officer—is key to a full and fair opportunity to litigate. Combining investigative, prosecutorial, and adjudicative functions in one person may constitute a denial of due process. *See Lui.* On the other hand, pure separation of the functions (as with courts) is not required. Agencies can appoint hearing officers from the same agency if they show that the functions as they are performed are adequately separated so that there is no prejudice. *See Lui; Thompson.*

There are several concerns about the independence of the City's hearing officer.

- The mayor cannot be an independent adjudicator. He has the power to conduct hearings and also to impose fees and fines. If the City budget relies on license fees or fines for revenue, the mayor, as hearing officer, may feel pressured to issue rulings that maximize revenue to the City, regardless of the evidence.

- The ordinances appear to commingle the functions of investigator, prosecutor, and adjudicator. For example, the mayor has the power to enter, or authorize any law enforcement officer to enter, licensed premises to enforce the City ordinances. § 2-1. Thus, the mayor appears to act as an investigator.

- The mayor appears to be both prosecutor and adjudicator. He is charged with giving notice and he signs the notice form, both of which are prosecutorial functions. The mayor also acts as hearing officer, an adjudicatory function.

- The mayor may influence the gathering of evidence, an investigative function. As hearing officer, the mayor is to admit into evidence reports from the police or other investigative bodies and may be inclined to give undue weight to the findings of city agencies that presumably report to him, and city employees preparing the reports may be inclined to slant the reports against licensees.

- The mayor may have access to information outside the hearing. Because the mayor has the duty to maintain records relating to action on liquor licenses and the authority to investigate license applicants, he/she may have access to the files prior to the hearing and thus to inadmissible evidence or at least to evidence that the licensee does not know has been considered.

Applicants should conclude that the commingling of the investigative and adjudicatory functions in the City's procedures is suspect and likely violates due process. To ensure that City procedures afford due process, the City should make several changes:

- The City should hire an independent hearing officer, perhaps not a City employee. Or the City should change the procedures so that the hearing officer has no role in law enforcement or investigation and no role in prosecuting the case.

- If the mayor remains as hearing officer, the City should ensure that the head of the police department does not report to the mayor and that the mayor cannot view the evidence prior to the hearing.

- These changes will affect both time- and cost-effectiveness. Hiring an independent hearing officer not employed by the City will clearly incur additional costs for the City. It may also add to the time needed prior to a hearing if there is a time lag in engaging an independent hearing officer.

- Alternatively, restructuring the mayor's duties as Commission chair may meet the due process requirements with less cost. Such restructuring will require time to redraft the ordinances and, presumably, some time to enact them. Once enacted, the changes may or may not affect the time-effectiveness of the procedures, depending on what they are.

c. *Evidence*

The more an agency acts like a court, the more a court is likely to grant preclusive effect to its decisions. *See Thompson*. One aspect of court-like process is the opportunity to present evidence through witnesses and exhibits, subject to cross-examination and objections. *Id.* Allowing hearsay evidence is not *per se* a violation of due process, but due process requires that evidence be evaluated as a whole. The standard is not whether the Rules of Evidence apply but whether the hearing is fair. Further, there must be adequate assurance of the truthfulness of the proceeding. *Trenton Nursing Home*. Due process requires that the accused be able to challenge the evidence presented. *Id.* (discussing case in which opponent of hearsay evidence had a right to submit its expert's report and case in which opponent could challenge hearsay (a records summary) with the original evidence).

- Applicants might note that LCO procedures that are indicative of due process include permitting licensees to present evidence, having witnesses testify under oath, making objections, and cross-examining witnesses. Hearings are also recorded by a court reporter. (§§ 2-3, 4). The City bears the burden of proof by a preponderance of the evidence. (§ 2-4).

- However, the City's procedures require the hearing officer to admit into evidence the police report or the report of any investigative body. Such a report is hearsay—an out-of-court statement being offered for the truth of the matter asserted. Yet there is no assurance that the licensee can challenge the evidence unless given the opportunity to cross-examine the preparer of the report.

- Accordingly, City procedures do not provide safeguards for the challenge of hearsay evidence similar to those in the cases discussed in *Trenton Nursing Home*. Depending on the type of hearsay in, for example, a police report, the opponent may or may not have adequate opportunity to challenge the evidence. There is no reason to believe that the contents of such reports are otherwise available to the accused or are based on information in the hands of the accused as was the case in *Lui*. Nor is there assurance that the preparer of a police report has "sufficient truthfulness." *See Trenton Nursing Home*.

- Applicants should recommend that the City revise its procedures to require that the police or other investigators appear in person before the hearing officer and be subject to cross-examination.

- Additional due process concerns arise from the facts that the hearing is to be informal and that the Franklin Rules of Evidence do not apply. *See id.*

- While due process does not require all the procedures of court, it is troublesome that the ordinances allow the City to present evidence through "other means" without specifying what those "other means" are. Any "other means" of presenting evidence must satisfy due process.

43

- Applicants should conclude that it is questionable whether the City procedures meet the "sufficient truthfulness" standard. *See Trenton Nursing Home.*

- The procedures should be rewritten to provide that the evidence as a whole must be probative and meet the "sufficient truthfulness" test. One option would be to delete the phrase "through other means" in § 2-4 and replace it with language using the "sufficient truthfulness" test. Complying with this standard may require additional time and impose costs on the City because the investigator/police officer will have to testify in person, taking him/her from job duties and/or possibly requiring the City to pay overtime.

- The City may continue to provide an informal hearing in which the Rules of Evidence do not apply so long as the evidence as a whole meets due process.

- The ordinances place the burden on the City to prove a violation by a preponderance of the evidence. § 2-4. This provision may not be required as part of due process but helps ensure that the licensee has a full and fair opportunity to be heard. Accordingly, applicants should conclude that no change is necessary regarding the allocation of the burden of proof.

- Likewise, there is no need to change the requirements that the licensee have the chance to cross-examine the City's witnesses and present evidence.

d. Prehearing discovery

One aspect of acting like a court is affording litigants the opportunity for prehearing discovery. *See Thompson.* Franklin state courts may not require prehearing discovery as an element of due process, but it is more likely that an agency decision will be given preclusive effect if the proceedings include some amount of prehearing discovery. Again, the standard for a reviewing court is whether the procedures, taken as a whole, provide for a full and fair opportunity to be heard. *Id.*

- As written, the City procedures are silent on prehearing discovery. Indeed, the hearing is to be conducted within five business days of the request for a hearing. Such short notice of the hearing offers little opportunity to inspect the evidence to be presented even if it were available.

- This issue is a close one. Applicants may conclude that the failure to provide prehearing discovery and the short prehearing period may violate due process, especially because the current notice form fails to provide the licensee with enough information to defend against the charges. The lack of prehearing discovery may be another factor courts would consider, along with the other

procedures that arguably violate due process, to conclude that the City procedures are so lacking as to not warrant preclusive effect. Applicants may conclude that if the notice provisions are made to be more informative about the
charges and if the other recommended changes are made, due process may not
require prehearing discovery.

- Astute applicants will recommend that the City change its procedures to provide more time between notice of the violation and the hearing or a chance to
  request more time to allow for prehearing discovery. The City might also
  change its procedures to permit some prehearing inspection of evidence.
  These changes will affect the timeliness of the proceedings but will not significantly impact the City's costs.

e. *Right to counsel*

While the *Thompson* court appears to require the right to counsel as an aspect of due
process, *Kord* (cited in *Trenton Nursing Home*) is not as clear on the issue. The *Kord*
court reviewed the right to counsel as one of the several factors to be considered in a
due process challenge to an agency decision. Here, the ordinances are silent on a licensee's right to counsel.

- Again, this is a close call. Some applicants may conclude that there is no due
  process right to counsel. Better applicants might conclude that providing licensees with the right to counsel would help ensure that agency procedures
  meet due process requirements. However, astute applicants may note that the
  short time between notice and hearing, without provision for continuances,
  may undermine any such right to counsel. It is unrealistic to believe that a licensee could find counsel who would be prepared in just five business days.

- Applicants might conclude that the City need not make any changes. However, better applicants will note that though the City need not provide counsel, it
  also should not preclude the right to counsel. Therefore, the City might permit
  extensions of time to make the right to counsel meaningful.

- On the other hand, applicants might recommend that the City amend its ordinances to provide that the licensee may be represented by counsel at the licensee's expense. This would require more time before the hearing.

- Applicants should conclude that such changes will affect the timeliness of the
  procedures, likely by extending the time to hearing. Extending the time may
  be necessary to better ensure preclusion. Most of the suggested changes will

not affect the cost of the procedures, although adding a right to legal representation could increase costs and increase the complexity of cases.

3. Procedures should be cost- and time-effective.

Applicants are told to consider the City's goals of cost- and time-effectiveness. *Lui* notes two means of financing hearings (via filing/licensing fees). Applicants need not determine budget figures or make cost projections, but should acknowledge that some procedures will be costly (i.e., hiring an independent hearing officer) and identify which are necessary and which are not. The points listed above incorporate time- and cost-effectiveness considerations.

III.   Conclusion

Applicants should conclude that the City needs to make several changes to its hearing procedures if it wishes to increase the likelihood that Commission decisions will be given preclusive effect. The City must make its Notice of Liquor Control Violation more informative. It should also provide for an independent hearing officer or restructure the mayor's duties so that the mayor is independent, eliminate its procedure for admitting police or other investigative reports without the preparer of the report being subject to cross-examination, and not prevent licensees from having counsel. Certain issues/procedures present a closer call as to whether changes are needed: whether the City should permit prehearing discovery or disclosure, grant the right to counsel, and be willing to extend some deadlines to accommodate counsel and prehearing disclosure. If added, such changes would increase the likelihood that the City's procedures would be granted preclusive effect. Most of these procedural changes will have minimal financial impact on the City, except possibly for hiring an independent hearing officer. Almost all the changes will increase the time needed for the hearing.

State of Franklin v. McLain

State of Franklin v. McLain

FILE

LIBRARY

POINT SHEET

Instructions

The back cover of each test form contains the following instructions:

You will have 90 minutes to complete this session of the examination. This performance test is designed to evaluate your ability to handle a select number of legal authorities in the context of a factual problem involving a client.

The problem is set in the fictitious state of Franklin, in the fictitious Fifteenth Circuit of the United States. Columbia and Olympia are also fictitious states in the Fifteenth Circuit. In Franklin, the trial court of general jurisdiction is the District Court, the intermediate appellate court is the Court of Appeal, and the highest court is the Supreme Court.

You will have two kinds of materials with which to work: a File and a Library. The first document in the File is a memorandum containing the instructions for the task you are to complete. The other documents in the File contain factual information about your case and may include some facts that are not relevant.

The Library contains the legal authorities needed to complete the task and may also include some authorities that are not relevant. Any cases may be real, modified, or written solely for the purpose of this examination. If the cases appear familiar to you, do not assume that they are precisely the same as you have read before. Read them thoroughly, as if they all were new to you. You should assume that the cases were decided in the jurisdictions and on the dates shown. In citing cases from the Library, you may use abbreviations and omit page references.

Your response must be written in the answer book provided. If you are taking the examination on a laptop computer, your jurisdiction will provide you with specific instructions. In answering this performance test, you should concentrate on the materials in the File and Library. What you have learned in law school and elsewhere provides the general background for analyzing the problem; the File and Library provide the specific materials with which you must work.

Although there are no restrictions on how you apportion your time, you should be sure to allocate ample time (about 45 minutes) to reading and digesting the materials and to organizing your answer before you begin writing it. You may make notes anywhere in the test materials; blank pages are provided at the end of the booklet. You may not tear pages from the question booklet.

This performance test will be graded on your responsiveness to the instructions regarding the task you are to complete, which are given to you in the first memorandum in the File, and on the content, thoroughness, and organization of your response.

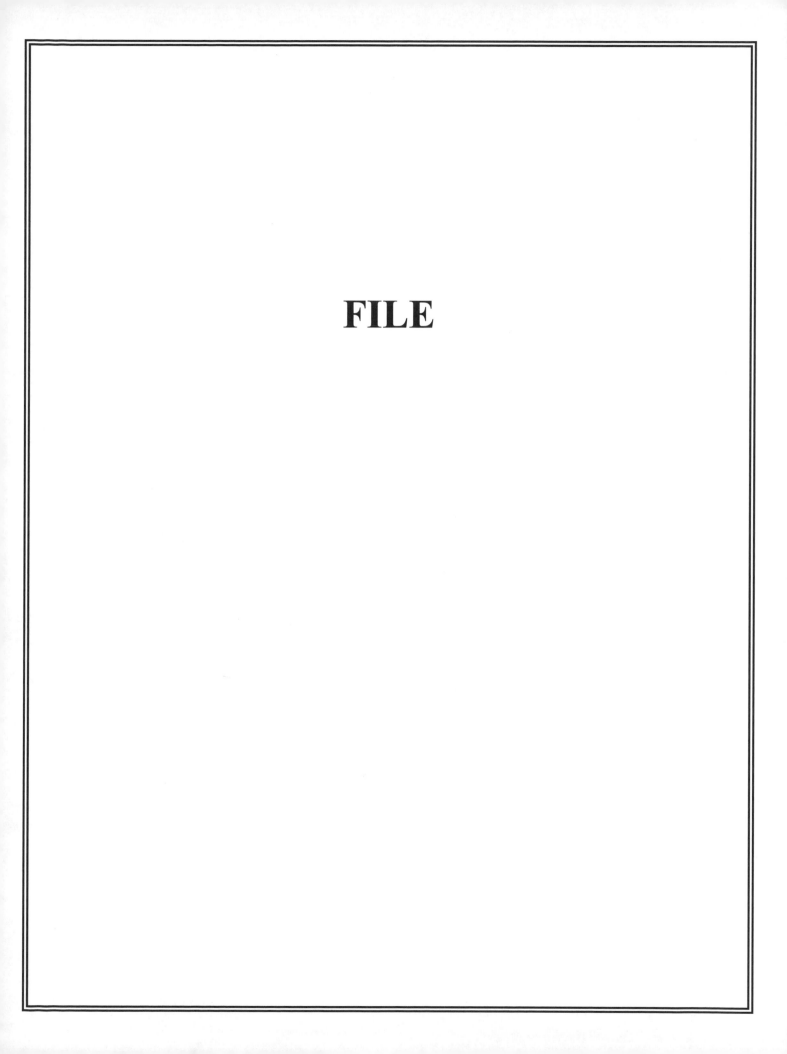

FILE

Selmer & Pierce, LLP
Attorneys at Law
412 Yahara Place
Centralia, Franklin 33703

MEMORANDUM

To: Applicant
From: Marcia Pierce
Date: February 23, 2010
Re: State v. Brian McLain

We have been appointed by the court to represent Brian McLain, who is indigent. The State of Franklin has charged McLain with three felony counts: possession of methamphetamine with intent to distribute, possession of equipment to manufacture methamphetamine, and manufacture of methamphetamine. The evidentiary hearing on our motion to suppress concluded yesterday. The judge wants our post-hearing brief before the end of the week.

I have attached the relevant portions of the transcript from the evidentiary hearing. Please draft the argument section of our brief. We need to make the case that Officer Simon had no reasonable suspicion that would justify the stop of McLain's vehicle on the night in question.

In addition to the motion to suppress, I've moved to dismiss Count Two of the criminal complaint, possession of equipment to manufacture methamphetamine, on the ground that it is a lesser-included offense of Count Three, manufacture of methamphetamine. Please draft that argument as well.

Do not prepare a separate statement of facts; I will draft it. However, for both of our arguments, be sure to provide detailed discussion and analysis, incorporating the relevant facts and addressing the applicable legal authorities. Be sure to anticipate and respond to the State's likely arguments.

STATE OF FRANKLIN
DISTRICT COURT FOR BARNES COUNTY

State of Franklin,	)	
Plaintiff,	)	**CRIMINAL COMPLAINT**
	)	
v.	)	**Case No. 09-CR-522**
	)	
Brian McLain,	)	
Defendant.	)	
	)	

The State of Franklin, County of Barnes, by District Attorney Sarah Russell, hereby alleges as follows:

1. Count One. That on October 5, 2009, the defendant, Brian McLain, did knowingly possess more than 15 grams but less than 100 grams of methamphetamine, a controlled substance, in the City of Centralia, County of Barnes, Franklin, with intent to distribute or deliver, in violation of the Franklin Criminal Code § 42.

2. Count Two. That on October 5, 2009, the defendant, Brian McLain, did possess equipment or supplies with the intent to manufacture methamphetamine, a controlled substance, in the City of Centralia, County of Barnes, Franklin, in violation of the Franklin Criminal Code § 43.

3. Count Three. That on October 5, 2009, the defendant, Brian McLain, was knowingly engaged in the manufacture of methamphetamine, a controlled substance, in the City of Centralia, County of Barnes, Franklin, in violation of the Franklin Criminal Code § 51.

November 17, 2009

Sarah Russell

Sarah Russell
Barnes County District Attorney
State of Franklin

State of Franklin v. McLain

STATE OF FRANKLIN
DISTRICT COURT FOR BARNES COUNTY

State of Franklin,　　　　　　　　　　)
　　　　　Plaintiff,　　　　　　　　　)
　　　　　　　　　　　　　　　　　　)
v.　　　　　　　　　　　　　　　　　)　　　　　Case No. 09-CR-522
　　　　　　　　　　　　　　　　　　)
Brian McLain,　　　　　　　　　　　　)
　　　　　Defendant.　　　　　　　　　)

MOTION TO SUPPRESS EVIDENCE
AND TO DISMISS COUNT TWO OF THE COMPLAINT

Defendant Brian McLain, by and through his attorney, Marcia Pierce of Selmer & Pierce, LLP, moves the Court as follows:

1.　　　To suppress all evidence obtained as a result of the search of his vehicle and a shed located in an alley next to 1230 8th Street, Centralia, Franklin, on October 5, 2009, on the ground that the investigating officer lacked reasonable suspicion to stop the defendant's vehicle and, as a result, both the stop and the subsequent search violated the defendant's Fourth Amendment rights under the United States Constitution. *See State v. Montel* (Franklin Ct. App. 2003).

2.　　　To dismiss Count Two of the criminal complaint as multiplicitous. The charge of "Possession of Equipment or Supplies with the Intent to Manufacture Methamphetamine," Fr. Crim. Code § 43, is a lesser-included offense of Count Three of the complaint, "Manufacture of Methamphetamine," Fr. Crim. Code § 51. Prosecution of both charges is, therefore, multiplicitous and violates the defendant's right not to be put in jeopardy of life and limb twice for the same offense as guaranteed by the double jeopardy and due process provisions of the United States Constitution. *See State v. Decker* (Franklin Sup. Ct. 2005).

Dated: February 2, 2010

　　　　　　　　　　　　　　　Respectfully submitted,

　　　　　　　　　　　　　　　Marcia Pierce

　　　　　　　　　　　　　　　Marcia Pierce
　　　　　　　　　　　　　　　Selmer & Pierce, LLP
　　　　　　　　　　　　　　　Counsel for Defendant

5

Transcript of Call to Centralia Police Department CrimeStoppers Hotline

October 5, 2009, 10:22 p.m.

Operator: CrimeStoppers Hotline. How may I direct your call?

Caller: Um, I'd like to report some criminal activity.

Operator: What is your location, sir?

Caller: I'm at the Oxford Street Shop-Mart. There's a guy here, and he's gotta be a meth dealer. I mean, he just bought two boxes of Sudafed cold medicine and some coffee filters, and I heard him ask the cashier if Shop-Mart had quit selling engine-starter fluid.

Operator: Can you describe this individual?

Caller: Well, he's kinda scuzzy looking, if you know what I mean. You know, shifty looking. He's a white guy, maybe mid-20s, with dark hair and one of those goatees. He's wearing jeans and a dark hooded sweatshirt.

Operator: I'll notify the officer on call. What is your name, sir?

Caller: Hey, I don't want to get involved. I don't need any grief. I just called because this guy is clearly up to something. He just left the store and is walking toward a red Jeep Cherokee in the parking lot.

Operator: Is there any other person with this individual?

Caller: Hey, I gotta go. I told you what I saw. [phone disconnected]

6

Excerpts from Suppression Hearing Transcript
February 22, 2010

Direct Examination of Officer Ted Simon by Assistant District Attorney Lynn Ridley

Q: Please state your name and occupation for the record.

A: Officer Ted Simon. I have been a police officer with the Centralia Police Department for 12 years, the last five in the narcotics division.

Q: Describe your training and experience in dealing with narcotics.

A: In addition to my five years in the division, I've attended Federal Bureau of Investigation courses every two years and have done additional training sponsored by the State of Franklin crime laboratory. I've been involved in over 200 narcotics arrests, including over 50 arrests for possession and manufacture of methamphetamine.

Q: Were you on duty on October 5, 2009?

A: Yes. I worked second shift, from 3 p.m. to 11 p.m.

Q: Sometime after 10 p.m. did you receive a call from dispatch?

A: Yes, at approximately 10:25 p.m. on October 5, I received a dispatch call indicating that a suspicious man had been seen at the Oxford Street Shop-Mart purchasing items that the caller said were used to make methamphetamine—coffee filters, two boxes of Sudafed cold medicine—and that the individual had also asked if engine-starter fluid was sold at Shop-Mart. Based on my experience and training, I know that all of those items are frequently used to manufacture methamphetamine; in fact, because of the increase in methamphetamine use, some stores, including Shop-Mart, won't let you buy more than two boxes of a cold medicine containing pseudoephedrine, such as Sudafed, at a time.

Q: Did the caller describe this suspicious individual?

A: Yes, I was informed by dispatch that the individual was a white male in his mid-20s dressed in jeans and a dark hooded sweatshirt. The caller also stated that the individual had dark hair and a goatee, and that he had been seen leaving the store and walking to a red Jeep Cherokee in the Shop-Mart parking lot.

Q: Did you take any action in response to this call?

A: Yes, I drove my squad car to the Shop-Mart, arriving at 10:28 p.m.—I had been only a few blocks away when I received the call.

Q: Did you find an individual matching the description there?

A: Not in the Shop-Mart parking lot. However, across Oxford Street, I saw a red Jeep Cherokee parked in front of Cullen's Food Emporium. There was no one in the vehicle, but after a minute I observed a white male with dark hair and a small beard, wearing jeans and a dark hooded sweatshirt, come out of Cullen's with a small paper bag in his hand. He got into the driver's seat of the red Jeep Cherokee.

Q: What happened next?

A: The individual appeared to be reaching over into the backseat, moving something around. He then started the vehicle and drove away. I followed him for a mile or so, until he stopped in front of an apartment building at 1230 8th Street. A man who had been sitting on the stoop stood up, walked over to the Jeep, and appeared to have a brief conversation with the driver. The Jeep Cherokee then pulled away from the curb and turned into the alley that runs between number 1230 and the next apartment building.

Q: What is the neighborhood like around 8th Street?

A: Well, in the last year we've seen an increase in calls and reports of criminal activity on 8th Street and the surrounding area. Only two months before we had busted a guy who had been growing marijuana plants in the basement of his apartment building on 8th Street, just a few blocks north of where the Jeep Cherokee stopped.

Q: Okay. Now, what did you do after the vehicle entered the alley?

A: I activated the squad car's lights and turned into the alley behind the Jeep Cherokee. The Cherokee came to a complete stop. I got out of the squad car and approached the vehicle. There was only the driver in the vehicle. I asked him for his driver's license so I could identify him. He took his license out of his wallet and gave it to me.

Q: Did you then identify the driver by his driver's license?

A: Yes, the name on the license was Brian McLain and the photo matched the driver.

Q: Do you see the driver, Brian McLain, in the courtroom today?

A: Yes, he is seated at the near side of the defense table.

Q: Let the record indicate that the witness has identified the defendant, Brian McLain.

Court: So noted.

Q: What happened next?

A: He demanded to know why I had stopped his vehicle. I responded that I had reason to believe that he had been purchasing items used in the manufacture of methamphetamine and I requested consent to search his vehicle.

8

Q: How did the defendant respond to that request?

A: He was angry and said, "Go ahead, I don't have anything to hide." He then made some derogatory comments to the effect that the police should be out catching "the real criminals." A search of his vehicle revealed a paper bag in the backseat like the one I had seen him carrying when he left Cullen's Food Emporium. Inside it was a box containing 50 matchbooks. I also found a plastic Shop-Mart bag containing a receipt dated October 5, 2009, coffee filters, a package of coffee, and two boxes of Sudafed cold tablets. Each box contained 20 tablets. In the glove box I found a plastic baggie containing what appeared to be one marijuana cigarette.

Q: What did you do then?

A: I informed the defendant that I was placing him under arrest. I handcuffed him, read him the Miranda warnings, and transported him to the Centralia West Side Police Station for booking. I found $320 in cash in his wallet. During questioning, the defendant directed us to a shed behind the building at 1230 8th Street where we found what is commonly referred to as a "meth lab": apparatus used to remove the pseudoephedrine in cold tablets and produce methamphetamine for sale to drug users. The defendant's meth lab contained equipment and materials used in producing methamphetamine, some of which showed recent use. Also, we found a glass beaker holding 18 grams of a whitish powder. Testing by the Franklin Crime Lab found it to be street-grade methamphetamine.

Q: Do you have an opinion, based on your training and experience, as to the street value of 18 grams of methamphetamine?

A: Yes, based on my experience, about $2,500.

Q: Based on your experience, is this an amount that would be kept for personal use only?

A: Absolutely not. It's more than 150 sales.

Assistant District Attorney Ridley: Thank you. No further questions.

Cross-Examination by Attorney Marcia Pierce

Q: Officer, had you responded to reports of criminal activity at the Oxford Street Shop-Mart before?

A: Sure, it's a busy place. I respond to a call there about once a month.

Q: And hadn't all those calls, before the night of October 5, 2009, been reports of shoplifting and, let me see here, three reports of vandalism?

A: Yes, that sounds accurate.

Q: So this was the first time you'd had a report of someone purchasing items for the manufacture of methamphetamine at that Shop-Mart store?

A: Yes, it was.

Q: Those other calls, for shoplifting and vandalism, were all made by individuals identifying themselves as either a Shop-Mart manager or an employee, weren't they?

A: Yes, they were.

Q: But the individual making the call to CrimeStoppers on October 5th didn't leave his name or otherwise identify himself, did he?

A: No, he didn't.

Q: When you reached the Shop-Mart just five minutes after you were dispatched, did you look for the person who made the report?

A: No, I was looking for the red Jeep Cherokee.

Q: Buying coffee filters is not illegal, is it?

A: No.

Q: Nor is buying cold medicine?

A: No.

Q: What about asking a store employee if the store stocks engine-starter fluid?

A: No, that's not illegal.

Q: Did the anonymous CrimeStoppers caller mention that, in addition to the coffee filters, the defendant purchased a package of coffee at the same time?

A: No, that wasn't in the report I received.

Q: Does the Shop-Mart sell food?

A: Well, it sells some snack items.

Q: But it's not a grocery store that sells meat and fresh produce, is it?

A: No, it's mainly a convenience store.

Q: So there wouldn't be anything unusual about someone stopping by the Shop-Mart and then going to Cullen's Food Emporium to buy groceries, would there?

A: No, I suppose not.

Q: Franklin law doesn't prohibit an individual from buying more than two boxes of Sudafed cold medicine, does it?

A: No, it doesn't.

State of Franklin v. McLain

Q: So it's only a Shop-Mart policy to allow a maximum purchase of two boxes at a time, isn't it?

A: Yes, that's true.

Q: Isn't it true that two boxes, containing a total of 40 tablets, would not be enough to produce any significant quantity of methamphetamine?

A: By itself, maybe.

Q: Did the defendant ever exceed the speed limit or violate any motor vehicle law during the entire time that you followed him?

A: No, not that I could observe.

Q: You stated that two months before you arrested the defendant, your department arrested a man for growing marijuana in his apartment building on 8th Street, right?

A: Correct.

Q: But you had never arrested an individual on 8th Street for maintaining a meth lab before?

A: No, that was the first meth operation we discovered on 8th Street.

Q: You also arrested my client for possession of marijuana?

A: Yes.

Q: And you were wrong about that?

A: The Crime Lab tests came back negative for marijuana.

Atty. Pierce: Thank you. No further questions.

Redirect by Assistant District Attorney Ridley

Q: Have you had any reports of criminal activity that originated from the Oxford Street Shop-Mart that turned out to be erroneous?

A: No. Since I've been assigned to this beat, every report I've received in regard to that Shop-Mart has resulted in a criminal report being filed or an arrest.

Attorney Ridley: Thank you.

Court: The witness is excused.

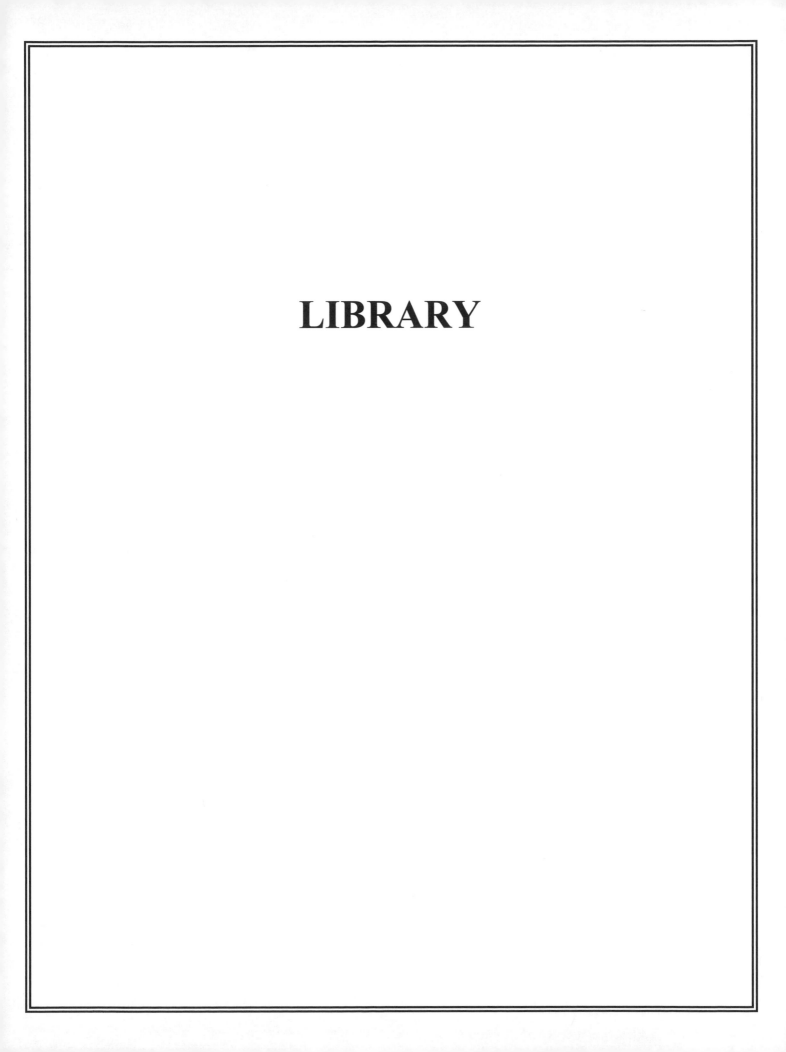

LIBRARY

§ 42. Possession with intent to distribute or deliver methamphetamine

(1) Except as authorized by this chapter, it is unlawful for any person to knowingly possess, with intent to distribute, a controlled substance, to wit, methamphetamine. Intent under this subsection may be demonstrated by, *inter alia*, evidence of the quantity and monetary value of the substances possessed, the possession of paraphernalia used in the distribution of controlled substances, and the activities or statements of the person in possession of the controlled substance prior to and after the alleged violation.

> (a) If a person knowingly possesses, with intent to distribute, 15 or more grams but less than 100 grams of methamphetamine, the person is guilty of a felony.

§ 43. Possession of equipment or supplies with intent to manufacture methamphetamine

(1) No person shall knowingly possess equipment or chemicals, or both, for the purpose of manufacturing a controlled substance, to wit, methamphetamine. . . .

> (b) A person who commits an offense under this section is guilty of a felony.

§ 44. Possession of precursor chemicals for methamphetamine production

(1) It is unlawful for any person to possess ephedrine, pseudoephedrine, red phosphorus, lithium metal, sodium metal, iodine, anhydrous ammonia, or their salts, isomers, or salts of isomers with intent to use the product to manufacture a controlled substance, to wit, methamphetamine. . . .

§ 51. Manufacture of methamphetamine

(1) It is unlawful for any person to knowingly manufacture methamphetamine. "Manufacture" means to produce, compound, convert, or process methamphetamine, including to package or repackage the substance, either directly or indirectly by extraction from substances of natural origin or by means of chemical synthesis. Any person who violates this subsection is subject to the following penalties: …

> (b) A person who manufactures 15 or more grams but less than 100 grams of methamphetamine is guilty of a felony.

State v. Montel
Franklin Court of Appeal (2003)

We granted the state leave to appeal an interlocutory order granting the defendant's motion to suppress evidence obtained by police as the result of a *Terry* stop.

Responding to reports of gunfire at 220 North Street, Franklin City Police, led by Officer Tom Kane, spoke with Sam Barber, who told them that two men had shot at him through a fence while he was in his yard. He said he did not see the shooters, but a witness told police he had seen a white Mazda speed away shortly after the shots were fired. Officer Kane knew that Barber was a gang member and that his gang and a rival gang were involved in recent shootings.

Later that day, Officer Kane asked Barber if he had any further information about the shooting. Barber said that he had nothing to add about his own shooting, but that he did have information about another shooting that same day. Barber said that his cousin told him that she witnessed gunfire on Elm Street, in the same neighborhood, and that the shots came from two cars, a white Mazda and a blue Honda with license plate SAO905. Barber refused to give police his cousin's name or any information about her. Using the license number, Officer Kane learned that the Honda belonged to Ray Montel, who Kane knew had recently been arrested in a nearby town on a firearms charge, and who was also known to be a member of the rival gang. The police were unable to locate Montel that evening, and did not find any evidence of the Elm Street shooting, such as bullet damage or spent shell casings. Nor were there any calls to 911 to report the shooting. A week passed with no further investigation of the Elm Street shooting. Then, Officer Kane and his partner saw Montel drive by. They stopped the car and questioned Montel, who denied any knowledge of either shooting. The officers found two guns in the car, and Montel was charged with various firearms offenses.

Montel moved to suppress all evidence gathered in connection with the stop of the car. The trial court granted the motion, holding that "once the tip of the Elm Street shooting proved unreliable, the officers' mere hunch that Montel was involved in criminal activity was not enough to establish a reasonable and articulable suspicion of criminal activity adequate to stop his car."

The sole issue on appeal is whether the police acted reasonably in stopping Montel and his passengers. Our review is *de novo*.

The Fourth Amendment protects individuals from unreasonable searches and seizures. Police, however, have the right to stop and interrogate persons reasonably suspected of criminal conduct. Police may make a brief investigatory stop if they have a reasonable

16

suspicion that criminal activity may be afoot. Such stops by police are often called "*Terry* stops" after the leading case, *Terry v. Ohio*, 392 U.S. 1 (1968). The test is whether the officers have "a reasonable suspicion, grounded in specific and articulable facts, that the person [is] involved in criminal activity" at the time. *Id.* To determine whether the suspicion is reasonable, courts will look at the totality of the circumstances of each case.

A tip from a source known to police—especially one who has provided information in the past—may be sufficient, in and of itself, to warrant a *Terry* stop. But an anonymous tip is different; it must be corroborated, such as by investigation or independent police observation of unusually suspicious conduct, and must be "reliable in its assertion of illegality, not just in its tendency to identify a determinate person." *Florida v. J.L.*, 529 U.S. 266, 272 (2000).

In *State v. Sneed* (Franklin Ct. App. 1999), the defendant was stopped after briefly visiting a house that police had under surveillance after receiving a tip from an untested confidential informant that heroin dealing was taking place there. We held that the police did not have reasonable suspicion to stop the defendant, noting that there was no testimony that the area was known for drug trafficking or that there had been short-term traffic to the house. The officers in *Sneed*, as here, based their stop solely on information received from an informant without having

that information verified by independent investigation.

The state argues that the tip here was reliable because of the officers' interactions with Barber, and because Barber was able to report a crime supposedly witnessed by his cousin. But this is not a case involving a "personal observation" or "firsthand account" of a crime, as in those cases finding that the facts justified a *Terry* stop. The "tip" was hearsay. There was no way of knowing Barber's cousin's state of mind at the time she gave her information, or whether she could reliably and accurately relate events.

Most importantly, the police had specific reasons to doubt the veracity of the tip about the Elm Street shooting by the time they stopped Montel: no physical evidence of gunfire had been found, no 911 calls or other reports about the supposed shooting had been made, and the officers' investigation had not uncovered any other evidence that the shooting had occurred. In fact, the investigation undermined the tip's reliability. Officer Kane testified at the suppression hearing that it was "typical" for neighborhood shootings to be reported to 911, and for evidence such as "ballistics damage or shell casings" to be found in the area, or reported gunshot wounds. He said their investigation of the Elm Street shooting had found no such evidence.

As noted, when police stop someone in reliance on a tip, "reasonable suspicion" that a crime has been or is about to be committed "requires that the tip be reliable in its assertion of illegality." *J.L.,* 529 U.S. at 272. The license plate number provided a solid means of identifying Montel, but it did not corroborate the tip's assertion that he had been involved in a shooting on Elm Street. The fact that the area of Franklin City where Montel's car was stopped is a high-crime area did not warrant the stop. *See State v. Washington* (Franklin Ct. App. 1988). A person's mere presence in a high-crime area known for drug activity does not, by itself, justify a stop.

Because the tip relating to the identification of the cars had a relatively low degree of reliability, more information was necessary to establish the requisite quantum of suspicion. The tip, standing alone, was insufficient to provide reasonable suspicion for the officers' stop of the Montel vehicle.

In the end, the police had little more reason to suspect Montel of specific criminal activity when they stopped him than they did before receiving the hearsay tip. They suspected him of being affiliated with a gang and knew of his recent arrest. And they knew that there had been gang violence in the neighborhood. But the government does not suggest that the police had information tying Montel personally to any of this violence. The only possible crime to which the police could tie Montel—the Elm Street shooting—was the one that appeared, in all likelihood, never to have occurred. The dis-

trict court correctly suppressed the evidence derived from the stop.

Affirmed.

State of Franklin v. McLain

State v. Grayson
Franklin Court of Appeal (2007)

PER CURIAM. We granted Ron Grayson, the defendant in this drug-possession case, leave to appeal from an order denying his motion to suppress evidence obtained by police in the course of an investigatory stop. The facts are undisputed. An anonymous caller reported to police that Grayson would be leaving an apartment building at a particular time in a particular vehicle with a broken right taillight. The caller also said that Grayson would be traveling to a particular motel and would be carrying cocaine in a briefcase.

Police proceeded to the apartment complex where they observed a vehicle matching the caller's description. They saw a man leave the apartment, carrying a backpack, and enter the vehicle and drive off. The officers followed the car as it took the most direct route to the motel reported by the caller. Police stopped the vehicle "just short" of the motel and, during a weapons search, discovered illegal drugs on the driver.

The law on the subject of the sufficiency of anonymous tips as supporting the "reasonable suspicion" necessary to make a valid investigative stop is well-known and need not be repeated here. *See State v. Montel* (Franklin Ct. App. 2003). The sole question here is whether the anonymous tip, as corroborated by independent police work, exhibited sufficient indicia of reliability to provide reasonable suspicion to make the stop. We consider it a close question. But we are satisfied that the stop was appropriate under the totality of the circumstances.

Although not every detail of the tipster's "story" was verified, the other information was sufficiently corroborated—in particular, the man left the apartment building described by the tipster, entered a vehicle matching the description provided by the tipster, and followed a route consistent with that predicted by the tipster. We believe these facts meet the "independent police corroboration" requirement and we therefore affirm the trial court's order.

Affirmed.

State v. Decker
Franklin Supreme Court (2005)

Defendant George Decker was charged with first-degree burglary and second-degree assault. He moved to dismiss the charges as multiplicitous, claiming that the latter charge is a lesser-included offense of the former. The court of appeal affirmed the district court's denial of Decker's motion to dismiss. We reverse.

The complaint charged that Decker entered a hotel room registered to his girlfriend, Mary Carls, through a locked door and without her permission. Once in the hotel room, Decker assaulted Carls. Hotel security caught Decker and detained him until he was arrested.

Where the same event or transaction gives rise to two statutory offenses, courts must determine if one constitutes a lesser-included offense of the other. This analysis begins with a comparison of the elements of both offenses, known as a "strict elements" test. If the elements of the "greater" crime necessarily include the elements of the "lesser" crime, then the latter offense is a lesser-included offense and prosecution of both crimes violates double jeopardy. *Blockburger v. United States*, 284 U.S. 299 (1932). This test is codified in Franklin Criminal Code § 5(2). A lesser-included offense is necessarily included within the greater offense if it is impossible to commit the greater offense without first having committed the lesser offense.

If, however, each of the offenses contains at least one element that the other does not, the test is not satisfied. *Id.* For example, in *State v. Jackson* (Fr. Ct. App. 1992), a crack cocaine pipe containing cocaine residue was found on the defendant. He was tried for possessing the cocaine inside the pipe in an amount less than five grams. He moved the court for a jury instruction on the lesser-included offense of possessing drug paraphernalia, rather than cocaine. The court denied the motion and the defendant was convicted for possessing cocaine. Affirming the district court's ruling, the court of appeal stated:

> Allied offenses of similar import are offenses the elements of which correspond to such a degree that the commission of one will result in the commission of the other. The elements of drug possession and possession of paraphernalia do not so correspond. One may be in possession of drugs, but not paraphernalia. One may possess paraphernalia without possessing drugs. The offenses are not therefore allied offenses of similar import because one offense may be committed without the other.

State of Franklin v. McLain

Here, our comparison begins with the elements of first-degree burglary, a violation of Franklin Criminal Code § 23. To extract the elements, we determine what the statute requires. Section 23 specifies that a burglary is committed when "a defendant knowingly enters an occupied structure with the intent to remain therein unlawfully with the intent to commit a crime of violence . . . including assault and causes serious bodily injury to that person." Thus we can define the elements in this case as the defendant (1) knowingly, (2) entered and remained unlawfully, (3) in a building or occupied structure, (4) with intent to cause bodily injury, and (5) causing serious bodily injury to that
person.

The elements of second-degree assault, a violation of Franklin Criminal Code § 12, are that the defendant (1) with intent to cause bodily injury to another person, (2) caused serious bodily injury to that person.

Therefore, under § 23, the elements of burglary include the elements of assault. Thus, assault is a lesser-included offense of first-degree burglary. *See State v. Astor* (Fr. Ct. App. 1996) (to satisfy first-degree burglary, "the State must prove each and every element of the offense of assault and the fact-finder must determine . . . an assault was committed during the burglary"; if so, the same assault cannot constitute a separate offense). Although the elements of first-degree burglary include, in almost identical form, the elements of assault, Franklin case law does not require a strict textual comparison such that only where *all* the elements of the compared offenses coincide *exactly* will one offense be deemed a lesser-included offense of the greater. Instead, if, in comparing the elements of the offenses in the abstract, the offenses are so similar that the commission of one offense will necessarily result in commission of the other, then the offenses are multiplicitous.

Because the elements of first-degree burglary necessarily include the elements of assault, assault is a lesser-included offense of first-degree burglary. We therefore conclude that it was error to deny the motion to dismiss.

Reversed.

POINT SHEET

State of Franklin v. McLain
DRAFTERS' POINT SHEET

In this performance item, applicants' firm represents Brian McLain, who has been charged with violating various sections of the Franklin Criminal Code dealing with methamphetamine, a controlled substance. The charges are based on evidence seized from McLain after police, acting on an anonymous tip, stopped him for investigatory purposes. The tip was called in to the Franklin "CrimeStoppers Hotline" stating that a man had been seen at a convenience store purchasing items which, although innocent in themselves, are known ingredients of methamphetamine production, and leaving the scene in a red Jeep Cherokee. A Franklin police officer, responding to the tip, spotted McLain, who generally matched the personal description given by the tipster, and who was driving a red Jeep Cherokee in a relatively high-crime area. After brief questioning, McLain gave consent for the officer to search his car. The officer found the goods described in the tip, together with a small plastic bag containing what appeared to be a marijuana cigarette. McLain was arrested and booked, at which time police discovered $320 in cash in McLain's wallet. McLain then directed the police to a "meth lab" where they found chemicals and equipment that had been used to manufacture methamphetamine as well as 18 grams of the drug.

McLain was charged with three felony counts: possession of methamphetamine with intent to distribute, possession of equipment with intent to manufacture methamphetamine, and manufacture of methamphetamine—all in violation of the Franklin Criminal Code. He has moved to suppress all evidence seized by police on the ground that the officer lacked reasonable suspicion to stop him on the evening in question. He has also moved to dismiss the charge of possession of equipment with intent to manufacture methamphetamine on the ground that it is a lesser-included offense of manufacture of methamphetamine. Applicants' task is to draft the arguments in support of both motions.

The File consists of a memorandum from the supervising attorney describing the assignment (the task memo), the criminal complaint, the motion to suppress evidence and to dismiss Count Two, the transcript of the call to the Franklin CrimeStoppers Hotline, and portions of the transcript of the evidentiary hearing. The Library contains the relevant Franklin statutes and three cases—two relating to anonymous tips and investigatory stops, and one dealing with lesser-included offenses.

The following discussion covers all the points the drafters intended to raise in the problem. Applicants need not cover them all to receive passing or even excellent grades. Grading is left entirely to the discretion of the user jurisdictions.

I.   Format and Overview

The task memo directs applicants not to prepare a separate statement of facts; however, applicants are expected to draft a detailed analysis in which they incorporate the relevant facts and address the applicable legal authorities. Applicants' work product should be written in persuasive "argument" form, pointing out (a) the legal standards governing the issues and (b) why, based on the relevant facts of record, those standards are or are not met in this case.

As stated in the task memo, applicants have two motions to discuss: a motion to suppress evidence on the ground that there was not reasonable suspicion for the officer to stop McLain and a motion to dismiss one of the three counts on multiplicity grounds.

II.   Discussion

A. The Motion to Suppress

Applicants are asked to draft the argument portion of the brief in support of McLain's motion to suppress all evidence resulting from the stop. The legal standards applicable to investigatory stops by police (often called "*Terry* stops" after the leading case, *Terry v. Ohio*, 392 U.S. 1 (1968)) are described in *State v. Montel* (Franklin Ct. App. 2003). The Fourth Amendment protects individuals from unreasonable searches, but, under *Terry*, police officers have the right to stop and interrogate persons "reasonably suspected of criminal conduct"; the basic test is whether the officers have "a reasonable suspicion, grounded in specific and articulable facts, that the person [is] involved in criminal activity" at the time. To make that determination, courts will consider the totality of the circumstances of each case.

- Similar to the facts in *Montel*, the officer stopped McLain after an anonymous tip was called in to the Franklin CrimeStoppers Hotline. While a tip from a recognized (and familiar) police informant may be sufficient, in and of itself, to justify a *Terry* stop, where the tipster is anonymous, or unknown to the officers, there must be corroboration—usually by investigation or independent police observation of unusually suspicious conduct.

- Other important considerations in evaluating an anonymous tip are (a) whether the tipster's information is based on his or her personal observation or "firsthand account" of a crime (or, for example, whether it is hearsay); (b) the strength and reliability of the tip with respect to its assertion of illegal activity, not just its tendency to identify a determinate person; and (c) the time that has elapsed between the reported crime and the stop.

- Here, the relevant facts are as follows:
  - The officer had information that an anonymous person had telephoned a report that a "scuzzy looking" white male, "maybe mid-20s," with dark hair and a goatee, wearing jeans and a dark hooded sweatshirt, was seen purchasing two packages of Sudafed cold medicine and some coffee filters at Shop-Mart, a convenience store, and asking the cashier whether the store had stopped selling automobile engine-starter fluid.
  - The tipster asserted that the man was "clearly up to something," and he told the hotline that the man was leaving the store and heading toward a red Jeep Cherokee in the parking lot.
  - Officer Simon, who took the report from the dispatcher, was aware, as a trained and experienced police officer, that cold medicine such as Sudafed can be processed to produce a key element of methamphetamine, and that coffee filters and engine-starter fluid are also used in the process.
  - Simon responded promptly to Shop-Mart and saw a man (McLain) matching the tipster's description come out of a grocery store across the street from the convenience store carrying a small paper bag.
  - McLain got into a red Jeep Cherokee parked in front of the store and drove off, with Simon following in his squad car. Simon saw McLain stop in front of an apartment building, talk briefly with a man there, and pull the Jeep into an adjoining alley, where Simon initiated the *Terry* stop.

After recognizing the general principles applicable to investigatory (*Terry*) stops, the argument should make the following points:
- There was no reason—other than the brief anonymous telephone call to the hotline—to suspect McLain of any criminal activity whatsoever.

- While information provided to police from known informants may be considered sufficiently reliable to justify a *Terry* stop, an anonymous tip must be corroborated by independent observation or investigation before police may reasonably execute an investigatory stop.

- Here, neither Simon nor any other officer undertook any independent investigation. Simon made no independent observations, other than to note, while following McLain's car, that (a) he matched the tipster's description, (b) he was driving in an area Simon knew had been the subject of some unknown number of criminal activity reports in the past year (Simon himself had made a marijuana arrest there), and (c) McLain had had a brief conversation with a man in front of a building. These facts do not constitute sufficient corroboration.

  - In support of their arguments, applicants should cite *State v. Washington* (quoted in *State v. Montel)*, which held that even where the officers knew that the neighborhood in which they encountered the defendant was a high-crime area known for drug activity, that fact alone did not provide police with reasonable suspicion to make an investigatory stop.

  - Indeed, here, while there had been reports of criminal activity in the area, none of them related to large-scale drug operations.

    - And the only other "evidence" Simon had was the anonymous report that McLain had, perfectly legally, purchased two packages of cold medicine and some coffee filters, and had asked the store clerk about engine-starter fluid.

Further, applicants should recognize that an anonymous tip must be "reliable in its assertion of illegality, not just in its tendency to identify a determinate person." *Florida v. J.L.* (cited in *State v. Montel*).

- The argument can be made that identifying McLain is really all the tip did in this case, because the only other information was that he had made a few purchases of concededly legal items at Shop-Mart.

- Other applicants may emphasize that the tip here was of such a "low degree of reliability" that "more information was necessary to establish the requisite quantum of suspicion" and that there is no such evidence or information in the record. *See Montel*.

- Applicants might note that in contrast to the defendant in *Montel*, whom the arresting officer knew to be a gang member charged with a weapons offense, McLain was unknown to Officer Simon, who had no reason to suspect that he was involved in dealing methamphetamine or any other illegal activity.

- However, astute applicants should anticipate that the prosecution will likely argue that Officer Simon's training and experience may well constitute the type of "independent observation" that can provide the corroboration necessary to legitimize the stop. Applicants should argue that the cases make no mention of training and experience as a substitute for actual, situation-specific independent investigation and observation.

- In addition, it can be argued that there is scant evidence that the 8th Street area, where McLain was stopped, has a reputation for drug activity. In *State v. Sneed* (cited in *Montel*) the court, in granting the motion to suppress, emphasized that a tip about drug activity at a particular house in a particular neighborhood did not provide reasonable suspicion where there was no evidence at the hearing that the area "was known for drug trafficking." Again, applicants should point out that all the officer in this case knew was that there had been several reports of criminal activity in the area—one involving cultivation of marijuana—but nothing to indicate the production of methamphetamine as suggested by the tip in this case.

- Further, Officer Simon testified that the only arrests made at the Shop-Mart have been for vandalism and shoplifting. There is no evidence of suspicious meth-related activity or purchases.

- Applicants are instructed to anticipate the State's principal arguments and briefly challenge them. In particular, they should anticipate the State's likely reliance on the *per curiam* opinion in *State v. Grayson* (Franklin Ct. App. 2007). In *Grayson*, the court held that the tip was adequately corroborated by "independent police work" where the officers observed a man meeting the tipster's description driving a car that met the tipster's description to a destination predicted in the tip. This ties in with a likely argument by the State that the tip's accuracy is enhanced because it was the result of the tipster's "personal observation"—which the *Montel* court recognizes as sometimes being a significant factor in determining the reliability of an anonymous tip.

- There is, however, a difference in the nature of the tips in *Grayson* and in the instant case. In *Grayson*, the tipster alleged knowledge of actual criminal activity—that the defendant was in possession of an illegal drug, which he was transporting to a specific address; and the police officers' observations corroborated most aspects of the tip. Here, the tip alleged only conduct that was perfectly legal—buying medicine, coffee filters, etc.—and better applicants should at least attempt to distinguish *Grayson* on that basis.

B.   The Motion to Dismiss Count Two of the Complaint

The charges in counts one, two, and three of the complaint arise from the chemicals, drug-manufacturing apparatus, and 18 grams of methamphetamine found in McLain's "meth lab" after his arrest. The task memo instructs applicants to draft the argument in support of defendant's motion to dismiss the "manufacturing equipment" count (Count Two) on the ground that it is a lesser-included offense of manufacture of methamphetamine (Count Three), and that therefore the complaint contains multiplicitous counts. A multiplicitous complaint raises double jeopardy concerns due to the possibility that the defendant will receive more than one sentence for a single offense.

- *State v. Decker* (Franklin Sup. Ct. 2005) provides the legal framework for analyzing whether one charge is a lesser-included offense of another. *Decker* follows the "strict elements" test established by the leading case, *Blockburger v. United States*, 284 U.S. 299 (1932). Under the strict elements test, where two or more offenses arise from the same act or transaction and the elements of the "greater" crime necessarily include the elements of the "lesser" crime, the latter offense is a lesser-included offense. Under *Blockburger*, which is codified in Fr. Crim. Code § 5(2), the court compares the elements of both offenses. If the comparison establishes that the elements of one offense are subsumed within those of the other, the former is a lesser-included offense, and a prosecution for both offenses places the defendant in double jeopardy. As an introductory matter, applicants should argue that both counts arise from the same course of conduct: McLain's alleged operation of a meth lab. Following the court's approach in *Decker*, applicants should examine the criminal complaint against McLain and the relevant sections of the Franklin Criminal Code and then identify the distinct elements of each charged offense.

- Count Two charges McLain with possession of equipment with the intent to manufacture methamphetamine, a violation of Fr. Crim. Code § 43. The elements of that offense are that the defendant

    (a) knowingly

    (b) possessed equipment or chemicals, or both,

    (c) for the purpose of manufacturing a controlled substance, to wit, methamphetamine.

- Count Three charges a violation of § 51, manufacture of methamphetamine. The elements of that offense are that the defendant

    (a) knowingly

    (b) engaged in the manufacture of methamphetamine.

- The intent element is identical for both offenses. A textual comparison of the elements demonstrates that the lesser offense contains the same intent element as the greater offense. Both offenses require that the person who commits either crime do so "knowingly."

- Astute applicants will recognize that the elements of possession of equipment do not fall as neatly into the elements of the greater offense, manufacture of methamphetamine, as do the elements of the burglary and assault charges at issue in *Decker*.

- At first glance, it is the lesser offense, possession of equipment with the intent to manufacture methamphetamine, which requires an element not present in the greater offense—the possession of equipment and supplies; section 51 provides simply that "[i]t is unlawful for any person to knowingly manufacture methamphetamine."

- The question then becomes whether, under the statutes, a person is able to manufacture methamphetamine without possessing the laboratory equipment and supplies used to make it, and the answer is "no." Or, as stated in *Decker*, "it is impossible to commit the greater offense without first having committed the lesser offense."

- Applicants should take care to distinguish *State v. Jackson* (Fr. Ct. App. 1992), cited in *Decker*. In *Jackson*, the defendant was charged with possessing cocaine in the form of residue found inside a crack cocaine pipe. He appealed the trial court's denial of his motion for a jury instruction on the offense of possession of drug paraphernalia, arguing that it was a lesser-included offense of cocaine possession. In rejecting this argument, the court of appeal explained, "One may be in possession of drugs, but not paraphernalia. One may possess paraphernalia without possessing drugs." In short, one offense could be committed without also committing the other offense.

- By contrast, in McLain's case, the lesser offense is composed of some, but not all, of the elements of the greater offense, so that it is impossible to commit the greater offense, the manufacture of methamphetamine, without also first committing the lesser, possession of equipment and supplies with the intent to manufacture methamphetamine.

Accordingly, there is a reasonable argument to be made that under the *Blockburger* test, the court should dismiss Count Two as multiplicitous.

Logan v. Rios

Logan v. Rios

FILE

LIBRARY

POINT SHEET

Instructions

The back cover of each test form contains the following instructions:

You will have 90 minutes to complete this session of the examination. This performance test is designed to evaluate your ability to handle a select number of legal authorities in the context of a factual problem involving a client.

The problem is set in the fictitious state of Franklin, in the fictitious Fifteenth Circuit of the United States. Columbia and Olympia are also fictitious states in the Fifteenth Circuit. In Franklin, the trial court of general jurisdiction is the District Court, the intermediate appellate court is the Court of Appeal, and the highest court is the Supreme Court.

You will have two kinds of materials with which to work: a File and a Library. The first document in the File is a memorandum containing the instructions for the task you are to complete. The other documents in the File contain factual information about your case and may include some facts that are not relevant.

The Library contains the legal authorities needed to complete the task and may also include some authorities that are not relevant. Any cases may be real, modified, or written solely for the purpose of this examination. If the cases appear familiar to you, do not assume that they are precisely the same as you have read before. Read them thoroughly, as if they all were new to you. You should assume that the cases were decided in the jurisdictions and on the dates shown. In citing cases from the Library, you may use abbreviations and omit page references.

Your response must be written in the answer book provided. If you are taking the examination on a laptop computer, your jurisdiction will provide you with specific instructions. In answering this performance test, you should concentrate on the materials in the File and Library. What you have learned in law school and elsewhere provides the general background for analyzing the problem; the File and Library provide the specific materials with which you must work.

Although there are no restrictions on how you apportion your time, you should be sure to allocate ample time (about 45 minutes) to reading and digesting the materials and to organizing your answer before you begin writing it. You may make notes anywhere in the test materials; blank pages are provided at the end of the booklet. You may not tear pages from the question booklet.

This performance test will be graded on your responsiveness to the instructions regarding the task you are to complete, which are given to you in the first memorandum in the File, and on the content, thoroughness, and organization of your response.

FILE

Dowell, Brown & Pope
Attorneys at Law
944 Metro Square Plaza
Bedford, Franklin 38701

MEMORANDUM

To: Applicant
From: Norman Brown, Supervising Attorney
Re: Logan v. Rios
Date: February 23, 2010

We represent Trina Rios, owner of Trina's Toys, a business in Bedford, Franklin. She has been sued by Karen Logan. Logan claims to have been injured when she slipped and fell while shopping at Trina's Toys. I've attached the complaint. We answered the complaint, denied the key allegations, and raised the affirmative defense of contributory negligence. We have conducted some discovery and investigation.

Under the local rules, we must attend an early dispute resolution (EDR) conference, conducted by an EDR judge. Although we have not completed our discovery, these settlement conferences are conducted early. Local Rule 12 describes the purpose of this conference.

In preparation for the EDR conference, please draft Item 6 of the EDR statement. I will use your draft to prepare the final submission. Item 6 of the EDR statement requires us to candidly "discuss . . . the strengths and weaknesses of" our case in the statement. As directed in Item 6, use the jury instructions to organize your discussion of the claim and affirmative defense. You will need to carefully review the evidence gathered to date and identify and evaluate the proof available for each legal element of the claim and the affirmative defense. Where relevant, provide citations to case law that supports your analysis; you need not provide citations to the factual record.

Do not address the other items required by the statement and do not address Logan's damages; I will prepare the portion of the statement concerning her medical condition, including her pain and suffering and medical costs.

Green County Local Rule 12. Early Dispute Resolution

Before trial, the parties shall participate in Early Dispute Resolution (EDR). EDR promotes direct communication between parties about possible claims, defenses, and supporting evidence, under the supervision of the EDR judge, a neutral evaluator. The EDR conference gives the parties an opportunity to narrow the issues and possibly settle the case with the assistance of the EDR judge. During the conference, the EDR judge may require the parties to assess all claims and defenses with the aim of settling the case. The EDR judge may meet with the parties separately or together. The conference discussion is confidential and will not be admissible at trial.

Five days prior to the EDR conference, each party must submit an EDR statement using Form 12. The EDR statement assists the EDR judge in evaluating each party's case. It may be used solely by the EDR judge, and is confidential, and may not be used at trial or shared with the other party or parties.

Form 12: Early Dispute Resolution Statement

Each party must provide the following information concerning the case:

1.   Name of party and trial counsel.

2.   Short description of the case.

3.   Legal theories presented by the case.

4.   Evidentiary issues likely to be raised at trial.

5.   Damages sought.

6.   A candid discussion of the strengths and weaknesses of the party's claims, counterclaims, and/or defenses and affirmative defenses. Parties are advised to use the jury instructions to identify each element of the claims, counterclaims, and/or defenses and affirmative defenses stated. For each element that must be proven, parties should discuss the specific strengths and weaknesses of the evidence gathered to date relating to that element in light of the jury instructions and any commentary thereto.

7.   The approximate number of witnesses to be called and the length of time that the party estimates will be needed for the trial.

STATE OF FRANKLIN

IN THE CIRCUIT COURT OF GREEN COUNTY

Karen Logan,)
           Plaintiff,)
v.)
)   2009-CV-3420
Trina Rios,)
doing business as Trina's Toys,)   COMPLAINT
           Defendant)

1. Plaintiff Karen Logan, a resident of Green County, Franklin, on January 27, 2009, entered the defendant's premises, Trina's Toys, located at 727 Mill Street, City of Bedford, County of Green, Franklin, during business hours, for the purposes of shopping in the store.

2. Defendant Trina Rios, a resident of Green County, Franklin, owns the building at 727 Mill Street, Bedford, Franklin, and conducts a business there under the name Trina's Toys.

3. On the date mentioned, the defendant had a duty to exercise ordinary care to see that her premises were reasonably safe for persons lawfully on the premises, including the plaintiff.

4. In violation of this duty, the defendant negligently permitted and maintained on the business premises the following unsafe conditions, creating an unreasonable risk of injury to persons lawfully on the premises, including the plaintiff: water accumulating on the floor where customers shopped and failure to warn that water had accumulated on the floor.

5. On January 27, 2009, the plaintiff was injured when she slipped and fell, owing to the unsafe conditions alleged in Paragraph 4.

6. As a proximate result of the negligence of the defendant, the plaintiff suffered an injury to her ankle, which has caused her great pain and suffering, lost wages, and a lost scholarship. The plaintiff has also incurred medical, hospital, and related expenses.

Wherefore the plaintiff requests judgment against the defendant in the sum of $30,000 or more, including costs of suit and such other and further relief as this court deems just and proper.

Dated: July 15, 2009

Barbara Santos

Barbara Santos, attorney for Karen Logan, Plaintiff

LING'S INVESTIGATIVE SERVICES
Suite 330
1800 Jenson Avenue
Bedford, Franklin 38701

I was asked to investigate certain aspects of an incident that occurred at Trina's Toys on January 27, 2009, on which date Karen Logan alleges she fell. Logan claims she hurt her ankle when she slipped and fell in a puddle of water in the store. Logan filed suit against Trina Rios on July 15, 2009. She claims the ankle injury caused her to lose her part-time job at Fresh Grocers and to lose her basketball scholarship at Franklin State University.

I contacted Joe Nguyen, who was Logan's supervisor at Fresh Grocers. Nguyen confirmed that Logan had worked part-time at the office of Fresh Grocers for the six months prior to her alleged fall, working about 15–20 hours a week, and earning $9/hour entering data into a computer. He confirmed that her employment was terminated February 2, 2009, after she failed to report to work for three days and failed to call in. Nguyen said he knew nothing about her falling or having hurt her ankle.

I tried to contact the women's basketball coach at Franklin State University (FSU), but he would not talk to me without a subpoena. However, I read back issues of the FSU student newspaper online. For the 2008–09 academic year, Logan was a second-year basketball player for FSU on scholarship. According to the articles I read, she did not get much playing time. I also found an article that reported that she was dropped from the team a couple of weeks before her visit to Trina's Toys due to "academic difficulties." I did confirm that Logan is currently enrolled at FSU.

Rios's employees Nick Patel and Naomi Feldman confirm that, on the date of the incident, Feldman called Green County Emergency Services and paramedics responded and took Logan to the emergency room. I cannot learn anything more about her medical condition without a medical release signed by Logan.

Patrick Ling

Patrick Ling

December 11, 2009

Excerpts from 1/14/10 Deposition of Karen Logan

EXAMINATION BY NORMAN BROWN, COUNSEL FOR TRINA'S TOYS

Attorney:	Please state your name, address, occupation, and age.
Logan:	Karen Logan, 2044 North Fifth Street, Apt. 23, Bedford, Franklin, student at Franklin State University. I am 20 years old.
Attorney:	Were you at Trina's Toys on January 27, 2009?
Logan:	Yes, my little sister had a birthday coming up and I wanted to get her a gift.
Attorney:	Were there other customers there at the time?
Logan:	A mom and her little boy, a toddler, who kept getting in and out of his stroller, and some other people.
Attorney:	What time did you arrive at the store that day?
Logan:	Around 11:30 in the morning. I was just looking around, walking up and down some aisles, and then I fell.
Attorney:	Where were you when you fell?
Logan:	I had just turned into the games and puzzles aisle and down I went.
Attorney:	As you turned into the aisle, what were you doing?
Logan:	Well, I had just been playing Wii bowling at a Wii display at the end of the aisle.
Attorney:	Tell me more about that. What is a "Wii"?
Logan:	A Wii is a video gaming system. You hold a controller and move as if you were really bowling; the action shows up on the video screen. There was a sign inviting people to "test your Wii bowling skills." So I did. When I finished, I started walking down the aisle where the games were so that I could check them out.
Attorney:	Did you look at the floor as you proceeded down the aisle?
Logan:	No, I was looking at the games on the shelves.
Attorney:	Was there anything blocking your view of the floor?
Logan:	No, but why would I look at the floor? I was looking at the games.
Attorney:	Was there any problem with the lighting in the aisle where you fell?
Logan:	I don't think so. The whole store was brightly lit.
Attorney:	Had you been in this aisle prior to falling?
Logan:	No, I was at the end of the aisle Wii bowling. I then walked down the game aisle, took a few steps, and fell.
Attorney:	Tell me how you fell.

Logan: I took a few steps into the aisle, saw the games ahead, started toward them, and then I felt my right foot sort of slide, and then twist around, and then it just slipped out from under me, and that's when I landed in the puddle.

Attorney: Do you know what caused you to fall?

Logan: Yeah, there was water on the floor.

Attorney: How much water was there?

Logan: I fell into a puddle of water, a couple of feet long, just a trail of water.

Attorney: How wide was the trail of water?

Logan: Several inches, maybe a foot.

Attorney: How deep was the water?

Logan: Oh, pretty thin. The floor there was level. There was just a thin puddle of water.

Attorney: What happened after you fell?

Logan: I took a minute to catch my breath. I felt sort of jolted. Then my right ankle began to hurt, really badly. I had been sitting there for a minute or so, when a customer asked if I was okay. I said, "No, I fell and I'm hurt." I started to get up, but she said I should wait and she would get help. I took off my shoes while I sat there.

Attorney: Did she get help?

Logan: A store employee came up and asked if I was okay. I said, "No, I fell and I'm hurt." He helped me get up and get to a chair near the front of the store. He brought my shoes and backpack to me—I had taken off my pack after I fell.

Attorney: Describe the shoes you were wearing. Were they high heels?

Logan: They were backless sandals with heels not more than three inches high. I had just gotten them the week before the accident.

Attorney: What kind of sole and heel were on the sandals—leather, rubber, what?

Logan: Leather, I'm pretty sure.

Attorney: What do you mean by backless?

Logan: You just slide your feet into the sandals; there is no strap around the heel.

Attorney: Had you ever worn the shoes before?

Logan: Yes, at least three times. They're very comfortable. Everyone wears them.

Attorney: Had it been raining or snowing that day?

Logan: No. I remember it was mild. And it was sunny.

Attorney: Do you know how the water got on the floor?

Logan v. Rios

Logan:	No.
Attorney:	Were you carrying a water bottle on the date you fell?
Logan:	Yeah, I always carry one. I had it in the mesh pocket of my backpack.
Attorney:	How much water did the bottle contain?
Logan:	It was the size I usually buy at the grocery store, a 16-ounce bottle.
Attorney:	When you left your apartment, was the water bottle full?
Logan:	Yes. I just grabbed an unopened bottle as I left my apartment.
Attorney:	Did you drink any water from the bottle before you arrived at Trina's Toys?
Logan:	Maybe. I don't remember.
Attorney:	Did you spill water on the floor in the aisle where you fell?
Logan:	Of course not. The bottle was in a pocket in my backpack. I told you that.
Attorney:	Do you know how the water got on the floor in the aisle where you fell?
Logan:	Someone spilled something, but I don't really know. I know that the little boy who was in and out of the stroller had a sippy cup with him.
Attorney:	A sippy cup?
Logan:	You know, a cup with a lid for toddlers. It has a slot in the lid so the toddler can drink but won't spill all over. It's a step between a baby bottle and a regular cup.
Attorney:	But you didn't see the little boy spill or drop the sippy cup?
Logan:	I wasn't paying too much attention to him.
Attorney:	Regarding your water bottle, was it still in your backpack after you fell?
Logan:	Absolutely.
Attorney:	Did you see anyone—including the little boy—spill where you fell?
Logan:	Not that I saw, but I wasn't watching people to make sure they didn't spill.
Attorney:	By the way, did you use your cell phone while in the store?
Logan:	I called a friend right after I bowled on the Wii to tell him what my score was.
Attorney:	Were you talking on the phone when you fell?
Logan:	No; I hung up just as I started down the aisle.

*   *   *   *

Attorney:	You said you lost wages as a result of your ankle injury?
Logan:	Yes, I had been working 20 hours a week at Fresh Grocers, entering data on the computer. I had been there for six months at the time of the accident.
Attorney:	Do you still work there?

31

Logan: No, they told me I could not work anymore because I fell and was hurt.

Attorney: How did the fall affect your being able to work there?

Logan: I don't know. I missed a couple days of work and then I came with my ankle all wrapped up and I was on crutches. They said I could not work there anymore.

Attorney: Did your work at Fresh Grocers require you to stand?

Logan: No, I sat at a computer.

Attorney: You said you missed a couple days of work. Did you contact your supervisor at Fresh Grocers to let him know that you would be absent?

Logan: No, I was in pain and was overwhelmed by school and getting used to crutches.

* * * *

Attorney: Is it your claim that you lost your basketball scholarship because of this injury?

Logan: Yes, it is. The coach said I wasn't contributing to the team anymore. The season was well under way and I couldn't practice due to the injury, and that obviously affected my playing. So this fall and the injury made me lose my scholarship.

Attorney: When did you learn that you lost the scholarship?

Logan: I don't remember the exact day.

Attorney: Did the coach give any reason for your losing the scholarship other than that you weren't contributing to the team anymore?

Logan: Not that I recall. I was really upset.

Attorney: Didn't the coach tell you your grades were the reason you lost the scholarship?

Logan: I don't remember him saying anything about my grades.

Attorney: Well, how were your grades last year?

Logan: They were good until this injury caused me to miss a lot of my classes.

32

Excerpts from 1/15/10 Deposition of Nick Patel

EXAMINATION BY BARBARA SANTOS, COUNSEL FOR KAREN LOGAN

Attorney: Please tell me your name, address, and occupation.

Patel: Nicholas Patel, but I go by Nick. I live in Bedford, 835 Jefferson Street. I work part-time at Trina's Toys and I go to school at Franklin State University.

Attorney: Were you working at Trina's Toys on January 27, 2009, the day Ms. Logan fell?

Patel: Yes; I clean up, stock shelves, and wait on customers.

Attorney: What were your duties regarding cleaning the store at the time Ms. Logan fell?

Patel: Every evening after we close, I sweep and mop the entire floor. In the morning, before we open, I dust and wipe down the counter area. Then I clean anything else my boss tells me to. So, on the night of January 26, 2009, the night before Ms. Logan fell, I swept and mopped the floor.

Attorney: Did you see Ms. Logan fall?

Patel: No, I heard a customer say that someone had fallen and needed help, so I went to see what had happened.

Attorney: What did you see?

Patel: I saw a girl, about my age, sitting on the floor in aisle 3, with her shoes off, rubbing her right foot and saying she was hurt. I later found out she was Karen Logan. There was a water bottle next to her on the floor. Also, I saw her cell phone and her shoes on the floor right next to her.

Attorney: Did you see any water?

Patel: Yes, she was sitting in a puddle of water.

Attorney: Describe the water.

Patel: It was a thin puddle, about a couple feet long.

Attorney: Are you sure it was water?

Patel: Well, it certainly looked like it. I cleaned it up later, and it cleaned up just like water—no color or odor.

Attorney: When was the last time you were in aisle 3 before you saw Ms. Logan?

Patel: I was in aisle 3 a couple of times that morning, restocking games. She fell around noon; I guess I had been there just before we opened at 10 a.m. I don't remember being in aisle 3 after we opened. I mainly stayed at the counter. We had a steady stream of customers in and out of the store.

33

Attorney:	How often are you supposed to patrol all the aisles?
Patel:	Once every hour.
Attorney:	Did you do so at 11 a.m.?
Patel:	No.
Attorney:	Why not?
Patel:	My girlfriend called me and I guess I just forgot. And we were busy.
Attorney:	Did you see any water on the floor when you were in aisle 3 around 10 a.m.?
Patel:	No.
Attorney:	Are there any sources of water in the store? Any squirt guns or water-related games?
Patel:	No, not in the main part of the store where customers are. There's a bathroom in the back. And the squirt guns are not filled with water. Besides, we only sell them in summer.
Attorney:	Any water leaks in the store's ceiling?
Patel:	No.
Attorney:	Do you know how the water got on the floor?
Patel:	I think Ms. Logan spilled it. I saw a water bottle next to her on the floor. It was empty. I put it in her backpack when I helped her up—I could tell the bottle was empty.
Attorney:	Did you or anyone else see her spill water?
Patel:	I didn't see her spill, and I don't know of anyone else who saw her spill, either.
Attorney:	So you have no reason to conclude that she spilled her water other than that you saw the water bottle?
Patel:	No, I guess not.
Attorney:	How many other customers were there in the store between 10 a.m. and noon?
Patel:	I don't know; a handful. Only one, two or three at a time, but there was a constant flow of customers. One would leave and another come in. I stayed busy at the counter. Maybe 10 or 12 customers altogether.
Attorney:	It's a toy store, so is it fair to say there were children in the store during that time?
Patel:	Yes, there are always kids in the store.
Attorney:	So it is possible that a child spilled something in the store?
Patel:	I suppose so, but I doubt it.

Logan v. Rios

Attorney:	Was there any warning sign in aisle 3, indicating that there was water on the floor?
Patel:	No. We didn't know there was any water there, so how could we put out a sign?
Attorney:	Does the store have any warning cones or signs to put out?
Patel:	No. We don't have spills like that.
Attorney:	Had anyone told you or any employee that there was water on the floor?
Patel:	No. If they had, I would have checked it out and cleaned it up.
Attorney:	Are you aware of anyone else having fallen in the store?
Patel:	No.
Attorney:	Do you have any other knowledge of what might have caused Ms. Logan to fall other than the water on the floor?
Patel:	Well, she had been wearing these shoes—sandals, sort of, with high heels—that looked pretty hard to walk on—not too steady. And she had a backpack and it weighed a ton—I had to pick it up and take it to her. So maybe she lost her balance because of the sandals and the backpack and then fell. Or maybe she just twisted her ankle on those sandals and then she spilled some water so we would think she fell on the water. Or maybe she spilled some water and fell on it.
Attorney:	Did you see Ms. Logan fall?
Patel:	No, I just saw her after she fell.
Attorney:	Do you know if anyone saw her fall?
Patel:	Not that I'm aware of.
Attorney:	Did she tell you why she fell?
Patel:	She said she slipped on the water and then she pointed to the water.
Attorney:	Do you have any reason to believe she was lying?
Patel:	No. I just don't know where the water came from.
Attorney:	What products are displayed in aisle 3?
Patel:	That's the aisle with puzzles, games, and video games.
Attorney:	Are there any overhead displays?
Patel:	No, but we try to display the puzzles and games so that they are attractive to customers. We had a computer-animated display of games right in the middle of the aisle near where I found Ms. Logan. At the head of the games aisle we had a Wii on display for customers to play some of the Wii sports video games.
Attorney:	Were there any displays sticking out from the shelves?

Patel:	No. Not that I remember—not in that aisle.
Attorney:	What is the composition of the floor in aisle 3—carpet, tile, what?
Patel:	It is tile. It is easy to clean up. I mop it up every evening and so I know it is real level there. We even make sure we use a cleaner that does not make the floor slippery. The boss, Trina, wants to be sure kids don't slip and fall.
Attorney:	Is it fair to say that if wet, the tile floor would be slippery?
Patel:	I suppose so.
Attorney:	Describe the lighting in aisle 3.
Patel:	Overhead lights. We want the customers to be able to see the toys without any trouble, so it is pretty bright.
Attorney:	Were there any other employees on duty that day?
Patel:	Yes, the boss, Trina, was in the back storeroom all morning checking inventory. Naomi Feldman and I were at the counter.

*   *   *   *

LIBRARY

FRANKLIN SUPREME COURT APPROVED JURY INSTRUCTIONS

Excerpts from Jury Instruction 35: Premises Liability with Contributory Negligence Claimed

The plaintiff seeks to recover damages for an injury that occurred while on the defendant's premises. In order to recover damages, the plaintiff has the burden of proving by a preponderance of the credible evidence that

1.   There was a condition on the defendant's property which presented an unreasonable risk of harm to people on the property.

2.   The defendant knew or in the exercise of ordinary care should have known of both the condition and the risk.

3.   The defendant could reasonably expect that people on the property would not discover such danger and the defendant failed to warn of the unreasonable risk of harm to people on the property.

If you find that the defendant had or should have had notice of a condition that presented an unreasonable risk of harm and failed to use ordinary care to prevent harm under the circumstances, then the defendant was negligent.

*   *   *   *

If you find that the plaintiff has proved that the defendant was negligent, then you should consider the defendant's affirmative defense of contributory negligence. In order to defeat the plaintiff's claim, the defendant must prove by a preponderance of the credible evidence that

The plaintiff was guilty of negligence that was a direct and proximate cause of the occurrence and the resulting injuries and damages, if any, sustained by him or her, in that the plaintiff [*insert the ways in which the plaintiff was negligent here*].

If the defendant proves all of these items by a preponderance of the credible evidence, your verdict should be for the defendant.

*   *   *   *

Logan v. Rios

Commentary (Duty of Owner of Land): The Franklin Supreme Court has eliminated the distinction between licensees and invitees.

The Court has ruled that the owner of a premises, though not an insurer of his customers' safety, owes his customers the duty to exercise reasonable care to maintain his premises in a reasonably safe condition for use by his customers. In determining what constitutes reasonable care, one issue is the length of time an unsafe condition has existed. In *Owens v. Coffee Corner* (Fr. Ct. App. 2007), the premises owner was liable for coffee that had "just spilled" because it was reasonably foreseeable that coffee-shop customers would spill coffee. On the other hand, the owner of a camera shop was not liable for soda that had "just spilled," because it was not reasonably foreseeable that soda spills would occur in a camera shop, where no refreshments were available. *Chad v. Bill's Camera Shop* (Fr. Ct. App. 2006). In *Rollins v. Maryville Mini-Golf Park* (Fr. Ct. App. 2002), the owner of a mini golf and recreation park was liable when a ketchup spill went unnoticed for an hour because the park had a snack bar, the owner knew that children frequently spilled food items, and the owner had an hour to discover and remove the spill that created the unreasonable risk.

A business owner is not liable for harm caused by a condition on his premises that is open and obvious, nor must the owner warn of conditions that are open and obvious. *Townsend v. Upwater* (Fr. Sup. Ct. 2000). Whether a condition is open and obvious may present a question of fact for the trier of fact to determine. The test to determine if a condition is open and obvious is objective. The court does not consider whether the plaintiff actually saw the alleged condition and the risk posed but whether an average user with ordinary intelligence would have been able to discover the risk presented upon casual inspection. *Roth v. Fiedler* (Fr. Sup. Ct. 1987).

There is one exception to the "open and obvious" rule: the "distraction exception" set forth in *Ward v. ShopMart Corp.* (Fr. Sup. Ct. 1991). The distraction exception applies when the owner has reason to suspect that guests or workers may not appreciate the danger or obvious nature of the condition because they are distracted or preoccupied. In *Ward*, carrying a large mirror distracted the plaintiff, preventing him from seeing a concrete post located in a doorway. Although ordinarily a post in the middle of a doorway would be an open and obvious condition, the distraction exception applied because it was foreseeable that customers would be leaving the store carrying large, unwieldy packages. In *Gardner v. Wendt* (Fr. Sup. Ct. 2000), the distraction exception applied when the plaintiff had failed to look at the floor he was walking on and fell over a box left in the aisle because he was distracted by holiday decorations. The box in the aisle was an open and obvious condition. The Court reasoned, however, that where the owner has created a distraction, such as blinking lights or a mobile suspended from the ceiling, the owner has reason to suspect that individuals on the premises might not appreciate the danger or obvious nature of an unsafe condition. In such cases, the owner has a duty of reasonable care.

The distraction exception does not apply, however, where those claiming injury created the distraction. In *Brown v. City of De Forest* (Fr. Ct. App. 2005), the plaintiff could not recover where she had tripped on an uneven sidewalk while chasing after a runaway child. She admitted that her attention was diverted from the sidewalk by her concern for the child. The court held that the distraction exception did not apply because the distraction was the result of the plaintiff's concern for the child and her own inattentiveness to where she was going, and the city could not be held responsible.

Commentary (Contributory Negligence): If the jury determines that the plaintiff's contributory negligence is a proximate cause of the injury claimed, the jury must find for the defendant and against the plaintiff. The term "contributory negligence" means negligence on the part of the plaintiff that proximately caused the alleged injury. Contributory negligence is a complete bar to recovery.

Commentary (Burden of Proof): Proof by a preponderance of the credible evidence means that the jury must be persuaded, considering the evidence, that the proposition on which the party has the burden is more probable than not. The jury must evaluate the quality of the evidence, including witness testimony, and the weight to be given it.

Commentary (Proximate Cause): Proximate cause means a cause that, in the natural or ordinary course of events, was a substantial factor in producing the plaintiff's injury.

POINT SHEET

Logan v. Rios

DRAFTERS' POINT SHEET

The task for the applicants in this performance test item is to prepare the initial draft of one part of the Early Dispute Resolution (EDR) statement that the supervising attorney will submit to the EDR judge, on behalf of the firm's client, Trina Rios, the defendant in a slip-and-fall case. Plaintiff Karen Logan was shopping at Trina's Toys, the toy store owned by Trina Rios, when she slipped on a small puddle of water and fell in one of the aisles, injuring her ankle in the process. As a result, Logan sued Rios, claiming that Rios violated her duty as a premises owner. Rios pled an affirmative defense of contributory negligence, which, if proven, would be a complete bar to Logan's recovery under Franklin law.

The File contains the instructional memo from the supervising attorney, Local Rule 12 concerning EDR conferences, Form 12 (the form to be completed for the EDR statement), the plaintiff's complaint, the defendant's investigator's report, and excerpts of the depositions of the plaintiff, Karen Logan, and Nick Patel, an employee of the defendant.

The Library includes a Franklin Supreme Court Approved Jury Instruction concerning the premises liability of property owners. The Jury Instruction contains commentary on the duty of property owners and the affirmative defense of contributory negligence.

The following discussion covers all the points the drafters of the item intended to incorporate, but applicants may receive passing and even excellent grades without covering them all. Grading is left entirely to the discretion of user jurisdictions.

I.   Overview

Applicants are expected to draft one component of the EDR statement in accord with the description set forth in Form 12, item 6:

> A candid discussion of the strengths and weaknesses of the party's claims, counterclaims, and/or defenses and affirmative defenses. For each element that must be proven, parties should discuss the specific strengths and weaknesses of the evidence gathered to date relating to that element in light of the jury instruction and any commentary thereto.

Applicants are told to carefully review the evidence gathered to date and identify and evaluate the proof available for each legal element of the claim and the affirmative defense. They are told to organize the facts relating to each legal element as defined in the jury instruction, to address both strengths and weaknesses of the case, and to analyze the case in light of the evidence available to Logan and Rios. Note that applicants have been told not to discuss Logan's damages (e.g., pain and suffering and the costs of medical care, etc.). Except as described below, applicants who do discuss damages may receive less than full credit as a result of their failure to follow directions. Applicants have been told to limit themselves to the evidence gathered to date. Speculation regarding evidence that may come to light as discovery proceeds is beyond the scope of the call memo.

Applicants are expected to extract from the jury instruction the elements of proof of liability that the plaintiff must establish and each element of the defendant's affirmative defense. From the depositions and other evidence provided, applicants should identify the evidence that supports the elements. Using the law and facts, they should assess the strengths and weaknesses of the evidence in relation to their client's case. Applicants are told that the EDR statement is confidential and will not be shared with the other party. Thus, they should be candid. Applicants who ignore the weaknesses of Rios's case—both in terms of their assessment of Logan's case and in terms of Rios's affirmative defense of contributory negligence—should be penalized.

Although applicants are not given a specific organizational format, they are directed in the call memo to organize the facts relating to each element as set forth in the jury instruction and to assess the strengths and weaknesses of their case. The outline provided below is an example of an organizational structure that complies with that instruction. Applicants should include citations to the cases cited in the Commentary to Jury Instruction 35 where appropriate. They need not cite to the factual record; record references are provided for graders' convenience.

II. **Arguments concerning the strengths and weaknesses of defendant Rios's case including any affirmative defenses**

A. <u>There was a condition which presented an unreasonable risk of harm to people on the defendant's property: namely, the presence of water on the floor (Jury Instruction 35; Complaint ¶ 4)</u>

Strengths of Rios's case:
- Applicants might point out that an indisputably small and thin puddle of water on the middle of a floor in a well-lit store hardly constitutes an unreasonable risk of harm.

Weaknesses of Rios's case:

- Applicants should note that it is undisputed that there was water on the floor where there was customer traffic. (Patel Dep. Tr., Logan Dep. Tr.)
  - It is possible that a jury would find that *any* amount of water on a slippery tile floor constituted an unreasonable risk.
- It is also undisputed that there was no warning about the water on the floor—no employee saw it, and no signs or cones were posted. (Patel Dep. Tr.) Had there been some notice to customers that there was water on the floor, the condition would not have presented an unreasonable risk of harm.

B. <u>The defendant knew or in the exercise of reasonable care should have known of both the condition and the risk. (Jury Instruction 35; Complaint ¶ 4)</u>

Strengths of Rios's case:

- Patel, one of Rios's employees, was in the store at the time of the fall. Neither he nor Rios knew about the water and thus could not have prevented it or warned customers about it. (Patel Dep. Tr.)
- Further, it was not unreasonable that Rios and her employees were unaware of the water.
  - There are no sources of water in the area of the fall that would have caused water to accumulate there: no leaking ceiling, no squirt gun displays. In fact, aisle 3 was an area of puzzles and games. (Patel Dep. Tr.)
  - It was not raining or snowing on the day of the incident. (Logan Dep. Tr.)
  - Trina's Toys is not a store that sells refreshments or toys containing water, so it is arguably unexpected for there to be a spill on the floor.
  - Patel mops the floors at night, after the store closes, so the floors would presumably dry by the next morning.
  - No one reported to store employees that there was water in the aisle, even though the store had had a steady stream of customers that day. (Patel Dep. Tr.)
  - If a customer spilled the water, neither Rios nor Patel had knowledge of the spill. (Patel Dep. Tr.)
  - A key factor in determining whether a premises owner acted with reasonable care is the length of time an unsafe condition existed. (JI 35 Commentary) Here, even

47

if Logan relies on Patel's admission that no store employee had checked on the aisle for two hours (Patel was in the aisle just before the store opened at 10 a.m..; Logan fell before noon), there was no reason to anticipate spills in the toy store and thus no duty to periodically check for them. (Patel Dep. Tr.) (*Chad v. Bill's Camera Shop* (Fr. Ct. App. 2006))

- By contrast, the owner of a coffee shop was liable for a fall that occurred when coffee had "just spilled" because it was reasonably foreseeable that customers would spill coffee. *Owens v. Coffee Corner* (Fr. Ct. App. 2007).
- Unlike the mini-golf operator found liable for a fall caused by a liquid spill in *Rollins v. Maryville Mini-Golf Park* (Fr. Ct. App. 2002), Rios does not serve food in her establishment.

Weaknesses of Rios's case:

- There is no evidence to narrow the possible time period that the water was on the floor.
- It is undisputed that Patel failed to patrol the aisles each hour. (Patel Dep. Tr.)
  - Had he done so, he almost certainly would have found the water, as it was in plain view.
  - There were two other employees there—Rios herself and Naomi Feldman—who presumably were capable of checking the aisles themselves, but did not.
  - Trina's Toys is a store frequented by children, who, like the little boy in the store at the time of Logan's fall, could be expected to have various containers like baby bottles and sippy cups containing beverages that could spill.
  - Thus, a jury could conclude that two hours is too long for a puddle of water to be in a busy area of a toy store.

C. <u>The defendant could reasonably expect that people on the property would not discover the danger, and the defendant failed to warn that water had accumulated on the floor. (Jury Instruction 35) However, the defendant could not be liable for harm caused by a condition which was open and obvious, nor must the defendant warn of conditions on the premises that are open and obvious. (*Townsend v. Upwater*)</u>

Strengths of Rios's case:

- Water on the floor is usually an open and obvious condition.

  - Logan admitted that nothing blocked her view of the water. (Logan Dep. Tr.)

  - Logan admitted that she was not looking at the floor. (Logan Dep. Tr.)

- Logan also conceded that the store was brightly lit, so there is no evidence of a problem with the lighting that would have prevented a reasonable person from noticing the water. (Logan Dep. Tr., Patel Dep. Tr.)

- Logan had been on her cell phone just prior to the fall and may have been distracted by the call. (Logan Dep. Tr.)

Weaknesses of Rios's case:

- Rios failed to warn of the water. (Patel Dep. Tr.) In fact, the toy store is not equipped to warn of spills—it does not have warning signs or cones to put out on the floor. (*Id.*)

- The water, being odorless and colorless, may not have been readily apparent to customers. (*Id.*) Also, this was not a large spill but a thin "trail of water." (Logan Dep. Tr.)

- Rios's customers could not necessarily be expected to scour the store's floor searching for hazards. Many of Rios's customers are children who would be focusing on the toys displayed. Adults, too, would reasonably be expected to be looking at the toys on display, as Logan said she was doing just before the fall (e.g., Wii bowling game).

D. <u>If the defendant created a distraction in the area such that the defendant had reason to suspect that the plaintiff might not appreciate the obvious nature of the unsafe condition, the defendant had a duty to warn the plaintiff.</u> (*Ward v. ShopMart*)

Strengths of Rios's case:

- Had Logan been looking where she was walking, she would have seen the water, which was an open and obvious condition. (Logan Dep. Tr.)

- The store was well lit. (Logan Dep. Tr., Patel Dep. Tr.)

- The distraction exception should stay just that—an exception. If it is construed as applying to all stores that make an effort to attractively display merchandise, all retail stores will become insurers of their customers' safety.

Weaknesses of Rios's case:

- Although Rios has no duty to warn of open and obvious conditions, she does have a duty to warn if a customer is likely to be distracted and therefore fail to notice the dangerous condition. (*Ward v. ShopMart*)
  - Holiday decorations may constitute a distraction. If so, the "distraction exception" to the open and obvious rule applies and the defendant is not relieved of liability for the plaintiff's injury. (*Gardner v. Wendt*)
  - But *Gardner* is distinguishable—holiday decorations qualify as a distraction because they are not usually present.
  - In this case, the aisle where Logan fell—indeed, the entire store—is filled with merchandise that is meant to attract customers. (Patel Dep. Tr.)
    - The end of the aisle had a computer-animated display of games. (*Id.*) This display may have distracted Logan from noticing where she was walking.
    - She claims to have been looking at the merchandise ahead of her, further down the aisle. (Logan Dep. Tr.)
  - The store also had a Wii game available for play, which Logan had been playing just before her fall. (*Id.*) She may have been distracted by it.
  - If it was reasonable to expect that the store displays would distract Logan from watching for open and obvious conditions, Rios had a duty to warn of the puddle.
    - It is undisputed that there were no warnings about the water puddle that could have alerted Logan to it.
  - However, the distraction exception does not apply when those claiming injury created the distraction. In *Brown v. City of De Forest* (Fr. Ct. App. 2005), the plaintiff could not recover where she had tripped on an uneven sidewalk while chasing after a runaway child. She admitted that her attention was diverted from the sidewalk by her concern for the child. The court held that the distraction exception did not apply because the distraction was the result of the plaintiff's concern for the child and inattentiveness to where she was going, and the city could not be held responsible.
    - In light of Logan's questionable credibility as a witness (see below), a jury might find it more likely than not that she was still using her cell phone when she slipped and so, under *Brown*, the "distraction" was of her own making, and the exception would not apply.

50

E. <u>Defendant's Affirmative Defense: Contributory Negligence. The plaintiff was negligent in spilling the water on which she slipped, and that negligence was the proximate cause of her injury. (Jury Instruction 35)</u>

Strengths of Rios's affirmative defense:

- Franklin is a contributory negligence jurisdiction. Thus, any negligence by Logan that contributed to her fall is a complete bar to recovery.
- While Logan has denied that she spilled water on the floor, there is circumstantial evidence that she did so.
  - She admits that she had a water bottle with her in the store. (Logan Dep. Tr.)
  - The water bottle was on the floor next to her after she fell. (Patel Dep. Tr.)
  - According to Patel, the water bottle was empty when he put it in Logan's backpack after she fell. (*Id.*)
  - Logan claims the bottle was full when she left for the store. (Logan Dep. Tr.)
  - She is equivocal regarding how much water was in the bottle when she was in the store and whether she had consumed any of it. (*Id.*)
  - The fact that there was no reason for water to be in aisle 3 and that no other customer saw the water creates a strong circumstantial case that Logan herself spilled the water, fell, and then lied about it.
- Given the false and inconsistent statements that Logan has made about the impact her ankle injury had on her employment and her scholarship, the jury may well believe that Logan herself spilled the water that caused her fall.

Weaknesses of Rios's affirmative defense:

- No witness actually *saw* Logan spill the water.
  - Patel testified that he is unaware of any witnesses to Logan's fall who might be able to apportion some blame to her. (Patel Dep. Tr.)
  - Logan herself testified that she did not see anyone else spill any water, including the toddler using the sippy cup. (Logan Dep. Tr.)
- Nevertheless, while there were no witnesses, it cannot be ruled out that the toddler with the sippy cup or another customer with water caused the spill.

Logan v. Rios

F. <u>Defendant's Affirmative Defense: Contributory Negligence: The plaintiff was negligent in failing to exercise due care for her safety by wearing shoes that were unsafe, especially while carrying a heavy backpack, and that negligence was the proximate cause of her injury.</u> (Jury Instruction 35)

Strengths of Rios's affirmative defense:

- Logan was wearing shoes with approximately three-inch heels and leather soles, which she was wearing for only the fourth time. The shoes were backless, high-heeled sandals. (Logan Dep. Tr.)
- The shoes looked like they were "not too steady." (Patel Dep. Tr.)
- It is likely that the leather soles were slippery and that the shoes, along with the weight of the backpack, caused Logan to fall. She could have expected that her relative inexperience in those particular shoes coupled with the heavy backpack could potentially lead to slipping and falling under any conditions.

Weaknesses of Rios's affirmative defense:

- No one saw how or why Logan fell.
- It is undisputed that she fell where the water puddle was.
- Stores like Trina's Toys can reasonably anticipate that customers will be wearing a variety of footwear.

G. <u>Additional Strengths of Rios's Case</u>

- Logan has the burden of proving by a preponderance of the *credible* evidence, including testimony, that she was injured as a result of Rios's negligence. (Jury Instruction 35)
- Logan is vulnerable to impeachment as a witness.
- Rios will present evidence that Logan has lied about some of her damages, and therefore Logan's account of how she fell is suspect.
  - Logan lied about her injury causing the loss of her job.
    - According to Joe Nyugen, Logan's supervisor at Fresh Grocers, Logan lost her job because she failed to report to work for three days and failed to call in. Nyugen may testify that Logan was absent for three days without notice to her

52

employer and that the employer had no knowledge of her injury when it fired her. (Ling's report)

- Logan lied about her injury causing the loss of her basketball scholarship.
  - Logan claimed that she lost the basketball scholarship after the fall because she could not practice with her injured ankle. Rios may call university officials to show that Logan lost the scholarship prior to the injury and that the reason was "academic difficulties." (Ling's report)

Being able to show that Logan has lied about these facts will undermine the credibility of her testimony about the fall itself.

Applicant Identification

Jackson v. Franklin Sports Gazette, Inc.

Read the instructions on the back cover.
Do not break the seal until you are told to do so.

NATIONAL CONFERENCE OF BAR EXAMINERS

Instructions

The back cover of each test form contains the following instructions:

1.   You will have 90 minutes to complete this session of the examination. This performance test is designed to evaluate your ability to handle a select number of legal authorities in the context of a factual problem involving a client.

2.   The problem is set in the fictitious state of Franklin, in the fictitious Fifteenth Circuit of the United States. Columbia and Olympia are also fictitious states in the Fifteenth Circuit. In Franklin, the trial court of general jurisdiction is the District Court, the intermediate appellate court is the Court of Appeal, and the highest court is the Supreme Court.

3.   You will have two kinds of materials with which to work: a File and a Library. The first document in the File is a memorandum containing the instructions for the task you are to complete. The other documents in the File contain factual information about your case and may include some facts that are not relevant.

4.   The Library contains the legal authorities needed to complete the task and may also include some authorities that are not relevant. Any cases may be real, modified, or written solely for the purpose of this examination. If the cases appear familiar to you, do not assume that they are precisely the same as you have read before. Read them thoroughly, as if they all were new to you. You should assume that the cases were decided in the jurisdictions and on the dates shown. In citing cases from the Library, you may use abbreviations and omit page references.

5.   Your response must be written in the answer book provided. If you are taking this examination on a laptop computer, your jurisdiction will provide you with specific instructions. In answering this performance test, you should concentrate on the materials in the File and Library. What you have learned in law school and elsewhere provides the general background for analyzing the problem; the File and Library provide the specific materials with which you must work.

6.   Although there are no restrictions on how you apportion your time, you should be sure to allocate ample time (about 45 minutes) to reading and digesting the materials and to organizing your answer before you begin writing it. You may make notes anywhere in the test materials; blank pages are provided at the end of the booklet. You may not tear pages from the question booklet.

7.   This performance test will be graded on your responsiveness to the instructions regarding the task you are to complete, which are given to you in the first memorandum in the File, and on the content, thoroughness, and organization of your response.

Contents

Jackson v. Franklin Sports Gazette, Inc.

FILE

LIBRARY

Point Sheet

FILE

Jackson v. Franklin Sports Gazette, Inc.

BENSON & DEGRANDI
Attorneys at Law
120 Garfield Avenue
Franklin City, Franklin 33536

MEMORANDUM

From: Robert Benson

To: Applicant

Date: July 28, 2009

Re: *Jackson v. Franklin Sports Gazette, Inc.*

Our client, the *Franklin Sports Gazette*, has been sued by Richard "Action" Jackson, star third baseman for Franklin City's major league baseball team, the Franklin Blue Sox. The complaint alleges infringement of Jackson's right of publicity under Franklin's recently enacted right of publicity statute. I interviewed Jerry Webster, managing editor of the *Gazette*, and Sandi Allen, its vice president of marketing, and also compiled some background information on Jackson and the team. I have summarized my interview and research in the attached memorandum.

Given that the new Franklin right of publicity statute has not been tested in the courts, this will be a case of first impression. However, there has been considerable case law developed under the prior, and now preempted, common law right of publicity, which may or may not still be relevant precedent.

Please prepare a memorandum analyzing whether Jackson has a cause of action under the right of publicity statute and whether we have any legal arguments to oppose that cause of action under the statute and the relevant case law. You need not include a separate statement of facts, nor address any issue of damages. Rather, analyze Jackson's claims and our defenses, incorporating the relevant facts into your legal analysis and assessing our likelihood of success on each such basis. Draft the points of your analysis in separate sections using descriptive headings. Be sure to explain your conclusions.

1

MEMORANDUM

From: Robert Benson

To: Applicant

Date: July 28, 2009

Re: *Jackson v. Franklin Sports Gazette*—INTERVIEW AND RESEARCH SUMMARY

These notes summarize salient facts from my interview of the *Franklin Sports Gazette*'s managing editor, Jerry Webster, and its vice president of marketing, Sandi Allen, as well as background research on the Franklin Blue Sox.

The *Franklin Sports Gazette* is a weekly tabloid published in Franklin City and distributed throughout the state, dealing with Franklin's sports teams and events, including Franklin City's major league baseball team, the Franklin Blue Sox. The *Gazette* reports on Blue Sox games and team news, and is known for its incisive writing and action photography. The *Gazette* is sold by subscription and on newsstands.

Richard "Action" Jackson is the star third baseman of the Blue Sox, the only major league team for which he has played during his 12-year career. Jackson is a much-beloved fixture in the Franklin City sports scene, and is noted for his charitable endeavors and community service. It sometimes appears that the majority of fans at Blue Sox games are wearing apparel with Jackson's name, nickname, or unique double-zero number, "00," and Jackson has earned millions of dollars merchandising his name and likeness for products and services. He is reported to be among the top ten endorsement earners in baseball.

Five seasons ago, the *Gazette* published an account of a regular season Blue Sox game in which Jackson scored on a close play at home plate. The Blue Sox lost the game, which was wholly unmemorable in an unmemorable season—they finished in fifth place, last in the division. The story was accompanied by a photograph of Jackson sliding into home plate (the "Photo"). The Photo showed the opposing team's catcher's feet, and Jackson's back as he slid with one arm thrown up in the air. A spray of dirt from the slide obscured most of Jackson's body and uniform number, allowing only the second zero to be partially visible. No part of Jackson's face could be seen. The Photo won a third place award from the Franklin City Photographers' Association "Best Sports Photo of the Year" competition. Jackson is Caucasian, and a check of the relevant Blue Sox rosters shows that, at the time, the Blue Sox had three other players (two of whom are also Caucasian) who wore uniform numbers ending in zero—today, they have five other players with such numbers (all Caucasian). The Blue Sox have not changed the design of the team uniforms in 25 years, and their uniform design is one of the few in the major leagues which does not include the player's name on the back.

One month ago, the *Gazette* ran a print advertisement in the *Franklin City Journal*, a daily newspaper, soliciting subscriptions. The ad reproduced the Photo over text and a subscription coupon. Allen chose to use the Photo in the ad, with Webster's approval, for the reasons given in the attached memorandum, which also includes her draft of the ad. The ad was published with the text unchanged from the draft.

In the week following the ad's appearance, the *Gazette*'s new subscriptions, which resulted directly from the ad (as shown by use of the coupon in the ad), increased by 18% over new subscriptions during the previous week.

Two days ago, Jackson served a complaint on the *Gazette*, alleging that it had violated Jackson's right of publicity under Franklin's statute and had damaged him by depriving him of the license fee he would have reaped from this use of his image and of his ability to license the use of his image to other sports publications.

FRANKLIN SPORTS GAZETTE

Memorandum

From: Sandi Allen

To: Jerry Webster

Date: June 15, 2009

Re: Subscription ad

We want to liven up the print ad we run every Monday in the *Franklin City Journal*; the old ads, which are text only, are too staid. We've got this award-winning photo of Action Jackson from a few years ago, which conveys excitement, action, and the kind of sports coverage we stand for. Using the photo together with new text copy will, I think, result in a significant increase in subscriptions to the *Gazette*. The draft of the ad is attached. OK?

OK *DW* 6-15-09

[PHOTO WILL BE REPRODUCED HERE]

GET IN WITH THE ACTION!!!!!

SUBSCRIBE NOW TO THE *FRANKLIN SPORTS GAZETTE*!

Look at all you get:

> Great stories!
>
> Coverage of every Franklin team!!
>
> And award-winning photos like this that put you right in the middle of the action!!!

Use this coupon for our special offer: 26 weeks of the *Gazette* for only $24.99!

[COUPON WILL BE INSERTED HERE]

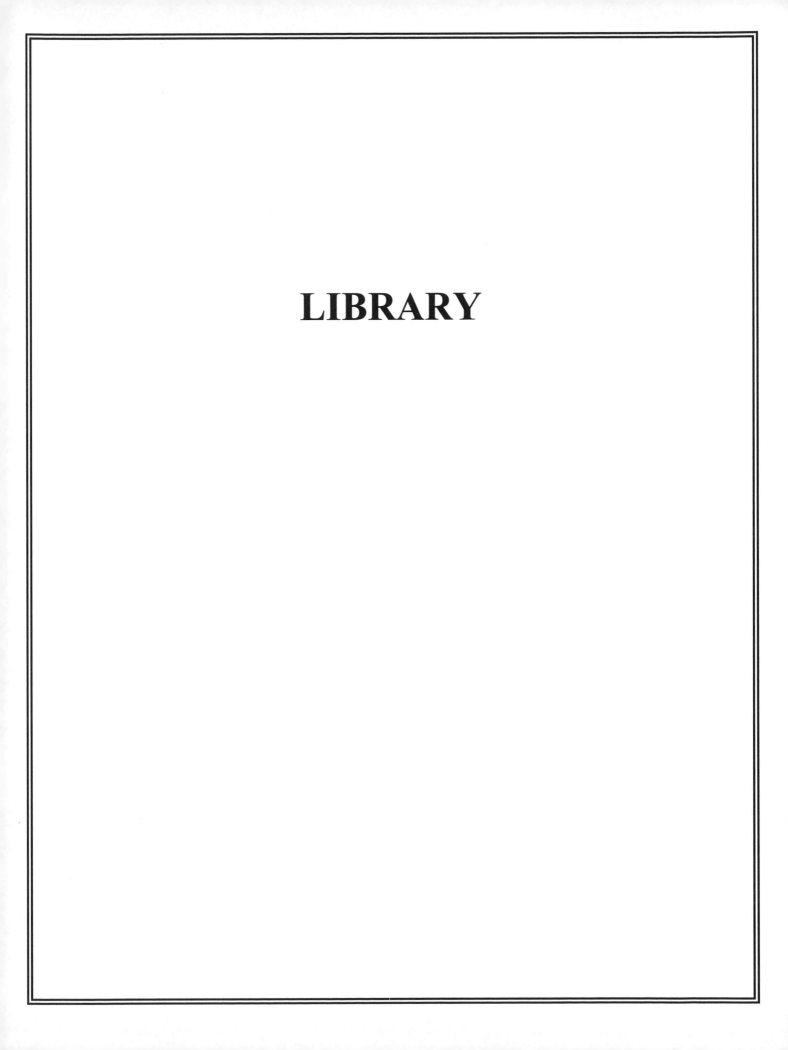

LIBRARY

FRANKLIN RIGHT OF PUBLICITY STATUTE

§ 62 RIGHT OF PUBLICITY—Use of Another's Persona in Advertising or Soliciting without Prior Consent

(a) <u>Cause of Action</u>. Any person who knowingly uses another's . . . photograph, or likeness, in any manner on or in products, merchandise, or goods, or for purposes of advertising or selling, or soliciting purchases of products, merchandise, goods or services, without such person's prior consent, . . . shall be liable for any damages sustained by the person or persons injured as a result thereof.

(b) <u>Definitions</u>. As used in this section, "photograph" means any photograph or photographic reproduction, still or moving, or any videotape or live television transmission, of any person, such that the person is readily identifiable.

(1) A person shall be deemed to be readily identifiable from a photograph when one who views the photograph with the naked eye can reasonably determine that the person depicted in the photograph is the same person who is complaining of its unauthorized use.

*   *   *   *

(d) <u>Affirmative Defense</u>. For purposes of this section, a use of a . . . photograph, or likeness, in connection with any news, public affairs, or sports broadcast or account, or any political campaign, shall not constitute a use for which consent is required under subsection (a).

*   *   *   *

(g) <u>Preemption of Common Law Rights</u>. This section preempts all common law causes of action which are the equivalent of that set forth in subsection (a).

EXCERPTS FROM LEGISLATIVE HISTORY

Franklin State Assembly, Committee on the Arts and Media, Report No. 94-176 (2008), pp. 4–5, on F.A. Bill No. 94-222 (Franklin Right of Publicity Act of 2008)

The common law of Franklin has recognized an individual's "right of publicity" for many decades. Starting in the 1950s, Franklin's courts recognized that an individual has both a property right and a personal right in the use of his or her "persona" for commercial purposes.

It is important to note that the right of publicity differs from, and protects entirely different rights than, a copyright. A copyright protects the rights of reproduction, distribution of copies to the public, the making of derivative works, public performance, and public display in an original work of authorship. Thus, for example, the copyright owner of a photograph may prevent others from reproducing the photograph without authorization. But the right of publicity protects the interests of an individual in the exploitation of his or her persona—the personal attributes of the individual that have economic value, which have nothing to do with original works of authorship. Thus, for example, even if authorization to use a copyrighted photograph is obtained from the copyright owner, commercial uses of that photograph which exploit the persona of the photograph's subject could infringe upon the subject's right of publicity. It is also important to note that the right of publicity is exclusively a matter of state law—unlike copyright, which is exclusively within federal jurisdiction. There is no federal right of publicity.

As developed by Franklin's courts, the elements of a common law cause of action for appropriation of the right of publicity are (1) the defendant's use of the plaintiff's persona, (2) appropriation of the plaintiff's persona to the defendant's commercial or other advantage, (3) lack of consent, and (4) resulting injury. Even after 50 years of development, the boundaries of Franklin's common law right of publicity are necessarily ill-defined, as the courts can deal only with the specific facts of individual cases that come before them. Given the expansion of our "celebrity culture," the opportunities for individuals to exploit this right have increased exponentially in recent years. Accordingly, the Committee concludes that there is a need to codify this increasingly important economic right.

While the Committee agrees with, and the proposed legislation codifies, the basic elements of the cause of action as understood at common law, the Committee is of the view that some of the common law cases went too far in upholding individual claims, while others did not go far enough. The Committee therefore intends that the legislation set forth the full extent of the right, thus preempting the common law cause of action in this area. Obviously, to the degree that prior common law decisions accord with the legislation's provisions, they continue to constitute good precedent which the courts may use for guidance in applying the legislation.

The legislation would achieve several goals in clarifying the law:

*   *   *   *

- The case law has, in a few opinions, dealt with the specificity with which an individual needs to be identifiable when his or her photographic image is used without consent. It is important that a single standard be used for such analysis. Accordingly, the legislation includes a subsection which explicitly sets forth the requirements for that identification.

- There has been some uncertainty as to whether news reporting organizations were liable for infringement of the right of publicity when they included an individual's picture or other indices of persona in ancillary uses. It is the Committee's view that the important right of freedom of the press, found in both the Franklin Constitution and the First Amendment to the United States Constitution, must supersede any individual claims based on "any news, public affairs, or sports broadcast or account, or any political campaign." Hence, the legislation includes an express exemption for such uses of an individual's persona.

*   *   *   *

The legislation is hereby favorably reported to the Assembly.

Holt v. JuicyCo, Inc., and Janig, Inc.
Franklin Supreme Court (2001)

The right of publicity, which exists at common law in Franklin, has been defined as the protection of an individual's persona against unauthorized commercial use. Since we recognized this right some 50 years ago, there has been an increasing number of cases dealing with it, reflecting the similarly increasing economic importance of the right.

The issue in this case is whether an individual's persona, as reflected in certain aspects of his visual image, is identifiable in an audiovisual work—and thus actionable if the other elements of the common law cause of action are met—even if his face and other more common identifying features are unseen.

Ken Holt, a Franklin resident, is a noted downhill skier, participating on the World Cup Ski Tour. He has a devoted fan following, due in large part to his dashing good looks and winning personality. As is the custom in downhill skiing races, when he is competing, Holt is completely covered up: he wears a body-clinging "slick" suit, boots, gloves, and a helmet with a tinted faceplate. In competition, Holt always wears a distinctive and unique gold-colored suit with purple stripes, adorned with patches from his sponsors. His name is emblazoned in large gold letters on his purple helmet.

And, as do all competitors, he wears a bib with his assigned number for that particular competition, so that he may be distinguished from other competitors.

JuicyCo manufactures a sports drink called PowerGold, which ostensibly aids in maintaining energy during athletic activity. JuicyCo markets PowerGold nationwide to consumers. Janig is its advertising agency.

In 1999, Janig produced a television commercial for PowerGold, using a video clip of a two-man race between Holt and another skier, for which it acquired the rights by license from the broadcast network that covered the race and owned the copyright in the clip (the network had obtained no rights from Holt, nor did it need to, as its coverage was newsworthy and authorized by the World Cup Ski Tour). Neither Janig nor JuicyCo sought permission from Holt or the other skier to use their images in the commercial. Janig used digital technology to modify aspects of Holt's appearance in the video clip: it deleted the patches on his suit, deleted his bib number, deleted the name "HOLT" from the helmet, and inserted the PowerGold logo on his helmet and chest. Voice-over narration was added describing the attributes of PowerGold.

12

Holt brought this action for violation of his common law right of publicity, claiming that his likeness was used for commercial purposes without his consent. He claimed that the use implied his endorsement of PowerGold, depriving him of endorsement fees from JuicyCo and precluding his endorsing competing sports drinks.

JuicyCo and Janig argued that there was no way to identify the skier in the commercial as Holt, given that his face, name, bib number, and sponsors' patches were not visible. JuicyCo and Janig moved to dismiss for failure to state a cause of action.

In considering a motion to dismiss for failure to state a claim, a court must accept the complaint's well-pleaded allegations as true and construe them in a light most favorable to the plaintiff. Dismissal of the complaint is proper if it appears certain that, under applicable law, the plaintiff is not entitled to relief under any facts which could be proved in support of the claim.

The district court dismissed the action on the grounds that Holt was not identifiable in the video clip, holding that he was unrecognizable as his face was not visible and his name, sponsors' patches, and bib number were deleted. The court of appeal affirmed. If the courts below were correct that, as a matter of law, the plaintiff was not identifiable, then in no sense has his right of publicity been violated.

We agree with the district court that Holt's likeness—in the sense of his facial features—is itself unrecognizable. But the question is not simply whether one can recognize an individual's features, but whether one can *identify* the specific individual from the use made of his image.

We hold that the lower courts' conclusion that the skier could not be *identifiable* as Holt is erroneous as a matter of law, in that it wholly fails to attribute proper significance to the distinctive appearance of Holt's suit and its potential, as a factual matter, to allow the public to identify Holt as the skier in the commercial. The suit's color scheme and design are unique to Holt, and their depiction could easily lead a trier of fact to conclude that it was Holt, and not another wearing that suit, appearing in the commercial and endorsing PowerGold. Whether it did or not is a factual, not a legal, question that will have to be decided at trial.

Reversed and remanded.

13

Brant v. Franklin Diamond Exchange, Ltd.

Franklin Court of Appeal (2003)

Barbara Brant was the star of the Franklin University intercollegiate diving team that won the national collegiate championships in 1995. She was the only diver in the championships to score a perfect "10" in a dive from the 10-meter board. She has retired from competitive diving and now lives in Franklin City, where she practices law.

The Franklin Diamond Exchange (the "Exchange") is a jewelry store in Franklin City. In 2002, it obtained the rights to reproduce a photograph of Brant's perfect dive from the copyright owner of the picture. The photograph shows Brant from the waist to the toes entering the water on the completion of her dive. Her head and torso, to her waist, have entered the water and are not visible. The picture does show her legs and the bottom of her bathing suit, which was a generic one-piece suit, of the same color, design, and cut as was required to be worn by all female divers who participated in the championships. Other than that part of Brant's body, the picture shows nothing but the surface of the swimming pool—there is no way to identify the venue, time, or event depicted. The Exchange used the photograph in an advertisement in the *Franklin City Journal* over the headline "Make a Splash! Give Her a Diamond!" with illustrations of four different diamond bracelets, their prices, and the name, address, and phone number of the Exchange.

Brant saw the advertisement and brought this action against the Exchange for violation of her common law right of publicity. The Exchange admitted that the photograph depicted Brant, but moved to dismiss for failure to state a cause of action. The Exchange argued that Brant's likeness was not identifiable from the photograph, and hence her right of publicity could not have been infringed. Brant opposed the motion, citing *Holt v. JuicyCo, Inc., and Janig, Inc.* (Fr. Sup. Ct. 2001) as authority for the proposition that one's face or similar identifying features need not be visible if the individual whose right of publicity is allegedly violated is nevertheless identifiable from the depiction used. The district court agreed and, after trial, awarded Brant $150,000 in damages. The Exchange appealed, alleging that the district court erred as a matter of law. For the reasons given below, we agree and reverse, with instructions to dismiss the complaint.

In *Holt*, the skier whose picture was used in

a commercial advertisement was identifiable because of his unique uniform which, though somewhat altered digitally, nevertheless remained basically the same and clearly visible in the depiction. Thus, the public to whom the advertisement was aimed could easily identify the figure depicted as Holt and no other skier.

Brant argues that, following *Holt*, there are two elements that can be used to identify the individual depicted in the picture as herself—her legs and the visible portion of her bathing suit. We disagree. *Holt* is inapposite and distinguishable on the facts before us. It strains credibility here to argue that Brant's legs, which have no unique scars, marks, tattoos, or other identifying features, are identifiable by the public compared to any other diver's legs. The only other visible element in the picture is her bathing suit from the waist down. But that suit was identical in color, design, and cut to those worn by every other diver in the meet.

In sum, even though the Exchange does not contest that it is Brant who appears in the photograph, there is no way that the public could conclude that this was a picture of Brant as opposed to any other diver. Neither her likeness nor any other identifying attribute was present in the photograph. Thus, there is no possibility that Brant could prove facts which support her claim under the law. Her right of publicity was not infringed.

The judgment of the district court is reversed, and the case remanded with instructions to dismiss the complaint for failure to state a cause of action.

Miller v. FSM Enterprises, Inc.

Franklin Court of Appeal (1988)

Jan Miller, a resident of Franklin City, is a world-class figure skater, an Olympic champion now on the professional tour. FSM Enterprises, Inc., is the publisher of *Figure Skating!* Magazine ("FSM"), a national monthly which is devoted to the sport. In the course of its normal news coverage of the sport, FSM ran a story on Miller's appearance at the World Professional Figure Skating Championships in January 1987, and included a photograph of Miller seemingly frozen in midair in one of her jumps off the ice (the "Photo").

In February 1987, FSM placed an advertisement soliciting subscriptions in several national sports magazines, all of which were distributed in Franklin. The advertisement included the Photo over text extolling the quality of FSM's coverage of the sport of figure skating. There was no mention of Miller's name in the text. Miller sued, alleging that the use of her image in that advertisement violated her common law right of publicity.

The defendant moved to dismiss for failure to state a cause of action, claiming that the use was for newsworthy purposes. The district court denied the motion, holding that the advertisement soliciting subscriptions was not for such purposes, but was rather for a commercial use wholly detached from news coverage. After a bench trial, the district court found that Miller's right of publicity had been infringed, and awarded damages of $250,000. This appeal followed, and we are called upon to decide an issue of first impression: the use of an individual's image in an advertisement by and for a news medium under Franklin's common law right of publicity.

The elements of a common law cause of action for violation of the right of publicity are (1) the defendant's use of the plaintiff's persona, (2) appropriation of the plaintiff's persona to the defendant's commercial or other advantage, (3) lack of consent, and (4) resulting injury.

The right is not without limitations, however. One of the most important is an exemption for news reporting. The guarantees of freedom of the press in the Franklin and United States Constitutions are such that no individual can complain of legitimate news reporting which reproduces any aspect of his or her persona—name, image, or the like. Thus, wisely, we think, Miller makes no complaint about the use of her image in the issue of FSM that reported on her participation in the skating championships, and explicitly agrees that the use of the Photo there was for a legitimate news report. She does, however, argue that the use in the advertisement soliciting subscriptions is a different matter, and one that is actionable.

Miller argues that this case is no different from *Jancovic v. Franklin City Journal, Inc.* (Fr. Sup. Ct. 1984). Jancovic was a star goalie for the Franklin City Foxes, a minor league hockey team. The Foxes had a rabid following in Franklin City, and had won the championship of their league. The *Journal* printed a special section devoted to the championship series, which featured many photographs of the team, including one of Jancovic making an acrobatic save of a shot by the opposition. The *Journal* then reprinted that photograph as a large poster, with no text on it whatsoever, and sold the poster to retail stores which then sold it to the public. Jancovic claimed that his common law right of publicity was violated by the *Journal*'s poster sales. The Franklin Supreme Court agreed.

The Court held that, notwithstanding that the poster was manufactured and sold by an entity which functioned as a news organization, the poster as sold to the public had no relationship whatsoever to that function. Hence, the use did not qualify for the common law exemption for news reporting.

We think that this case is distinguishable from *Jancovic*, and that the use of Miller's image in the Photo when reproduced in the advertisement did not violate her right of publicity. In *Jancovic,* there could be no relationship in the mind of the consumer between the poster and the newspaper, and more particularly the news dissemination function of the newspaper. No part of the news story about Jancovic or his team—not even a caption for the photograph—was reproduced on the poster. Indeed, the purchasers would not have known that the newspaper had anything to do with the sale of the poster. The poster could just as easily have been manufactured and sold by a business selling sports memorabilia, and if it had been, there would have been no doubt that Jancovic's right of publicity had been violated.

But here, the use of Miller's image was incidental to the advertising of FSM in relationship to its news reporting function. The use illustrated the way in which Miller had earlier been properly and fairly depicted by the magazine in a legitimate news account. It informed the public as to the nature and quality of FSM's news reporting. Certainly, FSM's republication of Miller's picture was, in motivation, sheer advertising and solicitation. But that alone is not determinative of whether her right of publicity was violated. We think that the common law must accord exempt status to incidental advertising of the news medium itself. Certainly, that aspect of the exemption is limited—it can apply only when there can be no inference of endorsement by the individual depicted. So long as the Photo was used only to illustrate the quality and content of the periodical in which it originally appeared, and nothing more, Miller's rights were not violated. We might have concluded otherwise if the advertisement had somehow tied her explicitly to the solicitation for subscriptions (as, for example, by featuring her name in its headline or text) and thus implied an endorsement, for that implied endorsement would have met the requirement that the use of the persona be for the defendant's commercial advantage, beyond a reference to its newsworthy value. But such is not the case here.

Reversed and remanded with instructions to dismiss the complaint.

WEISS, J., dissenting:

I dissent. Miller is in part in the business of endorsing products, and this use implies her endorsement of the defendant's magazine. As the majority notes, if her name had been used in connection with the solicitation, there would have been no question that an endorsement was implied and her right of publicity violated. That her name was not used does not to my mind mean, as the majority would have it, that no endorsement was implied—a picture is, as we all know, worth a thousand words. The question of the use is one of degree, and here the use of her image seems to me to be trading on her persona for a purely commercial use as opposed to one that is intended to inform. I would affirm.

POINT SHEET

Jackson v. Franklin Sports Gazette, Inc.

Jackson v. Franklin Sports Gazette, Inc.
DRAFTERS' POINT SHEET

In this performance test item, applicants' law firm represents the *Franklin Sports Gazette*, a weekly tabloid sports newspaper. The *Gazette* has been sued by Richard "Action" Jackson, star third baseman of the Franklin Blue Sox, Franklin City's major league baseball team, for violation of his right of publicity under the recently enacted Franklin right of publicity statute.

The *Gazette* had, five years earlier, run a photograph of Jackson sliding into home plate ("the Photo") as part of its coverage of a Blue Sox game. In the Photo, Jackson's back was to the camera, his face and most of his body were obscured, and only the last digit of his uniform number was visible.

On June 15, 2009, the *Gazette*'s vice president of marketing sent a memo to its managing editor suggesting that the *Gazette* run a new advertisement in the *Franklin City Journal*, a daily newspaper, soliciting subscriptions. The advertisement showed the Photo over the headline "GET IN WITH THE ACTION!" and text that referred to the *Gazette*'s coverage as including "award-winning photos like this that put you right in the middle of the action!!!" After the advertisement ran in the paper as drafted, Jackson sued the *Gazette*.

The *Gazette* seeks the law firm's assistance in defending against the suit. Applicants' task is to draft an objective memorandum analyzing whether there is a cause of action under Franklin's right of publicity statute, identifying the *Gazette*'s possible legal arguments to oppose such a cause of action, and assessing the likelihood of success.

The File contains 1) the instructional memorandum, 2) a memorandum from the partner summarizing background research and interviews with the *Gazette*'s managing editor and vice president of marketing, 3) the memorandum from the vice president of marketing to the managing editor suggesting the advertisement, and 4) the advertisement itself. The Library contains 1) the Franklin right of publicity statute, 2) excerpts from its legislative history, and 3) three cases bearing on the subject.

The following discussion covers all the points the drafters intended to raise in the problem. Applicants need not cover them all to receive passing or even excellent grades. Grading is entirely within the discretion of the user jurisdictions.

I. FORMAT AND OVERVIEW

The assignment is to prepare a memorandum analyzing whether there is a cause of action under the recently enacted Franklin right of publicity statute. The analysis should be objective, noting the arguments on both sides of the issues presented and assessing the likelihood of success on each issue.

Jackson v. Franklin Sports Gazette, Inc., then poses two specific questions and one overarching legal issue for applicants:

1) Was Jackson identifiable in the Photo? If not, there is no possibility he could prove facts supporting one of the necessary conditions for a cause of action for violation of his right of publicity—the requirement that the individual's *persona* be used.

2) Even if he was identifiable in the Photo, is the use of the Photo by the *Gazette* excused under the statute's exemption for news reporting?

3) The answers to these questions must be informed by the degree to which the prior common law decisions are relevant and precedential under Franklin's new right of publicity statute.

No introduction or formal statement of facts is necessary, but applicants should incorporate the relevant facts into their analyses, using descriptive headings to separate the issues; those headings presented below are illustrative examples only, and not prescribed headings that applicants must use.

Applicants would likely review the elements of a cause of action under the right of publicity statute: 1) use of the plaintiff's persona, 2) appropriation of the persona for commercial or other advantage, 3) lack of consent, and 4) resulting injury. With respect to the second element, there is no doubt that the *Gazette* used the Photo for its commercial advantage. Likewise, elements 3 and 4 are not in dispute. The key issue is whether the first element has been met.

It is expected that applicants will conclude that there is a good, although not absolutely certain, argument that Jackson is not identifiable in the Photo. Thus, it is not possible to prove facts which meet the statutory requirement of identifiability necessary for a cause of action. On this issue, there is a strong argument that the existing common law precedents supporting the *Gazette*'s position remain good law, notwithstanding the preemption provision of the statute, as the decisions comport with the statute and its legislative history. In addition, there is a weaker, but plausible, argument that the use of the Photo comes within the news reporting exception of the statute. On this issue, the argument that the common law precedents remain good law, while plausible, is weak, given the language of the statute and legislative history.

II. DISCUSSION

A. Was Jackson identifiable?

The statute requires that the individual depicted in a photograph be "readily identifiable." § 62(b). It defines that term as meaning that a viewer can "reasonably determine that the person depicted in the photograph is the same person who is complaining of its unauthorized use." § 62(b)(1). Applicants should note that the common law right of publicity required that the plaintiff's persona be appropriated and argue that this is a standard similar to the standard in the statute. The legislative history of the statute indicates that prior common law decisions that accord with the new statutory provisions remain good precedent. This would indicate that the prior common law decisions on identifiability—*Holt v. JuicyCo, Inc., and Janig, Inc.,* and *Brant v. Franklin Diamond Exchange*—are still good law, as each appears to apply the equivalent of the new statutory standard, albeit not in so many words.

What features or attributes make an individual "identifiable"?

Jackson's face and most of his body are not visible in the Photo. Applicants should note that *Holt* teaches that facial representation is not necessary—there, the distinctive and unique garb of the athlete was sufficient to identify him in the minds of the public. On the other hand, *Brant* teaches that such "secondary" identification can only go so far—when an individual is depicted without any distinctive identifying features whatsoever, the right of publicity is not violated, for the public cannot identify the individual depicted as the individual making the claim. Accordingly, applicants must analyze whether Jackson is "identifiable" from any non-facial features in the Photo, such that a viewer could, in the words of the statute, "reasonably determine" that it is Jackson being depicted in the Photo.

Is Jackson "identifiable" from any non-facial features in the Photo?

Applicants should address the question whether there is any aspect of Jackson's depiction in the Photo that would allow the public to know that it is he, and not another player, being depicted. Applicants should state that a successful motion to dismiss requires that Jackson is *not* identifiable from the Photo. Applicants should apply the following analysis in concluding that Jackson's claim is unlikely to succeed:

- No part of Jackson's face or body can be identified.

- One possible identification that could be made is based on Jackson's uniform. But the uniform design has not changed in 25 years, and, by definition, a "uniform" is uniform— it is the same for all players on the team. Thus, the Photo could depict any player on the team. Applicants should support this analysis by referring to and analogizing with the use of a common swimsuit design by all competitors in *Brant*.

- Applicants should distinguish *Holt* by noting that the plaintiff there was "identifiable" by the *unique* aspects of his clothing (his gold racing suit), and argue that no similarly unique attributes are present here.

- Another possible identification that could be made is based on the partial visibility of Jackson's uniform number—the last zero in his double-zero number. But, at the time the Photo was taken, three other Blue Sox players had numbers ending in zero, and, at the time of the lawsuit, five other players did. Hence, the picture could have been of any one of four to six different individuals.

- The uniform number analysis requires further refinement—as parts of Jackson's unclothed body (one arm, his neck) are visible in the Photo, were those teammates whose numbers ended in zero of the same ethnic background as Jackson? As Jackson is Caucasian, if all the other teammates whose numbers ended in zero were non-Caucasian, that might be enough to find Jackson identifiable in the Photo. But the facts tell us that a sufficient number were also Caucasian (two of the three when the Photo was taken, and all five at the time of the lawsuit) as to preclude the possibility that Jackson could be reasonably identifiable in the Photo.

Is Jackson "identifiable" from the text of the advertisement?

- Applicants may note that Jackson may argue that the text of the advertisement, by its repeated use of the word "action," identifies the individual in the Photo as Jackson by using his nickname. This, it could be argued, is a secondary identifying feature like the distinctive outfit worn by the plaintiff in *Holt*. In response, applicants might observe that the statute's definition of what makes a person identifiable in a photograph is based solely on visual elements in the photograph itself. Hence, the use of "action" in the text does not affect the identifiability of the individual depicted in the Photo.

- Applicants might also note that Jackson could argue that the repeated use of the word "action" in the text of the advertisement and the reference to him in the memorandum from Sandi Allen to Jerry Webster show an intent to identify Jackson as the individual in the photograph, and therefore violate his right of publicity. The counterargument would be that use of "action" in the ad and the memo (with one exception, discussed below) was as a common noun, not the proper noun of Jackson's nickname: 1) if the headline in the ad had referred to Jackson, it would have said, "GET IN WITH ACTION," not "GET IN WITH *THE* ACTION" (emphasis added); 2) the memo referred to the Photo conveying "excitement, *action*, and the kind of sports coverage we stand for" (emphasis added), using the common noun "action" (with no initial capital letter) rather than the proper noun (with an initial capital letter); and 3) the text of the ad, referring to "put[ting] you right in the middle of the *action*" (emphasis added), also used the common noun, not Jackson's nickname. Hence, applicants could conclude that the public would understand the use in the ad in the sense of the common noun "action," and not as identifying Jackson himself.

- Finally, perceptive applicants will note that the memo's identification of the individual in the Photo as Action Jackson simply indicates the *Gazette*'s knowledge that the Photo depicts Jackson and not another player, and does not go to the question of the identifiability by the public of Jackson in the ad. Although the statute imposes liability on one who "knowingly uses" an individual's persona, a second requirement is that the individual be identifiable. As the court stated in *Brant*, that knowledge, and even its admission, does not make the individual "identifiable" by the public in the use itself.

In sum, applicants should conclude that there is a good argument, albeit not a certainty, that, under the statute and relevant and still-valid precedent, Jackson is not identifiable in the Photo and, as a result, he does not have a cause of action for violation of his right of publicity.

B. Was the use for news reporting?

Applicants should proceed in their analysis to note that, even if Jackson were "identifiable" in the Photo, the use could still be exempt because of the affirmative defense for "news

reporting" in the statute, § 62(d). As there seems to be prior common law precedent which would exempt the *Gazette*'s use in the subscription solicitation, applicants should first address whether the statute has changed the common law standard; if it has, the prior supporting case law no longer serves as precedent.

Did the statute change the common law standard of what constitutes news reporting?

Both the common law right and the new statutory right contain an exception for news reporting. *See* § 62(d); *Miller v. FSM Enterprises, Inc.* (Fr. Ct. App. 1988). As the common law developed, to be exempt the use had to be somehow related to news dissemination:

- In *Jancovic v. Franklin City Journal, Inc.* (discussed in *Miller*), a news photograph that was reproduced as a poster and sold as such by the newspaper, but without any reference to its news function, was held to violate the individual's common law right of publicity. The court held that it made no difference that the poster came from a news organization, as the lack of reference to the organization or its news activities removed the use from the exemption.

- Applicants should distinguish *Jancovic* on the grounds that the *Gazette*'s use did indeed refer to its news reporting activities. The text of the advertisement made direct reference to the activities and type of news coverage the *Gazette* provides ("great stories," "coverage of every Franklin team," "award-winning photos").

- Applicants will also note that a common law precedent, *Miller*, supports exemption for exactly the sort of use made here by the *Gazette*. In *Miller*, a magazine used a news photograph for a subscription solicitation, much like the use here. The court held (over dissent) that the relation of the photograph to the news function of the magazine was sufficient to qualify for the exemption, as the use was an example of the magazine's news coverage.

- Is *Miller* still good law under the statute? The statute grants an affirmative defense for use "in connection with any news, public affairs, or sports *broadcast or account*" (emphasis added). While this obviously applies to stories and news accounts, it is unclear as to whether it would extend to solicitations for subscriptions as was the case in *Miller*—could the solicitation, which illustrates the type of "news or sports accounts" the publication covers, itself be described as a "news . . . or sports . . . account"? Arguing against applying the *Miller* common law precedent is the plain language of the statute, which refers only to "account[s]" (in contrast, in *Miller*, the court was not construing statutory language but analyzing the issue in the context of whether the use of the plaintiff's image fell within the term "news reporting" under the common law). The legislative history could also be seen as, at best, ambiguous: 1) it notes that there was "uncertainty" as to whether uses "ancillary" to news reporting incurred liability, and 2) it emphasizes the "broadcast or account" language of the new statute. Hence, applicants should note the potential argument that the subscription solicitation furthers the goal of supporting news reporting by making the public aware of the *Gazette*'s coverage of issues of public interest, and thus the *Miller* rationale should be followed as good precedent, while also noting the weakness of the argument.

- The case for a valid affirmative defense could be seen as a toss-up at best. The statute speaks of the use of a photograph "in connection with any . . . sports broadcast or account." Is this language sufficiently broad to cover the advertisement? Is the term so ambiguous as to make resort to the legislative history necessary? Perceptive applicants will state that, while one could argue that the use of the Photo in the solicitation as an example of the *Gazette*'s content was intended to make the public aware of the *Gazette*'s coverage, one might just as easily argue that the statutory language is clear and includes only "account[s]" and not advertisements for the news medium itself.

If the statute adopted the common law standard for affirmative defense as set forth in *Miller*, did the *Gazette*'s specific use of the Photo meet that standard?

- Applicants should also note that the *Miller* precedent itself is not clear-cut and does not necessarily favor the *Gazette*. The *Miller* court opined that, if the use could be seen as an implied endorsement of the commercial purpose of the magazine, then the relation of the subscription solicitation to the news aspects would disappear and the use would violate the individual's right of publicity. The court gave as an example of such an impermissible implied endorsement the use of the individual's name in the text of the solicitation.

- The Gazette's advertisement did use Jackson's nickname ("Action") in both its headline and text, but, it could be argued, not as referring to the individual but rather to the common usage of the word "action," as previously noted. Hence, it could be argued, the use of the word would not be seen as an endorsement by Jackson. Again, applicants should note that the facts are ambiguous and this point could go against the *Gazette*.
- Perceptive applicants might conclude that the question could ultimately be whether it is the *Gazette*'s intent or the public's perception that determines the answer to whether an endorsement was implied.

Applicants should conclude that, while there is an argument to be made that Jackson's claim is not viable because the subscription solicitation falls within the statute's affirmative defense for "news reporting," that result is not certain, and good arguments could be made the other way that could defeat reliance on the "news reporting" affirmative defense.

Applicant Identification

MULTISTATE PERFORMANCE TEST

In re City of Bluewater

**Read the instructions on the back cover.
Do not break the seal until you are told to do so.**

NATIONAL CONFERENCE OF BAR EXAMINERS

Instructions

The back cover of each test form contains the following instructions:

1. You will have 90 minutes to complete this session of the examination. This performance test is designed to evaluate your ability to handle a select number of legal authorities in the context of a factual problem involving a client.

2. The problem is set in the fictitious state of Franklin, in the fictitious Fifteenth Circuit of the United States. Columbia and Olympia are also fictitious states in the Fifteenth Circuit. In Franklin, the trial court of general jurisdiction is the District Court, the intermediate appellate court is the Court of Appeal, and the highest court is the Supreme Court.

3. You will have two kinds of materials with which to work: a File and a Library. The first document in the File is a memorandum containing the instructions for the task you are to complete. The other documents in the File contain factual information about your case and may include some facts that are not relevant.

4. The Library contains the legal authorities needed to complete the task and may also include some authorities that are not relevant. Any cases may be real, modified, or written solely for the purpose of this examination. If the cases appear familiar to you, do not assume that they are precisely the same as you have read before. Read them thoroughly, as if they all were new to you. You should assume that the cases were decided in the jurisdictions and on the dates shown. In citing cases from the Library, you may use abbreviations and omit page references.

5. Your response must be written in the answer book provided. If you are taking this examination on a laptop computer, your jurisdiction will provide you with specific instructions. In answering this performance test, you should concentrate on the materials in the File and Library. What you have learned in law school and elsewhere provides the general background for analyzing the problem; the File and Library provide the specific materials with which you must work.

6. Although there are no restrictions on how you apportion your time, you should be sure to allocate ample time (about 45 minutes) to reading and digesting the materials and to organizing your answer before you begin writing it. You may make notes anywhere in the test materials; blank pages are provided at the end of the booklet. You may not tear pages from the question booklet.

7. This performance test will be graded on your responsiveness to the instructions regarding the task you are to complete, which are given to you in the first memorandum in the File, and on the content, thoroughness, and organization of your response.

i

In re City of Bluewater

Contents

FILE

MEMORANDUM

To:	Applicant
From:	Amy Gonzalez, City Attorney
Date:	July 28, 2009
Re:	Water Dispute

The City of Bluewater is in the process of annexing a 500-acre tract of land located here in Bluewater County adjacent to the existing city limits. Annexation is the process by which land is brought into the City and made subject to its taxing and service authority. The tract is the site for the future Acadia Estates subdivision. Once the tract is annexed into the City and the subdivision is built, the City intends to provide water, sewer, fire, and other municipal services to the subdivision pursuant to the City's standard Service Plan and collect revenue for those services. The revenue will be important to our city finances.

However, we have just received a demand letter from the attorneys for Turquoise Water Supply Corporation (TWS) threatening to sue the City if the City proceeds with its plan to provide water and sewer services to the subdivision. TWS is a retail provider of water and sewer services in neighboring El Dorado County pursuant to a Certificate of Convenience and Necessity (CCN) issued by the Franklin Public Service Commission. It, too, wants to expand its revenue base.

TWS asserts that it has the exclusive right to provide water and sewer services to the subdivision under 7 U.S.C. § 1926(b), a federal statute that protects rural water and sewer suppliers that borrow money from the federal government to finance the costs of constructing their water and sewer facilities. TWS further asserts that the City is barred by state law from providing water and sewer services to the subdivision. If TWS were to litigate these issues and prevail, the City would still be able to annex Acadia Estates, but it would be prohibited from providing water and sewer services to the subdivision.

This issue has not been litigated in Franklin federal district court, but I have attached two cases—one from a federal district court in Columbia and one from the Fifteenth Circuit Court of

In re City of Bluewater

Appeals—which may be helpful in evaluating and responding to TWS's contentions. Our legal assistant has assembled some background information, also attached.

Please draft a letter responding to TWS's attorneys' demand letter. We need to
- address each of TWS's contentions, and
- persuasively set forth our position that the City has the exclusive right to provide water and sewer services to the Acadia Estates subdivision.

Do not prepare a separate statement of facts. You should thoroughly analyze and integrate both the facts and the applicable legal principles in making your arguments.

MEMORANDUM

To: Amy Gonzalez
From: Rhonda Hostetler, Legal Assistant
Date: July 27, 2009
Re: Preliminary Research—Dispute with Turquoise Water Supply Corporation

The following is a summary of my preliminary research findings regarding Turquoise Water Supply Corporation (TWS):

- TWS is a private, nonprofit water supply corporation formed in 1985 to "develop and provide an adequate rural water supply to serve and meet the needs of rural residents," pursuant to Franklin Code § 1324.

- Since its inception, TWS has provided water and sewer services to certain rural areas of neighboring El Dorado County pursuant to a Certificate of Convenience and Necessity obtained in 1987 from the Franklin Public Service Commission.

- In 1990, TWS obtained federal loans and grants under 7 U.S.C. § 1926(a) to finance improvements of its water system. Using part of those federal loans, TWS constructed a water plant, a sewage treatment plant, and related facilities capable of providing water and sewer services to approximately 150 homes in a rural pocket of El Dorado County called Ironwood (located five miles away from the site of Acadia Estates).

- In 1996, TWS installed a six-inch-diameter water line along Franklin Highway 45, about three miles from the Acadia Estates tract, and began serving an additional 100 homes along that corridor.

- As a result of these expansions over time, TWS currently provides water and sewer services to approximately 250 rural residents and a handful of small commercial enterprises.

- The current outstanding balance on TWS's 40-year federal loans is approximately $1.4 million.

I've also spoken with engineer Angie Halloway in the City's Public Works Division and Greg Carrigan in the City's Planning Division and confirmed the following:

- When completed, the Acadia Estates subdivision will require water and sewer capacity sufficient to serve the planned development, including water lines that are at least 12 inches in diameter.

- The City has existing water lines and a sewage treatment plant less than a quarter mile from the proposed site of the subdivision. Within a few months of annexation, the City will be able to construct a 12-inch-diameter water line from its existing water facilities as well as the necessary sewer lines to serve the Acadia Estates tract using funds borrowed from the federal government for water and sewer improvements, pursuant to 7 U.S.C. § 1926(a).

- The City's federal loans were taken out in 1997 and 2003 and are for the standard 40-year term. The estimated outstanding balance is at least $4 million.

- TWS's nearest water and sewer facilities are located approximately three miles from the proposed Acadia Estates subdivision. To serve the subdivision, TWS would have to construct significant additional infrastructure, including a water well, one or more water storage tanks, and related water distribution facilities, as well as a sewage treatment plant to handle the residential wastewater generated by the subdivision. The design and construction of such facilities would likely take a minimum of two years to complete.

Bowman & Bowman
Attorneys at Law
3200 Allen Parkway
Cypress, Franklin 33027

July 24, 2009

Amy Gonzalez, City Attorney's Office
1900 Phoenix Place
Bluewater, Franklin 33070

Re: Turquoise Water Supply—Acadia Estates

Dear Ms. Gonzalez:

We are writing on behalf of our client, Turquoise Water Supply Corporation, to inform you of TWS's exclusive right to provide water and sewer services to the proposed Acadia Estates subdivision. We have learned that the City intends to provide water and sewer services to the subdivision. The City has no right under state or federal law to serve the subdivision. TWS holds a Certificate of Convenience and Necessity ("CCN") and thus has the exclusive right to serve the quadrant of El Dorado County near the proposed Acadia Estates subdivision. On July 20, 2009, TWS filed an application with the Franklin Public Service Commission to expand its service area to include Acadia Estates, pursuant to Franklin Code § 457. Once the application is granted, TWS's service area will include Acadia Estates. We understand that the City intends to annex the Acadia Estates tract. Please be advised that even if the City proceeds with the proposed annexation, TWS will nonetheless have the federally protected right, pursuant to 7 U.S.C. § 1926(b), to provide water and sewer services to the Acadia Estates subdivision through its existing water line along Highway 45 and through an expansion of its sewage treatment facilities, which is already under way and scheduled to be completed by January 2011. *See Glenpool Utility Auth. v. Creek County Rural Water Dist.* (10th Cir. 1988).

In addition, the City is precluded under state law from serving the tract. *See* Franklin Code §§ 450(b) & 675. TWS demands that the City modify its proposed Service Plan for the Acadia Estates tract to exclude water and sewer services, as such services will be provided by TWS. If the City refuses to comply, TWS will pursue all available legal remedies, including the filing of a federal lawsuit.

Sincerely,

Henry Bowman

Henry Bowman, Esq.

5

BLUEWATER TRIBUNE

The voice of rural Franklin

July 14, 2009

500-Home Planned Community to Become Newest Addition to City of Bluewater

A.C. Homes, a well-established real estate developer in Franklin, is asking the City of Bluewater to annex a 500-acre tract of land just outside the city limits. The requested annexation will encompass a large planned residential development called Acadia Estates.

When completed, the Acadia Estates subdivision could offer as many as 500 single-family homes, two or more condominium and/or apartment complexes, and related commercial development. Acadia Estates will include a traditional grocery-store-anchored retail center, as well as a "town square" comprising small specialty stores. The planned community will include strategically located space for recreational activities and amenities, connecting bike and walking paths, and office space for residents who work at home.

"This planned development will create a fully integrated community where people can live, work, and play," said Andrew Christianson, founder and president of A.C. Homes.

Christianson declined to comment on the development's projected costs, but said homes would range in price from $200,000 to $500,000.

If approved, Acadia Estates would be A.C. Homes's first development in Bluewater County. Christianson said that he is still working with city officials to hammer out the details of the various phases of development entailed in constructing a planned community of this size. The city council will consider granting consent to the annexation of the 500 acres of land comprising Acadia Estates in early October. A.C. Homes is also in discussions with the Bluewater Independent School District about the possibility of building a school within the development.

Christianson said construction of the necessary water and sewer infrastructure could begin as early as January 2010 and be completed by April 2010, with home construction anticipated to commence shortly thereafter and be completed by December of that year, although the precise timing will depend on how quickly the necessary development agreements and construction-drawing approvals can be obtained.

6

DRAFT SERVICE PLAN FOR ANNEXED AREA
Annexation Case No. A2009, City of Bluewater, Franklin

ACREAGE TO BE ANNEXED: 500 acres [legal description omitted]

DATE OF ADOPTION OF ANNEXATION ORDINANCE: _____

SERVICES TO BE PROVIDED UPON ANNEXATION:

Municipal services to the acreage described above shall be furnished by or on behalf of the City of Bluewater, Franklin (the City), at the following levels and in accordance with the following schedule:

A. Police & Fire Services

The City will provide police and fire protection, as well as ambulance service, to the newly annexed tract at the same or a similar level of service now being provided to other areas of the City with similar topography, land use, and population.

B. Water Service

The proposed area of annexation does not have a certificate of convenience and necessity (CCN), and once the area is annexed, the City can serve it in the future. The area will be provided with water service within three months of the effective date of annexation.

C. Sewer Service

Once the area is annexed, the City will have the right to provide sewer service to the proposed area of annexation. Sewer service will be provided to the area within three months of the effective date of annexation.

D. Maintenance of Water and Sewer Facilities

Any and all water or sewer facilities owned or maintained by the City at the time of the proposed annexation shall continue to be maintained by the City. Any and all water or wastewater facilities which may be acquired subsequent to the annexation of the proposed area shall be maintained by the City to the extent of its ownership. The City Council believes that, with minor extensions to its existing water and sewer systems, the City can adequately accommodate the projected water and sewer needs in the area proposed to be annexed.

* * *

In re City of Bluewater

8

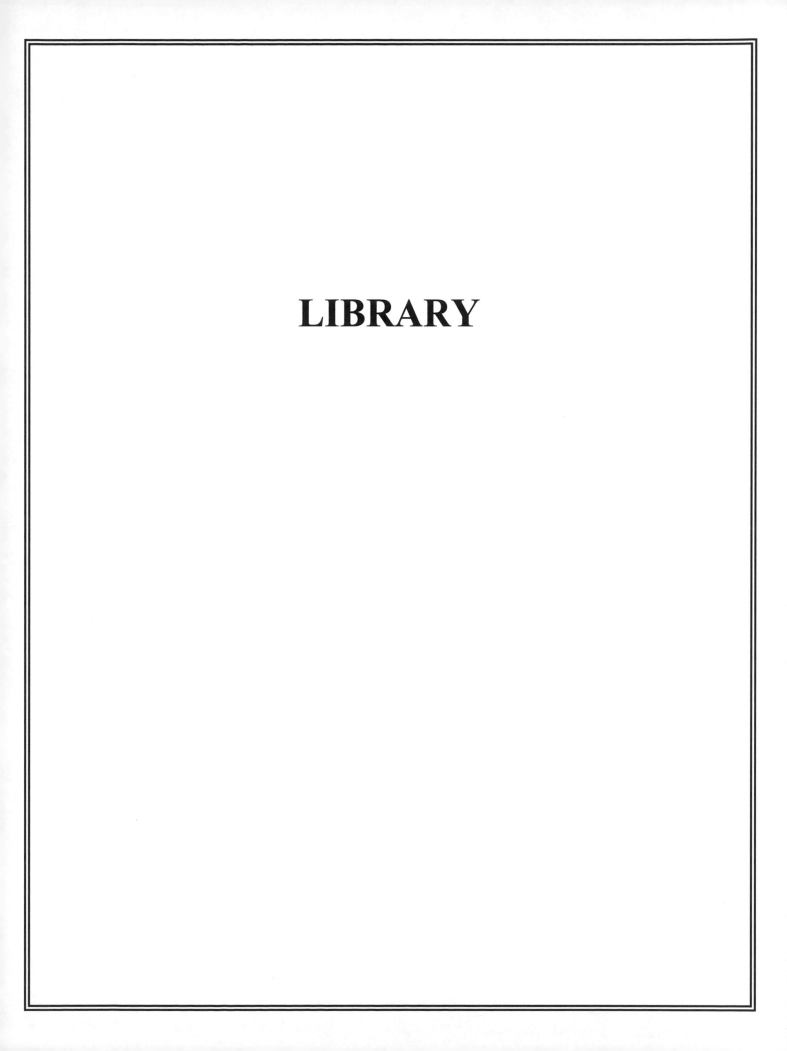

LIBRARY

UNITED STATES CODE
CONSOLIDATED FARM AND RURAL DEVELOPMENT ACT
7 United States Code § 1921 *et seq.*

*　*　*　*

7 U.S.C. § 1926 Water and Waste Facility Loans and Grants

(a) The Secretary [of Agriculture] is authorized to make or insure loans to associations, including corporations not operated for profit . . . and public and quasi-public agencies, to provide for the . . . development, use, and control of water and the installation or improvement of drainage or waste disposal facilities . . . for serving farmers, ranchers, farm tenants, farm laborers, and rural businesses, and other rural residents, and to furnish financial assistance or other aid in planning projects for such purposes.

(b) The service provided or made available through any association shall not be curtailed or limited by inclusion of the area served by such association within the boundaries of any municipal corporation or other public body . . . during the term of such loan . . . .

FRANKLIN CODE

Chapter 19. Water Utilities

§ 450. Certificate of Convenience and Necessity Required

(a) A water supply corporation may not render retail water or sewer service directly or indirectly to the public without first having obtained from the Franklin Public Service Commission a Certificate of Convenience and Necessity demonstrating that present or future public convenience and necessity require or will require such service.

(b) A person or entity may not construct facilities to provide water or sewer service or otherwise provide such service to an area for which a water supply corporation already holds a Certificate of Convenience and Necessity absent the certificate holder's written consent.

*　*　*　*

§ 453. Requirement to Provide Continuous and Adequate Service

Any water supply corporation that possesses a Certificate of Convenience and Necessity must provide continuous and adequate service to every customer whose use is within the certificated area.

*　*　*　*

§ 457. Amendments to Certificate of Convenience and Necessity

The holder of a Certificate of Convenience and Necessity may, by written application, seek authorization from the Franklin Public Service Commission to expand or modify the service area covered by the existing Certificate of Convenience and Necessity. In determining whether to amend a Certificate of Convenience and Necessity, the Commission shall ensure that the applicant possesses the capability to provide continuous and adequate service.

* * * *

§ 675. Provision of Water and Sewer Services Outside of City Limits

Any city that owns or operates a water supply or sewer system may extend the system into, and furnish water and sewer services to any person within, any territory adjacent to the city, and may install within that territory necessary equipment, provided, however, that the extension of a water supply or sewer system shall not enter into any territory served by the holder of a Certificate of Convenience and Necessity unless such certificate holder requests the extension of water or sewer services from the city.

In re City of Bluewater

Fountain Water Supply, Inc. v. City of Orangevale

United States District Court, Northern District of Columbia (2003)

Fountain Water Supply, Inc. (Fountain), is a nonprofit rural water association that provides retail water service to rural customers. It furnishes service in an area that is 18 miles by 36 miles surrounding the City of Orangevale (City). The City is a municipality that also operates a water supply system and supplies water to customers inside its city limits.

Fountain sued the City alleging violation of 7 U.S.C. § 1926(b). Section 1926(b) prevents municipalities from curtailing the service area of rural water service providers who are indebted to the United States. Fountain claims that the City has encroached on its service area by providing water to customers located approximately 1.5 miles outside of the City's limits.

The City has filed a motion for summary judgment, contending that under Columbia law, Fountain does not have the legal right to serve the four customers in the disputed area because it never secured an exclusive "service area" pursuant to Columbia law. The City further disputes the extent to which Fountain was providing or making available water services in the disputed area.

The questions before the court are (1) whether Fountain is entitled to the protections of § 1926(b), and (2) whether the City's conduct in providing water and sewer services to four customers within Fountain's service area violates or potentially violates the protections afforded to Fountain by the statute.

Although the answer to the first question involves primarily interpretation of federal statutes, the answer to the second question involves an interplay between federal law and state law. The court addresses first the question of whether Fountain is entitled to whatever protections § 1926(b) affords under the circumstances.

One portion of the Consolidated Farm and Rural Development Act (the "Act") authorizes the United States Secretary of Agriculture to make or insure loans to rural water associations to provide water service and other essential community facilities to farmers and other rural residents. 7 U.S.C. § 1926(a). The specific provision of § 1926 in question here is subsection (b), which protects a borrowing association, and consequently the federal government as a secured party on loans to the association, from municipal curtailment of the association's service area, which is the association's financial base. This provision not only encourages rural water development, but also provides the federal government greater security for its loans by ensuring that the borrower's financial base will not be lost to another provider.

To prevail on a claim that a municipality or other entity has violated § 1926(b), a rural water association must establish that (1) it is an "association" within the meaning of the Act, (2) it has a qualifying outstanding federal loan obligation, and (3) it has provided service or made service available in the disputed area. The parties do not dispute that Fountain is an "association" within the meaning of the Act. As of July 1, 1992, it had a qualifying outstanding federal loan in the amount of $2,030,000. Thus, the issue on appeal is whether Fountain has provided service or made service available in the disputed area.

The statute does not specifically define the terms "provided" and "made available." Therefore, the Court must look to state law governing the way in which a water association provides service to potential customers to determine whether a qualifying association has provided service or made service available to the disputed area.

Making service available has two components: (1) the legal right under state law to serve an area; and (2) the physical ability to serve an area, which is also known as the "pipes-in-the-ground" test. The state-law and pipes-in-the-ground tests are not independent tests, but prongs of a single test for "made service available."

a. Legal authority to serve

Columbia law requires a water service provider to obtain written authorization from the Columbia Public Service Commission prior to constructing or operating a water distribution system in a particular area. Columbia Water Code § 287.02.

The City concedes that Fountain sought and obtained the necessary approvals from the Columbia Public Service Commission to serve the area in dispute. However, the City asserts that it nonetheless has the exclusive right to serve customers within two miles of its city limits pursuant to Columbia Government Code § 357A, which provides that "water services shall not be provided within two miles of a city by a rural water district." That may well be. However, Fountain is not a rural water district but rather a rural water association. For public policy reasons, the Columbia legislature deemed that this rule should not apply to

14

rural water associations. Thus § 357A is inapplicable to the case at hand.

b. Physical ability to serve

Turning to the "pipes-in-the-ground" test, the court finds that genuine issues of material fact preclude summary judgment on the question of encroachment upon Fountain's protected service area. Although the record includes maps of where Fountain's and the City's respective water lines run, the court finds the information provided by the maps and other exhibits does not remove all doubts about whether Fountain was physically able to provide service when the City began serving the four customers in the disputed area.

Accordingly, the City's motion for summary judgment is denied, and this matter will proceed to trial on the issues stated above.

Klein Water Company v. City of Stewart

United States Court of Appeals for the Fifteenth Circuit (2005)

Klein Water Company is a Columbia nonprofit water supply corporation. Klein provides rural water service to a portion of Dodge County, Columbia, and is regulated by the Columbia Public Service Commission. Klein is financed, in part, by federal loans made pursuant to the Consolidated Farm and Rural Development Act, 7 U.S.C. § 1921 *et seq.* The City of Stewart (City) is a municipality that owns and operates its own water distribution system and sewage treatment plant. The City provides water to businesses and residences in and around its incorporated and annexed boundaries and also has a series of federal loans under 7 U.S.C. § 1926(a).

Klein unsuccessfully sought declaratory and injunctive relief against the City, alleging that the City had extended water distribution facilities over a portion of Klein's territory in violation of 7 U.S.C. § 1926(b). In some instances, Klein alleged, the City had annexed the areas in which it had begun providing water service into its City limits, and in other instances, it had simply begun providing water service to customers outside of the City limits and within Klein's service area.

On appeal, Klein contends that (1) § 1926(b) provides no statutory protection to municipalities and protects only rural water associations against encroachment by municipalities, and (2) application of a "pipes-in-the-ground" test is contrary to law and to the purpose of § 1926(b) where a rural water association has a defined territorial boundary.

We first review the district court's holding that Klein does not qualify for § 1926(b) protection. Section 1926(b) was enacted to encourage rural water development by protecting associations' customer bases and thereby safeguarding the financial viability of rural associations and the repayment of federal loans.

To prevail, Klein must show that it is entitled to § 1926(b) protection by establishing that (1) it is an "association" within the meaning of the Act, (2) it has a qualifying outstanding federal loan obligation, and (3) it has provided service or made service available in the disputed area. The district court held that both Klein and the City were "associations" for purposes of the Act, and that both parties had qualifying loans. The court held, however, that, unlike the City, Klein had not provided service or made service available in the disputed areas, and thus was not entitled to § 1926(b) protection.

Section 1926(a) indicates that the term "associations" includes "corporations not operated for profit . . . and public and quasi-public agencies . . . ." Congress intended that municipalities be viewed as "associations" for purposes of the Consolidated Farm and Rural Development Act. A city is a public agency. Further, as an entity created for the purpose of providing a public water supply to a designated geographic area, Klein is an "association" under the Act.

Neither party challenges the district court's finding that both parties have qualifying federal loans. Therefore, the central issue in determining whether Klein is entitled to § 1926(b) protection is whether it has provided service or has made service available within the disputed territories. The district court, in construing the term "made available," rejected Klein's argument that having a precisely drawn service area suffices to fulfill the third requirement for statutory protection. Rather, the court concluded that an association makes service available prior to the time a municipality begins providing service to a disputed area

when it actually has water lines adjacent to or within the area at issue before municipal service begins. The court found that Klein had not provided service or made service available under this test and therefore did not satisfy the third prerequisite for § 1926(b) protection, whereas the evidence established that the City had satisfied this test. On appeal, the parties agree that Klein has not actually provided water service in the disputed areas.

We look to the state law governing the way in which a water district must provide service to potential customers to determine whether Klein has provided service or made service available in the disputed areas. Under Columbia law, a water supply corporation must obtain written authorization from the Columbia Public Service Commission prior to constructing or operating a water distribution system in a particular area. Columbia Water Code § 287.02. Klein admits that it has not obtained written authorization from the Columbia Public Service Commission to construct facilities or to serve customers within portions of the disputed areas, and has had no requests for service from potential customers in the areas at issue. In our view, these concessions distinguish this case from other cases in which courts have upheld water districts' rights to § 1926(b) protection from municipal encroachment based on the fact that the water districts were actually and actively providing service, or clearly had made service available.

In *Glenpool Utility Authority v. Creek County Rural Water District* (10th Cir. 1988), the Tenth Circuit addressed the issue of whether a municipality had the exclusive right to provide water service to a newly annexed territory. There, the rural water association had been incorporated to provide water service within specific territorial limits, including an area known as Eden South, and had obtained a federal loan to construct its rural water system. The City subsequently annexed new territory into its city limits, including the area of Eden South. The City was aware at the time of annexation that the rural water district claimed the exclusive right to serve Eden South and that it was, in fact, providing water service there.

In *Glenpool*, the district court found that the rural water association had a water line that ran within 50 feet of the Eden South property and that any prospective user within the rural water association's territory could receive water service from the association simply by applying for service. Because the association would then be obligated to provide the service, the district

court found that it could and would provide water service to Eden South within a reasonable time of an application for such service.

On appeal, the Tenth Circuit concluded that the association had "made service available" to the disputed area by virtue of its lines adjacent to the property and its responsibilities to applicants within its territory. The court further held that § 1926(b) prohibited the City from using annexation of Eden South as a "springboard" for providing water service to the area and thereby curtailing or limiting the service made available by the association.

Glenpool teaches that the question of whether an association has made service available is resolved by answering whether the facilities exist on, or in proximity to, the location to be served. If an association does not already provide service, to be eligible for § 1926(b) protection the association must either (1) have existing water lines within or adjacent to the property claimed to be protected by § 1926(b) prior to the time an allegedly encroaching competitor begins providing service, or (2) be able to provide such service within a reasonable period of time.

Based on the location of Klein's distribution lines, which are located more than a mile from the disputed areas, there is no question that it had not made service available prior to the time that the City began providing service to the disputed properties. Nor has Klein demonstrated that it could make service available within a reasonable amount of time. Further, uncontroverted evidence demonstrates that (1) Klein had no facilities in the disputed areas or adjacent to the disputed areas (the nearest Klein facilities range from 1.2 to 1.4 miles away), (2) Klein did not have the financial wherewithal to extend its existing facilities to the disputed areas, and (3) even with sufficient funding it would take at least 12 months for Klein to construct the water lines necessary to serve residents in the disputed areas who were in need of water service at the time that the City began providing such service. The City, on the other hand, could meet residents' needs immediately.

Klein is unable to show that it has provided service or made service available in the disputed areas, and is therefore not entitled to the § 1926(b) protection which might otherwise have been available. The City was entitled to provide service to residents in the disputed areas.

In sum, an association's ability to serve is predicated on the existence of facilities within or adjacent to a disputed property. By its clear terms, § 1926(b) does not provide an automatic, exclusive right to serve, but rather provides protection only if certain conditions are met. Among those conditions is that an association has at least made service available or is capable of making service available within a reasonable period of time. In this case, Klein has not established its authorization to serve the disputed properties or its ability to provide the service. Not having facilities available, and not having requested authority from the Columbia Public Service Commission to construct such facilities, Klein has shown that its availability of service is merely speculative.

Affirmed.

POINT SHEET

In re City of Bluewater
DRAFTERS' POINT SHEET

In this performance test item, applicants are employed by the City Attorney's Office for the City of Bluewater, Franklin. The City has received a demand letter from the attorneys for Turquoise Water Supply Corporation (TWS), the provider of water and sewer services to rural residents in a neighboring county, asserting that TWS is entitled to provide water and sewer services to a 500-acre tract of land adjacent to Bluewater's existing city limits, which the City is in the process of annexing. Annexation is the process by which land is brought into the City and made subject to its taxing and service authority, thereby providing additional tax revenue for the City. The tract of land in dispute is the future site of the 500-home Acadia Estates subdivision, which is slated to be constructed over the next 18 months. Applicants' task is to prepare a persuasive letter responding to TWS's attorneys' contentions that TWS qualifies as a federally indebted "association" whose water and sewer service area is entitled to protection against municipal curtailment, pursuant to 7 U.S.C. § 1926(b) of the Consolidated Farm and Rural Development Act.

The File consists of the instructional memo from the supervising attorney, a memorandum of preliminary research findings, TWS's demand letter, a newspaper article, and the City's proposed Service Plan for the Acadia Estates subdivision. The Library contains excerpts from the Consolidated Farm and Rural Development Act (the Act), excerpts from the Franklin Code, and two cases bearing on the subject.

The following discussion covers all the points the drafters intended to raise in the problem. Applicants need not cover all of them to receive passing or even excellent grades. Grading is entirely within the discretion of the user jurisdictions.

I.   Overview

The task is to write a persuasive letter to TWS's attorneys responding to the assertions made in TWS's demand letter, specifically the claim that TWS has the exclusive right to provide water and sewer services to the proposed Acadia Estates subdivision. Applicants should base their arguments on the Consolidated Farm and Rural Development Act, 7 U.S.C. § 1921 *et seq.*, and the state statutes that govern a water supplier's right to serve a particular geographic area (Franklin Code Ch. 19 §§ 450(b) and 675).

23

Applicants are expected to exhibit a good deal of judgment in what the response letter says and how it says it, as there are no formatting instructions provided except that they are to respond to TWS's attorneys' arguments and argue that the City has the exclusive right to provide service to Acadia Estates. Applicants are instructed not to prepare a separate statement of facts. Their answers should be in the form of a letter to opposing counsel, using fairly formal language but not relying on legal jargon. They must "analyze and integrate" the facts and legal principles in formulating their arguments. This instruction from the supervising attorney is intended to require applicants to integrate the facts and the law, not merely recite them.

II.   The Statutes and Cases

The following points, which applicants should extract and use in formulating their arguments, emerge from the federal and state statutory provisions and the cases in the Library:

- The Consolidated Farm and Rural Development Act (the Act), 7 U.S.C. § 1921 *et seq.*, authorizes the Secretary of Agriculture to make or insure loans to nonprofit associations to provide water service and other related essential community facilities to farmers and other rural residents. 7 U.S.C. § 1926(a).

- The Act further protects a borrowing association, and consequently the United States government as a secured party on loans to the association, from municipal curtailment of the association's service area, which is the association's financial base.

  - Specifically, 7 U.S.C. § 1926(b) provides in relevant part:

    The service provided or made available through any association shall not be curtailed or limited by inclusion of the area served by such association within the boundaries of any municipal corporation or other public body . . . during the term of such loan.

- Because the Act does not specifically define the terms "provided" and "made available," courts must look to the state law governing the way in which a qualifying association provides water service to potential customers to determine whether that entity has provided service or made service available to the disputed area.

  - Making service available has two components: (1) the legal right under state law to serve an area; and (2) the physical ability to serve an area, which is also known as the "pipes-in-the-ground" test. The state-law and pipes-in-the-ground tests are not independent tests, but prongs of a single test for "made service available." *Fountain Water Supply, Inc. v. City of Orangevale* (N. Dist. of Columbia 2003).

24

- **Legal Right:** In Franklin, a water supply corporation must hold a Certificate of Convenience and Necessity (CCN) issued by the Franklin Public Service Commission in order to have the legal right to provide water and sewer services to a particular geographic area. Franklin Code Ch. 19 § 450. Once granted, the CCN imposes an obligation upon the holder to provide "continuous and adequate service to every customer" within the certificated area. *Id.* § 453.

  - A CCN may be amended by written application approved by the Commission, upon a finding by the Commission that the applicant "possesses the capability to provide continuous and adequate service." *Id.* § 457.

  - While a city need not obtain a CCN to provide service outside its boundaries, it is prohibited from providing service to an area for which a water supply corporation already holds a CCN, absent the certificate holder's written consent. *Id.* § 675.

- **Physical Ability to Serve ("pipes in the ground"):** Whether an association has made service available is also contingent on the existence of facilities in, or in proximity to, the location to be served. *Klein Water Co. v. City of Stewart* (15th Cir. 2005). If an association does not already have service in existence, the association must either have existing water lines within or adjacent to the property claimed to be protected by § 1926(b) prior to the time an allegedly encroaching association begins providing service, or be able to provide such service within a reasonable period of time, in order to be eligible for protection. *Id.*

III. Arguments to Be Addressed in Response Letter

In its demand letter, TWS contends that it is entitled to protection under 7 U.S.C. § 1926(b) and that, in any event, under state law (specifically, Franklin Code Ch. 19 §§ 450(b) & 675) the City is prohibited from providing water and sewer services to the subdivision. Each contention will be addressed in turn.

A. TWS's Federal Argument under 7 U.S.C. § 1926(b)

- In order to prevail on its claim that the City's plan to provide water and sewer services to Acadia Estates violates § 1926(b), TWS must establish the following: (1) it is an "association" within the meaning of the Act, (2) it has a qualifying outstanding federal loan

  obligation, and (3) it has provided service or made service available in the disputed area. *Fountain; Klein.*

25

(1) "Association" Requirement

- Here, as in *Fountain Water Supply*, it appears that TWS is an "association" within the meaning of the Act because it is a nonprofit water supply corporation organized to provide rural water and sewer services pursuant to Franklin Code § 1324 (cited in Preliminary Research Memorandum).

- However, the City also qualifies as an "association" under § 1926(b) because § 1926(b), by its terms, applies not only to private nonprofit corporations such as TWS but also to "public and quasi-public agencies" such as the City. *See Klein.*

- Moreover, the "association" requirement is just the first of three prerequisites for entitlement to § 1926(b) protection.

(2) Federal Indebtedness Requirement

- TWS is currently indebted to the federal government for loans taken out in 1990, to the tune of $1.4 million. (Preliminary Research Memorandum.)

- However, the City is also federally indebted by virtue of having obtained federal loans in 1997 and 2003 to finance water and sewer improvements. The amount of the City's present indebtedness is estimated to be at least $4 million and thus, under *Klein*, the City qualifies for § 1926(b) protection as well. (Preliminary Research Memorandum.)

(3) "Made Service Available" Requirement

- The core issue is whether TWS and/or the City have provided service or made service available in the disputed area.
- As set forth above, the Act does not define the terms "provided" and "made available." However, the cases provide considerable guidance on this issue and identify a two-prong test for determining whether service has been "provided" or "made available": (1) the legal right under state law to serve an area, and (2) the physical ability to serve an area ("pipes in the ground"). *Fountain*; *Klein*.

(a) State-Law Prong

- Although TWS contends that it has the right under Franklin law to provide service to the Acadia Estates subdivision, in fact it does not have that right at this time. Its application under Franklin Code Ch. 19 § 457 to expand the territory covered by its CCN to include Acadia Estates is pending before the Franklin Public Service Commission. (Demand letter.) Thus, TWS's present legal right to provide water and sewer services is limited to those portions of El Dorado County covered by its existing CCN. No portion of its existing CCN extends into Bluewater County.

    - Moreover, it is questionable whether TWS will even be able to secure the requested CCN amendment, notwithstanding its attorneys' posturing to the contrary in the demand letter, because amendment of a CCN is contingent upon being able to provide "continuous and adequate service." Franklin Code Ch. 19 § 457. As discussed below, it appears that TWS is not able to provide such service to Acadia Estates, nor will it be able to do so within a reasonable amount of time.

    - Thus, like the water association in *Klein*, TWS has not obtained the necessary state agency authorization to provide service to the disputed area.

- The City, in contrast, has the present legal right to provide service to the tract pursuant to Franklin Code Ch. 19 § 675, which authorizes a city that owns or operates a water supply or sewer system to "extend the system into, and furnish water and sewer services to any person within, any territory adjacent to the city," provided that the territory is not already served by the holder of a CCN.

    - The Acadia Estates tract is located "adjacent to" Bluewater's existing city limits and the tract is not being served by any CCN holder.

    - Note, however, that there is no Franklin equivalent of the Columbia statute that precludes rural water districts from providing water service within a

27

two-mile zone of a city. *Cf. Fountain* (discussing Columbia Government Code § 357A).

- Any attempt by an applicant to apply the Columbia two-mile-zone statute to the Acadia Estates dispute, or to assert the existence of an analogous Franklin statute, would be misguided.

- Thus, applying the state-law component of the "made service available" requirement to the facts presented in this item, the City is the only party that actually has a present right to serve the tract.

- Furthermore, even if TWS were to secure an amendment to its CCN before the City completes its annexation of the Acadia Estates tract, this alone would not be dispositive because whether an association has "made service available" involves *both* whether an association has the legal right to provide such service, as determined by applicable state law, *and* whether service is physically available by virtue of the association having water lines ("pipes in the ground") adjacent to the disputed property. *Fountain.*

(b) "Pipes-in-the-Ground" Prong

- The "pipes-in-the-ground" requirement involves an assessment of whether an association has the *physical* ability to actually supply water to a disputed area. *Fountain.*

- Whether an association has made service available depends on the existence of facilities in, or in proximity to, the location to be served. "If an association does not already provide service, to be eligible for § 1926(b) protection the association must either (1) have existing water lines within or adjacent to the property claimed to be protected by § 1926(b) prior to the time an allegedly encroaching competitor begins providing service, or (2) be able to provide such service within a reasonable period of time." *Klein* (citing *Glenpool Utility Auth. v. Creek County Rural Water Dist.* (10th Cir. 1988)).

28

- Important considerations are whether the federally indebted association is already providing water service to the disputed tract and whether the association has had any requests for service from potential customers in the area at issue. *Klein.*

- Here, as in *Klein*, TWS cannot overcome any of these hurdles. Its nearest existing facilities are located three miles from the proposed Acadia Estates subdivision and are inadequate to meet the needs of the subdivision.

  - TWS currently provides water and sewer services to only 250 residential customers in rural El Dorado County and a handful of commercial enterprises. Thus, its existing service area is only one-half the size of the future 500-home Acadia Estates subdivision.

    - Furthermore, TWS's existing six-inch-diameter water line along Highway 45 is inadequate to meet the needs of the subdivision, which requires water lines that are at least 12 inches in diameter. (Preliminary Research Memorandum.)

- Thus, unlike the association in the *Glenpool* case cited in the TWS demand letter (and distinguished by the court in *Klein*), TWS cannot argue that it has adequate water lines adjacent to the disputed area or that it is currently providing service to customers in the disputed area.

- Further, similar to the association in *Klein*, TWS has not received any requests for service from any potential customers in the disputed area.

- Finally, TWS cannot provide service within a reasonable amount of time.

  - According to the *Bluewater Tribune* article, construction of the necessary water and sewer infrastructure for Acadia Estates is slated to begin as early as January 2010 and to be completed by April 2010, with home construction to commence shortly thereafter and be completed by December of that year.

  - The City's technical personnel estimate that it would take a minimum of two years for TWS to design and construct the improvements and expansions needed to serve Acadia Estates, assuming TWS has sufficient funds to do so (which is

29

questionable, since TWS has had to borrow money from the federal government to finance prior expansions). (Preliminary Research Memorandum.)

- TWS's own attorneys concede that it would take 18 months (until January 2011) for TWS to construct the new sewage treatment plant needed to serve the subdivision. (Demand letter.)

- Even giving TWS the benefit of the doubt and assuming the accuracy of its own 18-month time frame, this would mean that TWS would not be capable of providing the necessary water and sewer infrastructure to Acadia Estates until a month after the subdivision is anticipated to be fully constructed.

- Thus, it is clear that TWS would not be able to provide service within the proposed development schedule, which contemplates completion of water and sewer lines by April 2010.

- Thus, like the association in *Klein*, TWS is unable to show that it has provided service or made service available in the disputed area, and it is therefore not entitled to the § 1926(b) protection that might otherwise have been available.

- In contrast, the City can provide service within a reasonable period of time and thus satisfy the "pipes-in-the-ground" test.

  - According to the information provided by the City's Planning and Public Works Divisions, the City has existing water and sewer facilities less than a quarter mile from the proposed site of the subdivision. (Preliminary Research Memorandum.)

  - The City's Service Plan further indicates that with "minor extensions to its existing water and sewer system," the City can accommodate the projected needs of the subdivision and make services available within three months after annexing the tract. This would allow development of the subdivision to proceed on schedule, with home construction being completed by approximately December 2010. (Draft Service Plan; *see also*

B. TWS's State-Law Arguments under Franklin Code Ch. 19 §§ 450(b) and 675

- TWS's demand letter cites Ch. 19 §§ 450(b) and 675 of the Franklin Code for the proposition that the City is prohibited under state law from providing water and sewer services to the Acadia Estates subdivision.

- Section § 450(b) prohibits the provision of water and sewer services as well as the construction of facilities for such services to areas already covered by another entity's existing CCN, absent the certificate holder's written consent.

- Similarly, § 675 prevents a city from serving adjacent areas outside of city limits that are serviced by a CCN holder unless the CCN holder requests the extension of water or sewer services from the city.

- TWS's state-law arguments rest on the presumption that TWS will, in fact, be granted an amendment to its CCN.

- For the reasons set forth above, namely TWS's inability to provide continuous and adequate service to the Acadia Estates subdivision as required by § 457, these arguments must fail.

IV.   Conclusion

By its clear terms, § 1926(b) does not provide an automatic, exclusive right to serve, but rather provides protection only if certain conditions are met. *Klein.* Among those conditions is that an association has made service available or is capable of making service available within a reasonable period of time. *Id.* In this case, as in *Klein,* TWS has not established a legal right under state law to serve Acadia Estates or the ability to actually provide service now or within a reasonable amount of time. Not having facilities available, and not having obtained the necessary CCN amendment to serve the Acadia Estates subdivision, TWS is not entitled to protection under federal or state law. Indeed, TWS may well be precluded by those very same statutes from attempting to interfere with the City's plans to serve the subdivision.

NOTES

Applicant Identification

Phoenix Corporation v. Biogenesis, Inc.

Read the instructions on the back cover.
Do not break the seal until you are told to do so.

NATIONAL CONFERENCE OF BAR EXAMINERS

INSTRUCTIONS

1. You will have 90 minutes to complete this session of the examination. This performance test is designed to evaluate your ability to handle a select number of legal authorities in the context of a factual problem involving a client.

2. The problem is set in the fictitious state of Franklin, in the fictitious Fifteenth Circuit of the United States. Columbia and Olympia are also fictitious states in the Fifteenth Circuit. In Franklin, the trial court of general jurisdiction is the District Court, the intermediate appellate court is the Court of Appeal, and the highest court is the Supreme Court.

3. You will have two kinds of materials with which to work: a File and a Library. The first document in the File is a memorandum containing the instructions for the task you are to complete. The other documents in the File contain factual information about your case and may include some facts that are not relevant.

4. The Library contains the legal authorities needed to complete the task and may also include some authorities that are not relevant. Any cases may be real, modified, or written solely for the purpose of this examination. If the cases appear familiar to you, do not assume that they are precisely the same as you have read before. Read them thoroughly, as if they all were new to you. You should assume that the cases were decided in the jurisdictions and on the dates shown. In citing cases from the Library, you may use abbreviations and omit page references.

5. Your response must be written in the answer book provided. If you are taking this examination on a laptop computer, your jurisdiction will provide you with specific instructions. In answering this performance test, you should concentrate on the materials in the File and Library. What you have learned in law school and elsewhere provides the general background for analyzing the problem; the File and Library provide the specific materials with which you must work.

6. Although there are no restrictions on how you apportion your time, you should be sure to allocate ample time (about 45 minutes) to reading and digesting the materials and to organizing your answer before you begin writing it. You may make notes anywhere in the test materials; blank pages are provided at the end of the booklet. You may not tear pages from the question booklet.

7. This performance test will be graded on your responsiveness to the instructions regarding the task you are to complete, which are given to you in the first memorandum in the File, and on the content, thoroughness, and organization of your response.

Contents

FILE

FORBES, BURDICK & WASHINGTON LLP

777 Fifth Avenue
Lakewood City, Franklin 33905

<u>MEMORANDUM</u>

To: Applicant

From: Ann Buckner

Date: February 24, 2009

Subject: *Phoenix Corporation v. Biogenesis, Inc.*

Yesterday, we were retained by the law firm of Amberg & Lewis LLP to consult on a motion for disqualification filed against it.

Amberg & Lewis represents Biogenesis, Inc., in a breach-of-contract action brought by Phoenix Corporation seeking $80 million in damages. The lawsuit has been winding its way through state court for almost six years. Phoenix is represented by the Collins Law Firm. There have been extensive discovery, motion practice, and several interlocutory appeals over the years, but the matter is now set for jury trial in a month and is expected to last six weeks. Two weeks ago, however, Phoenix filed a disqualification motion after Amberg & Lewis obtained one of Phoenix's attorney-client privileged documents—a letter from Phoenix's former president to one of its attorneys. Yesterday, I interviewed Carole Ravel, an Amberg & Lewis partner. During the interview, I learned some background facts; I also obtained a copy of the letter and Phoenix's brief in support of its disqualification motion.

Please prepare a memorandum evaluating the merits of Phoenix's argument for Amberg & Lewis's disqualification, bringing to bear the applicable legal authorities and the relevant facts as described to me by Ms. Ravel. Do not draft a separate statement of facts, but instead use the facts as appropriate in conducting your evaluation.

1

Buckner: Good to see you, Carole.

Ravel: Good to see you too, Ann. Thanks for seeing me on such short notice.

Buckner: My pleasure. What's the problem?

Ravel: The problem is a motion for disqualification. Here's the supporting brief.

Buckner: Thanks. Let me take a quick look. I'm unacquainted with the science, but the law is familiar. How can I help?

Ravel: To be candid, we've made a few mistakes, and I thought it would be prudent to consult with someone like you with substantial experience in representing lawyers in professional liability and ethics matters.

Buckner: Tell me what happened.

Ravel: Sure. Six years ago, Phoenix Corporation sued Biogenesis for breach of contract in state court, seeking about $80 million in damages. Phoenix is a medical research company; the Collins Law Firm represents it. Our client Biogenesis is one of the largest biotechnology companies in the world. Phoenix claims that Biogenesis breached a contract they entered into in 1978. There's a lot about this case that's enormously complicated and technical—all that science that you said you're unacquainted with—but the dispute is fairly simple. Under the agreement, Phoenix granted a license to Biogenesis to use a process that Phoenix invented for genetically engineering human proteins. In exchange, Biogenesis was obliged to pay Phoenix royalties on sales of certain categories of pharmaceuticals that were made using the licensed engineering process. Here is the dispute: While Biogenesis has taken the position that its royalty obligation is limited to the categories of pharmaceuticals specified, Phoenix claims that it extends to other categories of pharmaceuticals as well. If the jury agrees with Biogenesis, it owes nothing more. If the jury agrees with Phoenix, Biogenesis owes about $80 million beyond what it has already paid in royalties.

Buckner: That's how the brief sums it up, too.

Ravel:	Right. The factual background and procedur al history set out in the brief are accurate—but of course we disagree with Phoenix's argument about Biogenesis's royalty obligation.
Buckner:	Fine. But what about this Phoenix letter that's allegedly protected by the attorney-client privilege?
Ravel:	Here it is, a letter to Peter Horvitz, a Collins partner, from Gordon Schetina, who was then Phoenix's president.
Buckner:	Thanks. It certainly looks privileged.
Ravel:	It is. I can't deny it. But it's im portant. Let me go back to the 1978 agreem ent. Discovery in Phoenix's breach-of-cont ract action has established to our satisfaction that, by their conduct fro m 1978 to 1998, Biogenesis and Phoenix revealed that they understood that B iogenesis's royalty obligation was lim ited to the categories of pharmaceuticals s pecified in the agreement. During that period, Biogenesis made a lot of money and paid Phoenix a great deal in royalties. It was only in 1998 that Phoenix began to clai m that Biogenesis 's royalty obligation extended to other categories of pharmaceuticals—when it saw how much more in royalties it could obtain and became greedy to get them.
Buckner:	And the Schetina letter . . .
Ravel:	And the Schetina letter amounts to an admission by Phoenix that Biogenesis was correct in its understanding of its limited royalty obligation.
Buckner:	So how did you get it?
Ravel:	Phoenix's lawyers assum e that the Schetina letter was disclosed to us inadvertently during discovery, but they're wrong. The letter arrived on February 2, 2009, by itself, in an envelope with the Collins Law Firm's return address. My assistant opened the envelope and discovered the letter all by itself, with a note reading "From a 'friend' at the Collins Law Firm."
Buckner:	Do you know who the "friend" was?
Ravel:	No. But it's not hard to guess. Collins is in the process of laying off staff in an effort to increase profits. The letter was obviously sent by a disgruntled employee.
Buckner:	That makes sense. But what happened next?

3

Ravel:	When the letter arrived, my team and I were in full trial-preparation mode. Of course, I recognized that the letter appeared privileged on its face; it's a classic confidential communication from a client to an attorney. In our eyes, the letter was a smoking gun. It made our case and we wanted to use it.
Buckner:	So what happened?
Ravel:	We were pretty sure that we were within the ethical rules. But that same day, two of the associates on my team went out for lunch. As they were discussing the impact of the Schetina letter in what turned out to be too much detail, a man at a neighboring table asked whether they knew who he was. They said no, and the man said he was Peter Horvitz and stormed out. Horvitz called me within minutes, and he was furious. He demanded return of the letter and I refused. A few days later, he filed the disqualification motion.
Buckner:	I see. And precisely what is it you'd like us to do for you?
Ravel:	Ann, I'd like you to evaluate the merits of Phoenix's argument that we should be disqualified. Trial is only a month away, and Biogenesis would have to incur tremendous costs if it were forced to substitute new attorneys if we were disqualified. And let's be candid, we've been charged with a violation of an ethical obligation and might face some exposure as a consequence.
Buckner:	I understand, Carole. Let me do some research, and I'll get back to you.
Ravel:	Thanks so much.

PHOENIX CORPORATION
1500 Rosa Road
Lakewood City, Franklin 33905

January 2, 1998

CONFIDENTIAL

Peter Horvitz, Esq.
Collins Law Firm
9700 Laurel Boulevard
Lakewood City, Franklin 33905

Dear Peter:

I am writing with some questions I'd like you to consider before our meeting next Tuesday so that I can get your legal advice on a matter I think is important. I have always understood our agreement with Biogenesis to require it to pay royalties on specified categories of pharmaceuticals. I learned recently how much money Biogenesis is making from other categories of pharmaceuticals. Why can't we get a share of that? Can't we interpret the agreement to require Biogenesis to pay royalties on other categories, not only the specified ones? Let me know your thoughts when we meet.

Very   truly yours,

Gordon Schetina

Gordon Schetina
President

IN THE DISTRICT COURT OF THE STATE OF FRANKLIN
FOR THE COUNTY OF LANCASTER

PHOENIX CORPORATION,	)	**No. Civ. 041033**
	)	
Plaintiff,	)	**PLAINTIFF'S BRIEF IN SUPPORT OF**
	)	**MOTION TO DISQUALIFY COUNSEL**
v.	)	**FOR DEFENDANT**
	)	
BIOGENESIS, INC.,	)	
	)	
Defendant.	)	
	)	

I.   Introduction

The rule governing this m   otion is plai n: A trial court m   ay—and, indeed, m ust—disqualify an attorney who has violated an   ethical obligation by his or her handling of an opposing party's attorney-client privileged m aterial and has thereby threat ened that party with incurable prejudice. Just as plain is the result th at the rule co mpels here: Defendant's attorneys obtained one of plaintiff's attorney-client   privileged documents evidently by inadvertent disclosure. In violation of their ethical obligation, they chose to examine the document, failed to notify plaintiff's attorneys, and then refused to return the docum ent at th e latter's dem and. By acting as they did, they have threatened plain   tiff with incurable prejudice. Since   this Court cannot otherwise prevent this prejudice, it must disqualify them to guarantee plaintiff a fair trial.

II.   Factual Background and Procedural History

In 1977, P hoenix Corporation, a m edical research company, invented a process for genetically engineering human proteins—a process essential to the developm ent of entirely new categories of pharm aceuticals capable of m anaging or curing the m ost serious conditions and diseases afflicting human beings, including diabetes and cancer.

In 1978, Phoenix entered into an agreement with Biogenesis, Inc., one of the pioneers in the field of biotechnology: Phoe   nix licensed its invention to   Biogenesis, and Biogenesis obligated itself to pay Phoenix royalties on its sales of various categories of pharmaceuticals.

Between 1979 and 1997, Biogenesis produced dozens of pharm aceuticals and generated billions of dollars in revenue as a result of their sale. To be sure, Biogenesis paid Phoenix substantial royalties—but, as it turns out, far less than it was obligated to.

In 1998, Phoenix learned that Bioge nesis had not been paying r oyalties on its sales of all the categories of pharm aceuticals in questio n, but only categories specified in the 1978 agreement. For the f irst time, Biogenesis s tated its positio n that the a greement so lim ited its obligation. Phoenix rejected any such limitation.

Between 1999 and 2002, Phoenix attem pted to resolve its dispute with Biogenesis. Each and every one of its efforts, however, proved unsuccessful.

In 2003, P hoenix brought this action agai nst Biogenesis for br each of the 1978 agreement, seeking $80 million in dam ages for royalties Biogenesis owed but f ailed to pay. Between 2003 and 2009, Phoenix and Biogenesis have been engaged in extensive discovery and motion practice and in several interl ocutory appeals as they have prep ared for a jury trial, set to begin on March 30, 2009, and expected to last six weeks.

On February 2, 2009, P hoenix learned, fortuitously, that Biogen esis's attorneys, Amberg & Lewis LLP, had obtained a docum ent evidently through inadvertent di sclosure by Phoenix's attorneys, the Collins La w Firm, in the course of discovery. On its face, the docum ent showed itself to b e protected by the attorney-client privilege, reflecting a conf idential communication from Phoenix, by its then president Gordon Schetin a, to one of its attorneys, Peter Horvitz, seeking legal advice, and clearly the docu ment was not intended for the Am berg firm. Nevertheless, the Amberg firm failed to notify Collins about its receipt of the Schetina letter. A s soon as it learned what had transpired, Collins instructed the Amberg firm to return the letter, but the Amberg firm refused.

III.   Argument

A.   This Court Should Disqualify Amberg & Lewis from Representing Biogenesis Because It Has Violated an Ethical Obligation Threatening Phoenix with Incurable Prejudice in Its Handling of Phoenix's Attorney-Client Privileged Document.

The law applicable to Phoenix's motion to disqualify Amberg & Lewis from representing Biogenesis in this action is clear.

7

A trial court may, in the exercise of its inherent power, disqualify an attorney in the interests of justice. *Indigo v. Luna Motors Corp.* (Fr. Ct. App. 1998). The court may—and, indeed, must—disqualify an attorney who has violated an ethical obligation by his or her handling of an opposing party's attorney-client privileged material and has thereby threatened that party with incurable prejudice. *Id.* Although the party represented by the disqualified attorney may be said to enjoy an "important right" to representation by an attorney of its own choosing, any such "right" "must yield to ethical considerations that affect the fundamental principles of our judicial process." *Id.* As the court said, "The paramount concern, however, must be to preserve public trust in the scrupulous administration of justice and the integrity of the bar." *Id.*

As will be demonstrated, the law compels the disqualification of Amberg & Lewis.

1. Phoenix's Document Is Protected by the Attorney-Client Privilege.

To begin with, the Schetina letter is protected by the attorney-client privilege. Under Franklin Evidence Code § 954, the "client . . . has a privilege to refuse to disclose, and to prevent another from disclosing, a confidential communication between client and attorney. . . ." On its face, the Schetina letter reflects a confidential communication from Phoenix's then president, Schetina, to one of its attorneys, Horvitz, seeking legal advice.

2. Amberg & Lewis Has Violated an Ethical Obligation.

Next, Amberg & Lewis has violated an ethical obligation by handling the Schetina letter as it did. In the face of the inadvertent disclosure of attorney-client privileged material, such as evidently occurred in this case, the ethical obligation is plain under Franklin Rule of Professional Conduct 4.4: "An attorney who receives a document relating to the representation of the attorney's client and knows or reasonably should know that the document was inadvertently sent shall promptly notify the sender."

Because on its face the Schetina letter reflects a confidential communication from Phoenix's then president, Schetina, to its attorney, Horvitz, seeking legal advice, and is therefore protected by the attorney-client privilege, Amberg & Lewis should surely have known that the letter was not intended for it. The Amberg firm was at the very least obligated to notify Collins that it had received the letter. It should also have refrained from examining the letter, and should have abided by our instructions. On each point, the Amberg firm acted to the contrary, choosing to examine the letter, failing to notify Collins, and then refusing to return it at Collins's demand.

8

Even if it should turn out that Amberg & Lewis obtained the Schetina letter as a result of unauthorized disclosure as opposed to inadvertent disclosure, the outcome would be the same. In *Mead v. Conley Machinery Co.* (Fr. Ct. App. 1999) the Court of Appeal imposed an ethical obligation similar to that of Rule 4.4 to govern cases of unauthorized disclosure. It follows that the misconduct of the Amberg firm, as described above, would amount to an ethical violation if the letter's disclosure were unauthorized and not inadvertent.

3.   Amberg & Lewis Has Threatened Phoenix with Incurable Prejudice.

Finally, by its unethical actions, Amberg & Lewis has threatened Phoenix with incurable prejudice. The Schetina letter could well prejudice the jury in the midst of a long and complex trial, especially if it were cleverly exploited by Biogenesis. Whether or not any *direct* harm could be prevented by the exclusion of the letter from evidence—which Phoenix intends to seek in the coming days—the *indirect* harm that might arise from its use in trial preparation cannot be dealt with so simply: The bell has been rung, and can hardly be unrung, except by disqualification of Amberg & Lewis—an action that is necessary in order to guarantee Phoenix a fair trial.

Even if it should turn out that Amberg & Lewis obtained the Schetina letter by *unauthorized* disclosure as opposed to *inadvertent* disclosure, the result would not change. It is true that in *Mead v. Conley Machinery Co.*, the Court of Appeal suggested in a footnote that, in cases of unauthorized disclosure, the "threat of 'incurable prejudice'. . . is neither a necessary nor a sufficient condition for disqualification." But that suggestion is mere dictum, inasmuch as *Mead* did not involve the threat of *any* prejudice, incurable or otherwise.

IV.   Conclusion

For the reasons stated above, this Court should grant Phoenix's motion and disqualify Amberg & Lewis from representing Biogenesis in this action.

Respectfully submitted,

Date: February 9, 2009

Kimberly Block

Kimberly Block
COLLINS LAW FIRM LLP
Attorneys for Plaintiff Phoenix Corporation

10

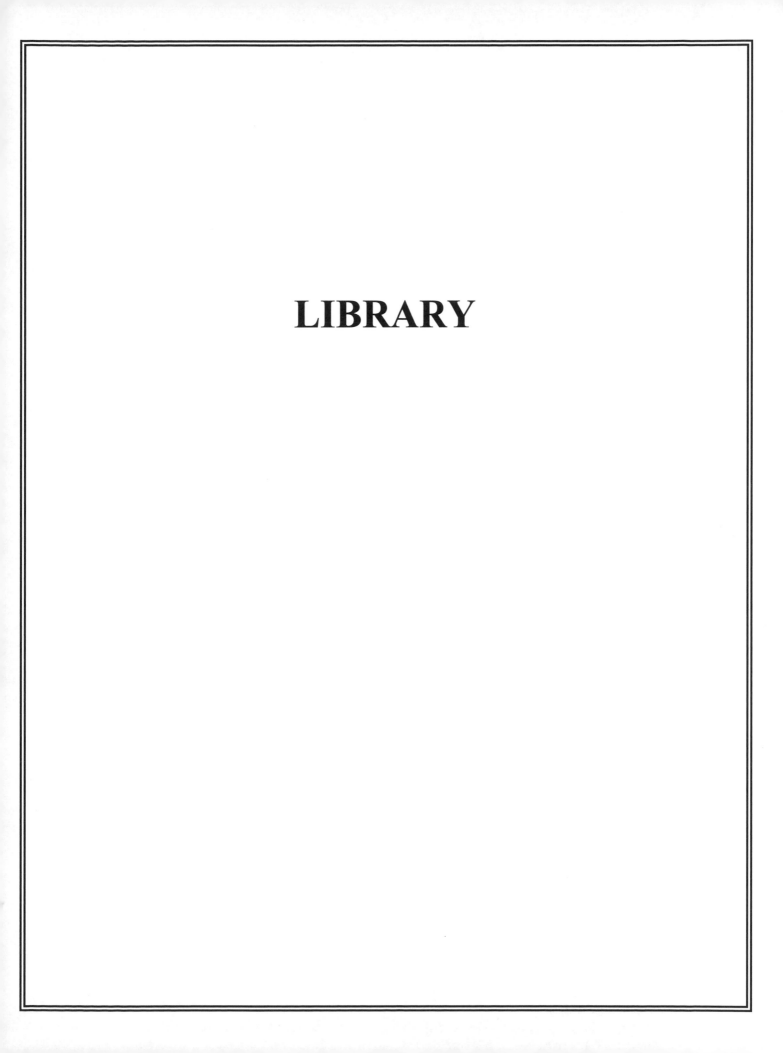

LIBRARY

RULE 4.4 OF THE FRANKLIN RULES OF PROFESSIONAL CONDUCT

Rule 4.4. Inadvertent disclosure of attorney-client document

An attorney who receives a document relating to the representation of the attorney's client and knows or reasonably should know that the document was inadvertently sent shall promptly notify the sender.

HISTORY

Adopted by the Franklin Supreme Court, effective July 1, 2002.

COMMENT

[1] Rule 4.4, which was adopted by the Franklin Supreme Court in 2002 in response to *Indigo v. Luna Motors Corp.* (Fr. Ct. App. 1998), recognizes that attorneys sometimes receive documents that were mistakenly sent or produced by opposing parties or their attorneys. If an attorney knows or reasonably should know that such a document was sent inadvertently, then this rule requires the attorney, whether or not the document is protected by the attorney-client privilege, to promptly notify the sender in order to permit that person to take protective measures.

[2] Rule 4.4 provides that if an attorney receives a document the attorney should know was sent inadvertently, he or she must promptly notify the sender, but need do no more. *Indigo v. Luna Motors Corp.*, which predated this rule, concluded that the receiving attorney not only had to notify the sender (as this rule would later require), albeit only as to a document protected by the attorney-client privilege, but also had to resist the temptation to examine the document, and had to await the sender's instructions about what to do. In so concluding, *Indigo v. Luna Motors Corp.* conflicted with this rule and, ultimately, with the intent of the Franklin Supreme Court in adopting it.

[3] Rule 4.4 does not address an attorney's receipt of a document sent without authorization, as was the case in *Mead v. Conley Machinery Co.* (Fr. Ct. App. 1999). Neither does any other rule.

13

Mead v. Conley Machinery Co., which also predated this rule, concluded that the receiving attorney should review the document—there, an attorney-client privileged document—only to the extent necessary to determine how to proceed, notify the opposing attorney, and either abide by the opposing attorney's instructions or refrain from using the document until a court disposed of the matter. The Franklin Supreme Court, however, has declined to adopt a rule imposing any ethical obligation in cases of unauthorized disclosure.

Indigo v. Luna Motors Corp.
Franklin Court of Appeal (1998)

The issue in this p ermissible interlocutory appeal is w hether the trial court abused its discretion by disqualif ying plaintiff's attorney for im proper use of atto rney-client privileged documents disclosed to her inadvertently. We hold that it did not. Accordingly, we affirm.

I

Plaintiff Ferdinand Indigo sued Luna Motors Corporation for da mages after he sustained serious injuries when h is Luna spo rt utility vehicle rolled over as he was driving.

In the course of routine docum ent production, Luna's a ttorney's paralegal inadvertently gave J oyce Corrigan, Indigo's attorney, a docum ent drafted by Luna's attorney and memorializing a co nference between the attorney and a high-ranking Luna executive, Raymond Fogel, stamped "attorney-client privileged," in which they discussed the strengths and weaknesses of Luna's technical evidence. As soon as Corrigan received the docum ent, which is referred to as the "techn ical evidence document," she ex amined it clo sely; as a result, she knew that it had been given to her inadvertently. Notwithstanding her knowledge, she failed to notify Luna's attorney. She subsequently used the document for im peachment purposes during Fogel's deposition, e liciting damaging admissions. Luna's attorney objected to Corrigan's use of the document, accused her of invading the attorney-client p rivilege,

and demanded the docum ent's return, but Corrigan refused.

In response, Luna f iled a m otion to disqualify Corrigan. After a hearing, the trial court granted the motion. The court determined that the technical evidenc e document was protected by the attorney-client privilege, that Corrigan violated her ethical obligation by handling it as she did, and that disqualification was the appropriate remedy. Indigo appealed.

II

It has long been settled in Franklin that a trial court may, in the exercise of its inherent power, disqualify an attorney in the interests of justice. *See, e.g., In re Klein* (Fr. Ct. App. 1947). Ultimately, disqualification involves a conflict between a clien t's right to an attorney of his or her choice and the need to maintain ethical stan dards of professional responsibility. The param ount concern, however, must be to pr eserve public trust in the scrupulous adm inistration of justice and the integrity of the bar. The important right to an attorney of one's choice must yield to ethical considerations that affect the fundamental principles of our judicial process.

Appellate courts review a trial court's ruling on disqualification for abuse of discretion. A court abuses its discre tion when it ac ts arbitrarily or without reason. As will appear, we discern no arbitrary or unreasonable action here.

A

Indigo's first claim is that th e trial court erred in determining that Corrigan violated an ethical obligation by handling the technical evidence document as she did.

From the Franklin Rules of Professional Conduct and related case law, we derive the following, albeit implicit, standard: An attorney who receives materials that on their face appear to be subject to th e attorney-client privilege, under circum stances in which it is clea r they were not intended for the receiving attorney, should refrain from examining the materials, notify the sending attorney, and await the instructions of the attorney who sent them.

Under this standard, Corrigan plainly violated an ethical oblig ation. She received the technical ev idence document; the document appeared on its face to be subject to the a ttorney-client privilege, as it was stamped "attorney-client privileged"; the circumstances were clear that the d ocument was not intended for he r; nevertheless, she examined the docum ent, failed to notif y Luna's attorney, and ref used to return it at the latter's demand.

B

Indigo's second claim is that the trial court erred in determining that disqualification of Corrigan was the appropriate remedy in light of her violation of her ethical obligation.

The trial court p redicated Corrigan's disqualification on the threat of incurable prejudice to Luna. Such a threat has long been recognized as a sufficient basis for disqualification. *See, e.g., In re Klein.* We find it m ore than sufficient here. Corrigan used the technical evidence do cument during the deposition of Luna executive Fogel, eliciting dam aging admissions. Even if Corrigan were proh ibited from using the document at trial, she could not effectively be prevented from capitalizing on its contents in preparing for trial and perhaps obtaining evidence of sim ilar force and effect.

III

The trial court concluded that disqualification was necessary to ensure a fair trial. It did not ab use its d iscretion in doing so.

Affirmed.

Mead v. Conley Machinery Co.
Franklin Court of Appeal (1999)

The issue in this p ermissible interlocutory appeal is whether th e trial court a bused its discretion by disqualif ying plaintiff's attorney on the ground th at the attorney im - properly used attorney-client privileged documents disclosed to him without authorization. *Cf. Indigo v. Luna Motors Corp.* (Fr. Ct. App. 1998) (inadvertent disclosure). We hold that it did and reverse.

I

Dolores Mead, a for mer financial consultant for Conley Machinery Com pany, sued Conley for breach o f contract. Without authorization, she obtained attorney-client privileged documents belonging to Conley and gave them to her a ttorney, William Masterson, who used them in deposing Conley's president over Conley's objection.

Conley immediately moved to disqualify Masterson. After an evidentiary hearing, the trial court granted the motion. Mead appealed.

II

In determining whether the trial court abused its discretion by disqualifying Masterson, we ask whether it acted arbitrarily or without reason. *Indigo*.

III

At the thre shold, Mead argues that the tr ial court had no authority to disqualify Masterson because h e did no t violate any specific rule am ong the Franklin Rules of Professional Conduct. It is true that Masterson did not violate any specific rule— but it is *not* true that the court was without authority to disqualify him. With or without a violation of a specific rule, a court m ay, in the exercise of its inherent power, disqualify an attorney in the interes ts of justice, including where necessary to guaran tee a fair trial. *Indigo*.

IV

Without doubt, there are situations in which an attorney who has been privy to his or her adversary's privileged docum ents without authorization must be disqualified, even though the attorney was not involved in obtaining the documents. By protect- ing attorney-client communications, the attorney-client privilege encourages parties to fully develop cases f or trial, increasing the chances of an informed and correct resolution.

To safeguard the attorney-client privilege and the litigation process itself , we believe tha t the following standard m ust govern: An attorney who receives, on an unauthorized basis, materials of an adverse party that he or she knows to be attorney-client privileged should, upon recognizing the privileged nature of the materials, either refrain from reviewing such materials or review them only to the ex tent required to determ ine how to proceed; he or she should n otify the adversary's attorney that he or she has such materials and should either follow instructions from the adversary's attorney with respect to the disposition of the materials or refrain from using the m aterials until a def initive resolution of the proper disposition of the materials is obtained from a court.

Violation of this standard, however, am ounts to only one of the facts and circumstances that a trial court must consider in deciding whether to order disqualification. The court must also consider all of the oth er relevant facts and circumstances to determ ine whether th e interests of justice require disqualification. Specifically, in the exercise of its discretion, a trial court should consider these factors: (1) the attorney's actual or c onstructive knowledge of the m aterial's attorney-client privileged status; (2) the prom ptness with which the attorney notif ied the opposing side that he or she had received such material; (3) the extent to which the attorney reviewed the material; (4) the s ignificance of th e material, i.e., the extent to whic h its d isclosure may prejudice the party moving for disqualification, and the extent to which its return or other m easure may prevent or cure that prejudice; (5) the extent to which the party moving for disqualification m ay be at fault for the unauthorized disclosure; and (6) the extent to which the party opposing disqualification would suffer prejudice from the disqualification of his or her attorney.[1]

Some of these facto rs weigh in favor of Masterson's disqualification. For exam ple, Masterson should have known after the m ost cursory review that the docu ments in question were protected by the attorney-client privilege. Nevertheless, he did not notify Conley upon receiving them. Also, it appears that he thoroughly reviewed them, as he directly referenced specific portions in his response to Conley's disqualification motion. Finally, Conley was not at fault, since Mead copied them covertly.

Other factors, however, weigh against Masterson's disqualification. The information in the docum ents in question would not significantl y prejudice Conley, reflecting little m ore than a paraphrase of a handful of Mead's allegations. The court may exclude the docum ents from evidence and thereby prevent any prejudice to Conley—all without disqualifying Masterson. Exclusion would prevent ringing fo r the jury any bell that could not be unrung. To be sure, it would not erase the docum ents from M asterson's mind, but any harm arising from their presence in Masterson's m emory would be minimal and, indeed, speculative. In contrast, Mead would suffer serious hardship if Masterson were disqualified at this time, after he has determ ined trial strategy, worked extensively on trial preparation, and readied the matter for trial. In these circu mstances, disqualification may confer an enormous, and unmerited, strategic advantage upon Conley.

In conclusion, because the facto rs against Masterson's disqualification substantially outweigh those in its favor, the trial court abused its discretion in disqualifying him.

Reversed.

---

[1] In *Indigo v. Luna Motors Corp.*, we recently considered the issue of disqualification in th e context of *inadvertent* disclosure of a document protected by the attorney-client privilege as oppo sed to *unauthorized* disclosure. The an alysis set out in the text above renders explicit what was implicit in *Indigo*, and is generally applicable to d isqualification for inadvertent disclosure as well as unauthorize d disclosure. Although we found the threat of "incurable prejudice" decisive in *Indigo*, it is n either a n ecessary nor a sufficient condition for disqualification.

POINT SHEET

DRAFTERS' POINT SHEET

About six years ago, Phoenix Corporation, a medical research company represented by the Collins Law Firm , brought a b reach-of-contract action in state co urt seeking about $80 million in damages against Biogenesis, Inc., a biotechnology company represented by Amberg & Lewis LLP. A jury tr ial is set to begin in a month and is expected to last six weeks. Two weeks ago, however, Phoenix filed a m otion to disqualify Amberg & Lewis as Biogenesis's attorneys. Phoenix claims that Amberg & Lewis violated an ethica l obligation threatening incurable prejudice through its handling of one of Phoeni x's attorney-client privileged documents, which Phoenix assumes was disclosed inadvertently.

Amberg & Lewis ha s retained applicants' law fir m to consult on the m otion for disqualification. Applicants' task is to prepare an objective memorandum evaluating the m erits of Phoenix's argument to disqualify.

The File contains the followi ng materials: a memorandum from the supervising attorney describing the assignment (task memo), the transcript of the client interview, the document that is the subject of the disqualif ication motion, and Phoenix's brie f in support of its m otion for disqualification. The Library contains Rule 4.4 of the Franklin Rules of Professional Conduct and two cases bearing on the subject.

The following discussion covers all of the poi nts the draf ters intended to rais e in the problem. Applicants need not cover them all to receive passing or even excellent grades. Grading is left entirely to the discretion of the user jurisdictions.

I. Overview

Applicants are given a general call: "Please prepare a memorandum evaluating the merits of Phoenix's argument for Amberg & Lewis's disqualification. . . ." To complete the assignment, applicants should identify and discuss two key i ssues: (1) whether Amberg & Lewis has violated the rules of professional conduct, and (2) whether disqualificati on is indeed the appropriate remedy on the facts as given.

There is no specific format for the assigned task. Applicants' work product should resemble a legal m emorandum such as one an a ssociate would draft for a supervising partner. Applicants may choose to follow the lead of P hoenix's motion to disqualify and organize their answer in response to each of the issues raised in Phoenix's supporting br ief. However, it should be an objective m emorandum; applicants who dr aft a m emorandum that is persuasive in tone have not followed instructions (j urisdictions may want to consid er whether points should be deducted from such papers). The task memorandum instructs applicants not to draft a statement of facts but to be sure to incorporate the relevant facts into their discussions.

Applicants should conclude that even if Amberg & Lewis has violated an ethical obligation (and it is not at all clear that it has), disqualification is not the appropriate remedy in this case.

II. Detailed Analysis

These are the key points that applicants should discuss, taking care to incorporate the relevant facts and explain and/or distinguish the applicable case law, in an objective memorandum evaluating the merits of Phoenix's argument to disqualify Amberg & Lewis:

As a preliminary matter, applicants should set forth the basis for why the Schetina letter may trigger disqualification under the Franklin Rules of Professional Conduct.

- Franklin Evidence Code § 954 provides that a client has a privilege to refuse to disclose, and to prevent another from disclosing, a confidential communication between client and attorney.
- It appears undisputed that the Schetina letter is protected by the attorney-client privilege under § 954.
    - It is a communication, labeled "CONFIDENTIAL," from Phoenix's then president, Schetina, to one of its attorneys, Horvitz.
    - Amberg & Lewis concedes that the letter is privileged.
    - Even if the Schetina letter were not privileged, it relates "to the representation of the attorney's client," which is the standard used in Rule 4.4. In other words, a document does not have to be attorney-client privileged for its handling by opposing counsel to constitute a violation of the Rule.
- In *Indigo v. Luna Motors Corp.* (Fr. Ct. App. 1998), the court affirmed the granting of a motion for disqualification in a case where an attorney inadvertently received privileged materials and did not return them forthwith to opposing counsel.

A. Whether Amberg & Lewis violated its ethical obligation by its handling of the Schetina letter

Applicants should incorporate into their discussion of this issue the following facts surrounding Amberg & Lewis's receipt of the Schetina letter:
- On February 2, 2009, Amberg & Lewis obtained the Schetina letter as a result of the letter's unauthorized disclosure by some unidentified person at the Collins Law Firm,

which represents Phoenix. (The letter arrive d in an envelope bear ing Collins's return address and was accom panied by a note reading "From a 'friend' at the Collins Law Firm.") The letter is dated January 2, 1998, and is labeled "CONFIDENTIAL."[2]

- Amberg & Lewis did not notify Collins of its receipt of the letter.
- Indeed, Amberg & Lewis would like to use the letter in its case again st Phoenix— Schetina's statement is essentially an admission that Biogenesis's interpretation of the royalty agreement is the correct one.
- Also on February 2, 2009, Phoenix learned, by chance, that Am berg & Lewis had obtained the Schetina letter, but assumed, incorrectly, that it had done so as a result of inadvertent disclosure by Collins in the c ourse of discovery. Collins instructed Amberg & Lewis to return the letter, but Amberg & Lewis refused.
- In response, Phoenix filed the present motion to disqualify Amberg & Lewis.

Phoenix's argument regarding Amberg & Lewis's handling of the Schetina letter

- In its brief, Phoenix's first argum ent assumes that the Schetina letter's disclosure was inadvertent and cites Rule 4.4 in sup port of its position that, at a m inimum, Amberg & Lewis was requ ired to "prom ptly notify the sender" (i. e., the Collin s Law Firm) after it received the Schetina letter.
- If the le tter's disclosure was una uthorized, Phoenix contends that *Mead v. Conley Machinery Co.* (Fr. Ct. App. 1999) "im posed an ethi cal obligation sim ilar to that of Rule 4.4 to govern cases of unauthorized disclosure."
  - Contrary to both Rule 4.4 and *Indigo*, Amberg & Lewis chose to exa mine the Schetina letter, failed to notify Collins of its receipt, and then refused to return it at Collins's demand.
  - So, either way, whether the disclosure was inadvertent or unauthorized, Phoenix argues that Amberg & Lewis has committed an ethical violation.

Application of Rule 4.4 and relevant case law

Applicants should realize that Phoenix's argument overstates its position and that it is not so clear that Amberg & Lewis has violated the Franklin Rules of Professional Conduct.

---

[2] The letter states in its entirety: "I am writing with some questions I'd like you to consider before our meeting next Tuesday so that I can get your legal advice on a matter I think is important. I have always understood our agreement with Biogenesis to re quire it to pay royalties on specified categories of pharmaceuticals. I learned recently how much money Biogenesis is making from other categories of pharmaceuticals. Why can't we get a share of that? Can't we in terpret the agreement to require Biogenesis to pay royalties on other categories, not only the specified ones? Let me know your thoughts when we meet."

- Rule 4.4 provides in its entire ty that "[a]n atto rney who receives a document relating to the representation of the attorney's client and knows or reasonably should know that the document was inadvertently sent shall promptly notify the sender."
- Thus, under Rule 4.4, an attorney receiv ing a document disclosed inadvertently need do no more than notify the sender.
- On its face, the tex t of the rule p ertains only to situ ations involving *inadvertent* disclosure. The comments to Rule 4.4 are very clear on this point. In short, Rule 4.4 does not address the ethical implications for cases of *unauthorized* disclosure of privileged communications.
- Accordingly, Amberg & Lewis's conduct is not forbidden by the plain language of Rule 4.4.

1. *Indigo v. Luna Motors Corp.* is not dispositive.

- In *Indigo*, the plaintiff's attorney received an attorney-client privileged document during document production as a result of inadvertent disclosure. The attorney closely examined the document, which discussed the opposing side's technical evidence, and then used the docum ent at deposition to obtain dam aging admissions from the opposing party. Plaintiff's attorney refused opposing counsel's demands to return the document. The court held that this conduc t by plaintiff's atto rney constituted a violation of an ethical obligation and was grounds for disqualification.
- The *Indigo* court then articulated the following standard for how attorneys should proceed in such situations:
    - An attorney who receiv es materials that on their face appear to be sub ject to the attorney-client privilege, under circum stances in which it is clear they were not intended for the receiving a ttorney, should refrain from examining the materials, notify the sending attorney, and await the in structions of the attorney who sent them.
- The facts of the presen t case distin guish it from *Indigo*. Here, an unknown Collins employee intentionally sent the Schetina le tter to Am berg & Lewis. (Phoenix could not know this, because it is unaware of how Amberg & Lewis came into possession of the Schetina letter.)
    - Presumably, someone at Am berg & Lewis kept the envelope and note that cam e with the Schetina letter ("From a 'friend' at the Collins Law Firm ") and so it can easily prove that the disclosure was unauthorized, as opposed to inadvertent.
- More to the point, in adopting Rule 4.4, th e Franklin Supreme Court expressly pulled back from the holding in *Indigo*. *See* Rule 4.4, Comm ent 2. The Comment explains that when there is an inadvertent d isclosure, the attorney "must promptly notify the

sender, but need do no more. . . . *Indigo v. Luna Motors Corp.* conflicted with this rule and, ultimately, with the intent of the Franklin Supreme Court in adopting it."

- Thus, to the extent that it concluded otherwise, *Indigo* conflicts with Rule 4.4 and, ultimately, with the intent of the Franklin Supreme Court in adopting it. Rule 4.4 does not apply to unauthorized disclosure. Notwithstanding *Mead* (discussed below), the Franklin Supreme Court has declined to adopt a rule imposing any ethical obligation in such cases.

2. Application of *Mead*

- In *Mead*, the Franklin Court of Appeal held that an attorney who received privileged documents belonging to an adverse party through an unauthorized disclosure should do the following: "upon recognizing the privileged nature of the materials, either refrain from reviewing such materials or review them only to the extent required to determine how to proceed; he or she should notify the adversary's attorney that he or she has such materials and should either follow instructions from the adversary's attorney with respect to the disposition of the materials, or refrain from using the materials until a definitive resolution of the proper disposition of the materials is obtained from a court."

- But the court goes on to state that violation of this standard, standing alone, does not warrant disqualification.

- So, while *Mead* appears to require Amberg & Lewis to notify the Collins firm that it received the Schetina letter, following the offended law firm's instructions on what to do with the letter is optional—instead, Amberg & Lewis can wait for the court to weigh in on the issue.

  - But, under *Mead*, Amberg & Lewis must still refrain from using the materials until such court resolution is obtained.

  - In addition, astute applicants will point out that, while Amberg & Lewis wanted to use the Schetina letter in its case against Phoenix, Phoenix found out that Amberg & Lewis had the Schetina letter the *same day* that Amberg & Lewis received it (when Peter Horvitz, Phoenix's attorney, overheard the associates talking about the letter at lunch). Arguably, Amberg & Lewis could have notified the Collins firm that it had received the letter, if not for the fact that Horvitz found out about it before Amberg & Lewis had a chance to tell him.

- Again, applicants should note that *Mead* was decided in 1999, before the Franklin Supreme Court enacted Rule 4.4 in 2002. It could be implied that, had the court intended that there be an ethical rule regarding the use of privileged documents that were disclosed without authorization, it could have created one.

- In fact, Comment 3 to Rule 4.4 mentions the *Mead* case and then notes that "[t]he Franklin Supreme Court . . . has declined to adopt a rule imposing any ethical obligation in cases of unauthorized disclosure."

- As a consequence, *Mead* may lack continuing vitality on the ground that it is inconsistent with the Franklin Supreme Court's presumed intent not to impose any ethical obligation.

- That being said, it is also arguable that Amberg & Lewis did indeed violate an ethical obligation. Although the Franklin Supreme Court declined to adopt a rule imposing any ethical obligation in cases of unauthorized disclosure, it may have done so because it was satisfied with *Mead*, which had already imposed such an ethical obligation.

3. Even if there was no ethical violation, a violation of a rule is not necessary for disqualification.

- Language in both *Indigo* and *Mead* suggests that a motion for disqualification may be granted by a court even if there has been no rule violation. "It has long been settled in Franklin that a trial court may, in the exercise of its inherent power, disqualify an attorney in the interests of justice." *Indigo*, citing *In re Klein* (Fr. Ct. App. 1947). *See also Mead* ("[w]ith or without a violation of a specific rule, a court may . . . disqualify an attorney . . . where necessary to guarantee a fair trial") citing *Indigo*.

4. Conclusion of Issue A

- Phoenix's argument that Amberg & Lewis violated an ethical obligation by its handling of the Schetina letter fails insofar as it incorrectly assumes that Amberg & Lewis obtained the letter as a result of inadvertent, rather than unauthorized, disclosure.

- It appears that Amberg & Lewis would *not* have violated the ethical obligation imposed by *Indigo*. *Indigo* conflicts with Rule 4.4 and, ultimately, with the intent of the Franklin Supreme Court in adopting it, and therefore lacks continuing vitality.

- By contrast, Phoenix's argument that Amberg & Lewis violated an ethical obligation may succeed insofar as it assumes in the alternative that Amberg & Lewis obtained the letter as a result of unauthorized disclosure, depending, as indicated above, on whether *Mead* is still good law in light of the comments to Rule 4.4.

- Accordingly, there is a strong argument to be made that Amberg & Lewis has not violated the letter of the Professional Rules. Nevertheless, because the import of the *Mead* decision is uncertain, that does not end the inquiry and the court will still, most likely, go on to consider whether disqualification is required in the interests of justice.

B. Whether disqualification of Amberg & Lewis is the appropriate remedy

- A trial court may, in the exercise of its inherent power, disqualify an attorney in the interests of justice. It must exercise that power, however, in light of the important right enjoyed by a party to representation by an attorney of its own choosing. Such a right must nevertheless yield to ethical considerations that affect the fundamental principles of the judicial process. *Indigo*.

- Phoenix contends that Amberg & Lewis has threatened it with incurable prejudice and therefore disqualification must follow. In Phoenix's view, whether or not any *direct* harm could be prevented by exclusion of the Schetina letter from evidence, the *indirect* harm that might arise from its use in trial preparation cannot be dealt with so simply, inasmuch as "[t]he bell has been rung, and can hardly be unrung." (Pltf's br.)
    - It is true that in *Mead* the court suggested in a footnote that, in cases of unauthorized disclosure, the "threat of 'incurable prejudice'. . . is neither a necessary nor a sufficient condition for disqualification." But that suggestion is mere dictum, inasmuch as *Mead* did not involve the threat of *any* prejudice, incurable or otherwise (in *Mead*, the court described the document at issue as "little more than a paraphrase of a handful of [the plaintiff's] allegations").

- Applicants should conclude that disqualification is not mandated in this case.

- Even if Amberg & Lewis violated an ethical obligation, it should not be disqualified.

- Under *Mead*, disqualification in all cases of disclosure, whether inadvertent or unauthorized, depends on a balancing of six factors: (1) the receiving attorney's actual or constructive knowledge of the material's attorney-client privileged status; (2) the promptness with which the receiving attorney notified the opposing side of receipt; (3) the extent to which the receiving attorney reviewed the material; (4) the material's significance, i.e., the extent to which its disclosure may prejudice the party moving for disqualification, and the extent to which its return or other measure may cure that prejudice; (5) the extent to which the party moving for disqualification may be at fault for the unauthorized disclosure; and (6) the extent to which the party opposing disqualification would suffer prejudice from disqualification.
    - Contrary to any implication in *Indigo*, the threat of incurable prejudice is neither a necessary nor a sufficient condition for disqualification.

- The balance weighs *against* disqualification here.
    - As in the *Mead* case, where the documents were covertly copied, Phoenix is not at fault (Factor 5)—the Schetina letter was passed on to Amberg & Lewis by a disgruntled Collins employee. This favors disqualification.

- Furthermore, Amberg & Lewis knew or should have known of the letter's attorney-client privileged status (Factor 1), did not notify Collins of its receipt (Factor 2), and reviewed it thoroughly—in part because of its brevity (Factor 3). Concededly, these factors favor disqualification.
- But that being said, the Schetina letter nonetheless proves to be of dubious significance (Factor 4). True, it amounts to an admission by Phoenix that Biogenesis was correct in its understanding of its royalty obligation under the 1978 agreement. But its exclusion from evidence would prevent any prejudice to Phoenix. (Contrary to the situations in *Indigo* and *Mead*, where the attorneys in each case made use of the disclosed materials at depositions, here Amberg & Lewis has not yet made any use of the letter.) Moreover, any harm arising from any conceivable non-evidentiary use of the letter would be at best speculative.
- By contrast, Biogenesis would suffer substantial prejudice from Amberg & Lewis's disqualification, inasmuch as it would have to incur appreciable costs if it were forced to attempt to substitute new attorneys for a trial set to begin in a month after six years of preparation. These factors (Factors 4 and 6) disfavor disqualification—and they appear to predominate.
  - Biogenesis enjoys an "important right" to representation by Amberg & Lewis as its chosen attorneys. *Indigo*.
  - And there appear to be no "ethical considerations" so affecting the "fundamental principles of our judicial process" as to require that "right" to "yield." *Id.*
  - In sum, disqualification of Amberg & Lewis does not appear necessary to guarantee Phoenix a fair trial.
- Contrary to Phoenix's argument, which relies on language that appears in *Indigo*,[3] disqualification of Amberg & Lewis does not depend solely on the threat of incurable prejudice. Although Phoenix attempts to dismiss the court's analysis in *Mead* as mere dictum, the *Mead* court intended its analysis at least to clarify, and at most to supersede, its earlier language in *Indigo* in order to make plain that disqualification depends on a balancing of factors not reducible to the threat of incurable prejudice alone. In any event, there is no threat of incurable prejudice here. As stated, the exclusion of the Schetina

---

[3] In *Indigo*, the court relied on the opinion in *In re Klein*, which held that the threat of incurable prejudice "has long been recognized as a sufficient basis for disqualification." *Indigo*, citing *In re Klein*.

letter from evidence would avoid any prejudice, and any harm arising from its presence in the m emory of Am berg & Lewis attorneys would be at best speculative.

Applicant Identification

Ronald v. Department of Motor Vehicles

Read the instructions on the back cover.
Do not break the seal until you are told to do so.

NATIONAL CONFERENCE OF BAR EXAMINERS

INSTRUCTIONS

1.   You will have 90 minutes to complete this session of the examination. This performance test is designed to evaluate your ability to handle a select number of legal authorities in the context of a factual problem involving a client.

2.   The problem is set in the fictitious state of Franklin, in the fictitious Fifteenth Circuit of the United States. Columbia and Olympia are also fictitious states in the Fifteenth Circuit. In Franklin, the trial court of general jurisdiction is the District Court, the intermediate appellate court is the Court of Appeal, and the highest court is the Supreme Court.

3.   You will have two kinds of materials with which to work: a File and a Library. The first document in the File is a memorandum containing the instructions for the task you are to complete. The other documents in the File contain factual information about your case and may include some facts that are not relevant.

4.   The Library contains the legal authorities needed to complete the task and may also include some authorities that are not relevant. Any cases may be real, modified, or written solely for the purpose of this examination. If the cases appear familiar to you, do not assume that they are precisely the same as you have read before. Read them thoroughly, as if they all were new to you. You should assume that the cases were decided in the jurisdictions and on the dates shown. In citing cases from the Library, you may use abbreviations and omit page references.

5.   Your response must be written in the answer book provided. If you are taking this examination on a laptop computer, your jurisdiction will provide you with specific instructions. In answering this performance test, you should concentrate on the materials in the File and Library. What you have learned in law school and elsewhere provides the general background for analyzing the problem; the File and Library provide the specific materials with which you must work.

6.   Although there are no restrictions on how you apportion your time, you should be sure to allocate ample time (about 45 minutes) to reading and digesting the materials and to organizing your answer before you begin writing it. You may make notes anywhere in the test materials; blank pages are provided at the end of the booklet. You may not tear pages from the question booklet.

7.   This performance test will be graded on your responsiveness to the instructions regarding the task you are to complete, which are given to you in the first memorandum in the File, and on the content, thoroughness, and organization of your response.

Contents

FILE

Ronald v. Dep't of Motor Vehicles

LAW OFFICES OF MARVIN ANDERS
1100 Larchmont Avenue
Hawkins Falls, Franklin 33311

M E M O R A N D U M

To: Applicant
From: Marvin Anders
Date: February 24, 2009
Subject: Ronald v. Department of Motor Vehicles

Our client, Barbara Ronald, was arrested and charged with driving a motor vehicle with a prohibited blood-alcohol concentration. A blood test taken after her arrest indicates that she had a blood-alcohol concentration of 0.08 percent. Pursuant to § 353 of the Franklin Vehicle Code, the "Administrative Per Se" Law, the Franklin Department of Motor Vehicles (DMV) suspended her driver's license even though she has not yet had a criminal trial for driving with a prohibited blood-alcohol concentration.

Section 353 permits a driver whose license has been suspended to request an administrative hearing to vacate the suspension. The evidentiary portion of Ms. Ronald's hearing was yesterday. We must submit written argument to the administrative law judge on the issues we raised by the close of business today. Because this is an administrative proceeding—not a criminal prosecution for driving with a prohibited blood-alcohol concentration—the rules are different, particularly the rules of evidence. For example, the DMV may introduce hearsay evidence that would be inadmissible in court. Also, under § 353, the DMV need prove that Ms. Ronald was driving with a prohibited blood-alcohol concentration only by a preponderance of the evidence.

Please draft a persuasive memorandum for the administrative law judge arguing that:
1. The police officer did not have reasonable suspicion to stop Ms. Ronald;
2. The administrative law judge cannot rely solely on the blood test report to find that Ms. Ronald was driving with a prohibited blood-alcohol concentration; and
3. In light of all the evidence, the DMV has not met its burden of proving by a preponderance of the evidence that Ms. Ronald was driving with a prohibited blood-alcohol concentration.

Do not write a separate statement of facts. However, be sure to use the law and the facts to make the strongest case possible on each issue, anticipating and addressing the arguments that the DMV may be able to make in its favor.

1

Transcript of February 23, 2009, Administrative Hearing

Administrative Law Judge (ALJ): We're here for the hearing on the one-year suspension of Barbara Ronald's driver's license pursuant to Franklin Vehicle Code § 353. Attorney Jennifer Newman appears on behalf of the DMV, Marvin Anders on behalf of Ms. Ronald. Ms. Newman, you've got the burden; you go first.

Newman: Thank you. The DMV requests that the clerk mark as Exhibit 1 a Hawkins Falls Police Department Incident Report, by Officer Barry Thompson, regarding the incident involving Ms. Ronald on December 19, 2008. The DMV also requests that the Hawkins Falls Police Department Crime Laboratory § 353 Blood Alcohol Test, dated December 29, which is the document that triggered Ms. Ronald's driver's license suspension on January 9, be marked and admitted as Exhibit 2.

ALJ: Any objections to the admission of the police report and crime lab test results?

Anders: We don't object to admitting the police report. However, since the officer is here, I'll call him as a hostile witness and examine him on some details. We do dispute that he had reasonable suspicion to stop Ms. Ronald. We're also challenging the sufficiency of the § 353 test results as inadmissible hearsay, and we'll argue that they are not enough to support a finding that Ms. Ronald was driving with a blood-alcohol level of at least 0.08 percent.

ALJ: Ms. Newman?

Newman: It's the DMV's position that you should, at a minimum, consider the § 353 test results as evidence and that they are, in fact, enough to meet our burden, and that Officer Thompson did have reasonable suspicion to stop Ms. Ronald.

ALJ: The police report is admitted. Since this is an administrative hearing, I'll receive the § 353 test results, and you can argue their impact in a written memorandum.

Newman: With that, the DMV rests.

Anders: Your Honor, Ms. Ronald wants to testify briefly, and I'd like to call her.

[Witness takes the stand and is sworn and identified.]

Anders: Ms. Ronald, can you tell us what happened on the night of the incident?

Ronald: Yes. I went to the Lexington Club for a late supper. I had worked 18 hours at the Palace Hotel, where I'm the manager, dealing with a host of problems that came

2

out of nowhere. I had to go somewhere to unwind, and I was hungry. I had a salad and a piece of grilled fish and some white wine—no more than two glasses, just as I told the officer. I wasn't under the influence of anything. I was just drained. I left the Lexington Club after midnight. As I was driving down Highway 13, I saw a car following me so closely that I couldn't see it in my side mirrors. I became frightened, and I guess I must have begun to weave in my lane as I paid more attention to the car in my rearview mirror than to the road ahead. I was actually relieved when I saw the police lights. I immediately pulled over to the shoulder. I told the officer about the wine because I had nothing to hide. I was just very, very tired.

Anders: How do you think you did on the field sobriety tests that Officer Thompson had you perform—the coordination and balancing tests?

Ronald: Well, the officer told me I did not perform well. I myself think I did quite well, particularly since I'd been working for 18 hours. I was also wearing high heels, my arthritis was acting up, and traffic was whizzing by the side of the road where the officer had me perform the tests.

Anders: Thank you, Ms. Ronald. Your witness.

Newman: Ms. Ronald, how can you be sure you weren't under the influence of alcohol?

Ronald: I've worked in the hospitality business all my life. I've seen many people under the influence of alcohol. I know how they act. I simply wasn't acting that way.

* * * *

Anders: I'd like to call Officer Barry Thompson as a hostile witness. [Officer enters the room, takes the stand, and is sworn and identified.] Officer, do you remember your arrest of Ms. Ronald?

Thompson: Yes, I do.

Anders: After you first noticed her car, you followed her closely for nearly a mile. True?

Thompson: I wasn't tailgating her, but yes, I wanted to observe her carefully.

Anders: You had your high-beam headlights on?

Thompson: Yes. Again, to get a good look.

Anders: She wasn't going over the speed limit, was she?

Thompson: I don't recall.

Anders:	If she had been, you would have mentioned it in your report?
Thompson:	I probably would have.
Anders:	You said that her vehicle was weaving back and forth in its lane, correct?
Thompson:	Yes.
Anders:	But not until after you started following her?
Thompson:	I saw her weaving and it was 1:00 a.m., the time bars were closing.
Anders:	Did Ms. Ronald's vehicle ever travel out of her traffic lane?
Thompson:	I didn't see her cross into another lane, but she wasn't driving straight, either.
Anders:	You stopped her car on U.S. Highway 13, a major truck route, is that right?
Thompson:	Yes.
Anders:	Wasn't it quite busy that night?
Thompson:	I suppose so. It usually is.
Anders:	After you stopped her, you had her step onto the shoulder close to Highway 13?
Thompson:	Yes.
Anders:	She was wearing fairly high heels, wasn't she?
Thompson:	Yes.
Anders:	Did you allow her to take her shoes off?
Thompson:	She never asked to take her shoes off.
Anders:	You asked her to stand on one foot?
Thompson:	Yes.
Anders:	And to walk a straight line while right next to Highway 13, the truck route?
Thompson:	On the shoulder, off the highway.
Anders:	Okay, Officer. Let me ask: you didn't smell alcohol on her breath, did you?
Thompson:	I don't recall.
Anders:	I have nothing further.
Newman:	I have no questions.
Anders:	We rest. [Witness steps down.]
ALJ:	I've got another hearing scheduled. Written arguments are due by the close of business tomorrow.

4

HAWKINS FALLS POLICE DEPARTMENT INCIDENT REPORT # 48012

Incident Date: December 19, 2008   **Arrest Time:** 1:15 a.m. **Incident Type:** Driving with blood-alcohol level of 0.08 percent or more (Fr. Veh. Code § 352) **Personal Injuries:** None
Incident Location: U.S. Highway 13 at Bellaire Blvd.   **Conditions:** Dark, clear, dry
Suspect: Barbara Ronald, white female, weight 145 lbs, height 5′9″, d.o.b. 9/15/1951, age 57
Suspect's Identification: Franklin driver's license, #W23152
Suspect's Address: 110 Merrill Crest Drive, Hawkins Falls, FR 33309
Motor Vehicle: License Plate: Franklin JSP-256 **Make/Model/Year:** Jaguar XJS V12 1992

Detailed Description of the Incident: This officer first observed suspect's vehicle pulling out from the Lexington Club parking lot at 1:00 a.m. at U.S. Highway 13 and Montview Way. The vehicle began to travel south on U.S. Highway 13; followed suspect in patrol car and observed her vehicle weaving back and forth in her lane. There was no debris or other material in the roadway that could explain such weaving. I activated the patrol car's overhead emergency lights, and suspect pulled over to the right shoulder near the corner of U.S. Highway 13 and Bellaire Boulevard about 1.4 miles from the Lexington Club; approached driver's window to ask for identification; as suspect handed over her driver's license, her eyes appeared bloodshot and watery; she said that she had been weaving back and forth because she had been scared by my headlights and was trying to see who was following her; on questioning, she admitted to having consumed two glasses of white wine.

I asked suspect to exit her vehicle and observed that her gait was unsteady. Based on these observations, I asked suspect to perform a series of field sobriety tests. When asked to walk a straight line and then stand on one foot, suspect performed poorly, lost her balance, and was distracted. As a result of her poor performance on the field sobriety tests, objective symptoms of intoxication, and poor driving, I formed the opinion that she had been driving with a blood-alcohol level of at least 0.08 percent, and placed her under arrest at 1:15 a.m.

I transported her to headquarters; she consented to a blood test. I then transported her to Mercy Hospital for the blood draw. We arrived at 2:05 a.m. and waited until a blood sample could be drawn by a technician at 2:50 a.m. I booked the blood sample into the evidence locker under HFPD No. 48012.

Reporting Police Officer: Barry Thompson, Badge No. 4693
Report Date/Time: December 19, 2008, 8:29 a.m.

EXHIBIT 1

Ronald v. Dep't of Motor Vehicles

HAWKINS FALLS POLICE DEPARTMENT
CRIME LABORATORY
VEHICLE CODE § 353 BLOOD ALCOHOL TEST RESULTS

This is to certify under penalty of perjury under the law of the State of Franklin that on December 21, 2008, I tested a sample of the blood of Barbara Ronald, entered as HFPD No. 48012, on the HemoAssay-Seven Chemical Testing Instrument. I attest that my analysis of the Ronald sample reflected a blood-alcohol concentration of 0.08 percent.

Daniel Gans signed by Charlotte Swain

Daniel Gans

Forensic Alcohol Analyst

(Fr. Bur. of Inv. Cert. #802)

Charlotte Swain

Charlotte Swain

Senior Laboratory Technician

I certify that this is a true and accurate copy of forensic alcohol test results performed at the Crime Laboratory of the   Hawkins Falls Police Department   , pursuant to F.C.R. § 121.

Tony Bellagio

Tony Bellagio

Records Custodian

Dated: December 29, 2008

EXHIBIT 2

LIBRARY

Ronald v. Dep't of Motor Vehicles

FRANKLIN VEHICLE CODE

§ 352 Driving with a prohibited blood-alcohol percentage

It is unlawful for any person who has 0.08 percent or more of alcohol in his or her blood to operate a motor vehicle.

§ 353 Administrative suspension of license by Department of Motor Vehicles for prohibited blood-alcohol level on chemical testing

(a) Upon receipt by the Department of Motor Vehicles of a laboratory test report from any law enforcement agency attesting that a forensic alcohol analysis performed by chemical testing determined that a person's blood had 0.08 percent or more of alcohol while he or she was operating a motor vehicle, the Department of Motor Vehicles shall immediately suspend the license of such person to operate a motor vehicle for a period of one year.

(b) Any person may request an administrative hearing before an administrative law judge on the suspension of his or her license under this section. At the administrative hearing, the Department of Motor Vehicles shall bear the burden of proving by a preponderance of the evidence that the person operated a motor vehicle when the person had 0.08 percent or more of alcohol in his or her blood.

(c) Any party aggrieved by a decision of an administrative law judge may petition the district court in the county where the offense allegedly occurred for review of the administrative law judge's decision.

FRANKLIN CODE OF REGULATIONS

§ 121 Forensic blood-alcohol testing

Forensic blood-alcohol testing may be performed only by a forensic alcohol analyst who has been trained in accordance with the requirements of the Franklin Bureau of Investigation. A forensic blood-alcohol analysis signed by such a forensic alcohol analyst and certified as authentic by a records custodian for the laboratory in which the analysis was performed may be admitted in any administrative suspension hearing without further foundation.

9

FRANKLIN ADMINISTRATIVE PROCEDURE ACT

§ 115 Hearsay evidence; admissible at administrative hearing

Hearsay evidence shall be admissible at an administrative hearing. If hearsay evidence would be admissible in a judicial proceeding under an exception to the hearsay rule under the Franklin Evidence Code, it shall be sufficient in itself to support a finding. If hearsay evidence would not be admissible in a judicial proceeding under an exception to the hearsay rule under the Franklin Evidence Code, it may nonetheless be used for the purpose of supplementing or explaining other evidence.

FRANKLIN EVIDENCE CODE

§ 1278 Hearsay definition

Hearsay is a statement, other than one made by the declarant while testifying at a judicial proceeding, offered in evidence to prove the truth of the matter asserted.

§ 1279 Hearsay rule

Hearsay is not admissible except as provided by this Code.

§ 1280 Hearsay rule: public-records exception

Evidence of a writing made as a record of an act, condition, or event is not made inadmissible by the hearsay rule when offered in any judicial proceeding to prove the act, condition, or event, if (a) the writing was made by and within the scope of duty of a public employee, (b) the writing was made at or near the time of the act, condition, or event, and (c) the sources of information and method and time of preparation were such as to indicate its trustworthiness.

Pratt v. Department of Motor Vehicles
Franklin Court of Appeal (2006)

The Department of Motor Vehicles (DMV) seeks review of a district court decision vacating the suspension of Jason Pratt's driver's license for the offense of driving a motor vehicle with a prohibited blood-alcohol concentration (PBAC). The DMV asserts that the court erred in concluding that Pratt's deviations within one lane of travel, with nothing more, failed to provide the police officer with reasonable suspicion to justify an investigative stop of the vehicle.

On February 2, 2004, Plymouth police sergeant Tom Kellogg was on patrol on Mill Street. There is no line or marking delineating the traffic lane from the parking lane on this street. The parking lane is bounded by the curb. Sergeant Kellogg testified that, at approximately 9:30 p.m., he was traveling southbound on Mill Street and observed Pratt's car traveling northbound, but that the car was "canted" such that it was driving at least partially in the unmarked parking lane.

After Pratt's car passed, Sergeant Kellogg turned around and began following it. He observed the car traveling in an "S-type" pattern—a smooth motion toward the right part of the parking lane and back toward the centerline. He stated that Pratt's car moved approximately 10 feet from right to left within the northbound lane, coming within one foot of the centerline and to within six to eight feet of the curb. Pratt's car repeated the S-pattern several times over two blocks. The movement was neither erratic nor jerky,

and Pratt's car did not come close to hitting any other vehicles or to hitting the curb. Sergeant Kellogg testified that the manner of Pratt's driving suggested that the driver was intoxicated, so he turned on his emergency lights and pulled Pratt's car over. As a result of the evidence obtained after the stop, Sergeant Kellogg arrested Pratt for violating § 352 of the Franklin Vehicle Code and the DMV suspended Pratt's driver's license.

At the administrative hearing, Pratt's primary defense was that Sergeant Kellogg had no reasonable basis to stop his vehicle. The administrative law judge (ALJ) held that Sergeant Kellogg's testimony of Pratt's "unusual driving" and "drifting within one's own lane" provided reasonable suspicion to justify the stop. Pratt sought review of the ALJ's decision in the district court. The district court reversed, holding that slight deviations within a single lane do not give rise to reasonable suspicion that a driver has a PBAC.

The issue is whether the traffic stop violated Pratt's constitutional rights because it was not based on reasonable suspicion. Although investigative stops are seizures within the meaning of the Fourth Amendment, in some circumstances police officers may conduct such stops even where there is no probable cause to make an arrest. *Terry v. Ohio* (U.S. 1968). Such a stop must be based on more than an officer's "inchoate and unparticularized suspicion or 'hunch.'" *Id.* Rather, the officer "must be able to point to specific and articulable facts which, taken together with rational inferences from those facts, reasonably warrant" the stop. *Id.* The DMV has the burden of establishing that an investigative stop is reasonable. *See Taylor v. Dept. of Motor Vehicles* (Fr. Sup. Ct. 1973).

The DMV contends that Sergeant Kellogg had reasonable suspicion to stop Pratt. It argues that, in and of itself, repeated weaving within a single lane (absent an obvious innocent explanation) provides reasonable suspicion to make an investigative stop. While we agree that the facts of the case give rise to a reasonable suspicion that Pratt was driving with a PBAC and that the investigative stop was reasonable, we reject a bright-line rule that weaving within a single lane alone gives rise to reasonable suspicion. Rather, our determination is based on the totality of the circumstances.

In *State v. Kessler* (Fr. Ct. App. 1999), a police officer observed the defendant's car traveling slowly, stopping at an intersection with no stop sign or traffic light, turning onto a cross street, and accelerating "at a high rate of speed" (but under the speed limit). The officer then saw the car pull into a parking lot where the driver opened the door and poured out a "mixture of liquid and ice" from a cup. When the officer identified himself to the driver, the driver began to walk away, at which point the officer made an investigative stop. We held that the stop was based on a reasonable suspicion, even though any of these facts alone might be insufficient to provide reasonable suspicion.

The DMV contends that repeated weaving within a single lane alone gives an experienced police officer reasonable suspicion to make an investigative stop. That view, however, conflicts with *Kessler*. Further, the DMV's proffered bright-line rule is problematic because movements that may be characterized as "repeated weaving within a single lane" may, under the totality of the circumstances, fail to give rise to reasonable suspicion. This may be the case, for example, where the "weaving" is minimal or happens very few times over a great distance. Because the DMV's proffered standard can be interpreted to cover conduct that many innocent drivers commit, it may subject a substantial portion of the public to invasions of their privacy. It is in effect no standard at all.

However, driving need not be illegal to give rise to reasonable suspicion. Thus, we adopt neither the bright-line rule proffered by the DMV that weaving within a single lane may alone give rise to reasonable suspicion, nor the bright-line rule advocated by Pratt that weaving within a single lane must be erratic, unsafe, or illegal to give rise to reasonable suspicion. Rather, we maintain the well-established principle that reviewing courts must determine whether there was reasonable suspicion for an investigative stop based on the totality of the circumstances. As the building blocks of fact accumulate, reasonable inferences about the cumulative effect can be drawn.

Sergeant Kellogg did not observe any actions that constituted traffic violations or that, considered in isolation, provided reasonable suspicion that criminal activity was afoot. However, when considered in conjunction with all of the facts and circumstances of the case, Pratt's driving provided Kellogg with reasonable suspicion to believe that Pratt was driving while intoxicated.

Moving between the roadway centerline and parking lane is not slight deviation within one's own lane. The district court also incorporated by reference Sergeant Kellogg's testimony regarding Pratt's drifting and unusual driving. Our read of Sergeant Kellogg's testimony does not support the view that Pratt's weaving constituted only slight deviation within one lane. After initially stating that he did not have an estimate of how many times Pratt's vehicle weaved, on cross-examination Sergeant Kellogg stated that Pratt's vehicle weaved "several" or "a few" times over several feet. The manner and frequency of Pratt's weaving are not the only specific, articulable facts here. When Sergeant Kellogg first observed Pratt's vehicle, it was "canted into the parking lane" and "wasn't in the designated traffic lane." Finally, we note that the incident took place at 9:30 at night. While this is not as significant as when poor driving takes place at or around "bar time," it does lend some further credence to Sergeant Kellogg's suspicion that Pratt was driving while intoxicated.

When viewed in isolation, these individual facts may not be sufficient to warrant a reasonable officer to suspect that Pratt was driving while intoxicated. However, such facts accumulate, and as they accumulate, reasonable inferences about the cumulative effect can be drawn. We determine, under the totality of the circumstances, that Sergeant Kellogg presented specific and articulable facts, which, taken together with rational inferences from those facts, gave rise to the reasonable suspicion necessary for an investigative stop. Accordingly, the stop did not violate Pratt's constitutional right to be free from unreasonable searches and seizures.

Reversed.

Schwartz v. Department of Motor Vehicles
Franklin Court of Appeal (1994)

On October 21, 1992, at 2:25 a.m., Dixon City Police Officer James Pisano observed Gil Schwartz's vehicle straddling the southbound lanes of Valley Road at 60 miles per hour. Officer Pisano stopped Schwartz's vehicle at that time and, after making contact with him, noted that Schwartz had slurred speech, bloodshot eyes, a strong odor of alcohol, and an unsteady gait. Officer Pisano then administered field sobriety tests on which Schwartz performed poorly. Officer Pisano then arrested Schwartz.

Officer Pisano had Schwartz's blood drawn at 3:45 a.m. at the Dixon City hospital. The blood-alcohol lab test disclosed a blood-alcohol concentration of 0.129 percent. The lab test results were immediately noted on the lab's internal records but, because of an error, not on the official § 353 report until November 29, 1992, over a month after Schwartz's arrest and blood draw.

Pursuant to § 353 of the Franklin Vehicle Code, the Department of Motor Vehicles (DMV) suspended Schwartz's driver's license. Schwartz challenged the suspension at an administrative hearing. At the hearing, Officer Pisano testified and the administrative law judge (ALJ) received the lab test report offered by the DMV showing Schwartz's blood-alcohol concentration. Schwartz did not offer any evidence of his own, but raised several evidentiary objections, including that the lab test report was hearsay. The ALJ overruled his objections,

concluded that the lab test report came within the public-records exception to the hearsay rule, Fr. Evid. Code § 1280, found that the DMV had proved by a preponderance of the evidence that Schwartz had operated a motor vehicle with a blood-alcohol concentration of at least 0.08 percent, and upheld the suspension.

Schwartz petitioned for review in the district court, seeking to overturn the ALJ's decision. The court concluded that the lab report did not come within the public-records exception to the hearsay rule because the results of the test were not recorded close in time to the performance of the test, as required, but more than a month later. The court thus ruled that the suspension was not supported by a preponderance of the evidence. The DMV appeals.

Under § 353 of the Franklin Vehicle Code, the ALJ was bound to uphold the suspension if he found by a preponderance of the evidence—that is, if he found it more likely than not—that Schwartz was driving with a blood-alcohol concentration of 0.08 percent or more. The DMV has now conceded that the § 353 analysis in this case does not satisfy the public-records exception to the hearsay rule because of the late recording of the results. Therefore, we must consider what weight to give it.

Pursuant to Franklin Administrative Procedure Act § 115, if the blood-alcohol analysis

14

satisfies an exception to the hearsay rule, it may conclusively establish a violation of § 352. If not, additional evidence is needed to support such a finding.

In this case, the lab test report supplements Officer Pisano's testimony. Although a chemical blood-alcohol test report is one means of establishing that a driver's blood-alcohol concentration was 0.08 percent or more, it is not the only means. Both parties are free to introduce circumstantial evidence bearing on whether the driver's blood-alcohol concentration was at least 0.08 percent. Officer Pisano testified that he observed Schwartz driving in an erratic and dangerous manner, and that Schwartz had bloodshot eyes, gave off a strong odor of alcohol, had an unsteady gait and slurred speech, and performed poorly on field sobriety tests. This evidence that Schwartz was driving while heavily intoxicated provided sufficient support for the ALJ's finding that Schwartz was driving with a blood-alcohol concentration of at least 0.08 percent.

We emphasize that our decision does not justify license suspensions based solely on circumstantial evidence. A police officer's observations, standing alone, cannot establish that a driver's blood-alcohol concentration is at least 0.08 percent or more. Here, however, the record contains a blood test report, which (though inadmissible in court because it does not meet the public-records exception) may still be used in an administrative proceeding "for the purpose of supplementing or explaining other evidence." Franklin APA § 115.

Thus, the ALJ could properly consider whether this blood test report, together with the police officer's observations, supported a finding on the critical fact of blood-alcohol concentration. We conclude that the ALJ's decision is properly supported by the record in this case.

Reversed.

Rodriguez v. Department of Motor Vehicles

Franklin Court of Appeal (2004)

Following suspension of his driver's license by the Department of Motor Vehicles (DMV), Peter Rodriguez sought review in the district court seeking to vacate the suspension. The district court vacated the suspension, and the DMV appeals. We affirm.

Rodriguez was stopped by Town of Ada Police Officer Mac Huber on June 20, 2003, after failing to stop at a stop sign. When Officer Huber observed that Rodriguez was exhibiting symptoms of intoxication, he arrested him. Rodriguez submitted to a blood test, which purportedly showed a blood-alcohol concentration of 0.17 percent.

The DMV suspended Rodriguez's driver's license. At the hearing on the suspension held pursuant to the "Administrative Per Se" Law (Fr. Veh. Code § 353), the DMV submitted Officer Huber's written police report describing in perfunctory fashion the circumstances of the stop and the arrest. The DMV also submitted a one-page document entitled "blood-alcohol test results," which stated that Rodriguez's blood had been tested and found to contain "0.17 percent alcohol." The blood-alcohol test report was on letterhead from the "Town of Ada Police Department Crime Laboratory." The report bore the signature of "Virginia Loew, Criminalist."

Rodriguez challenged the sufficiency of the blood-alcohol test report under § 115 of the Franklin Administrative Procedure Act. He contended that the DMV had failed to show that the blood-alcohol test report satisfied the public-records exception to the hearsay rule because the DMV did not establish that the report had been prepared by a person with an official duty to perform a forensic alcohol analysis, as required by § 121 of the Franklin Code of Regulations. The administrative law judge (ALJ) rejected the challenge to the report and found that Rodriguez was driving with a blood-alcohol level of 0.08 percent or more, a finding based solely on the report.

Section 115 of the Franklin Administrative Procedure Act provides: "Hearsay evidence shall be admissible at an administrative hearing. If hearsay evidence would be admissible in a judicial proceeding under an exception to the hearsay rule under the Franklin Evidence Code, it shall be sufficient in itself to support a finding. If hearsay evidence would not be admissible in a judicial proceeding under an exception to the hearsay rule under the Franklin Evidence Code, it may nonetheless be used for the purpose of supplementing or explaining other evidence."

Rodriguez maintains that there is not sufficient evidence to support the ALJ's finding that he was driving with a blood-alcohol level of at least 0.08 percent because the report purporting to show his blood-alcohol concentration at 0.17 percent was hearsay that would not have been admissible at a

16

judicial proceeding under the public-records exception.

As the proponent of the blood-alcohol test report, the DMV bore the burden of establishing the foundation for the public-records exception, which entailed findings that (1) the forensic alcohol analysis was performed within the scope of the public employee's duty, (2) the results were recorded close in time to the performance of the analysis, and (3) the analysis and results were generally trustworthy. *See* Fr. Evid. Code § 1280.

The DMV claims that it established the proper foundation for the public-records exception to the hearsay rule regarding the blood-alcohol test report because under § 664 of the Franklin Evidence Code, "[i]t is presumed that official duty has been regularly performed."

We generally agree with the DMV that when a blood-alcohol test is performed within the scope of a public employee's duty, under § 664 of the Franklin Evidence Code it is presumed that the results were recorded close in time to the performance of the blood test and that the test and its results were generally trustworthy, inasmuch as the public employee's duty imposes such requirements.

We disagree, however, with the DMV that Rodriguez's blood-alcohol test was performed within the scope of duty of the public employee in question. Indeed, we conclude that the public employee here was not authorized to perform the forensic alcohol analysis in the first place.

The performance of forensic alcohol analysis is subject to strict regulation by § 121 of the Franklin Code of Regulations. Section 121 authorizes *only* "forensic alcohol analysts" to perform forensic alcohol analysis— and none others, including "criminalists."

On this record, it is evident that the blood-alcohol test here was performed by a public employee who was not authorized to perform forensic alcohol analysis. Virginia Loew is identified solely as a "criminalist"—and criminalists, as is evident, are not authorized to perform such blood-alcohol analyses.

The DMV argues that *Schwartz v. Department of Motor Vehicles* (Fr. Ct. App. 1994) permits the ALJ to consider an otherwise inadmissible blood test report, together with other circumstantial evidence, including a police officer's observations of the driver. But *Schwartz* involved very different facts. The DMV in that case conceded that the blood test report did not come within the public-records exception to the hearsay rule. Because the blood test report, by itself, was insufficient to support a finding, the DMV took great pains to establish the police officer's observations in detail. Here, by contrast, the DMV provided only cursory proof of the officer's observations. Indeed, this case illustrates a danger in the *Schwartz* ruling, especially if it permits the DMV to "rescue" testing by an unqualified person with unscientific testimony. For these reasons, we reject the DMV's reliance on *Schwartz*.

In this case, it follows that the DMV failed to meet its burden of establishing the necessary foundation for the public-records exception to the hearsay rule with respect to the blood-alcohol test report. A police report void of detail and a blood test report that lacks proper foundation, even in combination, do not add up to the necessary quantum of evidence. Consequently, the DMV failed to prove by a preponderance of the evidence that Rodriguez had an excessive blood-alcohol concentration, and the district court did not err in granting Rodriguez's petition and vacating the suspension of his driver's license.

Affirmed.

POINT SHEET

Ronald v. Department of Motor Vehicles
DRAFTERS' POINT SHEET

In this performance test, applicants work for a sole practitioner who represents Barbara Ronald. The Franklin Department of Motor Vehicles (DMV) suspended Ronald's driver's license for one year under § 353 of the Franklin Vehicle Code for driving with a blood-alcohol level of 0.08 percent or more in violation of § 352 of the same code. Ronald requested an administrative hearing to challenge the suspension. The evidentiary portion of the administrative hearing occurred on February 23, 2009. By the close of business on February 24, counsel must submit written arguments to the administrative law judge (ALJ). Applicants have a single task, to draft a persuasive memorandum arguing that (1) the officer did not have a reasonable suspicion warranting the stop of Ronald's vehicle; (2) the ALJ cannot rely solely on a blood test report to make a finding that Ronald was driving with a blood-alcohol concentration of at least 0.08 percent; and (3) in light of all the evidence, the DMV has not met its burden of proving that Ronald was driving with a blood-alcohol concentration of that percentage.

The File contains the memorandum from the supervising attorney, the administrative hearing transcript, the police report, and the § 353 test results. The Library contains a selection of Franklin statutes, administrative code provisions, and three cases.

The following discussion covers all of the points the drafters intended to raise in the problem. Applicants need not cover them all to receive passing or even excellent grades. Grading decisions are entirely within the discretion of the user jurisdictions.

I.   Overview

Applicants' task is to prepare a persuasive memorandum setting forth three arguments for why the ALJ should vacate the suspension of Ronald's driver's license for driving with a prohibited blood-alcohol concentration. No specific format is given for the task. Applicants are instructed not to draft a statement of facts. However, applicants are told to incorporate the relevant facts into their arguments. In addition, applicants should anticipate the arguments that the DMV may make in support of the suspension.

Because this is an administrative proceeding, and not a criminal matter, applicants should recognize that the DMV has a lower burden of proof: it need prove that Ronald violated § 352 only by a preponderance of the evidence. With respect to the three issues, it is expected that applicants will make the following points:

1. The officer did not have a reasonable suspicion justifying the stop of Ronald's vehicle and the contrary case law (*Pratt v. Department of Motor Vehicles* (Fr. Ct. App. 2006)) is readily distinguishable.

2. The blood test report would not be admissible hearsay in a judicial proceeding as it does not fall within the applicable exception to the hearsay rule—the public-records exception. Therefore it cannot, by itself, support a finding that Ronald was driving with a prohibited blood-alcohol concentration.

3. The remaining evidence (the police report and testimony), coupled with the limited weight accorded to the blood test report, falls far below what is required (and thus the DMV cannot meet its burden of proof) to show that Ronald was driving a motor vehicle with a prohibited blood-alcohol concentration.

II.   Analysis

A.   Officer Thompson did not have reasonable suspicion to stop Ronald.

In *Pratt v. Department of Motor Vehicles* (Fr. Ct. App. 2006), the court discussed the circumstances under which a weaving automobile presents reasonable suspicion justifying a traffic stop.

- Driving does not have to be illegal to give rise to reasonable suspicion.
- Rather, reasonable suspicion exists when an officer can "point to specific and articulable facts which, taken together with rational inferences from those facts, reasonably warrant" the stop. *Pratt*, quoting *Terry v. Ohio* (U.S. 1968). Rejecting a bright-line rule for such situations, the court held that there was reasonable suspicion for stopping the defendant in *Pratt* based on his erratic driving.
- Under the totality of the circumstances test, the court concluded that Pratt's driving created a reasonable suspicion. Pratt's driving went beyond slight deviation within one lane—his vehicle moved from the parking lane to within one foot of the centerline and then to within six to eight feet of the curb. This conduct occurred several times. In addition, when first observed, Pratt's vehicle was not in the designated driving lane but was "canted" in the parking lane. And the incident occurred at 9:30 at night. Taken together, these facts and the reasonable inferences therefrom provided the officer with a reasonable suspicion to stop Pratt.

Applying the *Pratt* standard to the *Ronald* facts

Applicants should argue that the ALJ should reject the DMV's assertion that there was reasonable suspicion for the traffic stop of Ronald's vehicle.

22

- First, there was no traffic violation.
    - Officer Thompson admitted that had Ronald been speeding, he would have noted so in his report.
    - Ronald's vehicle never crossed into another lane.
- Second, there is an innocent explanation for the weaving of Ronald's vehicle.
    - Ronald testified that when she noticed that a vehicle was following her closely (so closely that she could not see it in her side mirrors), she became frightened and began "to weave in my lane as I paid more attention to the car in my rearview mirror than to the road ahead."
    - And she was very tired, having just finished working an 18-hour shift.
    - By contrast, in *Pratt*, the defense did not offer any innocent explanation for Pratt's erratic driving.
    - Further, unlike the situation in *State v. Kessler* (Fr. Ct. App. 1999) (discussed in *Pratt*), there are no actions by the driver that provide additional facts supporting reasonable suspicion. In *Kessler*, the driver did not break any traffic laws, but did stop at an intersection where there was no traffic signal, accelerated at a high rate of speed, and then pulled into a parking lot where the driver then poured a "mixture of liquid and ice" from a cup onto the ground. When the officer identified himself to the driver, the driver began to walk away and at that point the officer executed a *Terry* stop.
- Officer Thompson's account of the stop does not contradict or undercut Ronald's testimony that she began to weave in her lane because she was frightened by the car following her. In fact, his testimony corroborates her description of the stop.
    - A fair reading of both Officer Thompson's testimony and his police report supports the conclusion that Ronald did not begin to weave in her lane until Thompson began following her.
    - Unlike *Pratt*, where there was detailed testimony describing the extreme nature of how the defendant weaved in his lane, here there are no details about the weaving beyond Officer Thompson's statement that "I didn't see her cross into another lane, but she wasn't driving straight, either."
    - Also, Officer Thompson testified that he used his high-beam lights. This would distract Ronald and make it difficult for her to see who was following her so closely.
- While it is relevant that Officer Thompson saw Ronald's vehicle leave the Lexington Club at 1:00 a.m., the time that bars close in Hawkins Falls, without more, that fact is not enough to constitute reasonable suspicion for the traffic stop.

23

- Granted, in *Pratt*, the court noted that it is more suggestive of intoxication when poor driving occurs "at or around 'bar time.'"
- In short, there are only three facts weighing in favor of reasonable suspicion: that Ronald had left a restaurant where alcohol was served, that she was driving around "bar time," and that she was weaving within her lane (but only after being closely followed).
- Applicants should argue that when viewed in light of the totality of circumstances—Ronald broke no traffic laws, and began weaving only after Officer Thompson began to follow her so closely that his vehicle could not be seen in her side mirrors, and he had his high-beam lights on—the facts fall far short of establishing reasonable suspicion for the traffic stop.

B. The blood test report cannot, by itself, support a finding that Ronald was driving with a prohibited blood-alcohol concentration (0.08 percent or more).

- The relevant facts regarding the test of Ronald's blood are undisputed:
    - On December 19, 2008, at 2:50 a.m., a sample of Ronald's blood was drawn at Mercy Hospital in Hawkins Falls.
    - On December 29, 2008, the Crime Laboratory of the Hawkins Falls Police Department issued a "Vehicle Code § 353 Blood Alcohol Test Results" stating that Ronald's blood sample was subjected to a chemical test on December 21 and reflected a blood-alcohol concentration of 0.08 percent. The document bears the signature of Charlotte Swain, who is identified by the title of "Senior Laboratory Technician," and the name "Daniel Gans," who is identified by the title of "Forensic Alcohol Analyst." Gans did not sign the document. Rather, his name was signed by Swain.
- The burden is on the DMV to prove by a preponderance of the evidence, that is, to prove that it is more likely than not, that Ronald was driving with a blood-alcohol concentration of at least 0.08 percent. Fr. Veh. Code § 353(b); *Schwartz v. Dept. of Motor Vehicles* (Fr. Ct. App. 1994).
- The ALJ should give limited weight to the § 353 lab report as evidence that Ronald had a prohibited blood-alcohol concentration.
    - The § 353 lab report is hearsay: it is an out-of-court statement offered to prove the truth of the matter asserted—that Ronald was driving with a blood-alcohol concentration of 0.08 percent or more. *See* Fr. Evid. Code § 1278 (defining hearsay).

24

- The DMV asserts that the § 353 lab report should be considered as evidence and that, by itself, the lab report is sufficient to prove by a preponderance of the evidence that Ronald was driving with a prohibited blood-alcohol concentration.
- The § 353 lab report does not fall within an exception to the hearsay rule and therefore cannot, by itself, support a finding at an administrative proceeding.
    - Under § 115 of the Franklin Administrative Procedure Act, if hearsay evidence would be admissible in a judicial proceeding under an exception to the hearsay rule, it is sufficient to support a finding at an administrative hearing. *See Rodriguez v. Dept. of Motor Vehicles* (Fr. Ct. App. 2004).
    - Thus, the question is whether the § 353 lab report comes within the public-records exception of § 1280 of the Franklin Evidence Code. *Rodriguez*; *Schwartz*. Section 1280 provides: "Evidence of a writing made as a record of an act, condition, or event is not made inadmissible by the hearsay rule when offered in any judicial proceeding to prove the act, condition, or event, if (a) the writing was made by and within the scope of duty of a public employee, (b) the writing was made at or near the time of the act, condition, or event, and (c) the sources of information and method and time of preparation were such as to indicate its trustworthiness."
        - The report of a forensic alcohol analysis, when performed by an authorized person, comes within the public-records exception of § 1280 of the Evidence Code by virtue of the presumption of § 664 as described in *Rodriguez*, that the "official duty has been regularly performed."
        - However, under § 121 of the Franklin Code of Regulations, forensic alcohol analysis "may be performed only by a forensic alcohol analyst." *See also Rodriguez*.
        - The § 353 lab report proffered by the DMV bears the signature of Charlotte Swain, who is identified by the title of "Senior Laboratory Technician," not the requisite "Forensic Alcohol Analyst." *See Rodriguez*. The "signature" of Daniel Gans, a "Forensic Alcohol Analyst," was executed by Swain.
        - As a result, the § 353 lab report does not comply with the requirements of § 121 of the Code of Regulations. As in *Rodriguez*, "the public employee here was not authorized to perform the forensic alcohol analysis in the first place."
        - Therefore, the DMV cannot establish the necessary foundation for the public-records exception to the hearsay rule with respect to the § 353 lab report.
        - In addition, there is a question as to whether the § 353 lab report was prepared "at or near the time of the . . . event." Fr. Evid. Code § 1280.

25

- In *Schwartz*, the lab test results were recorded over five weeks after the defendant's arrest and blood draw, and the DMV conceded that, as a result of the delay, the § 353 lab report did not satisfy the public-records exception to the hearsay rule.

- Here, Ronald's blood sample was tested just two days after her arrest, and the § 353 lab report was completed and certified eight days later, on December 29, 2008, during a holiday week.

- While much shorter than the five-week delay in *Schwartz*, an applicant could argue that the delay in preparing the report places it outside of the public-records exception.

- Applicants who make this argument may receive some credit, but the delay should not be the sole focus of their public-records exception argument.

- Rather, the fact that the alcohol analysis was performed by a laboratory technician and not a forensic alcohol analyst categorically precludes the report from satisfying the public-records exception. *See Rodriguez*.

To recap, the § 353 lab report would be inadmissible to support a finding in a judicial proceeding because it does not satisfy the requirements of the public-records exception to the hearsay rule. Although hearsay is admissible in administrative proceedings such as Ronald's, it is accorded limited weight; it cannot support a finding by itself, but may be used only to supplement or explain other evidence. *See* Fr. Admin. Proc. Act § 115.

C. In light of all the evidence, the DMV has not met its burden of proving that Ronald was driving with a prohibited blood-alcohol concentration.

- Assuming, *arguendo*, that there was reasonable suspicion for the traffic stop, the DMV still cannot meet its burden to prove by a preponderance of the evidence that Ronald had a blood-alcohol concentration of 0.08 percent or more.

- The only evidence in addition to the problematic § 353 lab report of Ronald's possible intoxication is found in the police incident report and Officer Thompson's testimony.

- Officer Thompson's report notes that he observed Ronald's vehicle "weaving back and forth in her lane." When he stopped her vehicle, he noted that "her eyes appeared

26

bloodshot and watery" and that she told him that she had had two glasses of white wine. According to Officer Thompson, her gait was unsteady, she performed poorly on field sobriety tests, and she was distracted.

- Officer Thompson's incident report was undermined by the testimony of Thompson himself, who made admissions supporting Ronald's testimony.
  - At the hearing, he conceded that Ronald had not exceeded the speed limit and that he had been following her closely with his high beams on.
  - Furthermore, he agreed, upon questioning, that Highway 13 is a busy truck route, and that Ronald performed the balancing and coordination tests while wearing high heels and standing on the shoulder of a busy highway.
  - Most telling, he could not recall smelling alcohol on Ronald's breath, nor is there any mention of his smelling alcohol in his report.
- Ronald's counsel called Ronald herself, who testified as follows:
  - She had no more than two glasses of white wine at dinner.
  - She was not under the influence of alcohol, but was drained after working for 18 hours straight.
  - She weaved while she was driving because the police officer was following too closely and she became distracted and afraid.
  - She noted that when she performed the field sobriety tests she was wearing high heels, her arthritis was acting up, and "traffic was whizzing by the side of the road."
  - Finally, she averred that she was sure that she was not under the influence of alcohol because she had long worked in the hospitality business and knew how persons acted when they were under the influence.
- Without more, the circumstantial evidence proffered by the DMV (the police report and the testimony) is insufficient to show that it was more likely than not that Ronald was driving with a prohibited blood-alcohol concentration.
- In *Schwartz*, the arresting officer testified that the driver, after being stopped for driving in an erratic manner, exhibited "slurred speech, bloodshot eyes, a strong odor of alcohol, and an unsteady gait," and then performed poorly on field sobriety tests. The court of appeal held that this circumstantial evidence of intoxication, when supplemented by a blood test (which, as is the case here, did not meet the public-records hearsay exception, and therefore could not by itself prove intoxication), provided adequate support for the ALJ's finding that the driver had a blood-alcohol level of 0.08 percent or more.

27

- However, in *Rodriguez*, the court emphasized the danger of allowing the DMV to "'rescue' testing by an unqualified person with unscientific testimony." Thus, where the DMV proffered "only cursory proof of the officer's observations" of the driver's intoxication, a § 353 lab report that did not meet the exception to the hearsay rule could not be used to bolster the scant circumstantial evidence of intoxication even though, under APA § 115, such a blood test could be used "for the purpose of supplementing or explaining other evidence."
- Applicants should argue that the case at hand is much closer to *Rodriguez* than to *Schwartz*, and therefore the § 353 lab report cannot sufficiently buttress Officer Thompson's testimony.
  - Unlike the facts in *Schwartz*, there is no evidence that Ronald slurred her words during her interchange with Officer Thompson, or that she gave off any odor of alcohol—two clear symptoms of intoxication.
  - Ronald explained that she was tired, having just finished working 18 hours straight. Under the circumstances, her alleged poor performance on the field sobriety tests is reasonably explained by the facts that she has arthritis, was wearing high heels, and was forced to perform the tests next to a busy highway.
    - Such factors militating against intoxication were not present in *Schwartz*.
  - Moreover, the demeanor of the driver in *Rodriguez* was at least as suggestive of intoxication as Ronald's, but was nevertheless held insufficient.
- Even if, considered together, all of the evidence, including the flawed § 353 lab report, shows that it is *possible* that Ronald was driving with a blood-alcohol level of at least 0.08 percent, it fails to show that it is *more likely than not* that she was doing so.

Because the DMV has not carried its burden to prove by a preponderance of the evidence that Ronald was driving with a blood-alcohol level of at least 0.08 percent, the ALJ must vacate the suspension of her driver's license.

Applicant Identification

Bohmer v. Bohmer

**Read the instructions on the back cover.
Do not break the seal until you are told to do so.**

NATIONAL CONFERENCE OF BAR EXAMINERS

Bohmer v. Bohmer

INSTRUCTIONS

1.   You will have 90 minutes to complete this session of the examination. This performance test is designed to evaluate your ability to handle a select number of legal authorities in the context of a factual problem involving a client.

2.   The problem is set in the fictitious state of Franklin, in the fictitious Fifteenth Circuit of the United States. Columbia and Olympia are also fictitious states in the Fifteenth Circuit. In Franklin, the trial court of general jurisdiction is the District Court, the intermediate appellate court is the Court of Appeal, and the highest court is the Supreme Court.

3.   You will have two kinds of materials with which to work: a File and a Library. The first document in the File is a memorandum containing the instructions for the task you are to complete. The other documents in the File contain factual information about your case and may include some facts that are not relevant.

4.   The Library contains the legal authorities needed to complete the task and may also include some authorities that are not relevant. Any cases may be real, modified, or written solely for the purpose of this examination. If the cases appear familiar to you, do not assume that they are precisely the same as you have read before. Read them thoroughly, as if they all were new to you. You should assume that the cases were decided in the jurisdictions and on the dates shown. In citing cases from the Library, you may use abbreviations and omit page references.

5.   Your response must be written in the answer book provided. If you are taking this examination on a laptop computer, your jurisdiction will provide you with specific instructions. In answering this performance test, you should concentrate on the materials in the File and Library. What you have learned in law school and elsewhere provides the general background for analyzing the problem; the File and Library provide the specific materials with which you must work.

6.   Although there are no restrictions on how you apportion your time, you should be sure to allocate ample time (about 45 minutes) to reading and digesting the materials and to organizing your answer before you begin writing it. You may make notes anywhere in the test materials; blank pages are provided at the end of the booklet. You may not tear pages from the question booklet.

7.   This performance test will be graded on your responsiveness to the instructions regarding the task you are to complete, which are given to you in the first memorandum in the File, and on the content, thoroughness, and organization of your response.

Bohmer v. Bohmer

FILE

LIBRARY

POINT SHEET

Bohmer v. Bohmer

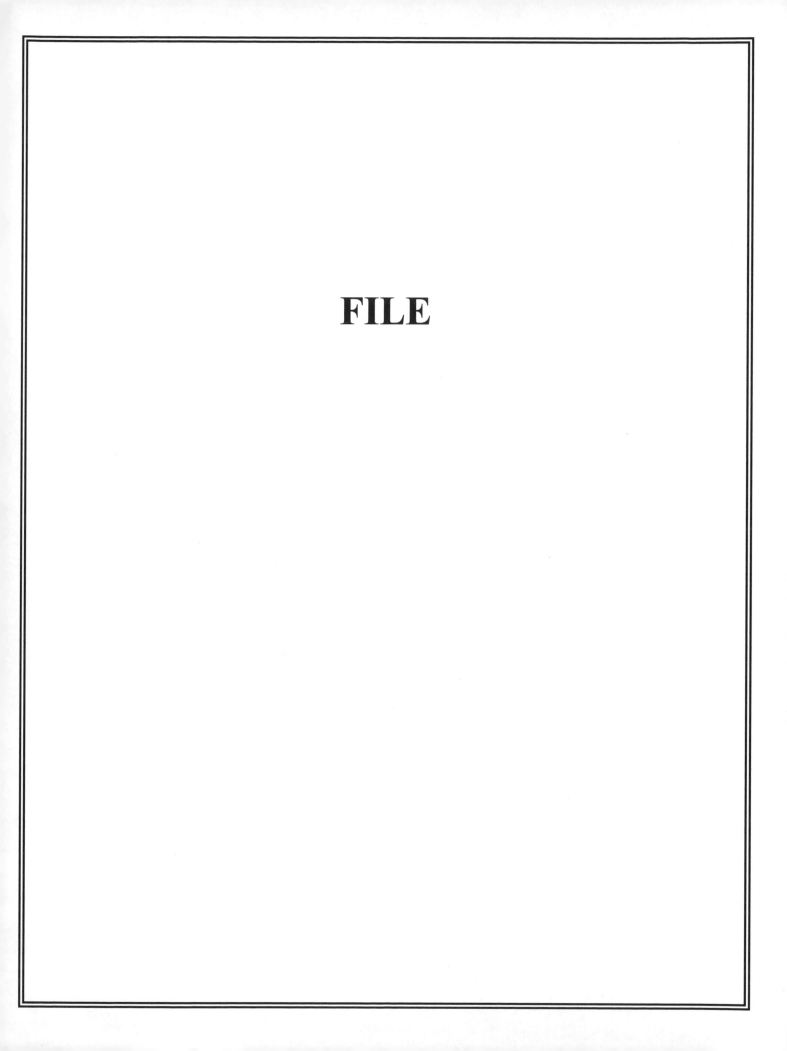

FILE

Bohmer v. Bohmer

Petrilla and Associates
Attorneys at Law
222 Van Every Place
Centralia, Franklin 33703

Office Memorandum

To: Applicant
From: Charles Petrilla, Managing Partner and Pro Bono Coordinator
Date: July 29, 2008
Re: Jessica Bohmer/Interstate Custody Case

Our law firm, as part of its pro bono program, has agreed to represent Jessica Bohmer in a child custody matter that her husband, Alex Bohmer, has filed in Franklin City, Franklin. Jessica currently lives with their six-year-old daughter, Carrie, in Columbia Heights, Columbia.

No divorce proceeding has yet been filed by either party. On June 30, 2008, Jessica's husband filed a child custody petition in Franklin District Court. We hope to convince the Franklin court that the case should be heard in Columbia where Columbia Legal Services is prepared to help Jessica file a custody action and obtain a civil protection order if necessary.

I just spoke to Columbia Legal Services this morning and will be talking to Jessica and Columbia Legal Services tomorrow. I want to be able to give them some answers regarding jurisdiction. To help me advise them, please prepare a memorandum analyzing the following two issues:

1. Whether Franklin or Columbia was the home-state jurisdiction under the Franklin Uniform Child Custody Jurisdiction and Enforcement Act (UCCJEA) at the time of the filing of the current custody case in Franklin.

2. Assuming for purposes of argument that the Franklin court decides that Franklin is the home-state jurisdiction, whether we are likely to be successful if we file a Motion to Decline Jurisdiction under the Inconvenient Forum provision of the Franklin UCCJEA.

Be sure to provide detailed discussion and analysis, incorporating the relevant facts and addressing the applicable legal authorities. I want to know the weaknesses as well as the strengths of a potential motion on Jessica's behalf. You need not prepare a separate statement of facts.

[Kathleen Murphy (KM), Columbia Legal Services attorney, and Charles Petrilla (CP), Franklin law firm partner, July 29, 2008]

KM: Charles, thanks very much for calling. I'm glad you've agreed to take Jessica's case because she needs representation in Franklin as well as in Columbia.

CP: Kathleen, I'm happy we can help. Thanks for faxing us a copy of the intake form and the Civil Protection Order issued in 2006 in Franklin against Jessica's husband, Alex. I've reviewed the intake form, but want to know if there have been any new developments. Have you filed a custody action on Jessica's behalf in Columbia?

KM: No, not yet. Jessica came into our office a little over two weeks ago seeking our help in obtaining sole custody of Carrie, and possibly with obtaining another civil protection order if Alex continues to threaten her. However, on June 30, 2008, Alex filed for custody of Carrie in Franklin District Court. We haven't actually seen a copy of Alex's complaint yet.

CP: I will get a copy from the court today and fax it to you. What are Jessica's concerns regarding having custody handled in Franklin?

KM: She's afraid to go back to Franklin City because of Alex's history of violence against her. She says that he owns a hunting rifle and she fears that he might use it to hurt her or Carrie. The most recent threatening episode was on February 1, 2008, when Alex became enraged when Jessica suggested a short visit to Columbia Heights to see her parents and Carrie, who was staying there with Jessica's parents. He ripped up several family photos. That really scared her—she left for Columbia the next day, on February 2, 2008, and hasn't been back since. Jessica also doesn't have the time or the money to go back and forth to Franklin City—the drive takes about an hour and a half, one way, and would require her to take time off from her new job.

CP: Does she intend to stay in Columbia?

KM: Yes. When she left Franklin on February 2, 2008, she didn't really have a plan. She told Alex that she would be back soon. However, after about three weeks in Columbia, she realized that she didn't want to go back to Franklin. She found a job and enrolled Carrie in the first grade in Columbia Heights. On March 1, 2008, she finally got up the courage and told Alex she wasn't coming back to Franklin but was going to stay with Carrie in Columbia.

CP: How did Alex react to that news?

KM: According to Jessica, he "flipped out." For weeks, he phoned her day and night, calling her all sorts of names. He also sent her a series of threatening e-mails like the one attached to the intake form.

CP: How does Jessica want to have the situation resolved?

KM: She wants sole custody of Carrie and wants to continue to live in Columbia, where her parents live. Having them nearby makes her feel safer, and they also help take care of Carrie. Jessica likes her new part-time job at a doctor's office and wants to enroll at the community college to finish her degree. Carrie's doing really well in school and has made a lot of friends. Carrie has told Jessica that she wants to stay in Columbia.

CP: We'll have to figure out which court should handle this matter. The UCCJEA is the law that controls which court has jurisdiction to hear custody cases. Both Columbia and Franklin adopted identical versions of this law. Let's see what the law is on this issue.

KM: We really hope that you can find a way to get the Franklin custody case resolved so that we can go forward here in Columbia. I will begin to prepare pleadings so that we can be ready to proceed in Columbia. Jessica is meeting with us tomorrow.

CP: Okay. I'll call you again tomorrow after we have done some research on our end.

Columbia Legal Services Intake Form

Date: July 14, 2008   **Intake Attorney:** Kathleen Murphy

I. Applicant Name: Jessica Bohmer

DOB: 5/30/1976 **Place of birth:** Columbia Heights, Columbia

Home address: 6226 Berkeley Blvd., Columbia Heights, Columbia 12111

Home telephone: 860-555-5688

Work address: Office of Stephen Tigani, MD, 10 Tulip Ave., Columbia Heights, Columbia

Work telephone: 860-555-3876

Is it safe to call the phone numbers listed? __X__ yes _____ no

Are the parties married? __X__ yes _____ no

If so, date and place of marriage: 3/29/2001, Columbia Heights, Columbia

Child(ren) in common. Include name, sex, and date and place of birth.

Carrie Bohmer, female, born 3/22/2002, Memorial Hospital, Columbia Heights, Columbia

Residence of applicant and child(ren) for the past 5 years. Include addresses, dates, and other people living with applicant.

1. 1/15/2003 to 5/31/2004: 28 Lanier St., Columbia Heights, Columbia; both parents and child;

2. 6/1/2004 to 5/30/2006: 1311 Taylor St., Franklin City, Franklin; both parents and child;

3. 5/31/2006 to 4/1/2007: 12 Ivy Lane, Franklin City, Franklin; mother and child only;

4. 4/2/2007 to 2/01/2008: 1311 Taylor St., Franklin City, Franklin; both parents and child (mother and child moved back with father);

5. 2/02/2008 to present: 6226 Berkeley Blvd., Columbia Heights, Columbia; mother, maternal grandparents, and child (mother moved in with her parents and child on February 2, 2008; child had been visiting her maternal grandparents since December 1, 2007).

What legal services is applicant seeking?

Jessica seeks to obtain sole custody of Carrie and protection from her husband's violence.

II. Opposing Party Name: Alex Bohmer

DOB: 10/18/1976 **Place of birth:** Columbia Heights, Columbia

Home address: 1311 Taylor St., Franklin City, Franklin 33068

Home telephone: 514-555-6999

4

Work address: Franklin Pharmaceutical Co., 101 Industrial Blvd., Franklin City, Franklin

Work telephone: 514-555-2339

Criminal history: n/a

Weapons: owns hunting rifle

Alcohol/drug use: drinks a few beers every weekend

Participation in drug/alcohol treatment: n/a

Participation in domestic violence intervention program: n/a

Has opposing party ever put his/her hands on applicant against applicant's will?
Yes

If yes, fill out Section III, Domestic Violence History

III. Domestic Violence History

Has applicant's spouse/partner forced applicant to do something by threatening applicant?

Yes, since Jessica was pregnant with Carrie, Alex has been physically and emotionally abusive. He has pushed her down, grabbed her, pulled her by the hair, slapped her in the face, and tried to choke her. He has refused to give her money, prevented her from going out with friends, and generally tried to interfere with her relationship with her large extended family.

What was the most recent incident?

On February 1, 2008, Alex got mad when Jessica told him she wanted to go for a short visit to Columbia to see Carrie and her family. He grabbed her by the shoulders and shook her. When she tried to get away, he got one of her family scrapbooks and took out several photos of her with her parents and ripped them up. Jessica was scared but managed to act calm. She left the next day for Columbia and told Alex she would be back in a few weeks.

What was the worst incident ever?

On Jessica's 30th birthday (5/30/2006), Alex pushed her down on the floor, then pulled her up and choked her. Jessica thought she was going to lose consciousness. She feared that he might really kill her. She had bruises on her neck and arms. She left the next day with Carrie and filed for a civil protection order, which was granted on 6/10/2006. She and Alex were separated for approximately 10 months before reuniting. She let the civil protection order lapse.

Bohmer v. Bohmer

Has/have applicant's child(ren) been abused by applicant's spouse/partner?

Alex has never attacked Carrie directly, but she has witnessed his violence against Jessica. When Alex, Jessica, and Carrie were living together as a family, Carrie frequently said that she was afraid "Daddy would get mad" at her, which Jessica interpreted as Carrie's fear that Alex would also hit Carrie. Carrie used to have nightmares, but those have subsided since she and Jessica moved out.

Additional history:

Jessica has never told anyone all the details about the abuse, although her family has suspected serious problems for a long time. Her family has witnessed the harassing phone calls Alex made after she moved to Columbia. Jessica wants to stay in Columbia because she has a place to live and a good part-time job, and because her mother is available to watch Carrie whenever needed. Jessica also plans to enroll in a community college here and complete her college degree.

Police reports: n/a

Hospital records: n/a

Prior Protection Orders: Yes, see Attachment A.

Date Issued	Jurisdiction	Disposition
6-10-2006	Franklin District Court	Consent Civil Protection Order, expired 6-9-2007

Other documents: See Attachment B.

IV. Income

Applicant employed: yes   **Approximate gross income:** $10,000

Opposing party employed: yes   **Approximate gross income:** $55,000

6

DISTRICT COURT OF FRANKLIN

Jessica Bohmer, Petitioner,   }
                    }   DV No. 0569-2006
      vs.   }
                    }

Alex Bohmer, Respondent.   }

CIVIL PROTECTION ORDER

Upon consideration of the petition filed in this case, and ☐ after a contested hearing, ☐ after a default hearing, ☒ by consent of the parties, the Court has determined:

☒ that the Petitioner has established by a preponderance of the evidence that there is good cause to believe that the parties have a family relationship and that the Respondent committed or threatened one or more acts of domestic violence within the meaning of Franklin Code § 12-105 *et seq.*, to wit, that the Respondent threatened to seriously harm the Petitioner and that he put his hands on Petitioner's neck in an attempt to choke her.

IT IS HEREBY ORDERED that for a period of 12 months from the date of this order:

☒   Respondent shall not assault, threaten, harass, or physically abuse Petitioner in any manner.

☒   Respondent shall stay at least 100 feet away from Petitioner's ☒ person, ☒ home, ☒ workplace, ☒ vehicle.

☒   Respondent shall not contact Petitioner in any manner, except by telephone; all telephone calls must be limited to reasonable hours of the day and must abide by the other provisions of this order.

☒   Respondent may not possess any firearms and must immediately turn over any such weapons he or she owns to the Franklin City Metropolitan Police Department.

THIS ORDER WILL EXPIRE IN 12 MONTHS UNLESS IT IS RENEWED BY THE COURT. FAILURE TO COMPLY WITH THIS ORDER IS A CRIMINAL OFFENSE AND CARRIES A PENALTY OF SIX MONTHS IN JAIL AND/OR A FINE OF $1,000.

_____   6-10-06

Respondent's signature *(required for a consent order only)*   Date

_____   6/10/2006

District Court Judge   Date

Bohmer v. Bohmer

To: jessicabohmer@mpt.com
From: alexbohmer@mpt.com
Date: March 10, 2008

Jessica,

You should think twice about leaving Franklin and taking Carrie. I mean business—if you don't come back soon, I guarantee you that you'll be sorry. I'm not going to sit still and let you walk all over me!

You know you can't take care of Carrie without me. Remember what happened the last time when you ran off and then came back begging for another chance? Besides, you're taking Carrie away from her life here—her school and her friends.

This is it, Jessica. I am not playing any more of your games. For Carrie's own good, I'm not going to let you cut me out of her life.

You know we could make this work if you would just try a little harder instead of quitting and running off to your parents every time we argue. I'm willing to meet you halfway—I know I've got a bad temper, and I've got an appointment with a therapist next week—but Carrie is my daughter and she needs her daddy as well as her mommy.

Alex

LIBRARY

Bohmer v. Bohmer

FRANKLIN UNIFORM CHILD CUSTODY JURISDICTION AND ENFORCEMENT ACT   (§ 16-101 *et seq.* (1999))

*   *   *   *

§ 16-102. Definitions.   In this Act:

*   *   *   *

(3) "Child custody determination" means a judgment, decree, or other order of a court providing for the legal custody, physical custody, or visitation with respect to a child. The term includes a permanent, temporary, initial, or modification order. . . .

*   *   *   *

(7) "Home State" means the State in which a child lived with a parent for at least six consecutive months immediately before the commencement of a child custody proceeding. . . . A period of temporary absence of any of the mentioned persons is part of the period.

*   *   *   *

§ 16-201. Initial Child Custody Jurisdiction.

(a) Except as otherwise provided . . . a court of this State has jurisdiction to make an initial child custody determination only if:

> (1) this State is the home State of the child on the date of the commencement of the proceeding, or was the home State of the child within six months before the commencement of the proceeding and the child is absent from this State but a parent continues to live in this State;

> (2) . . . or a court of the home State of the child has declined to exercise jurisdiction on the ground that this State is the more appropriate forum under § 16-207 . . . .

* *   *   *

§ 16-207. Inconvenient Forum.

(a) A court of this State which has jurisdiction under this [Act] to make a child custody determination may decline to exercise its jurisdiction at any time if it determines that it is an inconvenient forum under the circumstances and that a court of another State is a more

9

appropriate forum. The issue of inconvenient forum may be raised upon motion of a party, the court's own motion, or request of another court.

(b) Before determining whether it is an inconvenient forum, a court of this State shall consider whether it is appropriate for a court of another State to exercise jurisdiction. For this purpose, the court shall allow the parties to submit information and shall consider all relevant factors, including:

(1) whether domestic violence has occurred and is likely to continue in the future and which State could best protect the parties and the child;

(2) the length of time the child has resided outside this State;

(3) the distance between the court in this State and the court in the State that would assume jurisdiction;

(4) the relative financial circumstances of the parties;

(5) the nature and location of the evidence required to resolve the pending litigation, including testimony of the child; and

(6) the familiarity of the court of each State with the facts and issues in the pending litigation.

(c) If a court of this State determines that it is an inconvenient forum and that a court of another State is a more appropriate forum, it shall stay the proceedings upon condition that a child custody proceeding be promptly commenced in another designated State and may impose any other condition the court considers just and proper.

Bohmer v. Bohmer

In re Marriage of Mills
Franklin Court of Appeal (2002)

William and Jennifer Mills were married in 1993. They have two children. The parties separated in November 1999, when William moved from the family home to a nearby town in Franklin where he had secured a new job. Jennifer and the children remained in the family home in Franklin City.

In June 2000, the children went to Columbia for an extended visit to Jennifer's sister's farm. On August 10, 2000, Jennifer decided to leave Franklin with her mother and permanently move to Columbia and did so with the children. Thereafter, she rented a house, enrolled the children in school, and found a new job in Columbia. Jennifer has resided in Columbia with the children and her mother since moving there. However, Jennifer did not have an explicit conversation with William about her permanent relocation until sometime during the fall—the exact date is disputed, but both agree it was no earlier than November 1, 2000.

On April 1, 2001, William filed a petition in Franklin District Court seeking custody of the parties' two children.[1]

Jennifer moved to dismiss the petition, arguing that the Franklin court lacked subject matter jurisdiction to determine custody of the parties' children, on the grounds that Columbia was the children's "home state." The trial court granted the motion, concluding that it lacked subject matter jurisdiction under the Franklin Uniform Child Custody Jurisdiction and Enforcement Act (UCCJEA), § 16-101 *et seq.* William appeals. We affirm.

Under the UCCJEA, a Franklin court has subject matter jurisdiction to make a child custody determination if Franklin is the "home state" of the child. "Home state" is defined as the state in which a child lived with a parent for at least six months immediately before the commencement of a child custody proceeding. *See* UCCJEA § 16-102(7). Any period(s) of temporary absence are considered part of and included in the calculation of the six-month home-state requirement. *Id.*

On appeal William contends that the district court should have asserted jurisdiction under the UCCJEA to decide custody of the children because the children were only temporarily absent from Franklin and temporary absences are considered time in the home state. Specifically, he argues that when Jennifer left the state on August 10, 2000, she did so with the intent of returning to Franklin, and that she did not inform him that she intended to remain in Columbia with the children until at the earliest November 1, 2000. He thus maintains that the children's absence from Franklin was only a "temporary absence," and that they should be considered to have resided in Franklin until November 1, 2000.

---

[1] It is not unusual for child custody actions to be undertaken without a request to dissolve the marriage.

While we agree that intent is a significant consideration in determining whether an absence from a state is a "temporary absence," we do not believe that the significance of intent can or should be restricted to the intent existing at the time of leaving. If it were so restricted, then an absence that began with intent to return would remain a "temporary absence" even long after a decision had been reached to permanently relocate and such relocation to another state had in fact occurred. We believe instead that an absence from a state is no longer "temporary" once the absent person has formed the intent to reside permanently in another state and is in fact doing so with such intent.

In this case the children's presence in Columbia beginning in June 2000 was originally intended to be temporary. However, the parties had separated some seven months earlier and, as of August 10, 2000, Jennifer moved to Columbia intending to permanently relocate there with the parties' children. She has since resided there with them, with that intent. We conclude that the relevant six-month period began to run on August 10, 2000. We therefore agree with the trial court that Columbia, and not Franklin, was the children's "home state" when William filed his April 1, 2001, petition for custody, and that under UCCJEA § 16-201(a), the Franklin court did not have jurisdiction to make a child custody determination. In so concluding, we reject William's contention that the children's absence from Franklin must be considered a "temporary absence" until Jennifer expressly informed him in November that her earlier move to Columbia, of which he was aware, had been made with the intent that she and the children would remain in Columbia permanently.

Affirmed.

In re Marriage of Brickman and Young
Franklin Supreme Court (2003)

Mark Brickman commenced this action seeking to modify custody of his four minor children. His former wife, Ruth Young, moved to dismiss under the Franklin Uniform Child Custody Jurisdiction and Enforcement Act (UCCJEA) on the ground that Franklin is an inconvenient forum. She appeals the district court's denial of her motion, as affirmed by the court of appeal. We granted review, and now reverse and remand.

BACKGROUND

Brickman and Young married on October 1, 1988, in Livingston, Franklin. Thereafter, they separated and reconciled numerous times before finally separating in 1996.

Brickman repeatedly battered Young during the marriage, and Young obtained several court-issued protection orders during their multiple separations. Brickman pled guilty to domestic assault in 1990, 1991, 1994, and 1996. The record details Brickman's violations of the protection orders, as well as several incidents involving Brickman's violent behavior after the parties' final separation and before Young's move to Columbia.

In its March 23, 1998, marriage dissolution decree, the Franklin District Court, among other things, awarded custody of the parties' four children to Young. Shortly thereafter, Young relocated to the State of Columbia with her children. In response, Brickman filed a motion in Franklin District Court seeking to modify the court's decree and to obtain custody. Young then subsequently filed a motion requesting the Franklin District Court to decline jurisdiction as an inconvenient forum to allow the Columbia court to assume jurisdiction over the parties' ongoing child custody and visitation arrangements. Brickman opposed the motion. The Franklin District Court denied the motion; the court of appeal affirmed, and we granted review.

DISCUSSION

In this case of first impression we examine the provisions of the Franklin UCCJEA that allow a court to decline to exercise jurisdiction over child custody proceedings when the court determines that it is an inconvenient forum under the circumstances and that a court of another state is a more appropriate forum in which to make the child custody determination.

The Franklin UCCJEA sets forth six specific factors to be considered, which we discuss in turn below. We note that, while some factors may weigh more heavily than others, *all* must be considered by the court. The law does not allocate a burden of proof to either party, but directs the court to conduct an evaluation based upon the relevant information available to determine whether it is appropriate for another state to exercise jurisdiction.

The first inconvenient forum factor inquires "whether domestic violence has occurred and is likely to continue in the future and which State could best protect the parties and the child." UCCJEA § 16-207(b)(1). The UCCJEA places domestic violence at the top of the list of factors that courts are required to evaluate when determining whether to decline jurisdiction as an inconvenient forum for a child custody proceeding. With regard to this factor, the court should determine whether the parties are located in different states because one party is a victim of domestic violence or child abuse. If domestic violence or child abuse has occurred, the issue is which forum can provide greater safety.[1]

Given the high propensity for recidivism in domestic violence, we hold that when a court finds that domestic violence has occurred or that a party has fled the state to avoid further violence or abuse, the court is authorized to consider whether the party and the child might be better protected if further custody proceedings were held in another state. This factor alone is not dispositive under the UCCJEA; however, courts should give greater weight to this factor than to any other individual factor when considering jurisdictional issues under the UCCJEA.

Brickman asserts on appeal that his last act of reported domestic violence occurred in 1996 and claims that there has been "no apparent problem" during the past three years.

But Brickman's criminal record of domestic violence reveals a pattern of recurrent wife-battering of escalating intensity, which includes severely beating Young during her pregnancies. The record also establishes that Brickman has perpetrated serious injury upon his ex-wife and has exhibited obsessive and controlling behavior. Brickman testified at the May 2001 hearing that he had not received any type of psychological counseling since his last incarceration in 1996 for domestic violence. Moreover, he made no showing to the district court that his potential for future violence has abated.

This history of serious domestic violence and the threat of future domestic violence by Brickman leads us to conclude that with regard to this factor, Columbia is the state that would best protect Young and the children.

The second statutory factor asks how long the children have resided outside Franklin. UCCJEA § 16-207(b)(2). The district court relied heavily on the fact that the children have spent the majority of their lives in Franklin and on the extensive history of the parties in the Franklin courts. However, the four children, ranging in age from four to eleven at the time of the hearing, have now lived in Columbia for five years. Young tes-

---

[1] The compelling need to protect victims from further domestic violence is supported by the research findings of the United States Department of Justice. Those findings suggest that termination of an abusive relationship actually poses an increased risk of escalation in domestic violence. Although divorced women and separated women comprise only 10 percent of all women in America, they account for three-quarters of all battered women and report being battered 14 times as often as women still living with their partners. Divorced or separated men, as opposed to husbands living with their wives, commit 79 percent of all spousal violence.

14

tified that the children "have significant connections to family, school, and community" in Columbia and have developed relationships that have enhanced their sense of security and well-being, which is "a contrast from the isolation they experienced while living in Franklin." Because it has been the children's home for the past five years, we conclude that, on this factor, Columbia would be an appropriate forum for child custody proceedings.

The third factor evaluates the distance between the courts, which is approximately 400 miles in this case. UCCJEA § 16-207(b)(3). Young testified that the drive between her home and the court in Franklin takes about eight hours each way. As the primary custodial parent, Young must either bring the children with her to court proceedings or arrange for their care in her absence. Because the distance between the Franklin and Columbia courts creates a transportation inconvenience that must be borne by one of the parties, we conclude that the facts suggest that Brickman, as the noncustodial parent, may be in the better position to undertake the necessary travel.

The fourth factor concerns the relative financial circumstances of the parties, which the district court found to be disparate. UCCJEA § 16-207(b)(4). The court determined that Brickman enjoys an annual income of $41,797 while Young has an annual income of $6,500. We conclude that this factor weighs in favor of transfer to Columbia's jurisdiction.

The fifth factor examines the traditional bases for determining venue and inquires about the nature and location of the evidence required to resolve the pending litigation, including testimony of the children. UCCJEA § 16-207(b)(5). Notwithstanding Young's testimony that all current evidence regarding the children's mental health, medical, financial, and school records is in Columbia, the district court concluded that Franklin is just as convenient a forum as Columbia for review of pertinent child records. Although records may be easily transportable, the district court failed to address the convenience of the witnesses, the majority of whom reside in Columbia, including the four children. Three of the children are enrolled in school and receive therapeutic counseling in Columbia. Young maintains that Columbia is now the location of all witnesses and evidence regarding the children. Brickman did not refute Young's assertions regarding the location of evidence and witnesses. This factor weighs in favor of Columbia's jurisdiction.

The final factor is the familiarity of the court of each state with the facts and issues in the pending litigation. UCCJEA § 16-207(b)(6). There has been extensive litigation concerning this marriage in the Franklin court—the case file is now in its fifth volume. But while the Franklin court may be well versed in the conflict, Young argues persuasively that the Columbia court also has had an opportunity to at least become familiar with the facts and issues involved in the case, when she applied for and received a permanent protection order in 2001 from the Co-

15

lumbia court. Therefore, under this factor, while the Franklin court might be the more appropriate forum, we conclude that the Columbia court would not be an inappropriate forum.

CONCLUSION

Weighing all the factors together, and giving added weight to the first factor concerning the existence of past and danger of continuing violence, we conclude that Columbia is the more appropriate forum to resolve this custody dispute.

Accordingly, we reverse the court of appeal's affirmance of the district court's order and remand to the district court with instructions to stay further proceedings and to direct the parties to file in Columbia, the more appropriate forum.

Reversed and remanded.

Bohmer v. Bohmer

POINT SHEET

Bohmer v. Bohmer

Bohmer v. Bohmer

DRAFTERS' POINT SHEET

This performance test requires applicants, as associates of a Franklin law firm, to analyze the provisions of the Franklin Uniform Child Custody Jurisdiction and Enforcement Act (UCCJEA) and to predict whether the UCCJEA, and the Franklin cases interpreting it, will permit the firm to persuade a Franklin court that a state of Columbia court is the preferable venue to address a child custody dispute. The child's mother, Jessica Bohmer, is the firm's client. Jessica is still married to six-year-old Carrie's father, Alex Bohmer. Jessica has recently relocated from Franklin to Columbia with Carrie because of her concerns about Alex's violence.

The File contains an instructional memo from the managing partner, a transcript of a telephone call between the partner and a Columbia legal services attorney representing Jessica there, a Columbia Legal Services intake form, a Civil Protection Order, and a copy of an e-mail from Alex to Jessica. The Library includes excerpts from the UCCJEA and two Franklin cases.

The following discussion covers all of the points the drafters intended to raise in the problem. Applicants need not cover them all to receive passing or even excellent grades. Grading is entirely within the discretion of the user jurisdictions.

I. Format and Overview

Applicants' work product should resemble a legal memorandum that an associate would write to a partner. Applicants should thoroughly discuss the two issues raised in the instructional memo, identifying the specific UCCJEA provisions and case law supporting their analyses and conclusions and incorporating all relevant facts. Applicants are told to address and analyze potential weaknesses as well as strengths of Jessica's case. Those addressing only strengths should be downgraded. The issues that should be addressed are the following:

A. Whether Franklin or Columbia was the home-state jurisdiction under the Franklin UCCJEA at the time of the filing of the custody case in Franklin.

Applicants should conclude that Franklin was the home-state jurisdiction at the time Alex filed his custody suit in Franklin. They should conclude this after reading § 16-102, which defines the key concept of home-state jurisdiction; § 16-201, which prioritizes home-state jurisdiction; and *In re Marriage of Mills* (Franklin Ct. App. 2002).

Mills sets forth a test for determining whether a stay is a temporary absence or a permanent relocation to another state. The *Mills* court ruled that it is best to look at the intent of the absent parent to determine whether the move is a permanent relocation. Further, a move can begin as a temporary absence and can change to a permanent relocation because of a change in the parent's intentions. Home-state jurisdiction remains in the left-behind jurisdiction for six months from the time of the absent parent's intention to make the move permanent.

> B. **Assuming that Franklin is the home-state jurisdiction, whether the Franklin court is likely to grant a motion to decline jurisdiction under the UCCJEA's inconvenient forum provision, thus allowing a Columbia court to decide the Bohmer custody action.**

Applicants should analyze the UCCJEA inconvenient forum provision (§§ 16-207, 16-201(a)(2) (a court with home-state jurisdiction may decline in favor of another jurisdiction)) and *In re Marriage of Brickman and Young* (Franklin Sup. Ct. 2003). Applicants should discuss each of the six factors in § 16-207(b) in light of the facts and apply the appropriate standard as set forth in *Brickman*. They should conclude that the firm can make a strong argument that the Franklin court should decline jurisdiction to allow the Bohmer custody action to be heard in Columbia. However, they should also recognize that Jessica's case is not as compelling as that of the mother in *Brickman*, and thus the outcome of such a motion cannot be predicted with certainty.

II. Detailed Analysis

> A. **Whether Franklin or Columbia was the home-state jurisdiction under the UCCJEA when Alex filed the custody action in Franklin.**

Under the UCCJEA, the "home state" is the state in which a child lived with a parent for at least six consecutive months immediately before the commencement of the custody proceeding. § 16-102(3). A temporary absence is considered part of the home-state period. *Id.*

Under § 16-201, to proceed with an initial custody case, the court must either be (1) the "home-state" jurisdiction (if a home-state jurisdiction exists) or (2) the court in whose favor the "home-state" court declined jurisdiction under the UCCJEA inconvenient forum provision, § 16-207. The home-state jurisdiction has priority over all other jurisdictions except under very limited circumstances, namely, if the home-state jurisdiction declines jurisdiction in favor of another, more appropriate state. The jurisdiction must have been the child's home state on the date of the commencement of the custody action, or must have been the child's home state within six months of the commencement of the action. § 16-201. If the latter situation applies, § 16-201 further requires that a parent must continue to live in the left-behind state.

A key determination is the date of a child's permanent relocation to another state. This is the date from which the six-month period begins to run resulting in establishing another state as the new home state.

1. **Establishment of new home state: determination if absence from state is temporary absence or a permanent relocation**

- The *Mills* court discusses the factors used to determine if a parent and child have relocated permanently. In *Mills,* the children's absence was originally intended to be temporary, but it became a permanent relocation when the mother moved to Columbia and engaged in activities that made it clear she intended to relocate there permanently: she rented a house, enrolled the children in school, and took a new job. She did not expressly tell the father of her intent to relocate until months later. The father filed for custody in the left-behind state within six months of the date the mother notified him that her move was permanent, but more than six months from the date she first moved to Columbia. The court concluded that Franklin was no longer the home state at the time the father filed for custody and therefore the Franklin court lacked custody jurisdiction under the UCCJEA.

- The intent of the parent who has left is a significant factor in deciding whether there is a temporary absence or a permanent relocation. The court looks to the party's actions to determine intent.

- If the parent is found not to have the requisite intent to relocate, then the absence is treated as if it did not exist in determining the period of home-state jurisdiction. *See Mills*; § 16-102(7).

- Thus, the first two months that Carrie was visiting her grandparents in Columbia (December 2007 and January 2008) are most appropriately treated as a temporary absence, that is, as if Carrie were still living in Franklin for purposes of determining the home state.

- However, a stay that begins as a "temporary absence" can change and become a permanent relocation. *See Mills*. The nature of Carrie's stay with her grandparents changed, but only after February 2, 2008, when Jessica joined Carrie in Columbia and decided to relocate there.

- Franklin would continue to be the home state for six months from the time that Jessica formed the intent to relocate to Columbia and began to take steps to do so.

- Note that under *Mills*, the date that the absent parent expressly informs the other parent of the permanent nature of the move is relevant, but not controlling in deciding the date on which the absence transformed from a temporary to a permanent move. In *Mills*, the left-behind father in Franklin claimed that the key date was the date on which his wife *expressly* told him that her earlier move to Columbia was permanent, which he claimed was less than six months before his custody filing in Franklin. The *Mills* court rejected this argument, concluding that under the facts of the case it should have been clear to the father at an earlier date that the mother's move was permanent—the mother and children had been living in Columbia for months, the kids were enrolled in Columbia schools, etc.

- The period for calculating if Columbia is the home state begins to run from one of the following: February 2 (when Jessica went to Columbia), late February (when Jessica decided not to return to Franklin, began looking for a job, and enrolled Carrie in school), or March 1 (when Jessica told Alex of her decision to stay).

- Under *Mills*, the most relevant time would be late February when Jessica made a decision to stay in Columbia and began to act upon it. However, under any one of these dates, Franklin would still remain Carrie's home-state jurisdiction on the date Alex filed for custody (June 30) because fewer than six months had passed.

  - An argument that December 1, 2007 (when Carrie left to visit her grandparents), was the relevant date for determining whether Columbia would be the home state on June 30, 2008, would <u>not</u> be meritorious.

- In short, the requisite events to start the "home-state" clock ticking in Columbia did not occur until sometime after February 2, the day that Jessica left Franklin for Columbia. Thus, Columbia could not have become the new "home-state" jurisdiction for six months from that date—sometime after August 2, at the earliest. This means that the Franklin court had the right to proceed under "home-state jurisdiction" authority in Alex's June 30 custody case because at most only five months had passed, not the six months needed to establish a new home state in Columbia.

- Jessica sent Carrie to stay in Columbia with her parents on December 1, 2007; Jessica and Alex remained in Franklin; after Alex tore up the family photos, Jessica went to Columbia on February 2, 2008, telling Alex she would stay with her parents for a short visit but would return to Franklin in a few weeks.

- Jessica did not return as promised, but decided sometime later in February to separate from Alex and stay in Columbia. She enrolled Carrie in school in Columbia, found a job, and made plans to enroll in a community college. On March 1 Jessica told Alex that she did not intend to return to Franklin.

- On June 30, 2008, Alex filed for custody in Franklin district court. This date is: seven months from December 1, 2007, when Carrie left Franklin for Columbia; five months from February 2, when Jessica left Franklin for Columbia; and four months after Jessica told Alex on March 1, that she intended to stay in Columbia.

- If the objective test of "physical presence of the child within the jurisdiction" were the rule, then Columbia would arguably be the home state because more than six months had passed since December 1, 2007, when Carrie went to stay with her grandparents in Columbia.

- Here, it is not absolutely certain if February 2, later in February, or March 1 is the relevant date for determining if Carrie's living status has changed. The best answer is that the date that Jessica decided not to return to Franklin is the relevant date; but even assuming it is the earlier date of February 2, Franklin was still the home state on June 30, when Alex filed the custody petition. Columbia would not become the home state until sometime after July 1 at the earliest.

- Therefore, under the UCCJEA, Franklin has jurisdiction to the exclusion of any other state, unless it is an "inconvenient forum" under § 16-207.[1]

B. **Assuming that Franklin is the home state, whether a motion to decline jurisdiction under the UCCJEA's inconvenient forum provision would be likely**

---

[1] Under sections of the UCCJEA that were not included in the Library, there is one other circumstance where it would be appropriate to depart from the home-state jurisdiction: if "emergency jurisdiction" were appropriate in another jurisdiction. This issue is not raised by this problem and the Library does not contain legal authority for discussion of this issue.

to succeed, thus allowing a Columbia court to decide the Bohmer custody case.

UCCJEA § 16-207(a), as interpreted by *Brickman,* provides the criteria for analyzing whether the Franklin court should decline to exercise jurisdiction over the custody case despite the fact that Franklin is the home state. Applicants must discuss the strengths and weaknesses of Jessica's case in light of the court's analysis in *Brickman.*

Section 16-207(b) states: "A court of this State which has jurisdiction under this [Act] to make a child custody determination may decline to exercise its jurisdiction at any time if it determines that it is an inconvenient forum under the circumstances and that a court of another State is a more appropriate forum. The issue of inconvenient forum may be raised upon motion of a party, the court's own motion, or request of another court."

Section 16-207 requires the home state court to determine whether a court of another state would be a more appropriate forum by considering six factors. Although the first factor carries more weight, no single factor is dispositive.

Factor One: Whether domestic violence has occurred and is likely to continue in the future and which state could best protect the parties and the child

In *Brickman,* the court of appeal reversed the trial court's denial of the mother's (Young's) motion to decline jurisdiction. It found that the trial court failed to make findings regarding Brickman's acts of domestic violence before concluding that Young had not shown that she and the children would be safer if the custody case were transferred to Columbia. The court then detailed the couple's extensive history of domestic violence in Franklin.

A finding of past domestic violence can be the basis for a Franklin court to yield jurisdiction to another state, although first the court must consider evidence regarding all of the other jurisdictional factors enumerated by § 16-207(b). The *Brickman* court emphasized that the Franklin UCCJEA places domestic violence at the top of its list of factors—if it is present, the court may consider which of two competing states can best protect the victim from further abuse unless issues arise from consideration of other factors that outweigh the safety considerations.

Here, there is a credible history of Alex's abusive behavior toward Jessica. This is set out in the telephone transcript, the legal services intake form, the civil protection order, and Alex's e-mail. The parties had a 10-month separation followed by reconciliation, past physical violence in Carrie's presence, numerous incidents that Jessica shared with the legal services attorney at intake, and Alex's possession of a rifle. In addition, there were several recent incidents: Alex was increasingly unpredictable around Jessica, he had torn up family photos in anger, and he had sent a series of threatening e-mails after Jessica told him that she intended to stay in Columbia. Jessica says she fears for her safety and is afraid to return to Franklin.

However, these facts do not weigh as heavily in favor of Jessica as was the case in *Brickman*, where the evidence of domestic violence was more compelling than here. In *Brickman,* there was an escalating pattern of violence, including the husband severely beating his wife during pregnancy, resulting in four criminal convictions and incarceration. Here, there is an established pattern of violence that led to the issuance of the Franklin protection order in 2006 and to a temporary separation. Jessica's current fears are based on an incident in which Alex shook her and ripped up family photos, after which she moved to Columbia because she feared further violence. He sent her an e-mail message, saying "I mean business" and "I guarantee you that you'll be sorry," which sounds ominous but is not explicitly threatening. Parts of the message are conciliatory and express concern for Carrie; Alex says that he is "willing to meet you [Jessica] halfway" and that "Carrie is my daughter and she needs her daddy as well as her mommy." Moreover, the *Brickman* court relied in part on the fact that the offender "had not received any type of psychological counseling since his last incarceration" and had failed to show "that his potential for future violence has abated." If Alex can show that he attended the therapist appointment mentioned in his e-mail, he may be able to make the showing that Brickman failed to make.

In sum, although Jessica has some strong evidence of domestic violence, it is not as strong as that in *Brickman*.

FACTOR FAVORS JESSICA, BUT NOT TO THE EXTENT IN *BRICKMAN*

Factor Two: The length of time the child has resided outside this state

The *Brickman* children spent the most recent five years in Columbia; before that they had lived in Franklin. They had many connections in Columbia, but had lived in relative isolation in Franklin. The court found that this factor favored finding jurisdiction in Columbia.

Here, Carrie has spent seven consecutive months in Columbia; she was born in Columbia and lived there for her first year before she and her parents moved to Franklin; and many of Jessica's extended family members live in Columbia. Jessica can testify that these relationships give her a sense of security and well-being in contrast to the fear and anxiety she felt living in Franklin where she was relatively isolated because Alex discouraged any relationships with friends or family in Franklin.

NEUTRAL —OR SLIGHTLY FAVORS JESSICA

Factor Three: The distance between the court in this state and the court in the state that would assume jurisdiction

In *Brickman*, Young's Columbia home and the Franklin court were 400 miles apart. As the custodial parent, Young would have had to bring the children to court or arrange for their care. The court concluded that Brickman, the noncustodial parent, should bear any transportation inconvenience as he was "in the better position to undertake the necessary travel."

Here, it is 100 miles or an hour-and-a-half drive between the Franklin and Columbia courts. Because Jessica has physical care of Carrie, under *Brickman*, it would be reasonable to require Alex to bear the burden of traveling to Columbia. However, the distance is not nearly as burdensome as it was in *Brickman*. Furthermore, Jessica and Carrie live with Jessica's parents, who could presumably watch Carrie. Finally, Jessica is only working part-time, so she may be able to make the trip without missing work.

NEUTRAL

Factor Four: The relative financial circumstances of the parties

Brickman's annual income was $41,000 and Young's only $6,500. Presumably, the father's greater income made travel easier for him, but the court did not discuss this in detail.

Here, Jessica has a relatively new part-time job at a doctor's office earning $10,000 per year. Because she is a new employee, her job status may be particularly vulnerable. Alex has a presumably stable job with Franklin Pharmaceutical Co. making $55,000 per year.

FAVORS JESSICA

Factor Five: The nature and location of the evidence required to resolve the pending litigation, including testimony of the child

This factor examines the traditional bases for determining venue and inquires about the nature and location of the evidence required to resolve the pending litigation, including the testimony of the children. In *Brickman*, the court recognized that records can be transported to new courts easily, and that virtually all the witnesses lived in Columbia. Brickman did not refute Young's assertions. Therefore, the court held that this factor favored Young.

Here, the relevant evidence and witnesses appear almost equally split between Franklin and Columbia: Carrie, Jessica, and Jessica's parents and extended family are in Columbia; Carrie was born in Columbia and lived there until she was one year old; and Carrie has had extended visits with her grandparents there. On the other hand, Alex lives in Franklin; Carrie also lived there for four years; and her former preschool and friends are in Franklin. Jessica claims that they were isolated in Franklin because of Alex's abusive behavior and therefore she could argue that there is minimal evidence in Franklin. At best, it is not a clear-cut factor in favor of either party.

NEUTRAL

Factor Six: Each state court's familiarity with the facts and issues in the pending litigation

In *Brickman*, there was extensive litigation concerning the marriage in the Franklin court—the case file filled five volumes. In contrast, there was only a civil protection order in Columbia. However, despite the extensive litigation history in Franklin, the Franklin Supreme Court was satisfied that Columbia was the appropriate forum under the circumstances.

Here, there is past litigation in Franklin in that a protection order was issued against Alex in 2006. But that order did not address custody of Carrie and there is no prior custody case in either jurisdiction. The parties lived longer in Franklin as a couple than in Columbia, but got married and initially lived in Columbia. There appear to be more witnesses and possible evidence of Carrie's welfare in Columbia. Current threats might be better addressed in Columbia. A certified copy of the Franklin protection order could be obtained easily and introduced in Columbia.

NEUTRAL—OR SLIGHTLY FAVORS JESSICA

III.   Conclusion

Even though Franklin is the UCCJEA home state, applicants should conclude that the Franklin court is likely to decline jurisdiction in favor of Columbia based on the overarching factor of safety and security for Jessica and Carrie in light of Alex's abusive behavior and the threat that it may continue. Although the evidence of domestic violence is not as extensive as in *Brickman*, the totality of circumstances favors Jessica and there is no other factor that outweighs the issue of her sense of safety for herself and Carrie. Therefore, it would be reasonable for the Franklin court to follow *Brickman* and rule in Jessica's favor on the firm's motion to decline jurisdiction. This initial custody case is more appropriately addressed in Columbia.

Bohmer v. Bohmer

Applicant Identification

Williams v. A-1 Automotive Center

**Read the instructions on the back cover.
Do not break the seal until you are told to do so.**

NATIONAL CONFERENCE OF BAR EXAMINERS

INSTRUCTIONS

1. You will have 90 minutes to complete this session of the examination. This performance test is designed to evaluate your ability to handle a select number of legal authorities in the context of a factual problem involving a client.

2. The problem is set in the fictitious state of Franklin, in the fictitious Fifteenth Circuit of the United States. Columbia and Olympia are also fictitious states in the Fifteenth Circuit. In Franklin, the trial court of general jurisdiction is the District Court, the intermediate appellate court is the Court of Appeal, and the highest court is the Supreme Court.

3. You will have two kinds of materials with which to work: a File and a Library. The first document in the File is a memorandum containing the instructions for the task you are to complete. The other documents in the File contain factual information about your case and may include some facts that are not relevant.

4. The Library contains the legal authorities needed to complete the task and may also include some authorities that are not relevant. Any cases may be real, modified, or written solely for the purpose of this examination. If the cases appear familiar to you, do not assume that they are precisely the same as you have read before. Read them thoroughly, as if they all were new to you. You should assume that the cases were decided in the jurisdictions and on the dates shown. In citing cases from the Library, you may use abbreviations and omit page references.

5. Your response must be written in the answer book provided. If you are taking this examination on a laptop computer, your jurisdiction will provide you with specific instructions. In answering this performance test, you should concentrate on the materials in the File and Library. What you have learned in law school and elsewhere provides the general background for analyzing the problem; the File and Library provide the specific materials with which you must work.

6. Although there are no restrictions on how you apportion your time, you should be sure to allocate ample time (about 45 minutes) to reading and digesting the materials and to organizing your answer before you begin writing it. You may make notes anywhere in the test materials; blank pages are provided at the end of the booklet. You may not tear pages from the question booklet.

7. This performance test will be graded on your responsiveness to the instructions regarding the task you are to complete, which are given to you in the first memorandum in the File, and on the content, thoroughness, and organization of your response.

Williams v. A-1 Automotive Center

FILE

LIBRARY

POINT SHEET

FILE

Miller & Killebrew LLP
Attorneys at Law
450 Flamingo Drive, Suite 1000
Clear Bay, Franklin 33002

MEMORANDUM

To: Applicant
From: Tania Miller
Re: Williams v. Biggs d/b/a A-1 Automotive Center
Date: July 29, 2008

_____

We represent Robert Williams in a dispute with A-1 Automotive Center (A-1), concerning repairs that A-1 made to his minivan. He wants us to file a lawsuit on his behalf.

I believe Mr. Williams may be able to sue A-1 for fraud. I'm attaching notes of my interview with Mr. Williams and my memorandum to the file identifying four potentially actionable statements.

Please complete the following tasks:

1. Write a memo analyzing which of the four statements are actionable and which are not, and explaining the reasons for each of your conclusions.

2. For each statement that you determine to be actionable, draft a separate cause of action for fraud. Be sure to follow our firm's drafting guidelines for causes of action.

1

Miller & Killebrew LLP

OFFICE MEMORANDUM

To: Attorneys
From: Tania Miller
Re: Drafting Causes of Action
Date: September 5, 2004

In pleading a cause of action, firm practice requires attorneys to draft the minimum allegations necessary to plead the required legal elements of the claim, presented in separately numbered paragraphs. The practice of pleading the required legal elements minimizes the risk of the court dismissing an action for failure to state a claim.

For example, a complaint for negligence must usually allege four elements: that the defendant had a duty, that the defendant breached that duty, that the defendant's breach was the proximate cause of injury to the plaintiff, and that this injury caused the plaintiff to suffer compensable damages. The following complaint for negligence provides an example of a negligence pleading consistent with the firm's pleadings practice:

1.   When driving his car on the streets of Franklin City, Joe McMann owed other persons using the streets the duty to drive his car as a reasonable and prudent person would.

2.   On December 5, 2002, Joe McMann breached his duty by driving his car at a speed in excess of the posted speed limit and through a red light at the corner of First Avenue and K Street in Franklin City.

3.   When Joe McMann breached his duty, his car struck Sally Young, who was a pedestrian lawfully walking in a crosswalk at the intersection of First Avenue and K Street.

4.   As a result of Joe McMann's breaching his duty, Sally Young suffered serious bodily injury and other damages.

Client interview notes: Robert Williams
July 24, 2008

Met with new client Robert Williams this morning concerning his dispute with A-1 Automotive Center (A-1). A-1 is a small auto-repair shop located in Navasota, Franklin, which is owned and operated by Aaron Biggs.

Last month, Williams and his family were planning to leave for a one-week vacation in Ocean City, Columbia. He intended to drive to Ocean City in his 2003 Dodge minivan. At that time, the minivan had approximately 75,000 miles on the odometer and was in perfect working condition.

Williams saw an advertisement in a local newspaper in which A-1 offered an oil change and fluid check for $29.95, and decided to take advantage of it. On Thursday, June 5, 2008, he called A-1 and spoke with Biggs, who told him to bring in the minivan and said that A-1 would do the work right away.

When Williams arrived, he was informed by Biggs that his minivan would have to be test-driven. Williams told Biggs that he would like to go along. After waiting around for half an hour, however, he saw his minivan being driven around the corner by one of the shop's mechanics. When the mechanic returned from the test-drive, Williams saw him talking and joking about something with Biggs. A few minutes later, Biggs walked over and told Williams that although the minivan was shifting fine, there might be a little slippage in the transmission, and that A-1 would have to find what was causing the problem. Because Biggs could not estimate how long that would take, Williams took a bus home.

Williams was home no more than 15 minutes when he received a call from Biggs telling him that there were problems with the minivan's transmission. Biggs told Williams that he had "checked and found a notification from Dodge about a defect causing the gears to grind down." Williams expressed surprise that there could be any problem with the transmission when the vehicle had been running perfectly, and he told Biggs not to take the transmission out of the minivan until he arrived.

When Williams arrived at the shop about 45 minutes later, the transmission had already been removed from his minivan and disassembled. Biggs told Williams, "Your transmission is going to fail, and soon!" Biggs gave him the option of having his old transmission repaired for about $1,400 or purchasing a rebuilt transmission from A-1's stock at a cost of around $1,700. Although Williams originally had had no intention of putting a rebuilt transmission into his

3

minivan, at that point he felt he had no choice. He had no expertise in automotive repair, he was planning to leave for his vacation the next day, and Biggs told him that it would take three days to repair his own transmission but that a rebuilt transmission could be installed by that evening. Williams told Biggs to install the rebuilt transmission. Biggs then said, "It would also help if we installed an extra cooler to keep it from running hot." Williams told Biggs that if the minivan had needed an extra cooler, the manufacturer would have installed one. With that, Biggs dropped the subject.

Williams picked up the minivan that evening and paid the bill. As Williams left the shop, Biggs told him, "I guarantee the job."

Williams took the minivan home and parked it in his garage. Later that evening, he noticed transmission oil all over the garage floor. He decided to delay his vacation and take the minivan back to A-1. When Williams looked at his receipt, however, he discovered that it was stamped "NO GUARANTEE." The next morning, when he called A-1 to inquire why this was the case, Biggs told him that because he had elected not to have the extra cooler installed, A-1 could not guarantee the transmission. That same day, Williams took the minivan to Mission Dodge, a local dealership, and told them about his experience with A-1. Mission discovered that the minivan's transmission was in fact his original transmission and not a rebuilt one. (Domestic car manufacturers mark engine transmission casings with the vehicle's serial number.) Mission also told Williams that Dodge had not circulated any notification about any problems with the transmissions in its 2003 minivans. Mission charged Williams $128 to repair the transmission leak, which had been caused by A-1's improper reinstallation of the transmission.

On June 17, 2008, after he returned from vacation, Williams called A-1 and attempted to get his money back. Biggs told Williams that he would look into it. Williams called back several times to follow up with Biggs. Each time, Biggs told him that he was still looking into the matter. Williams came to us to bring suit.

Miller & Killebrew LLP
Attorneys at Law
450 Flamingo Drive, Suite 1000
Clear Bay, Franklin 33002

MEMORANDUM

To: File
From: Tania Miller
Re: Williams Matter
Date: July 25, 2008

Note to file—Further research needed to determine whether any of the following statements by Biggs might support a cause of action for fraud:

1. Biggs had "found a notification from Dodge about a defect causing the gears to grind down."

2. "Your transmission is going to fail, and soon!"

3. "It would also help if we installed an extra cooler to keep it from running hot."

4. "I guarantee the job."

RECEIPT

A-1 Automotive Center
4834 West Avenue
Navasota, Franklin 33017
(222) 555-2115
FIRST CLASS SERVICE

Invoice #:	I0023059
Date:	June 5, 2008
Page:	1

Customer: Robert Williams Address: 17159 Springfield Ct. City: Diamond Springs, FR 33015 Home Phone: (222) 555-3591 Work Phone: (222) 555-6705	Vehicle: 2003 Dodge Grand Caravan Minivan License: E47-S19 V.I.N.: JH5SV9257RS928599 Engine: V6/150hp/3.8L Mileage: 75,249
Parts	**Labor**
REBUILT TRANSMISSION, INCLUDING HOUSING, GEARS, SEALS, PLANETARY ASSEMBLY, SPRAGS, TORQUE CONVERTER, PAN GASKET, FILTER, BANDS, SOLENOID, AND FRONT PUMP; DRAIN AND REPLACE TRANSMISSION FLUID $1400.00	CUSTOMER REQUESTED WE REPLACE ORIGINAL TRANSMISSION WITH REBUILT TRANSMISSION INSTEAD OF REPAIRING ORIGINAL 6.25 hrs @ $60.00/hr $375.00

Labor:	$375.00
Parts:	$1400.00
Other Fees:	$0.00
Supplies:	$0.00
Subtotal:	$1775.00
Sales Tax:	$112.00
Total:	$1887.00
Paid:	$1887.00
Balance Due:	$0.00

NO GUARANTEE

Williams v. A-1 Automotive Center

LIBRARY

Foster v. Panera
Franklin Court of Appeal (2003)

This action was brought to recover damages for fraud. Plaintiff Danielle Foster appeals from the trial court's dismissal of the action for failure to state a claim against defendants Ted Panera and Abbey Furniture Company (collectively "defendants").

PLAINTIFF'S ALLEGATIONS

The pertinent allegations in the complaint are as follows:

On or about May 7, 2001, Foster told Panera, the store manager at Abbey Furniture Company, that she wished to purchase a certain set of bedroom furniture, which included a solid wood headboard. All of the items were present in the store except for the headboard. Panera told Foster that the headboard was at the store's warehouse and would be delivered to her with the other items.

Unknown to Foster, Panera made this representation knowing that it was false and intending to induce Foster's purchase of the furniture. Relying on this representation, Foster ordered and paid for the bedroom set, specifically including the solid wood headboard. She would not have ordered or purchased the bedroom set, nor any of its individual components, had she known that it would not include the matching headboard. When the furniture was delivered to Foster with a brass headboard, instead of the solid wood headboard, Foster telephoned

Panera, who apologized and said that the correct headboard would be delivered to her soon. However, during the ensuing weeks and months, Panera told Foster that the headboard was on order, under manufacture, in storage, or in delivery, providing various delivery dates. The solid wood headboard was never delivered.

Panera knew that these later representations were false and, in making them, intended that Foster would be induced to keep the furniture and refrain from canceling the order. Relying on Panera's statements, Foster kept the furniture and waited for delivery of the wood headboard. Had she known that the statements were false, she would have canceled the order, returned the furniture, and demanded a refund. But because she was the customer in this transaction and because Panera, as the store manager, presumably had familiarity with the whereabouts of store inventory, Foster relied on his representations as being true.

Foster has stored but has not used the furniture. Defendants have not removed it from Foster's home, nor have they refunded the purchase price. As a direct and proximate result of Panera's initial misrepresentation, Foster was induced to purchase the bedroom set and was damaged thereby.

As a direct and proximate result of Panera's later misrepresentations, Foster was induced to store unwanted furniture, and to refrain from canceling the contract and obtaining a refund, all to her damage in the amount of $3,500.

DEFENDANTS' MOTION TO DISMISS

Defendants filed a motion to dismiss the complaint on the ground that "the complaint fails to state a claim upon which relief may be granted against defendants." The motion was granted, and this appeal ensued.

ANALYSIS

In reviewing a trial court's grant of a motion to dismiss, we accept the plaintiff's allegations as true and give her the benefit of all fair implications therefrom. A complaint for fraud must allege the following elements: (1) a material misrepresentation of fact by the defendant, (2) made with knowledge of its falsity, (3) made with intent to deceive or induce reliance, (4) reasonable reliance by the plaintiff upon the misrepresentation, and (5) loss by the plaintiff as a proximate result of the misrepresentation.

Every element of the cause of action for fraud must be specifically pleaded and the facts constituting the fraud must be alleged with sufficient particularity to allow a defendant to understand fully the nature of the charge made. It is not sufficient to allege fraud in general terms, or in terms which amount to mere conclusions.

Defendants contend that the representations were not material and therefore cannot support an action for fraud. We disagree.

A representation is material if a reasonable person would consider it important in deciding to enter into the transaction. Here, the complaint indicates that Foster asked for a solid wood headboard, and that Panera repeatedly confirmed its eventual availability. A reasonable person seeking a solid wood headboard would have considered these assertions to be an important factor in the sale. The allegations thus clearly demonstrate that the representations were material.

CONCLUSION

Foster has properly stated a fraud claim. The judgment of the trial court dismissing the complaint is reversed, and the case remanded for proceedings consistent with this opinion.

Williams v. A-1 Automotive Center

Madison v. Brooks
Franklin Court of Appeal (2005)

This action was brought by plaintiff Jean Madison to rescind, on the ground of fraud, a written contract for the sale of certain plant nursery stock. The district court granted defendant Walter Brooks's motion to dismiss for failure to state a claim upon which relief could be granted. The sole question on appeal is whether a statement that is an expression of opinion may be actionable as fraud.

The complaint alleges that prior to executing the contract, Brooks told Madison that he had grafted 52,000 dormant buds in the trees comprising the nursery stock and that Madison "would surely see 60 to 70 percent of the dormant buds growing and producing trees." The parties stipulate that in fact only 30 percent of the dormant buds grew and produced trees.

Brooks contends that the so-called misrepresentation was the mere expression of an opinion and not a statement of a fact, and therefore could not constitute actionable fraud. He insists that a vendor has the right to freely express an opinion as to what will or will not happen in the future in relation to the sale of the property under consideration, and that such statements do not constitute actionable fraud.

As a general rule, fraud cannot be predicated upon the mere expression of an opinion which is understood to be only an estimate or a judgment. The person to whom such a statement is made has no right to rely upon the statement, and does so at his peril. For example, an auto dealer's representations that the vehicle "was a good car" and that it was "about the best one they had" were not actionable as fraud. *Bender v. Fiat Corp.* (Fr. Ct. App. 1986). Nor was the statement that certain seeds were "top quality tomato seeds" definitive enough as to how the product would perform but instead was merely the grower's opinion that the seeds were top quality. *Novotny v. Ford Farms* (Fr. Sup. Ct. 1999).

However, there is an exception to this rule where the opinion relates to a subject as to which the parties do not have equal knowledge or means of ascertaining the truth. Where the party making the misrepresentation has special knowledge of the facts underlying the opinion, or "is possessed of superior knowledge respecting such matters, with a design to deceive and mislead," the positive assertion of a matter, which stated in another form might be a mere opinion, may be actionable if the statement was false. *Novotny.* In *Novotny,* the grower also described the tomato seeds as "ones that would produce drought-resistant plants that would bear firm, uniform fruit that would not bruise during shipment." The court held that *this* statement could be the basis for a fraud action. *Id. See also Wong v. Hall Lumber, Ltd.* (Fr. Ct. App. 2004) (statement made by salesman that windows were coated in a preservative that would "protect against rot and decay for at least 10 years" constituted an actionable statement).

The complaint's allegations fall within the exception. In addition to alleging that Brooks told Madison that she "would surely see 60 to 70 percent of the dormant buds growing and producing trees," the complaint alleges that Brooks knew that the dormant buds were poorly handled and would almost certainly not grow properly. The complaint also alleges that Madison relied upon Brooks's skill in the business and that Madison, who was not an expert in the field of horticulture, did not possess reasonable means of ascertaining the truth of Brooks's statement.

When we review the granting of a motion to dismiss for failure to state a claim, we take the well-pleaded allegations of fact as true. Taking these allegations as true, the statement that Madison "would surely see 60 to 70 percent of the dormant buds growing and producing trees" would be equivalent to a misrepresentation of fact, satisfying that essential element of common law fraud.

Accordingly, the trial court should not have dismissed the complaint. We reverse and remand.

Rogers v. Statewide Insurance Co.
Franklin Court of Appeal (1995)

Plaintiff Michelle Rogers appeals from a judgment entered after the trial court granted defendant Statewide Insurance Company's motion to dismiss her complaint for failure to state a claim upon which relief may be granted. The sole issue on appeal concerns the circumstances under which an unfulfilled promise to perform is actionable as fraud at common law. We conclude that when the promise is made with no intent to perform, it constitutes a misrepresentation of fact. If the other elements of fraud are present, a cause of action for fraud exists.

Rogers alleges as follows: She was involved in an auto accident with Andy Bosch, an insured of defendant. Bosch's liability was reasonably clear. Rogers obtained an estimate of $3,200 to repair her vehicle. Statewide represented to her that she was authorized to have her vehicle repaired at Capitol Ford, that Statewide's obligation to indemnify her for her damages was reasonably clear, and that Statewide would pay her for all such repairs immediately upon their completion. Rogers relied on the representations and brought her vehicle to be repaired. However, Statewide refused to pay for the repairs or to indemnify her. Because Rogers lacked the funds to complete the repairs or to obtain the release of her vehicle, she was left without its use for an extended period of several weeks until Statewide eventually settled her claim.

The gist of Rogers's fraud claim is that Statewide said it *would* pay for her repairs *immediately upon their completion*, and that it failed to do so, that Rogers could not afford to have the repairs completed or redeem her vehicle, and that she lost the use of the car for several weeks. The critical alleged misrepresentation as to immediate payment upon completion did not involve a past or existing material fact. Rather, it involved a promise to perform at some future time.

A promise is a statement of intention to perform some action in the future. If the maker of a promise honestly intends to follow through on that intention at the time of the promise, the statement cannot give rise to an action for fraud. However, if at the time of making the promise the promisor has no plans to perform, he has misrepresented his present intention, which would be a misrepresentation of fact. It is that misrepresentation that can support an action for fraud. To state such a claim, one must specifically allege, among other things, that the promisor did not intend to perform at the time the promise was made. Rogers's complaint does not contain such an allegation. Therefore, the motion to dismiss was proper.

Affirmed.

POINT SHEET

Williams v. A-1 Automotive Center
DRAFTERS' POINT SHEET

This performance test requires applicants, as associates in a law firm, to analyze several potentially actionable statements and draft causes of action for fraud in a contemplated civil action arising from a dispute between the firm's client, Robert Williams, and A-1 Automotive Center (A-1) over work performed by A-1 on Williams's Dodge minivan. Williams has attempted unsuccessfully to resolve the matter, and he now wants the firm to file a lawsuit against A-1.

Drawing upon the materials in the File and Library, applicants must complete the following tasks: (1) write a memorandum analyzing the four statements made by A-1's owner to Williams to explain which are actionable and which are not; and (2) for each statement determined to be actionable, draft a separate cause of action for fraud.

The File contains the following materials: an instructional memorandum from the supervising attorney describing the assignment, the firm's guidelines for drafting causes of action, client interview notes, a memorandum from the supervising attorney identifying the four potentially actionable statements, and A-1's receipt for the alleged repairs. The Library contains three cases concerning the pleading requirements for a fraud cause of action.

The following discussion covers all of the points the drafters intended to raise in the problem. Applicants need not cover them all to receive passing or even excellent grades. Grading is entirely within the discretion of the user jurisdictions.

I.   Format

With regard to the first task—analysis of the four potentially actionable statements—no specific formatting guidelines are provided. However, based on the instructions in the supervising attorney's task memo, applicants are expected to discuss each statement in turn, determining whether it is actionable and explaining their conclusion as to each.

With regard to the second task, drafting the causes of action for fraud, the task memo instructs applicants to follow the firm's drafting guidelines for causes of action. Those guidelines require applicants to draft those minimum allegations necessary to plead the specific legal elements of the claim, presented in separately numbered paragraphs, in order to minimize the risk of A-1's filing a motion to dismiss for failure to state a claim. The drafting guidelines provide an example of a well-pleaded cause of action for negligence, identifying the elements of that claim and demonstrating how that claim should be pleaded consistent with the firm's pleadings practice.

II. Analysis of the Four Potentially Actionable Statements

The first case in the Library, *Foster v. Panera* (Fr. Ct. App. 2003), sets forth the five required elements of an actionable claim for fraud: (1) a material misrepresentation of fact by the defendant, (2) made with knowledge of its falsity, (3) made with intent to deceive or induce reliance, (4) reasonable reliance upon the misrepresentation by the plaintiff, and (5) loss by the plaintiff as a proximate result of the misrepresentation. A misrepresentation is material "if a reasonable person would consider it important in deciding to enter into the transaction." *Foster.* An opinion may be treated as a misrepresentation of fact when the parties are on unequal footing and the person making the statement has superior knowledge and/or experience. *Madison v. Brooks* (Fr. Ct. App. 2005). An unfulfilled promise made with no present intent to perform may constitute a misrepresentation of fact where the other elements of fraud are present. *Rogers v. Statewide Ins. Co.* (Fr. Ct. App. 1995).

The supervising attorney's memo to the file has identified four potentially actionable statements made by Aaron Biggs, A-1's owner, to Williams during the course of the parties' dealings; only two of these statements can support claims for fraud.

A. Actionable Statements

Applying the analysis in *Foster* and *Madison* to the facts presented here, applicants should conclude that the following statements *are* actionable:

(1) Biggs's statement that he had "found a notification from Dodge about a defect causing the gears to grind down."

- This statement was a material misrepresentation of fact. It was material in that a reasonable person would have considered it to be an important factor in authorizing the repairs to be undertaken. *Foster.* Furthermore, as confirmed by Mission Dodge, the statement was a <u>mis</u>representation because it was false.

- In *Foster*, the plaintiff's fraud cause of action was based on the defendants' repeated assertions that a solid wood headboard would be delivered to the plaintiff as part of the bedroom furniture set she purchased. The court concluded that a reasonable person looking for a bedroom set with a wood headboard would have considered the defendants' statements regarding the eventual availability of a wood headboard an "important factor" in purchasing the furniture.

- Here, too, a court would likely conclude that Biggs's statement concerning the alleged notification from Dodge about a defect in its transmissions to be an important factor in Williams's decision to authorize the repairs.

- The other elements of fraud are also present. Given that Mission Dodge informed Williams that no such defect notification had been issued by Dodge, it appears certain that Biggs uttered the statement knowing it was false and with the intent to deceive Williams. It was reasonable for Williams to rely on this statement by Biggs, the owner of the automotive repair shop. Finally, the misrepresentation caused Williams a loss of $1,887 for work that was not performed and an additional $128 paid to Mission Dodge to repair the leak caused by A-1's faulty re-installation of the transmission.

(2) Biggs's statement that "Your transmission is going to fail, and soon!"

- There appears to be little question that this statement is material; most consumers would deem it very relevant information that an experienced automotive mechanic had warned them that their transmission was about to fail.

- However, applicants should recognize that this statement is Biggs's opinion regarding the condition of the minivan's transmission. As a general rule, an action for fraud cannot be predicated upon the mere expression of an opinion that is understood to be only an estimate or a judgment and not a statement of fact. *Madison v. Brooks*. Indeed, the person to whom such a statement is made ordinarily has no right to rely on the statement, and does so at his peril. *Id.*

- An exception to this rule exists where the opinion relates to a subject as to which the parties do not have equal knowledge or means of ascertaining the truth. *Id.* Thus, "where the party making the misrepresentation has special knowledge of the facts underlying the opinion, or 'is possessed of superior knowledge respecting such matters, with a design to deceive and mislead,' the positive assertion of a matter, which stated in another form might be a mere opinion, may be actionable if the statement was false." *Id.* (quoting *Novotny v. Ford Farms*). So, a grower's statement that the tomato seeds were "ones that would produce drought-resistant plants that would bear firm, uniform fruit that would not bruise during shipment" could serve as the basis of an action for fraud. *Id.*

- Applying this standard, Biggs's statement that "Your transmission is going to fail, and soon" is distinguishable from the examples of inactionable opinions cited in *Madison* (that a vehicle was a "good car" (*Bender v. Fiat Corp.*) and that certain seeds were "top quality tomato seeds" (*Novotny v. Ford Farms*)). Those statements were not definitive enough about how the products would perform to take them out of the realm of mere opinion.

- Instead, Biggs's statement predicting the transmission's future nonperformance falls within the *Madison* exception to opinion statements, in that it was made by an individual (Biggs) who had expertise and knowledge superior to that possessed by Williams in a situation where the parties were not on equal footing. The facts indicate that Williams relied on Biggs's opinion in authorizing the alleged repairs, just as the inexperienced plaintiff in *Madison* relied upon the experienced defendant's assurance that 60 to 70 percent of the dormant buds would produce trees when purchasing the defendant's nursery stock.

- The Williams-Biggs interaction is also analogous to two cases cited in *Madison* where the defendants had special knowledge or expertise:

Novotny (grower's statement that seeds would produce "drought-resistant plants that would bear firm, uniform fruit that would not bruise during shipment" was actionable) and *Wong v. Hall Lumber Ltd.* (viable action for fraud existed where salesman stated that windows were coated with a preservative that would "protect against rot and decay for at least 10 years").

- Further, given the totality of the circumstances, it appears certain that Biggs's statement was also made with the intent to deceive (the fact that Biggs re-installed the minivan's original transmission gives lie to his statement that it was in imminent danger of failing), that Williams's reliance was reasonable (he was not knowledgeable about engine repair, nor was he in a position to get a second opinion when the transmission was already disassembled), and that Williams suffered loss as a result of Biggs's misrepresentations (the $1887 paid to A-1 and the $128 paid to Mission Dodge to fix the leak caused by A-1's faulty re-installation of the transmission).

B. Statements That Are Not Actionable

The following representations would *not* be considered actionable under *Foster*'s definition of materiality and the holding in *Rogers v. Statewide Insurance Co.*:

(1) Biggs's statement that "It would also help if we installed an extra cooler to keep [the transmission] from running hot."

- The facts indicate that this statement was made *after* Williams had authorized the transmission repairs to be made and that Williams in fact declined to have the cooler installed. Thus, an action based on this statement would fail to state a claim for fraud because according to the sequence of events, Williams did not rely on this statement in making his decision to have A-1 replace the transmission and he did not sustain any loss as a result because the cooler was never installed.

- Applicants could also receive credit for discussing whether or not this statement was material and concluding that it was not actionable because it was not an important factor in deciding whether to enter into the transaction. *See Foster*.

(2) Biggs's statement that A-1 would "guarantee the job."

- A promise is a statement of intention to perform some action in the future. *Rogers v. Statewide Ins. Co.* If the maker of the promise honestly intends to follow through on that intention at the time of the promise, the statement cannot give rise to an action for fraud. *Id.* However, an unfulfilled promise to perform may constitute a misrepresentation of fact if it is made with no intent to perform *and* if the other elements of fraud are present. *Id.*

- Biggs's statement that the work was guaranteed was a promise that he clearly did not intend to perform. (The facts that the receipt was stamped "No Guarantee" and that Biggs refused to refund any money to Williams because Williams had not agreed to have the extra cooler installed, both show that when Biggs stated that he guaranteed the work, he had no intent at all of making good on that promise.) Thus, at first blush, it would appear that his statement would be actionable.

- However, *Rogers* holds that an unfulfilled promise is actionable only where the other elements of fraud are present. Here, the harm had already been done when the statement was made, in that Williams had already authorized and paid for the alleged repairs. Clearly he could not have relied upon this statement in authorizing or paying for the transmission work.

III. Drafting the Fraud Causes of Action

The ask memo instructs applicants to draft a separate cause of action for fraud based on each statement that applicants determine to be actionable. As discussed above, only two of the four statements are actionable—Biggs's statement about the alleged notification from Dodge and Biggs's statement that the transmission would fail.

Foster v. Panera, Rogers v. Statewide Insurance Co., and *Madison v. Brooks* provide the legal framework for determining the elements and essential allegations necessary to sustain a fraud cause of action. Although applicants need not cite to the cases by name in this portion of their answer, they should incorporate the following pleading requirements and concepts into their work product:

- The elements of fraud are (1) a material misrepresentation of fact by the defendant, (2) made with knowledge of its falsity, (3) made with intent to deceive or induce reliance, (4) reasonable reliance upon the misrepresentation by the plaintiff, and (5) loss by the plaintiff as a proximate result of the misrepresentation. *Foster.*

- Every element of a cause of action for fraud must be specifically pleaded and the facts constituting the fraud must be alleged with sufficient particularity to allow the defendant to understand fully the nature of the charge made. *Id.* It is not sufficient to allege fraud in general terms, or in terms which amount to mere conclusions. *Id.*

Following the example of a well-pleaded negligence cause of action provided in the firm's drafting guidelines, applicants should craft separately numbered paragraphs identifying each element of both causes of action for fraud and the relevant facts in support thereof.

(1) A Material Misrepresentation

Applicants should quote or at least closely paraphrase the specific statements which form the basis for each fraud cause of action, and identify the facts surrounding each statement (e.g., the date, the sequence of events, and the fact that they were verbal statements made by A-1's owner, Biggs, to Williams). *See Foster* (requiring pleading with particularity to allow the defendant to understand the nature of the charge made).

(2) Made with Knowledge of the Misrepresentation(s)'s Falsity

Applicants should allege that Biggs made the statements with knowledge that they were false at the time he made them (e.g., Biggs knew that in fact Dodge had not issued any notification about problems with minivan transmissions; the fact that Biggs reinstalled Williams's original transmission belies Biggs's warning that the transmission was about to fail).

(3) Made with Intent to Deceive or Induce Reliance

It is sufficient for applicants to simply state that Biggs made the statements intending to induce Williams to agree to and pay for the proposed unnecessary repair work.

(4) Reasonable Reliance upon the Misrepresentation by the Plaintiff

The allegations for this element should indicate that (1) Williams relied on the representations of Biggs, a person with greater knowledge and expertise in the field of automotive repair, and (2) Williams's reliance was reasonable because he was the customer in this transaction and because of Biggs's superior knowledge, presumed expertise in the area of automotive repair, and position as the owner of the repair shop (in other words, the parties were on unequal footing), and (3) Williams would not have authorized the alleged repairs had he known that the statements were false.

(5) Loss by the Plaintiff as a Proximate Result of the Misrepresentation

It is essential that a plaintiff establish loss or harm that is proximately caused by his reasonable reliance on the defendant's representation. Following the lead provided in *Foster*, applicants should allege that "as a direct and proximate result" of Biggs's misrepresentations (or words to this effect), Williams was induced to authorize unnecessary transmission work that A-1, in fact, never performed, and that he was damaged at least in the amount he paid to A-1 for the alleged repairs ($1,887), plus the cost of the repair of the transmission leak by Mission Dodge ($128).

Applicant Identification

In re Velocity Park

Read the instructions on the back cover.
Do not break the seal until you are told to do so.

NATIONAL CONFERENCE OF BAR EXAMINERS

INSTRUCTIONS

1.   You will have 90 minutes to complete this session of the examination. This performance test is designed to evaluate your ability to handle a select number of legal authorities in the context of a factual problem involving a client.

2.   The problem is set in the fictitious state of Franklin, in the fictitious Fifteenth Circuit of the United States. Columbia and Olympia are also fictitious states in the Fifteenth Circuit. In Franklin, the trial court of general jurisdiction is the District Court, the intermediate appellate court is the Court of Appeal, and the highest court is the Supreme Court.

3.   You will have two kinds of materials with which to work: a File and a Library. The first document in the File is a memorandum containing the instructions for the task you are to complete. The other documents in the File contain factual information about your case and may include some facts that are not relevant.

4.   The Library contains the legal authorities needed to complete the task and may also include some authorities that are not relevant. Any cases may be real, modified, or written solely for the purpose of this examination. If the cases appear familiar to you, do not assume that they are precisely the same as you have read before. Read them thoroughly, as if they all were new to you. You should assume that the cases were decided in the jurisdictions and on the dates shown. In citing cases from the Library, you may use abbreviations and omit page references.

5.   Your response must be written in the answer book provided. If you are taking this examination on a laptop computer, your jurisdiction will provide you with specific instructions. In answering this performance test, you should concentrate on the materials provided. What you have learned in law school and elsewhere provides the general background for analyzing the problem; the File and Library provide the specific materials with which you must work.

6.   Although there are no restrictions on how you apportion your time, you should be sure to allocate ample time (about 45 minutes) to reading and digesting the materials and to organizing your answer before you begin writing it. You may make notes anywhere in the test materials; blank pages are provided at the end of the booklet. You may not tear pages from the question booklet.

7.   This performance test will be graded on your responsiveness to the instructions regarding the task you are to complete, which are given to you in the first memorandum in the File, and on the content, thoroughness, and organization of your response.

In re Velocity Park

In re Velocity Park

FILE

LIBRARY

POINT SHEET

FILE

In re Velocity Park

Hall & Gray LLP
Attorneys at Law
730 Amsterdam Ave.
Banford, Franklin 33701

M E M O R A N D U M

To: Applicant
From: Deanna Hall
Re: Liability waiver for Velocity Park
Date: February 26, 2008

Our client, Zeke Oliver, is about to open his new business venture, "Velocity Park," an outdoor skateboarding park (also referred to as a "skate park"). To reduce his liability to those who may be injured while skateboarding, Zeke has brought in a waiver form that he proposes to use. To help me advise him, please review his proposed waiver and prepare a memorandum:

- analyzing whether the proposed waiver will protect Velocity Park from liability for injuries occurring at the skate park;

- suggesting specific revisions to the proposed waiver, including replacement language as well as any changes in the waiver's design and layout (however, you should not redraft the entire waiver); and

- discussing whether any waiver will be enforceable if signed only by a minor.

1

Client Interview—Zeke Oliver
February 22, 2008

Atty: Zeke, come on in. How are things coming along with your new business?

Zeke: I am totally pumped! The construction is right on schedule, and on April 30, 2008, Velocity Park, Banford's first and only skateboarding park, will be open to the public!

Atty: Great. So what can I help you with today?

Zeke: Well, my brother told me that I should require everyone who uses the skateboard park to sign a liability waiver so if someone gets hurt, they can't sue me. I found an entry form from a triathlon in the state of Columbia that I entered last year. It had some stuff about waiving liability, so I just made some changes and added the Velocity Park logo. I was all set to send it to the printer, but then I thought that I should have you look it over first.

Atty: A liability waiver is an excellent idea. And you're right—waivers aren't necessarily interchangeable from one situation to another. Before we discuss your proposed waiver form, let's talk a bit about who will be using the skateboarding park and what activities they will be able to do there.

Zeke: Okay. According to my market research, I expect that most of Velocity Park's visitors will be teenagers and young adults. There will be a minimum age of 10 for using the park. It will have all the basic stuff skateboarders love: a large concrete bowl, a beginners' area, and jumps, sliding rails, and two half-pipes, so advanced skaters can do ollies, kickflips, grinds, and other stunts. I plan to hold skills clinics and offer private lessons. Also, I've hooked up with a couple of skateboard manufacturers to sponsor some competitions, although I don't have anything definite yet. By the way, I've brought a newspaper article that mentions the park.

Atty: Thanks. Will you charge admission for the park? What about equipment rentals?

Zeke: Admission will be $10 for a three-hour block of skateboarding. I want it to be affordable for teenagers. Right now, I have no plans to rent equipment, but the park will have a shop to sell boards, helmets, T-shirts, and accessories. Of course, there will be a concessions area for soft drinks and snacks.

Atty: I assume that skateboarders get a fair number of bumps and bruises. Do you have any particular concerns about injuries at your park?

Zeke: Injuries are just part of skateboarding. Usually they're nothing more than scrapes, bruises, and the occasional sprained wrist from taking a fall. There will be signs posted stating that skateboarders have to wear helmets while using the park.

Atty: Where will skateboarders fill out your waiver form? I notice that it's two pages—that's a fair amount of reading for a teenager waiting to get into the park.

Zeke: Hey, I thought I was doing well to have only a two-page waiver. If I included everything I wanted to, it would be five pages. Anyway, the waivers will be handed out where skateboarders pay the admission fee, and whoever is staffing the cash register will collect them. I suppose some kids may not read it closely, especially if they're anxious to get in and skateboard, but short of reading the waiver to them, I don't know how to get around that. Also the waiver can be printed off of the park's website.

Atty: Will your staff be trained to deal with medical emergencies?

Zeke: I'm in the process of putting together a first-aid station, but kids won't get much more than a bandage there. For anything more serious, staff will be trained to call the skateboarder's emergency contact or an ambulance. I'm not too worried about serious injuries. In my experience, skateboarders have a good sense of what tricks they can do safely. Besides, it's so much better to have kids skateboarding in a park designed for that purpose than on the streets.

Atty: Where do most skateboarders go now in Banford?

Zeke: It's really sad. As soon as the kids find a good place, like a parking lot or cul-de-sac with a nice incline, they get chased out by the neighbors. The city council doesn't like skateboarders either. It's voted to ban skateboarding downtown. That's why I'm opening the park. Unless kids can get to another town in the area with a skateboard park, there's no place to skateboard, apart from streets and driveways in the outlying neighborhoods. Eventually, if Velocity Park succeeds, I'd like to partner with the city of Banford to operate the park and make it free, but until then, I've got my work cut out for me just to make Velocity Park recoup its costs.

Atty: With your business experience, I'm sure it will turn a profit in no time. I'll review this liability waiver and see if it meets your needs. Then we'll meet next week to discuss it.

Zeke: Thanks. I appreciate it. I really need to have this taken care of before the park opens.

VELOCITY PARK
SKATEBOARDING
FOR A 21ST CENTURY WORLD

1500 North Street
Banford, Franklin 33712
(555) 555-1085

Welcome to Velocity Park! Before you hop on your skateboard and start work on your grinds, kickflips, and ollies, be sure to read and complete this form.

Admission Fees
$10 per skateboarder for a three-hour session in the park. $20 gets you an all-day pass. Unlimited monthly passes available for $75.

Hours of Operation
Monday–Friday, noon–8 p.m.
Saturday–Sunday, 10 a.m.–8 p.m.
Hours of operation subject to change without notice. Unanticipated closures will be posted at www.velocityparkskate.com.

Park Rules
➢ Must be 10 years of age or older to enter the skate park.
➢ Only skateboards and in-line skates may be used in the skate park.
➢ To enter and remain inside the skate park, you must wear a helmet.
➢ Inspect your equipment to make sure it is in good working order.
➢ Be considerate of fellow skateboarders, especially those who are younger and/or less skilled.
➢ No food, drink, or smoking allowed inside the skate park except in designated areas. No alcohol or drugs allowed.
➢ Skate park visitors must abide by staff instruction at all times.
➢ Velocity Park is not responsible for lost or stolen items.
➢ Failure to abide by these rules may result in expulsion from Velocity Park.

1. I understand and appreciate that participation in a sport carries a risk to me of serious injury and/or death. I voluntarily and knowingly recognize, accept, and assume this risk and hereby forever release, acquit, covenant not to sue, and discharge Velocity Park, its employees, event sponsors, and any third parties from any and all legal liability, including but not limited to all causes of action, claims, damages in law, or remedies in equity of whatever kind I have or which hereafter accrue to me, whether such injuries and/or claims arise from equipment failure, conditions in the

park, or any actions of Velocity Park, its employees, third parties, or other skateboarders. Velocity Park is not responsible for any incidental or consequential damages, including, but not limited to, any claims for personal injury, property damage, or emotional distress. This release is binding with respect to my heirs, executors, administrators, and assigns, as well as myself.

2. I have been informed of Velocity Park Rules and agree to abide by them.

3. In connection with any injury I may sustain, or illness or other medical condition I may experience during my participation in skateboarding or attendance at Velocity Park, I authorize any emergency first aid, medication, medical treatment, or surgery deemed necessary by attending medical personnel if I am not able to act on my own behalf.

4. In consideration of permission to use the skate park facility, I agree that Velocity Park, its agents, and its employees may use my appearance, name, and likeness in connection with my use of the facility in any Velocity Park publication, including news releases. I further agree that I am not entitled to any compensation for such use of my appearance, name, or likeness.

Name (please print):_____ Sex:_____ Age:_____

(Signed):_____ Date:_____

Emergency Contact Information
Name: _____ Phone No.:_____
Address: _____

How did you hear about Velocity Park?
_____

Would you like e-mail updates about Velocity Park events?   Yes   No
If yes, e-mail address: _____

SKATEBOARDING: OLD AND NEW INJURIES ON THE RISE

Each year in Franklin, skateboarding results in about 500 visits to hospital emergency rooms, with some 50 skateboarders (usually children and adolescents) requiring hospitalization, usually because of head injuries. Nationally, in 2007, some 15,000 emergency room treatments were skateboard-related. Wrist injuries are the most common, either sprains or fractures. Although rare, deaths from falls and collisions with motor vehicles can occur.

Protective gear, such as helmets, slip-resistant closed-toe shoes, and wrist guards can greatly limit the number and severity of injuries. However, according to J.P. Clyde, a professional skateboarder, injuries could be further reduced if skateboarders paid more attention to the surfaces they ride on. "Studies by the U.S. Consumer Product Safety Commission found that 35 percent of all skateboarding-related injuries could have been avoided if skateboarders really paid attention to the skating environment," he said. "One-third of injuries happen because there's a flaw in the riding surface, whether it's a street, a parking lot, or a skate park. Innocuous objects like pebbles, twigs, bottle tops, or other debris can cause a skateboarder to take a spill. Cracks, potholes, and ruts also pose hazards to the unwary skateboarder."

Dr. Sanford Takei, a sports medicine specialist, agrees. "Beginning skate-boarders—those who have been riding for less than a week—account for one-third of skateboarding injuries overall," he said. "Obviously, beginners fall more often and may not know how to fall correctly. When experienced riders are injured, it is usually from falls caused by rocks and other irregularities in the riding surface."

But what really has parents in Banford up in arms is a new trend in skateboarding-related injuries: injuries that occur when teenagers mix alcohol or marijuana and skateboards. There has been a rise in reports of teenagers gathering in the Library Mall, drinking alcohol and then skateboarding on home-made ramps and trying risky stunts. Maggie Alden, a student at Banford High School, said that she quit skateboarding in the Mall after seeing a rider fall and break his nose after colliding with another skateboarder. "Those guys are clueless about where they're going," Alden said. "Someone is always trying to start a fight or take someone else's skateboard," she added.

For his part, Zeke Oliver, owner of Velocity Park, which will be Banford's first skate park when it opens in April, appeared relaxed about the risks of skateboarding injuries and aggressive skateboarders. "Look, skateboarding is only going to grow in popularity," he said. "It's a great way for kids to get outside, blow off some steam, and get some exercise."

In re Velocity Park

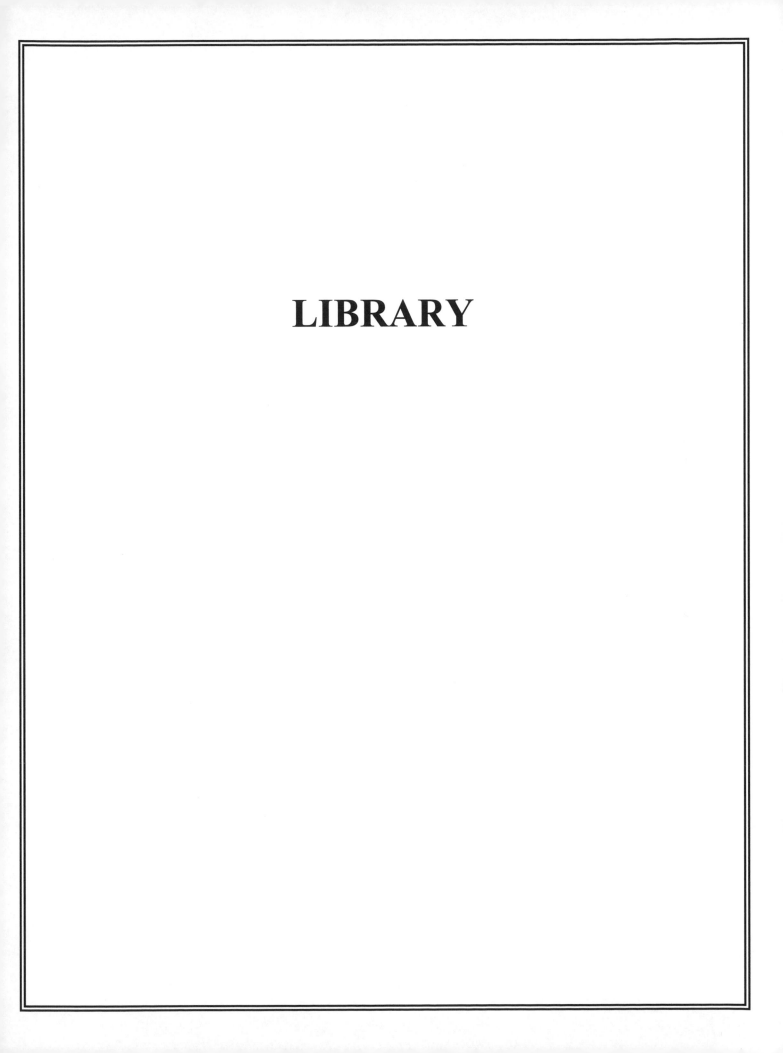

LIBRARY

§ 41 Contracts involving minors; limitations on authority of minor.

This section is intended to protect minors and to help parents and legal guardians exercise reasonable care, supervision, protection, and control over minor children.

(a) A minor cannot make a contract relating to real property or any interest therein.

*   *   *   *

(b)(1) The contract of a minor may be disaffirmed by the minor himself, either before his majority or within a reasonable time afterwards, unless the contract at issue is one for necessaries, such as food or medical care.

(b)(2) Where a minor enters into a contract, whether one for necessaries or not, said contract may be enforced against that individual if, upon reaching the age of majority, the individual expressly or implicitly ratifies the contract.

(b)(3) Subsections (b)(1) and (b)(2) shall not apply to contracts made on behalf of a minor by the minor's parent or guardian.

Lund v. Swim World, Inc.

Franklin Supreme Court (2005)

Tim Lund sued Swim World, Inc., for the wrongful death of his mother, Annie Lund, who suffered a fatal head injury at its facility. The trial court granted summary judgment to Swim World, ruling that the waiver signed by Lund released Swim World from liability. The court of appeal affirmed. For the reasons set forth below, we reverse.

Swim World is a swimming facility with a lap pool open to members and visitors. On May 3, 2001, Lund visited Swim World as part of a physical therapy program. Because Lund was not a Swim World member, she had to fill out a guest registration card and pay a fee before swimming.

The guest registration, a five-inch-square preprinted card, also contained a "Waiver Release Statement," which appeared below the "Guest Registration" section, requesting the visitor's name, address, phone number, reason for visit, and interest in membership. The entire card was printed in capital letters of the same size, font, and color. The waiver language read as follows:

WAIVER RELEASE STATEMENT. I AGREE TO ASSUME ALL LIABILITY FOR MYSELF, WITHOUT REGARD TO FAULT, WHILE AT SWIM WORLD. I FURTHER AGREE TO HOLD HARMLESS SWIM WORLD, AND ITS EMPLOYEES, FOR ANY CONDITIONS OR INJURY THAT MAY RESULT TO ME WHILE AT SWIM WORLD. I HAVE READ THE FOREGOING AND UNDERSTAND ITS CONTENTS.

The card had just one signature and date line. Lund completed the "Guest Registration" portion and signed at the bottom of the "Waiver Release Statement" without asking any questions.

After swimming, Lund used the sauna in the women's locker room. The bench she was lying on collapsed beneath her, causing her to strike her head against the heater and lose consciousness. Lund was rushed to the hospital but died the next day as the result of complications from her head injury.

The complaint alleged that Swim World was negligent in the maintenance of its facilities and that its negligence caused Lund's death.

Summary judgment is granted when there is no genuine issue of material fact and the movant is entitled to judgment as a matter of law. *Samuels v. David* (Franklin Sup. Ct. 1991). The case at bar turns on the interpretation of Swim World's waiver form and whether it relieves Swim World of liability for harm caused by its negligence.

Waivers of liability, also known as exculpatory contracts,[1] are permitted under Franklin law except when prohibited by statute or public policy. As no statute bars the contract at issue, we proceed to a public policy analysis of the exculpatory clause.

Public policy can restrict freedom of contract for the good of the community. Thus, claims that an exculpatory contract violates public policy create a tension between the right to contract freely without government interference and the concern that allowing a tortfeasor to contract away responsibility for negligent acts may encourage conduct below a socially acceptable standard of care.

We examine the particular facts and circumstances of the case when determining whether an exculpatory contract is void and unenforceable as contrary to public policy. Exculpatory contracts are generally construed against the party seeking to shield itself from liability. In *Schmidt v. Tyrol Mountain* (Franklin Sup. Ct. 1996), we set forth two requirements for an enforceable

exculpatory clause: "First, the language of the waiver cannot be overbroad but must clearly, unambiguously, and unmistakably inform the signer of what is being waived. Second, the waiver form itself, viewed in its entirety, must alert the signer to the nature and significance of what is being signed." *Id.* We also noted that a relevant consideration in the enforceability of such a clause is whether there is a substantial disparity in bargaining power between the parties.

Thus, a release having language that is so broad as to be interpreted to shift liability for a tortfeasor's conduct under all possible circumstances, including reckless and intentional conduct, and for all possible injuries, will not be upheld. Likewise, release forms that serve two purposes and those that are not conspicuously labeled as waivers have been held to be insufficient to alert the signer that he is waiving liability for other parties' negligence as well as his own.

In *Schmidt,* an action on behalf of a woman who fatally collided with the base of a chairlift tower while skiing, the plaintiff alleged that the defendant ski resort negligently failed to pad the lift tower. The resort moved for summary judgment, relying on the exculpatory clause in the ski pass signed by the skier. The waiver read, in part: "There are certain inherent risks in skiing and I agree to

---

[1] The words "release," "waiver," and "exculpatory agreement" have been used interchangeably by the courts to refer to written documents in which one party agrees to release another from potential tort liability for future conduct covered in the agreement.

hold Tyrol Mountain harmless for any injury to me on the premises."

The court in *Schmidt* held that the release was void as against public policy. First, the release was not clear; it failed to include language expressly indicating the plaintiff's intent to release Tyrol Mountain from its own negligence. Without any mention in the release of the word "negligence," and the ambiguity of the phrase "inherent risks in skiing," the court held that the skier had not been adequately informed of the rights she was waiving.

As to the second factor, the form, in its entirety, did not fully communicate its nature and significance because it served the dual purposes of an application for a ski pass and a release of liability. Furthermore, the waiver was not conspicuous, in that it was one of five paragraphs on the form and did not require a separate signature. In addition, we noted that there was a substantial disparity in bargaining power between the parties.

Following *Schmidt*, we hold that Swim World's exculpatory clause violates public policy. First, the waiver is overly broad and all-inclusive. The waiver begins: "I AGREE TO ASSUME ALL LIABILITY FOR MYSELF, WITHOUT REGARD TO FAULT. . . ." Here, it is unclear what type of acts the word "fault" encompasses; it could potentially bar any claim arising under any scenario.[2] We reject Swim World's claim that negligence is synonymous with fault and conclude that the word "fault" is broad enough to cover a reckless or an intentional act. A waiver of liability for an intentional act would clearly violate public policy. *See* Restatement (Second) of Contracts § 195(1) (term exempting party from tort liability for harm caused intentionally or recklessly is unenforceable on grounds of public policy).

Exculpatory agreements that, like this one, are broad and general will bar only those claims that the parties contemplated when they executed the contract. Here, we must determine whether the collapse of a sauna bench was a risk the parties contemplated when the exculpatory contract was executed. If not, the contract is not enforceable.

Here, given the broadness of the exculpatory language, it is difficult to ascertain exactly what was within Lund's or Swim World's contemplation. Nevertheless, it appears unlikely that Lund, when she signed the guest registration and waiver form, would have contemplated receiving a severe head injury from the collapse of a sauna bench.

---

[2] While including the word "negligence" in exculpatory clauses is not required, we have stated that "it would be helpful for such contracts to set forth in clear terms that the party signing it is releasing others for their negligent acts." *Schmidt*.

Further, Swim World's guest registration and waiver form failed to provide adequate notice of the waiver's nature and significance. Like the contract in *Schmidt*, the form served two purposes: it was both a "Guest Registration" application and a "Waiver Release Statement." The exculpatory language appeared to be part of, or a requirement for, a larger registration form. The waiver could have been a separate document, giving Lund more notice of what she was signing. Also, a separate signature line could have been provided, but was not. Clearly identifying and distinguishing those two contractual arrangements could have provided important protection against a signatory's inadvertent agreement to the release.

Another problem with the form is that the paragraph containing the "Waiver Release Statement" was not conspicuous. The entire form was printed on one card, with the same letter size, font, and color. It is irrelevant that the release language is in capital letters; *all* of the words on the form were in capital letters. Further, the only place to sign the form was at the very end. This supports the conclusion that the waiver was not distinguishable enough such that a reviewing court can say with certainty that the signer was fully aware of its nature and significance.

Finally, we consider the bargaining positions of the parties. This factor looks to the facts surrounding the execution of the waiver. We hasten to add that the presence of this factor, by itself, will not automatically render an exculpatory clause void under public policy.

Here, the record suggests that there was an unequal bargaining position between the parties. Lund had no opportunity to negotiate regarding the standard exculpatory language in the form. In his deposition, Swim World's desk attendant testified that Lund was simply told to complete and sign the form; the waiver portion was not pointed out, nor were its terms explained to her. No one discussed the risks of injury purportedly covered by the form. The desk attendant further testified that Lund did not ask any questions about the form but that there was pressure to sign it because other patrons were behind Lund waiting to sign in. These facts undeniably generate, at a minimum, a genuine dispute of material fact regarding the parties' disparity in bargaining power.

For these reasons we conclude that the exculpatory clause in Swim World's form violates public policy, and, therefore, is unenforceable.

Reversed.

Holum v. Bruges Soccer Club, Inc.

Columbia Supreme Court (1999)

Pamela Holum registered her seven-year-old son, Bryan, for soccer with Bruges Soccer Club, Inc. (the Club), a nonprofit organization that provides local children with the opportunity to learn and play soccer. Its members are parents and other volunteers. As part of the registration process, Mrs. Holum signed a release form whereby she agreed to release "the Club from liability for physical injuries arising as a result of [Bryan's] participation in the soccer club."

Bryan was injured when, after a soccer practice, he jumped on the goal and swung on it. The goal tipped backward and fell on Bryan's chest, breaking three ribs. Bryan's parents, Phil and Pamela Holum, sued the Club, alleging negligence on their own behalf and on behalf of Bryan. The trial court granted summary judgment to the Club, holding that the release signed by Bryan's mother barred the Holums' action against the Club.

The court of appeal affirmed in part and reversed in part. It held that the release barred Mr. and Mrs. Holum's claims. However, it went on to hold that the release did not bar Bryan's claim. Thus, while the parents' claims were barred, Bryan still had a cause of action against the Club, which a guardian could bring on his behalf, or which he could assert upon reaching the age of majority.

We agree with the court of appeal that the release applies to the injuries at issue. As to whether the release executed by Mrs. Holum on behalf of her minor son released the Club from liability for Bryan's claim and his parents' claims as a matter of law, we conclude that the release is valid as to all claims. Accordingly, we reverse that portion of the court of appeal decision holding that the release would not prevent Bryan from asserting a claim for his injuries.

We first consider whether the release is valid. In Columbia, with respect to adults, the general rule is that releases from liability for injuries caused by negligent acts arising during recreational activities are enforceable, whether the negligence is on the part of the participant in the recreational activity or the provider of the activity, in this case, the Club. This approach recognizes the importance of individual autonomy and freedom of contract.

For that reason, the release agreement is valid as to the parents' negligence claim. Mrs. Holum acknowledged that she read the agreement and did not ask any questions.

Mr. Holum did not sign the release, but he accepted and enjoyed the benefits of the contract. In fact, when the injury occurred, he was at the practice field, thereby indicating his intention to enjoy the benefits of his wife's agreement and be bound by it. It is well settled that parents may release their own claims arising out of injury to their minor children. Accordingly, we find that Bryan's parents are barred from recovery as to their claims.

Here, however, the release was executed by a parent on behalf of the minor child. The Holums contend that the release is invalid on public policy grounds, citing the general principle that contracts entered into by a minor, unless for "necessaries," are voidable by the minor before the age of majority is reached. The Club, however, argues that the public interest justifies the enforcement of this agreement with respect to both the parents' and the child's claims.

Organized recreational activities provide children the opportunity to develop athletic ability as well as to learn valuable life skills such as teamwork and cooperation. The assistance of volunteers allows nonprofit organizations to offer these activities at minimal cost. In fact, the Club pays only 19 of its 400 staff members. Without volunteers, such nonprofit organizations could not exist

and many children would lose the benefit of organized sports. Yet, the threat of liability deters many individuals from volunteering. Even if the organization has insurance, individual volunteers could find themselves liable for an injury.

Faced with the threat of lawsuits, and the potential for substantial damage awards, nonprofit organizations and their volunteers could very well decide that the risks are not worth the effort. Hence, invalidation of exculpatory agreements would reduce the number of activities made possible by the services of volunteers and their sponsoring organizations.

Therefore, although when his mother signed the release Bryan gave up his right to sue for the negligent acts of others, the public as a whole received the benefit of these exculpatory agreements. Because of this agreement, the Club can offer affordable recreation without the risks and overwhelming costs of litigation. Bryan's parents agreed to shoulder the risk. Accordingly, we believe that it is in the public interest that parents have authority to enter into these types of binding agreements on behalf of their minor children. We also believe that the enforcement of these agreements may promote more active involvement by participants and their families, which, in turn, promotes the overall quality and safety of these activities.

A related concern is the importance of parental authority. Parents have a fundamental liberty interest in the care, custody, and management of their offspring. Parental authority extends to the ability to make decisions regarding the child's school, religion, medical care, and discipline. Invalidating the release as to the minor's claim is inconsistent with parents' authority to make important life choices for their children.

Mrs. Holum signed the release because she wanted Bryan to play soccer. In making this family decision, she assumed the risk of physical injury on behalf of Bryan and the financial risk on behalf of the family as a whole. Apparently, she determined that the benefits to her child outweighed the risk of physical injury. The situation is comparable to Columbia Stat. § 2317, which gives parents the authority to consent to medical procedures on a child's behalf. In both cases, the parent weighs the risks of physical injury to the child and its attendant costs against the benefits of a particular activity.

Therefore, we hold that parents have the authority to bind their minor children to exculpatory agreements in favor of volunteers and sponsors of nonprofit sport activities where the cause of action sounds in negligence. These agreements may not be disaffirmed by the child on whose behalf they were executed. We need not decide here whether there are other circumstances, beyond the realm of nonprofit organizations, which will support a parent's waiver of a child's claims.

Accordingly, we hold that the release is valid as to the claims of both the parents and the minor child.

Affirmed in part and reversed in part.

POINT SHEET

In re Velocity Park
DRAFTERS' POINT SHEET

This performance test requires applicants, as associates at a law firm, to analyze the provisions of a liability waiver for a recreational activity. The client, Zeke Oliver, owns Velocity Park, set to be the first skateboarding park in Banford, Franklin, when it opens in April. Zeke has asked the law firm for advice regarding an appropriate liability waiver that users of the skate park will be required to sign in order to use the park.

In analyzing whether the waiver that Zeke provided is enforceable under Franklin law, applicants are expected to address both the waiver's language and its format. Applicants also must grapple with the issue of whether liability waivers signed only by minors will be enforced to bar actions for negligence arising from the minor's skateboarding injuries.

The File contains the task memorandum from the supervising partner, a client interview transcript, a liability waiver Zeke assembled by taking language from a triathlon entry form/liability waiver, and a newspaper article about the risks of skateboarding. The Library includes a Franklin statute regarding civil actions, a Franklin case, and a case from Columbia.

The following discussion covers all of the points the drafters intended to raise in the problem. Applicants need not cover them all to receive passing or even excellent grades. Grading is entirely within the discretion of the user jurisdictions.

I.   Format and Overview

Applicants' work product should resemble a legal memorandum such as an associate would write to a supervising partner. Applicants should analyze the waiver Zeke has proposed, identifying problems with its content and design that may preclude it from being found enforceable by a court. Applicants are told not to rewrite the entire waiver. However, if certain language is overbroad or ambiguous, applicants should suggest replacement language that better conforms to the standards set forth in the cases and explain why the changes are necessary for an enforceable waiver. Further, applicants should recognize that the reach of a waiver is tied to the characteristics of the activity (and potential injuries) at issue. Thus they should incorporate the relevant facts from the client interview and the news article in their analysis of the issues. The task memorandum does not require applicants to organize their answers in any particular order, but the order presented below is a logical manner in which to address the issues.

Applicants should conclude that (1) Zeke's proposed waiver contains significant content and format defects, and (2) while the precise issue has not been addressed by Franklin courts, it is unlikely that a court will enforce an exculpatory contract executed by a minor in this situation.

II. Discussion

In Franklin, a party may use an exculpatory contract to limit its liability exposure, but a court may refuse to enforce such a contract on the grounds that its terms violate public policy. A court considers two factors when determining whether an exculpatory contract is enforceable: whether the waiver of liability language is overly broad and ambiguous and whether the exculpatory clause is conspicuous such that it notifies the signer of the nature and significance of what is being waived. Courts will also consider a third, nondispositive factor: whether there exists a substantial disparity in bargaining power between the parties. *Lund v. Swim World, Inc.* (Franklin Sup. Ct. 2005).

A. Whether the Velocity Park Waiver Is Overly Broad and Ambiguous

Franklin courts construe the language of an exculpatory contract against the party seeking to enforce the contract. *Lund*. To survive a public policy challenge, the exculpatory contract must include a description that "clearly, unambiguously, and unmistakably inform[s] the signer of what is being waived." *Id.* (quoting *Schmidt v. Tyrol Mountain* (Franklin Sup. Ct. 1996)). In *Lund*, the deceased swimmer had signed a waiver in which she agreed "to assume all liability for myself, without regard to fault." The Franklin Supreme Court concluded that, by using only the word "fault," the exculpatory clause was overly broad because it could be construed as waiving any and all claims, even those for the defendant's intentional or reckless acts and omissions.

The key to determining whether the exculpatory language is overly broad is whether the risks that the parties contemplated at the time the waiver was executed can be ascertained. In *Lund*, the court held that the waiver's broad language prevented it from concluding that, at the time Lund signed the waiver, she anticipated the risk of a severe head injury when a sauna bench collapsed under her. Not only did the Swim World waiver refer generally to "fault," it failed to spell out any particular risks for which Lund was waiving the right to sue Swim World.

Here, the Velocity Park waiver fails to satisfy *Lund*'s requirement that exculpatory contracts "clearly, unambiguously, and unmistakably inform the signer of [the rights he or she is waiving]." The relevant paragraphs of the proposed waiver read as follows:

> 1. I understand and appreciate that participation in a sport carries a risk to me of serious injury and/or death. I voluntarily and knowingly recognize, accept, and assume this risk and hereby forever release, acquit, covenant not to sue, and discharge Velocity Park, its employees, event sponsors, and any third parties from any and all legal liability, including but not limited to all causes of action, claims, damages in law, or remedies in equity of whatever kind I have or which hereafter accrue to me, whether such injuries and/or claims arise from equipment failure, conditions in the park, or any actions of Velocity Park, its employees, third parties, or other skateboarders. Velocity Park is not responsible for any incidental or consequential damages, including, but not limited to, any claims for personal injury, property damage, or emotional distress. This release is binding with respect to my heirs, executors, administrators, and assigns, as well as myself.
>
> 2. I have been informed of Velocity Park Rules and agree to abide by them.

1. The language of the waiver is overbroad.

- Exculpatory clauses are strictly construed against the party seeking to shield itself from liability. *Lund*.

- The waiver at issue ostensibly releases Velocity Park from liability "from any and all legal liability, including but not limited to all causes of action, claims, damages in law, or remedies in equity of whatever kind . . . ."

- The phrase "any and all legal liability" would presumably cover injuries resulting from intentional and reckless acts, as well as from negligence. As stated in *Lund*, a release that is "so broad as to be interpreted to shift liability for a tortfeasor's conduct under all possible circumstances, including reckless and intentional conduct, and for all possible injuries, will not be upheld."

- Waivers are not effective to bar liability for intentional acts. *See Lund* (citing Restatement of Contracts (Second) § 195(1)).
- The word "negligence" need not appear in a waiver for it to be enforceable, but the better practice is to clearly state that by signing the waiver, the party is releasing others from negligence claims. *Lund*, fn.2.
- Thus, Zeke's waiver is too broad to inform a skateboarder of the precise rights waived.
- Further, the waiver attempts to be a release of claims against not just Velocity Park and its employees, but also against "any third parties."
  - This attempt to extend the waiver to unknown third parties is most likely unenforceable under *Lund*.
- The exculpatory clause also contains repetitive and confusing language (e.g., [I] hereby forever release, acquit, covenant not to sue, and discharge Velocity   Park . . ."), making it more likely that the average skateboarder at the park—according to Zeke, most Velocity Park visitors will be teenagers and young adults—will not carefully read or understand the agreement before signing it.

2. **The waiver fails to alert the signer to the risks involved in skateboarding.**

- Overbroad and general exculpatory agreements will be construed to bar only those claims that the parties contemplated when they executed the contract. *Lund*. A waiver that only vaguely refers to the activity at issue will not be deemed sufficient to inform the signer of the risks of the activity and the rights being waived. In *Schmidt v. Tyrol Mountain*, cited in *Lund*, a waiver's reference to the "inherent risks in skiing" was insufficient to inform the skier of the risks she was assuming.
- The Velocity Park waiver states that the signer "understand[s] and appreciate[s] that participation in a sport carries a risk to me of serious injury and/or death."

- This language is even more vague than the language in *Schmidt* ("the inherent risks in skiing"); it gives no information to the signer about particular risks associated with skateboarding.
- Thus the waiver should be revised to include language expressly informing the signer of specific skateboarding injury risks and possible causes.
  - *The Banford Courier* article states that the most common skateboarding injuries are wrist sprains and fractures, but serious head injuries may also occur.
- Applicants could redraft the Velocity Park waiver as follows: "I understand and appreciate that skateboarding carries a risk to me of injury from falls or collisions with objects or other skateboarders, including but not limited to bruises, abrasions, sprains and fractures (especially to the wrist), and head injuries, and that these injuries could be severe or even result in substantial disability or death."
  - A revised waiver could also mention something to the effect that using the half-pipes, jumps, etc., increases the risk of harm to the skateboarder.
  - A thorough waiver might also state that falls are likely due to debris on or irregularities in the riding surface (thus insulating Velocity Park for claims based on a skater falling because he or she ran over a piece of trash).
- The waiver also should clearly and expressly convey the risks of skateboarding in a park with other skateboarders.
- Applicants might note that many park users will be teenagers, so the language of the waiver should use terms understandable to someone of a relatively young age, even if the form will have to be signed by parents (*see* discussion *infra* II.D.).
- Moreover, given the rise in injuries associated with aggressive behavior in skateboarders (e.g., risky stunts, fights), the waiver should include language denying liability for injuries caused by Velocity Park's negligent failure to supervise skateboarders.

- Applicants could also note that there are other injuries that even a well-drafted waiver may not cover because they were not within the parties' contemplation when the waiver was executed. (For example, a skateboarder gets food poisoning from a hot dog sold by the Velocity Park concession stand.)

B.   Whether the Velocity Park Waiver Is Conspicuous

Second, a liability waiver must "alert the signer to the nature and significance of what is being signed." *Lund.* The exculpatory clause must be conspicuous to the signer; its format must visually communicate that the waiver language is important.[3] In *Lund*, the court noted that documents that serve two purposes generally are not sufficiently conspicuous, especially when there is only a single signature line, because the importance of the exculpatory clause may not be clearly distinguishable from the rest of the document. Further, the exculpatory clause in *Lund* was not conspicuous because it was in the same size, font, and color as the rest of the form.

- *Lund* provides specific examples of how a dual-purpose document may be improved.
  - The waiver could be a separate document.
  - There could be a separate signature line for the exculpatory clause.
- Zeke's form serves many purposes and the exculpatory clause is not conspicuous.
  - The form contains information on park hours, prices, and rules. It also has paragraphs whereby the skateboarder agrees to waive liability, consents to the use of his or her likeness, authorizes medical treatment, provides emergency contact information, and agrees to receive park e-mails.
  - There are headings for the sections regarding fees, hours, and park rules, but there is no heading for the exculpatory clause or the medical care and use of likeness paragraphs (although these paragraphs are numbered).

---

[3] Applicants are not expected to redraft the entire waiver or attempt to recreate it in a better format in their answer books (e.g., by redrafting the waiver language using a larger font). However, as directed by the task memo, they should suggest those changes that should be incorporated into the waiver's design and layout.

- The exculpatory clause is in a *smaller* font than is the first part of the form.

- There is only one signature line; arguably, the exculpatory clause, consent to medical treatment, and use of likeness parts warrant separate signatures.

- The clause does not have any language to the effect of "I have read this form and understand that by signing it I am waiving important rights." (Even the waiver in *Lund* contains the sentence "I have read the foregoing and understand its contents.") Adding such language would emphasize to the skateboarder the nature and significance of the waiver.

C.   Whether There Is a Disparity in Bargaining Power Between the Parties

The third public policy factor addressed in *Lund* is the question of whether there is a substantial disparity in bargaining power between the parties. In making this determination, the court will consider "the facts surrounding the execution of the waiver," including whether the signer has an opportunity to negotiate its terms. *Lund*.

- In *Lund*, there was no opportunity to negotiate the waiver's terms; Lund either signed or didn't swim.

- The Swim World employee did not alert Lund that the entrance form included a liability waiver, let alone explain its terms to her.

- The court also noted that there was not enough time to read Swim World's form and make a reasoned decision about the consequences of signing it, because there were other Swim World patrons waiting in line to check in.

- The court concluded that, at a minimum, there was a genuine dispute of material fact regarding the parties' disparity in bargaining power.

- Regarding the expected circumstances of skateboarders' execution of Zeke's proposed waiver, a substantial disparity of bargaining power could be found.

  - As in *Lund*, skateboarders will have to sign the exculpatory contract to use the park; there is no "opt-out" provision.

- Velocity Park would-be patrons, similar to the deceased in *Lund*, may be under pressure to sign the waiver as quickly as possible so as not to delay the entry of other skateboarders waiting in line.

- Applicants should suggest that park employees alert skateboarders and their parents (*see* below) to the form's liability waiver portion, warning them to carefully read it.

- They should also suggest that all patrons (and their parents) be told that if they have any questions about the waiver, they should ask park employees, who should be familiar with the waiver's terms.

- Also, Zeke should be sure to fully staff the park at peak times (e.g., opening and after school) when there might be many impatient kids and parents waiting in line.

- Applicants thus should suggest measures Zeke can take to minimize a substantial disparity in bargaining power between the parties. However, even if there is some disparity (i.e., patrons are not allowed to opt out of signing), it is unlikely that the presence of this one negative factor would lead a court to find an otherwise enforceable waiver void as against public policy. *See Lund.* Indeed, the *Lund* court appears to give more weight to the first two factors: whether the language is overbroad and ambiguous, and whether the form notifies the signer to the significance of what is being waived.

D. **Whether a Waiver Is Enforceable If Signed Only by a Minor**

- *Lund* does not address whether a release signed by a minor, or by a parent on a minor's behalf, would be contrary to public policy. Thus, it appears that the enforceability of waivers against minors is an issue of first impression in Franklin.

- The relevant case law on this issue is a Columbia case, *Holum v. Bruges Soccer Club, Inc.* (Col. Sup. Ct. 1999). *Holum* discusses the effectiveness of a waiver signed by a parent on behalf of her minor child as a condition of the child's participation in a soccer club. The court held that enforcing the waiver against the parents and the child was in the public's interest, largely because the defendant was a nonprofit soccer club that relied on volunteers to offer soccer to many children at low cost. The court reasoned that protecting the club and its volunteers from liability was critical to the existence of such recreational activities because volunteers might be reluctant to help if doing so meant subjecting themselves to liability. The court said that enforcing the club's liability waiver allocated the risk of injury from the club to parents, thereby benefiting the community as a whole by making soccer more accessible to all children.

- The court in *Holum* also emphasized that parents have authority to make decisions regarding the welfare of their children, comparing the club's waiver to the parents' statutory right to consent to medical procedures involving their children. The court assumed that a parent signing a release of future claims would be in a position to consider the alternatives and make a reasoned decision that the cost of waiving the right to sue was outweighed by the benefit to the child of being able to participate in the activity.

  - In *Holum,* the mother signed a release on behalf of her seven-year-old child. Most of the patrons at Velocity Park will be teenagers. Applicants will have to address how *Holum* applies where teenagers are involved and to an activity which, unlike the soccer club, is not sponsored by a volunteer-driven organization.

Application of *Holum* to the proposed Velocity Park waiver form

- Zeke's proposed waiver has a single line for the skateboarder's signature, and places for indicating sex and age. Zeke says in his interview that 10 is the minimum age to use the park and that he expects most skateboarders to be teens or young adults. In short, a substantial number of park patrons will be minors.

- Also, because beginning skateboarders account for one-third of skateboarding injuries, liability for claims by underage skateboarders is a real concern.

- The fact that Velocity Park is a for-profit enterprise weighs against enforcing a release that purports to waive a minor's right to sue for negligence under *Holum*.

  - While Zeke states that, at some point, he would like to partner with the City of Banford and make the skate park free, Velocity Park will clearly open as a for-profit business.

  - Thus, the rationale that enforceable liability waivers ensure volunteer participation and the provision of community-based recreation (so central in the *Holum* holding) is not a consideration here.

  - That does not mean that Velocity Park won't benefit Banford: it gives skateboarders a supervised space in which to skate and one that was expressly designed for that purpose. Thus, it will be an improvement over teens skateboarding in neighborhood cul-de-sacs and the Library Mall.

  - Applicants must recognize that *Holum,* a Columbia case, is persuasive only.

  - However, the *Holum* court based its holding equally on the fact that parents have authority to make life choices for their children and that they assume the risk of injury to their child in exchange for the privilege and benefit of participation in low-cost recreational sports.

- Applicants must grapple with the Franklin statute regarding enforceability of contracts entered into by minors. It seems clear that under § 41, a liability waiver signed by an underage skateboarder, without being co-signed by a parent or guardian, will not be enforceable.

  - For example, under § 41(b)(1), a minor can disaffirm a contract, unless the contract was for necessaries (e.g., food). Because skateboarding is not a necessary, an under-18 skateboarder could sign but then disaffirm a Velocity Park waiver. On the other hand, the waiver could be enforced against the skateboarder if he or she ratifies the agreement after turning 18 by, for example, continuing to use the park. (The assumption here is that once a waiver is signed, Velocity Park keeps it on file and a skateboarder doesn't need to sign a new one every time he or she uses the park.)

- Applicants should note that under *Holum*, parents in Columbia can waive claims on their own behalf and on behalf of their children for negligence that results in injuries to their children. Given that exculpatory contracts in Franklin will be enforceable if they meet the standards for scope and clarity in *Lund*, applicants should suggest that the Velocity Park waiver be signed by the parents of any skateboarder who is under 18. This will help insulate Velocity Park from negligence claims by injured skateboarders' parents.

Note: Applicants could receive extra credit for observing that, strategically, even if it is uncertain whether a waiver will be enforced, some provisions may be desirable to discourage people from suing the park after an injury.

Applicant Identification

In re Lisa Peel

**Read the instructions on the back cover.
Do not break the seal until you are told to do so.**

NATIONAL CONFERENCE OF BAR EXAMINERS

In re Lisa Peel

INSTRUCTIONS

1. You will have 90 minutes to complete this session of the examination. This performance test is designed to evaluate your ability to handle a select number of legal authorities in the context of a factual problem involving a client.

2. The problem is set in the fictitious state of Franklin, in the fictitious Fifteenth Circuit of the United States. Columbia and Olympia are also fictitious states in the Fifteenth Circuit. In Franklin, the trial court of general jurisdiction is the District Court, the intermediate appellate court is the Court of Appeal, and the highest court is the Supreme Court.

3. You will have two kinds of materials with which to work: a File and a Library. The first document in the File is a memorandum containing the instructions for the task you are to complete. The other documents in the File contain factual information about your case and may include some facts that are not relevant.

4. The Library contains the legal authorities needed to complete the task and may also include some authorities that are not relevant. Any cases may be real, modified, or written solely for the purpose of this examination. If the cases appear familiar to you, do not assume that they are precisely the same as you have read before. Read them thoroughly, as if they all were new to you. You should assume that the cases were decided in the jurisdictions and on the dates shown. In citing cases from the Library, you may use abbreviations and omit page references.

5. Your response must be written in the answer book provided. If you are taking this examination on a laptop computer, your jurisdiction will provide you with specific instructions. In answering this performance test, you should concentrate on the materials provided. What you have learned in law school and elsewhere provides the general background for analyzing the problem; the File and Library provide the specific materials with which you must work.

6. Although there are no restrictions on how you apportion your time, you should be sure to allocate ample time (about 45 minutes) to reading and digesting the materials and to organizing your answer before you begin writing it. You may make notes anywhere in the test materials; blank pages are provided at the end of the booklet. You may not tear pages from the question booklet.

7. This performance test will be graded on your responsiveness to the instructions regarding the task you are to complete, which are given to you in the first memorandum in the File, and on the content, thoroughness, and organization of your response.

In re Lisa Peel

FILE

LIBRARY

POINT SHEET

In re Lisa Peel

FILE

Black, Fernandez & Hanson LLP

Attorneys at Law
Suite 215
396 West Main Street
Greenville, Franklin 33755

MEMORANDUM

To: Applicant
From: Henry Black
Re: Peel subpoena
Date: February 26, 2008

Our client, Lisa Peel, has just been subpoenaed by the local district attorney to testify before a grand jury. The subpoena directs her to bring notes concerning any and all persons interviewed regarding an item she posted on her Web log (blog). These notes will reveal the identities of her sources for the information she posted on her blog. Peel promised to protect the confidentiality of her sources. She seeks our advice on whether she has grounds to resist the subpoena.

I am somewhat familiar with the Franklin Reporter Shield Act (FRSA). However, I do not know if the FRSA applies to Peel and her blog. Please draft an objective memorandum for me analyzing whether we can use the FRSA to move to quash Peel's subpoena.

You need not include a separate statement of facts, but be sure to use the facts in your analysis. Be sure to address both sides of the issue; that is, discuss any facts or law that may prevent Peel from claiming the protection of the FRSA.

Do not concern yourself with any First Amendment issues; another associate is researching those arguments.

Transcript of Interview with Lisa Peel

February 22, 2008

Attorney:	Lisa, nice to see you. What can I do for you?
Peel:	You can make this subpoena go away.
Attorney:	Tell me more. Why don't you start at the beginning?
Peel:	A couple of years ago, I retired from teaching, and my husband and I moved to Greenville here in Montgomery County. To find out more about my new community, I started attending the meetings of several public bodies—the library and school boards, the park district board, and the town council. The more I went, the more I got to know people, and the more I became part of the scene. People got to know and trust me. Soon, I realized that there was a lot going on that the public should know about.
Attorney:	Did you think about getting the local newspaper involved?
Peel:	Most of the towns in this county are too small to support a daily paper. So there is only one daily paper covering all of Montgomery County. The publisher believes the paper should boost the local communities, and he discourages the reporters from doing any stories and investigations that might portray the communities in a bad light.
Attorney:	So what did you do?
Peel:	About a year ago, I started an Internet blog. As you know, often the owner of the blog starts a discussion and others can post comments.
	On my blog, I posted the agendas of the Greenville town council, library and school boards, and sometimes the planning commission. After the meetings, I posted the minutes, my summary of the minutes, and my own commentary about how these decisions would affect the town. Within weeks, over 400 people visited the blog, and about a quarter of them commented on what I wrote or added questions that others would respond to. I actually had citizens engaged in learning what their government was doing.
	At first I updated the blog only occasionally. Then it generated so much interest that I decided to update it more often.
Attorney:	How often do you update it?

2

Peel: I generally post new items on Friday, but sometimes I may not get around to it until later in the weekend. I have movie reviews and gardening tips on the blog and also share news of my family. I post pictures of my pets and places where I've traveled. I'll also post announcements about the library's bake sale and events like that.

Attorney: Do your readers pay for access to your blog?

Peel: No, it's free. At first, I kept the blog wide open; anyone could access it and post anything—anonymously if they wanted to. But then I decided that letting anyone post anything might not be wise. So now, anyone can access it at no cost. But if you want to post a comment or a question, you have to register. Registering is also free. In the past two months, I've had over 3,500 registrants in this town of 38,000 people, and people have visited the site more than 15,000 times. I've also picked up a couple of local businesses, which pay me to post their ads on my blog.

Attorney: So, tell me about the subpoena.

Peel: One day, I got a call from an individual familiar with the school district administration. This person told me that the Greenville School District was losing the use of $10,000 worth of audiovisual and computer equipment purchased with district funds because the stuff was going to the home of the assistant superintendent. Well, $10,000 isn't a lot of corruption, I concede, but it is public money and it was intended to buy equipment for schoolchildren.

So I investigated and got confirmation from a couple of sources. I wrote a piece about what I found out and posted it on my blog. I brought you a hard copy of the posting. Now the Montgomery County District Attorney wants to know the sources of my information.

Attorney: Why not reveal your sources?

Peel: To get to the truth, especially the truth about public corruption, I have to talk to people on the inside. But insiders will never talk to me if they think their names will become public because they're worried about losing their jobs. So I get inside information from confidential sources, let people know about it by getting the word out, and suddenly the government starts investigating or the public starts asking questions.

3

Attorney:	Do you get paid for this work?
Peel:	Not much. The little income that comes from the sponsors' ads, I use for my expenses: computer upgrades, copy costs, telephone costs, gas for traveling, that sort of thing.
Attorney:	Do you know why the district attorney subpoenaed you?
Peel:	I have a couple of guesses. Now that I've exposed this scandal, he has to investigate. I suspect he is embarrassed to learn about this from my blog. Also, the district attorney is just being lazy. Think about it—how many people are in a position to know about this going on at the school? He just needs to start asking the right people and the information will come out. But, regardless of the reason, I have to protect my sources. I may be retired and this blog may be my hobby, but right now it is the only avenue for real news in this county.
Attorney:	I'm somewhat familiar with the Franklin Reporter Shield Act—we may have an argument that you are protected by it, but I doubt that "blogs" or "bloggers" are specifically mentioned in the Act. I am also concerned that you've never worked as a reporter before.
Peel:	But I work just like a real reporter. I attend public meetings, read agendas, minutes, budgets, etc. I make calls to the officials and other staff members and interview them. I then post the official agendas and minutes, along with my summaries and comments. The amount of time varies, but I usually spend 12-15 hours a week on my blog.
Attorney:	I see your point. Well, we'll do some research and get back to you soon.
Peel:	Thanks. I look forward to hearing from you.

$10,000 in School Equipment Diverted from Schools to Home of Assistant Superintendent

January 4, 2008: Greenville, Franklin

by Lisa Peel

The Greenville School District approved the purchase of $70,000 worth of new audiovisual and computer equipment for the schoolchildren of the Greenville School District this year, but not all of the equipment is in the schools. As the equipment arrived at the district offices, selected items were redirected to the home of Assistant Superintendent Frank Peterson, according to several sources closely associated with the school district. Sources estimate that Peterson has school district equipment worth over $10,000 at his home at the present time.

According to sources, who would speak only on the condition of anonymity, Peterson took selected items home "to test them out." But instead of returning these materials to the school, he kept them at his home.

At this time Peterson reportedly has at home two fully equipped desktop personal computers with two color printers, two laptop computers, one high-performance scanner, and a digital camera. He also has a classroom multimedia system in his home. That's $10,000 worth of *public* school equipment that he's using to create his own multimedia studio!

When asked for a response on Peterson's alleged activities, Greenville School Board President Annette Gross said, "We have policies in place to ensure that the public's dollars are spent according to budget."

Citizens should immediately ask President Gross for a full accounting of the purchases and for an investigation of Assistant Superintendent Peterson.

IN THE DISTRICT COURT FOR MONTGOMERY COUNTY
STATE OF FRANKLIN

SUBPOENA DUCES TECUM

In re Grand Jury Investigation   **Grand Jury Case Number 08-7703**

TO:

Lisa Peel
9853 S. Elm Street
Greenville, Franklin 33755

YOU ARE COMMANDED TO APPEAR before the Grand Jury duly empaneled in the above-captioned case at the Montgomery County Courthouse, Room 346, March 10, 2008, at 10:00 a.m. YOU ARE COMMANDED TO PRODUCE all reports, files, notes, and other documentation regarding Greenville School District equipment in the possession of Assistant Superintendent Frank Peterson, including all files, notes, reports, and any other documentation taken of or from any and all persons interviewed for or sources described or quoted in the GREENVILLE CITIZEN BLOG operated by Lisa Peel and dated January 4, 2008.

Subpoena requested by the Montgomery County District Attorney's Office.

DATE ISSUED: February 20, 2008

Elliot Wallace

Elliot Wallace
District Attorney

NOTICE:

FAILURE TO COMPLY WITH THIS SUBPOENA MAY RESULT IN FINES OR IMPRISONMENT OR BOTH.

BLOGS COMPETING WITH NEWSPAPERS AND NETWORKS

Blogs—slang for Web logs—started out as online personal diaries or journals but have rapidly become part of the everyday Web vernacular and are replacing news websites for many readers.

Blog owners or "bloggers" establish Web pages on which they post news items, commentary, information, and links to other sources for readers. Readers are often invited to respond. For example, the blogger might post a movie review, and ask readers to post their opinions. Or the blogger might comment on the latest appropriations bill before Congress and encourage readers to share their views with their representatives.

According to recent surveys, at least 8 million adults in the United States have created blogs, and 30 percent of Americans read one or more blogs regularly. Blogs cover every topic imaginable—technology, sports, medicine, art, entertainment, business, news, and politics. Of course, many blogs still serve as forums for sharing personal experiences, from weddings to the contents of a blogger's junk drawer.

Journalists and politicians have learned the power of blogs and recognize that they are now a force to be reckoned with. For example, during the 2006 Congressional campaigns, bloggers challenged many of the candidates' statements. Several major bloggers have received press credentials for political events. Most major news outlets have several staff bloggers. Blogging software is easy to use and inexpensive. Blogging is said to give a voice to those not given attention in the traditional media. It is just this ease of blogging that makes some professional journalists uncomfortable. "The blogger is the reporter, editor, and publisher. Where is the check on the blogger to ensure the truth?" asked Al Rains, Franklin Newspaper Association director. "Blogging isn't reporting, it's just writing. Any hack can offer half-baked commentary on the news of the day and post it online. How is that different from the millions of people who post items on their MySpace or Facebook pages?"

Other journalists see blogging as just another development in journalism—from newspapers to radio to TV to cable news, talk radio, and YouTube. "More means of sharing the news and inviting commentary is better than fewer means. I trust the public to learn from many sources and decide for themselves," says Tanya Browne, a journalism professor at Franklin University. "With so much media consolidation, there are many voices, especially local ones, that will be heard only through these 'alternative' forms of journalism."

LIBRARY

<h1 style="text-align:center">Franklin Reporter Shield Act</h1>

§ 900 Preamble

The primary purpose of this Act is to safeguard the media's ability to gather news. It is intended to promote the free flow of information to the public by prohibiting courts from compelling reporters to disclose unpublished news sources or information received from such sources.

§ 901 Definitions

As used in this Act:

(a) "reporter" means any person regularly engaged in collecting, writing, or editing news for publication through a news medium.

(b) "news medium" means any newspaper, magazine, or other similar medium issued at regular intervals and having a general circulation; a radio station; a television station; a community antenna television service; or any person or corporation engaged in the making of newsreels or other motion picture news for public showing.

(c) "source" means the person from whom or the means through which the information was obtained.

§ 902 Nondisclosure of source of information

No court may compel a reporter to disclose the source of any information or any unpublished material except as provided in this Act.

*　　*　　*　　*

Dictionary Definitions

The American Heritage Dictionary of the English Language (4th ed. 2000)

Blog: *noun* [shortened form of Web log], a website that contains an online personal journal with reflections, comments, and often hyperlinks provided by the writer.

Circulation: *noun*, movement in a circle or circuit, especially the movement of blood through blood vessels; .... free movement or passage; the passing of something, such as money or news, from place to place or person to person; the condition of being passed about and widely known, distribution; dissemination of printed material, especially copies of newspapers or magazines among readers; the number of copies of a publication sold or distributed.

Publication: *noun*, the act or process of publishing printed material; the communication of information to the public.

Publish: *verb*, to prepare and issue material for public disclosure or sale; to bring to public attention; to announce.

Reporter: *noun,* a writer, investigator, or presenter of news stories; a person who is authorized to write and issue official accounts of judicial or legislative proceedings.

During Terrence Johnson's trial for murder, Johnson served a subpoena *duces tecum* upon respondent Peggy Bellows, a newspaper photographer employed by the *Springfield Review*. The subpoena required Bellows to produce certain photographs that she took during a police search of Johnson's residence prior to his arrest. When Bellows refused to produce the photos, the trial court found her in civil contempt and sentenced her to jail. This appeal followed.

The sole issue on appeal is whether Bellows is a reporter whose unpublished photographs are protected by the Franklin Reporter Shield Act (FRSA). In Franklin, reporters have a statutory, qualified privilege protecting their sources and unpublished material from compelled disclosure. FRSA § 902. It is the burden of the party claiming the privilege to establish his or her right to its protection. *Wehrmann v. Wickesberg* (Fr. Sup. Ct. 2002).

We note at the outset that testimonial privileges, in general, are not favored because they "contravene a fundamental principle of our jurisprudence that the public has a right to every man's evidence." *United States v. Bryan*, 339 U.S. 323 (1950). The preamble to the FRSA, on the other hand, states that the FRSA seeks to promote the free flow of information to and from the media by protecting the media's confidential sources. Hence, competing interests must be addressed in determining the FRSA's scope.

We have found few cases that discuss who, beyond members of the traditional media, has status to claim the journalist's privilege. In 2002, the Franklin Supreme Court rejected using the FRSA to protect the identities of those paying for newspaper ads disguised as journalism. *St. Mary's Hospital v. Zeus Publishing* (Fr. Sup. Ct. 2002). The full page ads recounted a hospital's alleged illegal labor practices and urged a boycott. Similarly, the Columbia Supreme Court rejected the argument that defamatory messages posted on a sports Internet bulletin board (GolfNet) could be construed as "news" or as being "published at regular intervals," and therefore held that the poster of the messages was not protected by the Columbia Reporter Shield Act. *Hausch v. Vaughan* (Col. Sup. Ct. 1995).

In contrast to these cases, the Franklin Supreme Court did grant FRSA protection to a freelance writer for a magazine, *Kaiser v. Currie* (Fr. Sup. Ct. 2004), and to the author of a medical journal article, *Halliwell v. An-*

derson (Fr. Sup. Ct. 2002), holding that neither could be compelled to divulge their sources of information.

What we glean from these cases is that the test does not grant "reporter" status to any person simply because that person has a manuscript, a computer, a Web page, or a film. Rather, it requires an intent at the inception of the newsgathering process to disseminate investigative news to the public. Thus in *Hovey v. Fellenz* (Fr. Ct. App. 1989), the court held that the FRSA did not shield two reporters from having to testify about a crime that they happened to witness on their way home from work—when they witnessed the crime, they had no intent to disseminate news to the public. As we see it, the privilege is available only to persons whose purposes are those traditionally inherent to the press: gathering news for publication.

The FRSA defines a reporter as "any person regularly engaged in *collecting,* writing, or editing news for publication through a news medium." § 901(a) (emphasis added). Johnson claims Bellows is not covered by the FRSA for the simple reason that the Act doesn't mention "photographers." He claims that had the legislature intended to protect photographers, it would have included photographers in the statute.

Franklin law concerning statutory construc-

tion is clear. The principal rule of statutory construction is to ascertain and give effect to the legislature's intent. To determine the legislature's intent, courts first look to the statute's language. A court must give the legislative language its plain and ordinary meaning and construe the statute as a whole, giving effect to every word therein. When interpreting a statute, words and phrases must not be viewed in isolation but must be considered in light of other relevant provisions of the statute.

Where the language of the statute is clear and unambiguous, the only legitimate function of the courts is to enforce the law as enacted by the legislature. Courts should not depart from the plain language of the statute by reading into it exceptions, limitations, or conditions which conflict with the intent of the legislature. No rule of statutory construction authorizes the courts to declare that the legislature did not mean what the plain language of the statute says.

The record is clear from testimony of the *Springfield Review* editor that Bellows is employed as a photographer for the newspaper and that her permanent assignment is to "photograph newsworthy events." There is no dispute that the *Springfield Review*, a daily newspaper with a daily circulation of more than 100,000 readers, is a news medium. The record is also clear that, in her capacity as a photographer, Bellows does not write or edit.

The question then is whether she collects news by photographing newsworthy events. Where the legislature has supplied a definition, we are constrained to use only that definition. However, the legislature does not define the term "collecting" in the FRSA. In interpreting "the plain and ordinary meaning" of a word, where the legislature has not defined the term, courts may use a dictionary to assist in determining the plain and ordinary meaning. Turning to MERRIAM WEBSTER'S COLLEGIATE DICTIONARY 720 (10th ed. 1998), we find that collecting means "to bring together, gather, assemble." Taking photographs of events is one way to gather or assemble news. Bellows, by photographing newsworthy events, is regularly engaged in the gathering or assembling of news, and her activities fall within the statutory meaning of "collecting" news for publication.

Furthermore, extending the protections of the FRSA to photographers is consistent with the purpose of the Act. When it enacted the FRSA in 1948, the legislature stated the purpose of the Act as encouraging the free and unfettered flow of information to the public. The more recent amendments to the FRSA extend the protections to undisclosed materials as well as sources. *See* FRSA § 900. This provision protects the discretion of journalists to determine when and how to publish their materials.

Accordingly, Bellows meets the statutory definition of a reporter as she is a person regularly engaged in collecting news for publication through a news medium. Bellows is protected by the FRSA.

Reversed.

13

Lane v. Tichenor

Franklin Supreme Court (2003)

The sole question on appeal is whether the term "recreational purpose," as used in the Franklin Landowner's Recreational Immunity Act ("the Act"), § 730, includes hayrides. Lane brought this action against Tichenor for damages sustained during a hayride on Tichenor's land. On Tichenor's motion, the trial court dismissed the case and the appellate court affirmed.

The Act provides that landowners owe no duty of care to keep their premises safe for entry or use by any person for recreational purposes. The stated purpose of the Act is to "encourage owners of land to make land and water areas available to the public for recreational purposes by limiting their liability toward persons entering thereon for such purposes." § 730(1). Thus, the Act provides immunity only if the land is entered upon or used for a "recreational purpose."

The Act defines the term "recreational purpose" as follows: "'[r]ecreational purpose' includes any of the following, or any combination thereof: hunting, fishing, swimming, boating, snowmobiling, motorcycling, camping, hiking, cave exploring, nature study, water skiing, water sports, bicycling, horseback riding, and viewing or enjoying historical, archaeological, scenic or scientif-ic sites, or other similar activities." § 730(2)(c).

Lane argues that because hayrides are not listed among the items defined in the Act, the legislature meant to exclude them from the definition of "recreational purpose," and therefore the Act does not apply here. Tichenor responds that the term "other similar activities" indicates the legislature's intent to broadly define the term "recreational purpose."

In interpreting a statute, the court is constrained to ascertain and give effect to the intent of the legislature. The statutory language is the best indication of the drafters' intent. Where that language is unambiguous, courts must enforce the law as enacted. Each word in the statute, as well as the punctuation used, is to be examined. Where the statute enumerates various covered activities, such enumeration implies the exclusion of all others.

However, in this case the statutory language is not clear, and the enumeration is neither exclusive nor exhaustive. While the legislature provided a list of activities intended as a definition of "recreational purpose," the question is what the legislature meant by

14

"other similar activities." The question, more precisely, is whether hayrides fit within the phrase "other similar activities."

Where the language of a statute is unclear, the court may avail itself of external aids to interpret the statute. One such aid is the rules of construction of statutes, also called the canons of statutory interpretation. These rules or canons guide the court in ascertaining the intent of the legislature.

One canon, *ejusdem generis*, states that when general words follow particular and specific words in a statute, the general words must be construed to include only things of the same general kind as those indicated by the particular and specific words.

When we examine the items specifically enumerated in the Act, we find that the quality or characteristic common to all of them is the enjoyment of nature. While some may find enjoyment in fishing or hunting, others will find enjoyment in viewing historical or scientific sights, and still others in horseback riding or motorcycling. All of these activities take place outdoors and involve nature: the study of nature, the enjoyment of nature, or even travel through a natural setting.

Applying that quality to the present situation, a hayride is just another form of the enjoyment of nature. It is hard to see how hayrides are significantly different from horseback riding, motorcycling, or bicycling—all of which involve transporting oneself or others across the outdoors for enjoyment. One can imagine a group climbing onto a farm wagon, traveling along in the open, watching the stars, and communing with nature.

Lane further argues that while we should not apply this canon of construction at all, if we do, we must conclude that the quality common to all the enumerated or specific activities is that they occur by day. In this case, the hayride was conducted at night. However, we note that camping occurs overnight and that some fishing does as well. A starlit night far away from the lights and noise of a city, the crisp night air of an October evening, the snap and crackle of fall leaves accompanied by the sounds of night birds, the moonlight faintly illuminating old trees and fallen leaves, can all be enjoyed on a hayride at night under cover of darkness.

Because we hold that hayrides fall within the term "other similar activities" of the Act, we conclude that the trial court properly dismissed the case.

Affirmed.

15

NOTES

POINT SHEET

In re Lisa Peel

DRAFTERS' POINT SHEET

In this performance test item, applicants are employed by a law firm. Applicants' task is to prepare an objective memorandum evaluating whether a motion to quash will be successful with respect to a subpoena served on the firm's client, Lisa Peel. Peel operates an Internet Web log or "blog," which functions much as a newspaper, reporting news items and commentary; she is not a professional reporter. She recently posted to her blog a report that Greenville School District Assistant Superintendent Frank Peterson was using school district equipment in his home. The report was based on information from anonymous sources. Soon after the story was posted, Peel was served a subpoena duces tecum by the district attorney and ordered to appear before a grand jury and to bring notes and other documents concerning the sources of her information. Peel seeks the law firm's advice on whether there are grounds to resist the subpoena.

Applicants must analyze whether Peel is entitled to claim the protection of the Franklin Reporter Shield Act (FRSA), which provides that a reporter cannot be compelled to reveal his or her sources of information except as provided by the Act. The instructional memo instructs applicants not to address any First Amendment issues. To complete the assigned task, applicants must parse and interpret the statute and, in particular, the definitions of "reporter" and "news medium."

The File consists of the instructional memo from the supervising partner, a transcript of the interview with Peel, a copy of the item posted on the blog, the subpoena, and a news article about blogs. The Library consists of excerpts from the FRSA, several dictionary definitions, and two cases bearing on the subject.

The following discussion covers all of the points the drafters intended to raise in the problem. Applicants need not cover all of them to receive passing or even excellent grades. Grading is entirely within the discretion of the user jurisdictions.

I.   Overview

The task is to draft an objective memorandum assessing whether there are grounds to quash the subpoena. The work product should resemble a legal memorandum such as one an associate would prepare for a supervising partner. The key issue is whether Peel qualifies as a "reporter" as defined in the Act; if so, she cannot be compelled to reveal the sources of her report, except as provided in the Act.

This is primarily an exercise in statutory interpretation. Applicants should thus examine the definitions provided in the Act, determine the elements of the definitions that must be met if Peel is to be protected by the Act, and reach a conclusion regarding whether Peel's blogging activities meet each element. With respect to the key definitions in the Act, it is expected that applicants will arrive at the following conclusions:

- A "reporter" is any person regularly engaged in collecting, writing, or editing news for publication through a news medium.
  - Peel regularly engages or involves herself in collecting, writing, or editing the news, specifically, by attending meetings, analyzing public information, interviewing public officials, and writing summaries of and commentaries on their activities.
- The news written by Peel is published through a news medium.
  - A "news medium" is any newspaper, magazine, or other similar medium issued at regular intervals and having a general circulation.
  - Peel's blog is a publication issued at regular intervals and with a general circulation. Therefore, it qualifies as a news medium within the meaning of the Act.

II.   Relevant Facts

Applicants are instructed that they need not draft a separate statement of facts, but that they are expected to incorporate the relevant facts into their analysis. Some applicants may wish to set forth the facts at length. Others may wish to state only enough facts to set the scene and import other facts as necessary into their discussion of the issues.

A thorough discussion of whether Peel's blogging activities bring her within the Act's coverage would include the following facts:

- Peel began an Internet blog in which she publishes information about public bodies, including the agendas and minutes of public meetings, summaries of the meetings, and her own comments about the importance of these meetings.

- Peel attends meetings, obtains public documents, prepares summaries of the meetings and documents, and writes commentaries about the business of several public bodies. Peel's activities generally take about 12 to 15 hours per week.

- Peel's blog, the Greenville Citizen Blog, has at least 3,500 persons who are registered as readers. In order to post comments to the blog, readers must register with the blog; registration is free. There are likely many additional readers who are not registered.

- Peel usually posts items to the blog every Friday.

- There is no town newspaper and the only newspaper available is a countywide one that does not publish anything critical of the local communities.

- On January 4, 2008, Peel posted a news item to the blog reporting that Greenville School District Assistant Superintendent Frank Peterson was keeping school district audiovisual and computer equipment, worth approximately $10,000, in his home for his personal use.

- The blog posting about Peterson is based on information provided by confidential sources.

- The district attorney has subpoenaed Peel to appear before a grand jury and to bring notes concerning the source of her information about Frank Peterson.

III.   Analysis

Applicants are told to analyze applicable legal authority and explain how the facts and law support their conclusions. The instructional memo emphasizes that both sides of the issue should be addressed; that is, applicants should discuss not only those facts that support a motion to quash but also those facts that weigh against the motion's success. Applicants should take care to address each of the elements of the definition of a reporter found in the Act. One format is for each element of the definition to be the subject of a separate heading followed by analysis related to that heading. Alternatively, applicants may organize their work product in other ways. The headings appearing below are exemplars only and are not intended as the only acceptable headings.

Whether Peel engages in the activities of a reporter for the purposes of the FRSA

- At the outset, applicants should note that the person claiming the privilege under the FRSA has the burden to establish his or her right to its protection. *In re Bel-*

lows (Franklin Ct. App. 2005). Thus, in order to successfully resist the subpoena, the burden is on Peel to demonstrate that her blogging activities come within the ambit of the FRSA.

- The FRSA defines a reporter as "any person regularly engaged in collecting, writing, or editing news for publication through a news medium." FRSA § 901(a). Some of the terms in the statutory definition are further defined by statutes and others are not defined. Each of them must be interpreted.

  - In interpreting the FRSA, the court must ascertain and give effect to the intent of the legislature. Ordinarily the best indicator of the legislature's intent is the plain and ordinary meaning of the words used in the statute. Where the language is unambiguous, the court must rely on that language, giving effect to all the words in the statutory provision at issue. Where the legislature has defined terms, the court must use the definitions provided in the Act. *Bellows.*

  - NOTE: Applicants who rely on the dictionary definition of the term "reporter" have misconstrued the nature of statutory interpretation as explained in *Bellows*. The court is clear that where the legislature has defined a term, the court must rely on that definition.

    - Peel collects, writes, and edits news.

      - To collect news means to "gather or assemble" it. *Bellows.*

        - Peel gathers and assembles the news by obtaining public documents from public bodies, attending their meetings, and interviewing public officials.

      - Peel writes and edits the news by preparing summaries of minutes and other public documents and commentaries on the activities of several public bodies and posting them to her blog.

    - The term "news" is not defined in the Act. The plain and ordinary meaning of the term "news" involves activities of public bodies and the use of public monies.

      - Many of Peel's blog postings involve the activities of public bodies.

      - However, Peel's blog is not entirely devoted to news items. She posts recipes, gardening tips, and items about her family, as well as her vacation and pet photos, presumably none of which would be considered newsworthy.

- The FRSA describes a reporter as someone who "regularly engages" in news-gathering activities. FRSA § 901(a). The term "regular" is not defined. However, common usage of the term would include weekly activities of attending meetings and posting items to the blog.

- In addition, in *Bellows*, the court emphasized that the protections of the FRSA will be extended only to those individuals and organizations having "an intent at the inception of the news-gathering process to disseminate investigative news to the public."

  - Clearly Peel has the intent when she is attending civic meetings and interviewing officials to disseminate the news to the public via her blog. *Cf. Hovey v. Fellenz* (cited in *Bellows*) where two reporters were not entitled to claim the protection of the FRSA when they witnessed the commission of a crime on their way home from work.

- Nevertheless, Peel has no training as a reporter and she is not employed by the traditional media. By contrast, the person deemed a "reporter" for FRSA purposes in *Bellows* was a professional news photographer.

- Likewise, *Kaiser v. Currie* and *Halliwell v. Anderson*, two cases cited in *Bellows* as examples of situations in which the Franklin courts have granted FRSA protection, involved persons writing for traditional media: a magazine and a medical journal.

Whether Peel's blog qualifies as a "news medium" under the FRSA

- A reporter collects, writes, or edits news for publication through a news medium. FRSA § 901(a). Thus applicants must determine whether Peel's blog is a "news medium" for purposes of the FRSA.

  - The term "news medium" is defined in the FRSA as "any newspaper, magazine, or other similar medium issued at regular intervals and having a general circulation . . . ." FRSA § 901(b).

- Neither the term "Web log" nor "blog" is listed in the statute. Thus applicants must discuss whether an Internet blog like Peel's meets the definition of a "news medium."
  - The examples of news media provided in the statute are not an exhaustive or exclusive listing, because the definition includes the term "other similar medium." *See Lane v. Tichenor* (Franklin Sup. Ct. 2003).
  - Arguably, the use of the term "other similar medium" indicates the intent of the legislature to interpret "news medium" in a broad manner.
  - One canon of statutory construction, *ejusdem generis*, is helpful in interpreting the term "other similar medium." The canon states that when general words follow particular and specific words in a statute, the general words must be construed to include only things of the same general kind as those indicated by the particular and specific words. *Lane.*
    - In this case, one key quality common to the particular and specific words listed (i.e., newspapers and magazines) is that they are publications that occur on a regular basis.
    - However, it is also possible that the court may focus on the fact that newspapers and magazines are primarily print media.
    - Arguably, an indication that the legislature intended that the term "news medium" be interpreted in a broad manner is the long list of various forms of media listed in the statute; these media are not limited to print media, but encompass a broad range of means of communication. FRSA § 901(b).
    - And applicants could note that it is now common for newspapers and magazines to have online versions.
  - There is a strong argument that, like the listed forms of news media in § 901(b), Peel's blog is published at regular intervals and has a general circulation.
    - The word "publish" means "to prepare and issue material for public disclosure or sale; to bring to public attention; to announce." *American Heritage Dictionary.*

- Peel posts items to the blog in order to bring them to the attention of the public. This is analogous to the printing and distribution of a newspaper or magazine.
  - Indeed, she states that, because of her blog, "I actually had citizens engaged in learning what their government was doing." Peel interview.
- As a general rule, Peel posts new items to the blog on a regular basis—she tries to post new items every Friday. But sometimes it may be later in the weekend before new posts are on her website.
  - Thus, Peel's blog lacks the reliability of most traditional media (e.g., the morning newspaper or 11 p.m. news broadcast).
- Nonetheless, Peel's blog can be distinguished from the Internet bulletin board in *Hausch v. Vaughan* (Col. Sup. Ct. 1995). In that case, the Columbia Supreme Court, interpreting the Columbia Reporter Shield Act, held that messages posted to an Internet bulletin board, which were posted intermittently, failed to meet that Act's requirement that to be a news medium, the claimed "news" had to be "published at regular intervals."
  - Peel's blog is updated every week.
  - And, unlike an Internet bulletin board, Peel's blog is not designed to be primarily a forum for readers to post messages for others to read. (In fact, she modified her blog so that only registered users could post comments.) Her blog is intended to inform members of her community about local government activities.
- The term "circulation" is not defined in the Act, but the dictionary defines "circulation" as "the condition of being passed about and widely known, distribution; . . . the number of copies of a publication sold or distributed." *American Heritage Dictionary.*
- In order to post to the blog, a reader must register with the blog. This is an act like subscribing, although there is no cost. The current regis-

tration for the blog totals over 3,500, or almost 10 percent of the Greenville population.

- The large number of visitors (15,000) to Peel's blog indicates that, in addition to the more than 3,500 registered readers, there are many other regular or intermittent readers.

  - This relatively large readership is consistent with the statistics showing that millions of Americans either operate, read, or otherwise participate in blogs. *See America Today* article.

- Additionally, the fact that the legislature used a broad range of means of communication or types of media when defining "news medium" suggests that an Internet blog is a news medium.

  - Words in statutes are not to be viewed in isolation but in light of other relevant provisions of the statute. *Bellows.*

- Other news media included in the Act are radio, television, community antenna television, and newsreels. FRSA § 901(b).

  - Including a blog in the definition of "news medium" is consistent with the inclusion of more "modern" forms of communication in the Act.

    - Even though "blogs" and "bloggers" did not exist when the Franklin legislature enacted the FRSA in 1948, they are now, as indicated in the *America Today* article, a journalistic force to be reckoned with.

Whether including Peel's blogging activities within the coverage of the FRSA serves the legislative intent underlying the Act

- The intent of the legislature in enacting the statute was discussed in *Bellows.*

  - The Franklin legislature, in 1948, stated that the purpose of the Act was to encourage the free flow of information. *See* FRSA § 900 ("The primary purpose of this Act is to safeguard the media's ability to gather news. It is intended to promote the free flow of information to the public . . . .").

  - The purpose of promoting the free flow of information to the public applies here where Peel's blog is dedicated to that purpose, where the item posted on the blog reported on misconduct by a public official, where there is no town newspaper, and where the only newspaper in the county does not engage in investigative journalism.

IV. Conclusion

- Even though Peel is not a professional reporter employed by traditional media, because she is regularly engaged in collecting, writing, and editing the news for publication on her blog, which is a news medium, being published at regular intervals and having a general circulation, she should be deemed a reporter under the FRSA.

- Because she is a reporter under the FRSA, she cannot be compelled to reveal the identity of the source of the information for the article that appeared in the blog.

Therefore, it is probable that a motion to quash the subpoena based on the FRSA privilege will be successful.

In re Lisa Peel

Applicant Identification

Acme Resources, Inc. v. Black Hawk et al.

Read the instructions on the back cover.
Do not break the seal until you are told to do so.

NATIONAL CONFERENCE OF BAR EXAMINERS

INSTRUCTIONS

1. You will have 90 minutes to complete this session of the examination. This performance test is designed to evaluate your ability to handle a select number of legal authorities in the context of a factual problem involving a client.

2. The problem is set in the fictitious state of Franklin, in the fictitious Fifteenth Circuit of the United States. Columbia and Olympia are also fictitious states in the Fifteenth Circuit. In Franklin, the trial court of general jurisdiction is the District Court, the intermediate appellate court is the Court of Appeal, and the highest court is the Supreme Court.

3. You will have two kinds of materials with which to work: a File and a Library. The first document in the File is a memorandum containing the instructions for the task you are to complete. The other documents in the File contain factual information about your case and may include some facts that are not relevant.

4. The Library contains the legal authorities needed to complete the task and may also include some authorities that are not relevant. Any cases may be real, modified, or written solely for the purpose of this examination. If the cases appear familiar to you, do not assume that they are precisely the same as you have read before. Read them thoroughly, as if they all were new to you. You should assume that the cases were decided in the jurisdictions and on the dates shown. In citing cases from the Library, you may use abbreviations and omit page references.

5. Your response must be written in the answer book provided. If you are taking this examination on a laptop computer, your jurisdiction will provide you with specific instructions. In answering this performance test, you should concentrate on the materials in the File and Library. What you have learned in law school and elsewhere provides the general background for analyzing the problem; the File and Library provide the specific materials with which you must work.

6. Although there are no restrictions on how you apportion your time, you should be sure to allocate ample time (about 45 minutes) to reading and digesting the materials and to organizing your answer before you begin writing it. You may make notes anywhere in the test materials; blank pages are provided at the end of the booklet. You may not tear pages from the question booklet.

7. This performance test will be graded on your responsiveness to the instructions regarding the task you are to complete, which are given to you in the first memorandum in the File, and on the content, thoroughness, and organization of your response.

Acme Resources, Inc. v. Black Hawk et al.

FILE

LIBRARY

FILE

Peterson, Michaels & Williams
Attorneys at Law
1530 Lakeside Way
Franklin City, Franklin 33033

MEMORANDUM

To:	Applicant
From:	Conrad Williams
Date:	July 24, 2007
Re:	*Black Hawk et al. v. Acme Resources, Inc.* (Black Eagle Tribal Court);
	Acme Resources, Inc. v. Black Hawk et al. (U.S. Dist. Ct. for the Dist. of Franklin)

We represent Robert Black Hawk and seven other members of the Black Eagle Indian Tribe (the Tribe) in an action in Black Eagle Tribal Court (Tribal Court) against Acme Resources, Inc. (Acme). Acme's mining activities, specifically the extraction of coal bed methane, have caused our clients' water wells to begin to run dry. In the Tribal Court action we are seeking damages and an injunction ordering Acme to cease its operations on the Black Eagle Indian Reservation.

The coal bed methane underlies private land on the Reservation owned in fee simple by Patrick Mulroney, who is not a member of the Tribe. While Mulroney owns the surface of the land, the underlying minerals are owned by the Tribe. The Tribe granted Acme the right to extract the methane from under Mulroney's land in exchange for a royalty. At the same time, Mulroney granted Acme the right to use his land to build the infrastructure that is necessary for mining.

In response to our complaint in Tribal Court, Acme filed an answer denying liability and also denying the jurisdiction of the Tribal Court. No further proceedings have occurred in Tribal Court. Instead, Acme filed a separate federal action in U.S. District Court for the District of Franklin seeking both a declaratory judgment that the Tribal Court lacks jurisdiction in this matter and an injunction against prosecution of our Tribal Court action. (See attached complaint.)

I plan to respond to Acme's complaint by filing a motion with the federal court: (1) for summary judgment on the ground that the Tribal Court has jurisdiction; or, in the alternative (2) to stay or dismiss Acme's federal action on the ground that the Tribal Court should be permitted to

1

consider its jurisdiction over the matter. (See attached draft motion and affidavits of Robert Black Hawk and Jesse Bellingham, Ph.D.)

Please draft the argument sections of the brief in support of both points. Each distinct point in the argument should be preceded by a subject heading that encapsulates the argument it covers and succinctly summarizes the reasons the court should take the position you are advocating. A heading should be a specific application of a rule of law to the facts of the case and not a bare legal or factual statement of an abstract principle. For example, <u>improper</u>: The Police Did Not Have Probable Cause to Arrest Defendant. <u>Proper</u>: The Fact That Defendant Was Walking Alone in a High-Crime Area at Night Without Photo Identification Was Insufficient to Establish Probable Cause for His Arrest.

The argument under each heading should analyze applicable legal authority and state persuasively how the facts and the law support our clients' position. Authority supporting our clients' position should be emphasized, but contrary authority should also generally be cited, addressed, and explained or distinguished. Be sure to address the grounds asserted in Acme's complaint; do not reserve arguments for reply or supplemental briefs. No statement of facts is necessary, but be sure to incorporate the relevant facts into your argument.

Williams: Good afternoon, Mr. Black Hawk. What can I do for you?

Black Hawk: My neighbors and I are at the end of our ropes. We are all members of the Black Eagle Tribe and we are in bad shape. Our wells are running dry.

Williams: Do you know why?

Black Hawk: You bet we do. Two years ago, Acme Resources came onto our Reservation with promises of jobs and riches. Acme wanted to develop a huge coal bed methane field under the Reservation. The easiest access to the field is by way of Patrick Mulroney's land. None of us tribal members wanted it because we had heard of water problems associated with the development of coal bed methane.

Williams: I know that methane is a primary source of natural gas and that coal bed methane is simply methane found underground in coal seams. How does developing coal bed methane affect your water wells?

Black Hawk: Well, I read up on this. Both groundwater and methane flow through fractures in the coal seams—in fact, coal seams are often aquifers. To extract the methane, water is pumped out of the coal seam. As the water pressure decreases, the methane separates from the groundwater and can be piped out. Developing coal bed methane involves extracting huge quantities of groundwater to reduce the water pressure enough to release the methane gas in the coal seam. Since my neighbors and I all farm and ranch on land surrounding Mulroney's place, we were worried about our wells running dry because of the drop in water pressure.

Williams: And your worries came true.

Black Hawk: No kidding. We're running out of water for our livestock and our crops. We're going to go broke because our land just won't support us without water. A geologist who looked at it says that all wells on the Reservation are likely to be affected eventually. We tried to tell the Tribal Council before it voted on the Acme agreement, but the promises of easy money from Acme carried the day. Under the deal, the Tribe is getting a 20 percent royalty on all methane production.

Williams: So you want to see what we can do for you?

Black Hawk: Yes. We really are in a tough spot. Word about the water problem has spread around the Reservation and we believe the vast majority of our fellow tribal members have second thoughts about what the Tribal Council did. We have a Tribal Court and the judge is a fair man. He knows the history of our Tribe and tribal ways. We think that if he and a tribal jury could hear about our problems caused by Acme's extraction of the coal bed methane, we could win.

Williams: Well, I've litigated some in Tribal Court. I know there is no federal statute or treaty addressing the Tribal Court's civil jurisdiction. Your Tribe's constitution and code have some provisions in them about protecting the environment. Maybe that could be a hook for us. I'm somewhat worried about the Tribal Council approving the deal. Can you tell me what your losses have been?

Black Hawk: We neighbors got together with a farm finance guy from Franklin City. He estimates our losses to date to be $1.5 million, and they aren't done yet.

Williams: What about this Patrick Mulroney?

Black Hawk: Well, he's a non-Indian—not a member of our Tribe. Mulroney owns fee land within the Reservation that his family bought from Tribe members about a hundred years ago. Anyway, I'm surprised he went along with the Acme deal because he must be losing his water, too. But he's getting a lot of money from Acme and he's been talking for years about selling and moving somewhere warmer. With the money from the deal, he may not care anymore.

Williams: Okay. Let's get your neighbors in to discuss filing an action in Tribal Court to see what we can do.

Black Hawk: Great. I'll get in touch with everybody and call you.

IN THE UNITED STATES DISTRICT COURT
FOR THE DISTRICT OF FRANKLIN

Acme Resources, Inc., Plaintiff,	)))	Case No. CV 103-07
v.	)))	**COMPLAINT**
Robert Black Hawk, Stewart Marsh, Irene Martin, James Davis, Mary Gray, Katherine White Horse, Lester Stewart, and James Black Hawk, Defendants.	)))))	

Plaintiff Acme Resources, Inc., alleges:

1. This action involves the federal question of whether the Black Eagle Tribal Court can exercise jurisdiction over Acme Resources, Inc. (Acme), in an action brought by members of the Black Eagle Indian Tribe arising out of a controversy involving the development of coal bed methane underlying fee land owned by Patrick Mulroney, who is not a member of the Tribe.

2. This court has jurisdiction under 28 U.S.C. § 1331.

3. Defendants are all members of the Black Eagle Indian Tribe and brought an action against Acme in Black Eagle Tribal Court seeking damages and an injunction to stop Acme from developing the coal bed methane underlying Mulroney's land.

4. The Black Eagle Tribal Court lacks jurisdiction over Acme in the tribal court action because Acme is not a member of the Tribe. *Montana v. United States* (U.S. 1981).

Wherefore, Acme Resources, Inc., prays the Court enter judgment:

1. Declaring that the Black Eagle Tribal Court lacks jurisdiction over Acme in the tribal court action;

2. Enjoining the defendants from prosecuting the tribal court action; and,

3. Awarding Acme its costs and any other appropriate relief.

Dated: July 9, 2007

Respectfully submitted,

Frank Johnson

Frank Johnson
Franklin Bar #1012
Counsel for Acme Resources, Inc.

Acme Resources, Inc. v. Black Hawk et al.

Draft

IN THE UNITED STATES DISTRICT COURT
FOR THE DISTRICT OF FRANKLIN

Acme Resources, Inc., Plaintiff,	)	Case No. CV 103-07
	)	
	)	**MOTION FOR**
v.	)	**SUMMARY JUDGMENT,**
	)	**OR TO STAY OR**
Robert Black Hawk, Stewart Marsh, Irene Martin,	)	**DISMISS**
James Davis, Mary Gray, Katherine White Horse,	)	
Lester Stewart, and James Black Hawk,	)	
Defendants.	)	

The above-named defendants move the Court as follows:

1. To grant the above-named defendants summary judgment on the ground that there exists no genuine issue of material fact that the Black Eagle Tribal Court has jurisdiction over plaintiff Acme Resources, Inc., and the action pending before it under *Montana v. United States* (U.S. 1981), and that the defendants are entitled to judgment as a matter of law; or, in the alternative,

2. To dismiss or stay this action on the ground that Acme has failed to exhaust its remedies in the Black Eagle Tribal Court as required by *National Farmers Union Ins. Cos. v. Crow Tribe* (U.S. 1985).

This motion is supported by the affidavits of Robert Black Hawk and Jesse Bellingham, the pleadings on file, and a brief filed contemporaneously herewith.

Dated: July ____, 2007

Respectfully submitted,

_____
Conrad Williams
Franklin Bar # 1779
Counsel for Defendants

IN THE UNITED STATES DISTRICT COURT
FOR THE DISTRICT OF FRANKLIN

Acme Resources, Inc., 　　　　Plaintiff,	)	Case No. CV 103-07
	)	
v.	)	**AFFIDAVIT OF**
	)	**ROBERT BLACK HAWK**
	)	**IN SUPPORT OF**
Robert Black Hawk, Stewart Marsh, Irene Martin,	)	**DEFENDANTS' MOTION**
James Davis, Mary Gray, Katherine White Horse,	)	**FOR SUMMARY**
Lester Stewart, and James Black Hawk,	)	**JUDGMENT, OR TO**
Defendants.	)	**STAY OR DISMISS**

County of Custer ）
　　　　　　　　　） ss:
State of Franklin ）

Upon first being duly sworn, Robert Black Hawk says:

1. I am a member of the Black Eagle Tribe, a federally recognized Indian tribe.

2. I farm and ranch a 3,000-acre tract of land on the Black Eagle Reservation.

3. My land abuts land owned in fee simple by Patrick Mulroney. All of Patrick Mulroney's land is within the Black Eagle Reservation. Two years ago, Mulroney granted Acme Resources, Inc., permission to use his land to explore for and develop coal bed methane.

4. The Black Eagle Tribe leased the minerals under Mulroney's land to Acme, and Acme began developing the coal bed methane.

5. Within six months of the commencement of Acme's coal bed methane operation under Mulroney's land, the water wells on my land began to run dry. My neighbors have told me that their wells are also running dry.

6. I cannot economically use my land to grow crops and feed my cattle without water, and there is no other source of water reasonably available to me.

Dated: July 23, 2007

Robert Black Hawk

_____
Robert Black Hawk

Signed before me this 23rd day of July, 2007

Jane Mirren

_____
Jane Mirren
Notary Public

Acme Resources, Inc. v. Black Hawk et al.

Acme Resources, Inc.,	)	**Case No. CV 103-07**
Plaintiff,	)	
	)	**AFFIDAVIT OF JESSE**
v.	)	**BELLINGHAM, Ph.D.,**
	)	**IN SUPPORT OF**
Robert Black Hawk, Stewart Marsh, Irene Martin,	)	**DEFENDANTS' MOTION**
James Davis, Mary Gray, Katherine White Horse,	)	**FOR SUMMARY**
Lester Stewart, and James Black Hawk,	)	**JUDGMENT, OR TO**
Defendants.	)	**STAY OR DISMISS**

County of Custer)
) ss:
State of Franklin)

Upon first being duly sworn, Jesse Bellingham says:

1. I am a geologist and have a Ph.D. in geology from the University of Franklin.

2. I was employed by Beta Resources in its mineral exploration department for twenty years before I began my own forensic geology firm, Bellingham Geologic Consulting.

3. I was engaged by the defendants to conduct a study to determine the cause of the water wells running dry on the Black Eagle Reservation and have completed my study.

4. Coal bed methane development requires the extraction of huge quantities of water from the land. Based on my investigation of (a) the records of the water produced from the defendants' land over the last ten years, (b) geological studies of the area, and (c) my knowledge and experience with coal bed methane development, it is my professional opinion that coal bed methane development activity by Acme Resources, Inc., is causing the defendants' wells to run dry.

5. Due to the nature of the groundwater system underlying the Black Eagle Reservation, my professional opinion is that it is likely all wells on the Reservation will run dry over the next five years if Acme's coal bed methane development continues.

Dated: July 23, 2007

Jesse Billingham
_____
Jesse Bellingham, Ph.D.

Signed before me this 23rd day of July, 2007

Jane Mirren

Jane Mirren
Notary Public

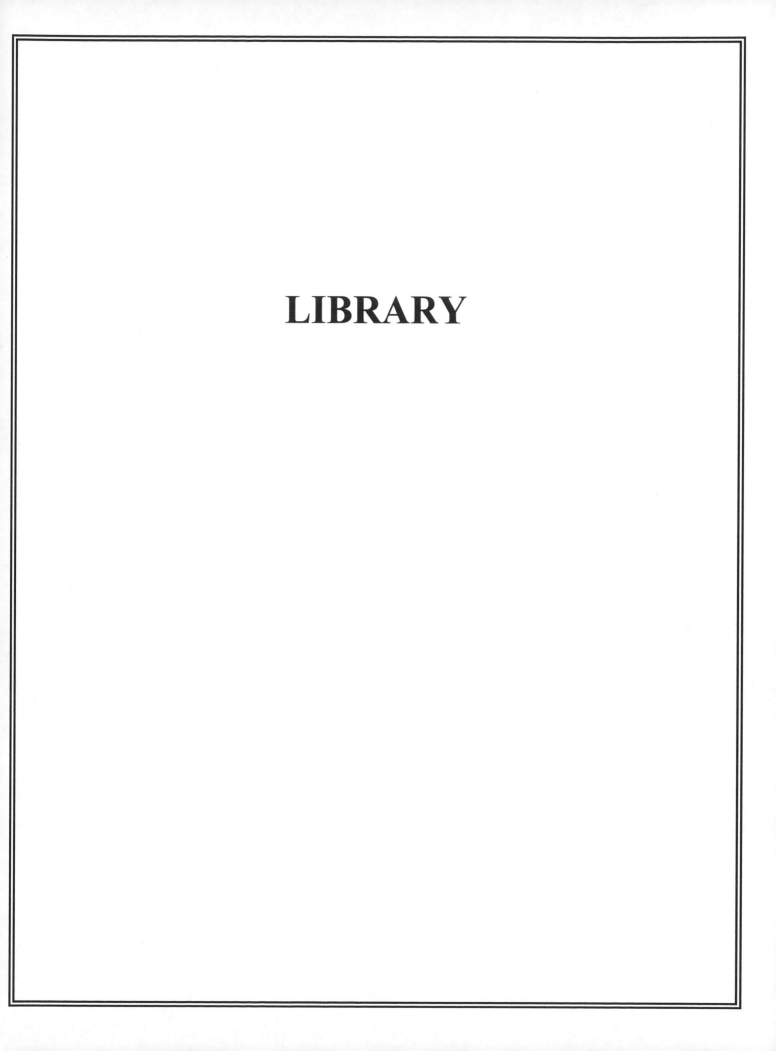

LIBRARY

Article IV, Black Eagle Tribal Constitution

Section 1

The land forms part of the soul of the Black Eagle Tribe. The land of the Black Eagle Reservation shall be preserved in a clean and healthful environment for the benefit of the Tribe and future generations. The Tribal Council shall have power to enforce, by appropriate legislation, the provisions of this section.

Black Eagle Tribal Code

§ 23-5 Protection of Reservation Environment

(1) Recognizing that a clean and healthful environment is vital to the economic security of the Black Eagle Tribe, no person shall pollute or otherwise degrade the environment of the Black Eagle Reservation.

(2) Any person harmed by a violation of subsection (1) may bring a civil action in Black Eagle Tribal Court for damages and other appropriate relief against the person responsible for the violation.

Acme Resources, Inc. v. Black Hawk et al.

AO Architects v. Red Fox et al.

United States Court of Appeals (15th Cir. 2005)

The question in this appeal is whether a tribal court may exercise civil jurisdiction over a nonmember of the tribe in a wrongful death action arising from injuries on nonmember fee land.[1]

The Church of Good Hope, composed of tribal members, owns a parcel of land in fee simple on the Red River Indian Reservation in the State of Columbia. The Church built a meeting hall designed by AO Architects, a firm with offices in Columbia City, Columbia. The Church acted as its own general contractor for the project. AO was not asked to, and did not, supervise the construction. The meeting hall served the Church. However, from time to time the Red River Tribe leased the hall for general tribal meetings in which tribal leaders were elected and other tribe business was conducted.

After a very heavy snowfall in January 2003, the meeting hall's roof collapsed during a general tribal meeting. Five tribe members were killed and many more were injured. The families of those killed brought wrongful death actions in tribal court against AO Architects alleging negligence in the design of the meeting hall roof. Before responding to the complaint filed in tribal court, AO filed a complaint in federal district court claiming that the tribal court did not have jurisdiction over it or the action pending in tribal court. The district court granted a preliminary injunction to AO Architects against further proceedings in the tribal court. The tribe members appealed. For the reasons set forth below, we vacate the preliminary injunction and remand for further proceedings consistent with this opinion.

Standard of Review

Whether a tribal court may exercise civil jurisdiction over a nonmember of the tribe is a federal question. *National Farmers Union Ins. Cos. v. Crow Tribe* (U.S. 1985). We review questions of tribal court jurisdiction and exhaustion of tribal court remedies *de novo*. A district court's order regarding preliminary injunctive relief is reviewed for abuse of discretion.

Governing Law

Analysis of Indian tribal court civil jurisdiction begins with *Montana v. United States* (U.S. 1981). In *Montana*, the United States Supreme Court held that, although the tribe retained power to limit or forbid hunting or fishing by nonmembers on land still owned by or held in trust for the tribe, an Indian tribe could not regulate hunting and fishing by non-Indians on non-Indian-owned fee land within the reservation. In what is often referred to as *Montana*'s "main rule," the Court stated that, absent express

---

[1] The terms "nonmember fee land" and "non-Indian fee lands" refer to reservation land acquired in fee simple by persons who are not members of the tribe.

authorization by federal statute or treaty, the inherent sovereign powers of an Indian tribe do not, as a general proposition, extend to the activities of nonmembers of the tribe.

The Court acknowledged, however, that "Indian tribes retain inherent sovereign power to exercise some forms of civil jurisdiction over non-Indians on their reservations, even on non-Indian fee lands." *Id.* The Court set out two instances in which tribes could exercise such sovereignty: (1) "A tribe may regulate, through taxation, licensing, or other means, the activities of nonmembers who enter consensual relationships with the tribe or its members, through commercial dealings, contracts, leases, or other arrangements"; and (2) "A tribe may also retain inherent power to exercise civil authority over the conduct of non-Indians on fee lands within its reservation when that conduct threatens or has some direct effect on the political integrity, the economic security, or the health and welfare of the tribe." *Id.*

In *Strate v. A-1 Contractors* (U.S. 1997), the Court held that a tribal court had no jurisdiction to hear a personal injury lawsuit between non-tribal members arising from a car accident that occurred on a state highway running through a reservation. The road upon which the accident took place, although on tribal land, was subject to a right-of-way held by the State of North Dakota. The Court determined that this right-of-way rendered the stretch of road "equivalent, for nonmember governance purposes, to alienated, non-Indian land."

The Court declined to comment on the proper forum when an accident occurs on a tribal road within a reservation.

Strate also considered whether either of the two *Montana* exceptions conferring tribal court jurisdiction applied. In determining that the case was not closely related to any consensual relationship between a nonmember and the tribe or a tribe member, the Court noted that the event at issue was a commonplace state highway accident between two non-Indians. Therefore, even though it occurred on a stretch of highway running through the reservation, it was "distinctly non-tribal in nature." *(Cf. Franklin Motor Credit Co. v. Funmaker* (15th Cir. 2005), also finding no consensual relationship under *Montana* because there was no "direct nexus" between the lease entered into by Franklin Motor Credit and the tribe and the subsequent products liability claim against Franklin Motor Credit by a tribe member injured while driving one of the leased vehicles.)

Turning to the second *Montana* exception for activities that directly affect the tribe's political integrity, economic security, or health and welfare, the Court in *Strate* also concluded that the facts did not establish tribal civil jurisdiction. The Court recognized that careless driving on public highways running through the reservation would threaten the safety of tribal members. However, if the assertion of such broad public safety interests were all that *Montana* required for jurisdiction, the exception would swallow the rule. Instead, the

11

exception must be interpreted with its purpose in mind, which was to protect tribal self-government and control of internal relations. "Neither regulatory nor adjudicatory authority over the state highway accident at issue is needed to preserve 'the right of reservation Indians to make their own laws and be ruled by them.'" *Strate* (quoting *Montana*).

Exhaustion of Tribal Remedies

In *National Farmers*, the Supreme Court applied a tribal exhaustion doctrine requiring that a party exhaust its remedies in tribal court before seeking relief in federal court. This doctrine is based on a "policy of supporting tribal self-government and self-determination," and thus a federal court should ordinarily stay its hand "until after the tribal court has had a full opportunity to determine its own jurisdiction." *Id.* In other words, the tribal court should be given the first opportunity to address its jurisdiction and explain the basis (or lack thereof) to the parties. In such cases, the proceedings in federal court are stayed (or dismissed without prejudice) while the tribal court determines whether it has jurisdiction over the matter.

The Supreme Court has emphasized that the exhaustion doctrine is based on comity. The comity doctrine reflects a practice of deference to another court and is not a jurisdictional prerequisite. Thus, where it is clear that a tribal court lacks jurisdiction, the exhaustion doctrine gives way for it would serve no purpose other than delay. *See Strate*. In the present case, tribe members allege that there has been no exhaustion of tribal remedies because AO Architects commenced this federal action without affording the tribal court the opportunity to consider the jurisdictional issues.

Disposition

Here, the accident occurred on nonmember fee land, and AO Architects is not a member of the tribe. This would suggest under *Montana*'s main rule that the tribal court would lack jurisdiction. Moreover, on the record before us, it appears that AO Architects did not perform any services on the reservation, and that its contract was with a nonmember of the tribe, the Church of Good Hope.

Yet AO Architects must have known that it was designing a building for use of large gatherings on the reservation, and it may well have known that the facility would be used by the tribe for general meetings involving governance functions. The consequences of AO Architects' actions in designing the building would certainly be felt on the reservation. We are mindful of the two exceptions to *Montana*'s general rule against extending a tribe's civil jurisdiction to nonmembers of the tribe in the absence of express Congressional authorization or any treaty provision granting a tribe jurisdiction.[2] As discussed above, those exceptions are that a tribe may have jurisdiction over (1) nonmembers who enter into consensual relationships with the

---

[2]The parties concede that no federal statute or treaty bears on the question before us.

tribe or its members, or (2) activities that directly affect the tribe's political integrity, economic security, or health and welfare. Either or both of the exceptions may have application here.

The record comes to us on appeal from a preliminary injunction. The proceedings were abbreviated, and we are uncertain on the record before us whether the tribal court would have jurisdiction under either of the *Montana* exceptions and whether AO Architects must first exhaust its tribal court remedies before seeking relief in federal court.

Therefore, we vacate the preliminary injunction and remand to the district court to develop a record and reach a reasoned conclusion on these issues of jurisdiction and exhaustion. We express no opinion on these questions.

Vacated and remanded.

NOTES

POINT SHEET

Acme Resources, Inc. v. Black Hawk et al.

Acme Resources, Inc. v. Robert Black Hawk et al.
DRAFTERS' POINT SHEET

This performance test requires applicants, as associates in a law firm, to draft a persuasive brief in a federal court action contesting whether an Indian tribal court may exercise civil jurisdiction over a nonmember of the tribe.

Applicants' law firm represents Robert Black Hawk and seven other members of the Black Eagle Indian Tribe (collectively, "tribe members" or "Black Hawk et al."). The tribe members have filed a lawsuit in tribal court against a mining company, Acme Resources, Inc.   (Acme), for damages caused by Acme's extraction of coal bed methane from under reservation land. The process used to develop the coal bed methane has depleted the water table, causing many of the tribe members' wells to begin to run dry, leaving them without water for their livestock or crops. A geologist predicts that all wells on the Reservation will go dry in five years if Acme's methane extraction continues.

In response to the Tribal Court complaint, Acme filed an answer denying liability and jurisdiction. At the same time, Acme commenced an action in federal court requesting a declaratory judgment that the Tribal Court has no jurisdiction over Acme and seeking an injunction against prosecution of the Tribal Court action. Applicants' task is to analyze the law relating to Tribal Court jurisdiction and draft the argument section of a brief in support of a motion for summary judgment in the federal action or to dismiss or stay the federal action to allow the Tribal Court to consider its jurisdiction first.

The File contains: (1) a memorandum from the supervising attorney describing the assignment; (2) a transcript of an interview with the client, Robert Black Hawk; (3) a copy of Acme's complaint filed in U.S. District Court; (4) a draft motion for summary judgment or, in the alternative, to dismiss or stay; (5) an affidavit signed by Robert Black Hawk; and (6) an affidavit by a geologist who has studied the cause of the Reservation water table depletion.

The Library contains excerpts from the Black Eagle Tribal Constitution and Tribal Code, and a Fifteenth Circuit opinion relating to tribal court jurisdiction.

The following discussion covers all the points the drafters intended to raise in the problem. Applicants need not cover them all to receive passing or even excellent grades. Grading is entirely within the discretion of the user jurisdictions.

I. Format and Overview

The supervising attorney's memo requests that applicants draft two arguments: that the court should grant summary judgment to the defendant Tribe members because there is no genuine issue of material fact that the Tribal Court has jurisdiction over Acme; and that, as an alternative basis for relief, the district court should stay or dismiss (without prejudice) Acme's action in federal court to allow the Tribal Court to consider the question of its jurisdiction.

The memorandum provides the template for applicants' argument section of the brief in support of the draft motion. Jurisdictions will have to decide how to weigh the subjective component of "persuasiveness." One guide is that an applicant's work product is not considered responsive to the instructions if it is in the form of an objective memo that takes the on-the-one-hand/on-the-other-hand approach. The argument section of the brief should be broken into its major components with well-crafted headings that summarize applicants' arguments. The arguments should weave the law and facts together into a persuasive statement of the argument, citing to the appropriate authorities and including contrary authorities that are to be addressed, explained, or distinguished. Applicants are instructed that a statement of facts is not necessary.

Applicants should argue that under the two *Montana* exceptions to the general rule against tribal court jurisdiction over nonmembers, the Black Eagle Tribal Court has jurisdiction over Acme. Acme entered into a "consensual relationship" with the Tribe through the lease agreement giving Acme the right to mine the methane gas under the Reservation. Acme's methane operations also threaten the Tribe's economic security by depleting its water supply. Thus, the district court should grant defendants' summary judgment motion. Further, applicants should argue that the Tribal Court has not yet had an opportunity to rule on the jurisdictional issue, and under the exhaustion rule of *National Farmers Union,* the district court should stay or dismiss the federal action to allow the Tribal Court to address the jurisdiction issue first.

II. The Facts

Applicants are to incorporate the relevant facts into the argument sections of their briefs, emphasizing those facts favorable to tribe members' position.

- The eight defendants, Black Hawk et al., are all members of the Black Eagle Tribe (the Tribe) and operate farms and ranches within the Black Eagle Reservation.

- Black Hawk et al. are neighbors of Patrick Mulroney, a nonmember of the Tribe who owns fee land within the Reservation.

- Acme, a mining company, is not a member of the Black Eagle Tribe.

- Mulroney granted a permit to Acme to use his land for the infrastructure necessary to explore for coal bed methane under his land. Acme pays Mulroney a royalty in exchange for access to his land.

- The Tribe owns the mineral rights to the methane under Mulroney's land. It leased to Acme the right to extract the methane in exchange for a 20 percent royalty for the Tribe.

- Acme's methane development requires pumping out huge quantities of groundwater. Within six months of the development of the coal bed methane field, the wells of Mulroney's neighbors, Black Hawk et al., began to run dry.

- Black Hawk and his co-defendants cannot survive economically without water to run their farms and ranches, and there is no other water reasonably available.

- Geologist Jesse Bellingham, Ph.D., defendants' expert, states that all Reservation wells will run dry within five years if the coal bed methane development continues.

- The Black Eagle Constitution recognizes the importance of preserving the Reservation's environment, and the Black Eagle Tribal Code authorizes a civil action by a party aggrieved by another's degradation of the environment.

- Black Hawk et al. brought an action in Black Eagle Tribal Court against Acme for damages and injunctive relief. Acme denied both liability and the Tribal Court's jurisdiction. No further proceedings have been held in tribal court.

- Acme filed an action in federal court seeking declaratory relief and an injunction against prosecution of the tribal court action.

- No federal statute or treaty addresses the Black Eagle Tribal Court's civil jurisdiction.

III. Legal Issues

Applicants must address two issues:

- Whether there is any genuine issue of material fact as to whether the Tribal Court has jurisdiction over the action pending before it and whether summary judgment should be entered in favor of Robert Black Hawk et al., and

- Whether the district court action should be dismissed or stayed because Acme failed to exhaust tribal court remedies before seeking relief in federal court.

Applicants might appropriately frame the questions in any number of ways, but should recognize the jurisdiction and exhaustion of tribal remedies issues.

IV.   Argument

To formulate a good argument, applicants must digest the legal authority contained in *AO Architects v. Red Fox et al.*, the Fifteenth Circuit decision, and the cases cited therein as well as the File materials. *AO Architects* summarizes the governing United States Supreme Court precedent regarding tribal court jurisdiction. The following argument headings are suggestions only and should not be taken by the graders as the only acceptable ones.

A.   Because Acme Entered Into a Consensual Relationship With the Black Eagle Tribe, and Because Its Mining Poses a Threat to the Tribe's Economic Security, There Is No Genuine Issue of Material Fact as to Whether the Tribal Court Has Jurisdiction Over Acme and, Therefore, Black Hawk Et Al. Are Entitled to Summary Judgment.

- Absent express authorization by Congress or a treaty provision authorizing jurisdiction over nonmembers, a tribal court may not exercise civil jurisdiction over a nonmember. *Montana v. United States*, 450 U.S. 544 (1981).
- There are two exceptions to this general rule: (1) the consensual relationship exception; and (2) the security of the tribe exception. If the controversy arises out of a consensual relationship between the nonmember and the tribe or its members, or if the nonmember's conduct directly threatens the political integrity, economic security, or health and welfare of the tribe, the tribal court may exercise jurisdiction over the nonmember. *Id.*

Applicants should argue that, although Acme is not a member of the Tribe and is engaged in activities on the surface of land held in fee simple by another nonmember (Mulroney), the controversy arises out of a consensual relationship (the lease agreement) and also threatens the economic security of the tribe (no water to raise crops or livestock). Applicants should use the facts in the File to argue that both *Montana* exceptions apply, and should distinguish *Strate* and *Funmaker*, cases cited in *AO Architects* in which the court declined to find a consensual relationship or tribal security exception, and thus found that the tribal court had no jurisdiction over nonmembers.

The Acme/Tribe Lease Constitutes a Consensual Relationship and Therefore the Tribal Court Has Jurisdiction Under the First *Montana* Exception.

- The first *Montana* exception confers civil jurisdiction over a nonmember where the nonmember has a consensual relationship with the tribe through commercial dealings. *AO Architects,* citing *Montana.*

- The Tribe/Acme lease satisfies this commercial dealing requirement: it is a direct business relationship between the Tribe and Acme. It gives Acme a sustained (as opposed to fleeting) presence within the Reservation, and it has significant (as opposed to minimal) financial and environmental implications for Tribe members and the Tribe as a whole.

  - The Acme/Tribe relationship is thus distinguishable from a "commonplace" reservation highway accident between two nonmembers that the *Strate* court rejected as an insufficient basis for conferring tribal jurisdiction.

- In *Franklin Motor Credit Co. v. Funmaker* (cited in *AO Architects*), the 15th Circuit Court of Appeals noted that tribal court jurisdiction will not be conferred under the consensual relationship exception unless there is a "direct nexus" between the underlying business relationship and the subject of the lawsuit against the nonmember.

  - Thus, in *Funmaker*, the court rejected tribal court jurisdiction over a car dealership's financing company in a products liability suit brought by a tribe member who was injured while driving a vehicle leased by the tribe and financed by the finance company.

- Here, by contrast, there is a "direct nexus" between Acme and the Tribe.

  - The Tribe and Acme entered into a lease agreement giving Acme the right to extract methane from mineral reserves belonging to the Tribe and located within the Reservation in exchange for a 20 percent royalty payment to the Tribe on all methane produced.

  - The subject of the Tribe members' lawsuit is the harm allegedly caused by Acme's methane mining.

- Applicants might anticipate that Acme will attempt to argue that the consensual relationship at issue, Acme's lease of the mineral rights, is a consensual relationship with the Tribe, and not with one Black Hawk et al., the parties suing Acme.

- However, the applicable case law does not suggest that there must be a direct match between the parties involved in the consensual relationship and the parties to the suit in tribal court. The key is that there be a consensual relationship with the tribe or its members and that there be a connection between the facts giving rise to the litigation in tribal court and that relationship. *See Funmaker.*

Acme's Mining Activities Threaten the Tribe's Economic Security by Depleting the Reservation Water Supply, Thereby Satisfying the Second *Montana* Exception.

The second *Montana* exception permits a tribal court to exercise civil jurisdiction over a nonmember of the tribe where the nonmember's conduct "on fee lands within [the tribe's] reservation . . . threatens or has some direct effect on the political integrity, the economic security, or the health and welfare of the tribe." *AO Architects* (quoting *Montana*). It is important that applicants recognize that a conclusory reference to the negative effect of Acme's activities on the Tribe is not sufficient. Rather, applicants are expected to identify the particular interest(s) of the Tribe (e.g., its economic security) that are at risk from Acme's extraction of coal bed methane.

- Black Hawk et al. have identified a real and substantial risk to the Tribe's economic security: if Acme's mining activities continue, it is likely that within five years all the wells on the Reservation will run dry. (*See* Bellingham Aff.)

- The fact that the wells of eight Tribe members with ranches and farms abutting Patrick Mulroney's land (the site of Acme's methane extraction) began running dry within six months of the start of Acme's mining operations shows the immediate impact that the mining has had and the potential magnitude of the risk. (*See* Black Hawk Aff.)

- The Black Eagle Tribal Constitution, article IV, § 1, stresses the importance of the environment to the Tribe: "The land of the Black Eagle Tribal Reservation shall be preserved in a clean and healthful environment for the benefit of the Tribe and future generations."

- The Tribal Code reiterates this concern for the environment and creates a cause of action in Tribal Court for any person harmed by those who "pollute or otherwise degrade the environment of the Black Eagle Reservation." Tribal Code § 23-5.

- Obviously, depleting the water table in order to extract coal bed methane degrades the environment of the Reservation.

- Moreover, without a stable and plentiful water supply, Tribe members will be unable to raise crops or livestock, in the absence of securing an alternate water supply that is economical and practical. Thus, the lack of water will directly threaten the Tribe's economic security.

- The specific risk here (which threatens the entire Tribe and is directly related to Acme's conduct) stands in sharp contrast to the interest in preventing careless driving on a reservation's public highways at issue in *Strate*, where the Supreme Court refused to find jurisdiction, reasoning that such a broad public safety interest, such as preventing auto accidents, would swallow the rule of *Montana*.

- Applicants may also argue that the Tribe's health and safety and welfare are threatened by Acme's depletion of the water table through its methane mining.

  - While Black Hawk's affidavit and interview focus on the threat to the Tribe's economic security (inability to support crops and livestock), applicants could reasonably argue that tribal health and safety may also eventually be at risk, especially given Bellingham's prediction that *all* wells will run dry in five years. In short, the Tribe could end up without adequate water for basic health and sanitation as a result of Acme's mining.

- Astute applicants might note that Acme could argue that even if the Tribe eventually has to find another source of water, for the term of Acme's lease, the Tribe will receive a royalty of 20 percent of all methane production. Presumably, that is a significant amount (in his interview notes, Black Hawk states that ". . . the promises of easy money carried the day").

- Applicants should contend that the royalty income from Acme cannot offset the permanent damage to the Reservation and the Tribe's long-term economic security if there is no water available on the Reservation.

- The fact that Acme's mining operation is based on land owned in fee simple by Patrick Mulroney, a nonmember of the Tribe, does not deprive the Tribal Court of jurisdiction.

- Acme is extracting coal bed methane that belongs to the Tribe and the aquifer being depleted by Acme's activities serves all the wells on the Reservation.

- The probability, as stated in the Bellingham Affidavit, that *all* the wells on the Reservation will run dry within five years, counters the argument that the economic security of the entire Black Eagle Tribe (as opposed to only the eight tribe members involved in the current litigation) is not at stake.

- Applicants could argue that the fact that the Tribal Council granted Acme a mining concession does not affect defendants' rights, as the Tribal Constitution and Tribal Code addresses threats to the Reservation's environment and provides an independent basis for Tribe members' standing to bring suit.

- In sum, contrary to what Acme alleges in its complaint, it is clear that the Tribal Court has jurisdiction because both exceptions to *Montana*'s main rule apply. Therefore, the court should grant summary judgment to Black Hawk et al.

B.   The Tribal Exhaustion Doctrine of *National Farmers Union* Requires the District Court to Dismiss or Stay Acme's Federal Action on the Grounds That the Tribal Court Has Not Been Afforded an Opportunity to Consider Its Own Jurisdiction.

Applicants' argument discussing the exhaustion rule should mention the following points:

- *National Farmers Union Ins. Cos. v. Crow Tribe*, 471 U.S. 845 (1985), announced a tribal exhaustion requirement: a tribal court should ordinarily first be given an opportunity to consider its jurisdiction before a party may seek relief in federal court. *See AO Architects*.

- The exhaustion rule is a prudential rule and is to be applied as a matter of comity (deference) unless it is clear that the tribal court lacks jurisdiction over the action involving the nonmember.

- Here, the Black Eagle Tribal Court has not had an opportunity to consider and rule on whether it has jurisdiction over Acme.
  - Acme has answered the complaint in Tribal Court, but no further proceedings have been held there.
- Applicants should argue that the Black Eagle Tribal Court has jurisdiction over the action before it because both *Montana* exceptions apply, and therefore Black Hawk et al. are entitled to summary judgment on that issue. In addition, applicants should state that if the court determines that it is unclear whether the Tribal Court has jurisdiction, the court should, consistent with the principle of comity discussed in *AO Architects* and *National Farmers Union*, dismiss or at least stay the action to give the Tribal Court an opportunity to consider the question.

Applicant Identification

In re Mistover Acres LLC

Read the instructions on the back cover.
Do not break the seal until you are told to do so.

NATIONAL CONFERENCE OF BAR EXAMINERS

INSTRUCTIONS

1. You will have 90 minutes to complete this session of the examination. This performance test is designed to evaluate your ability to handle a select number of legal authorities in the context of a factual problem involving a client.

2. The problem is set in the fictitious state of Franklin, in the fictitious Fifteenth Circuit of the United States. Columbia and Olympia are also fictitious states in the Fifteenth Circuit. In Franklin, the trial court of general jurisdiction is the District Court, the intermediate appellate court is the Court of Appeal, and the highest court is the Supreme Court.

3. You will have two kinds of materials with which to work: a File and a Library. The first document in the File is a memorandum containing the instructions for the task you are to complete. The other documents in the File contain factual information about your case and may include some facts that are not relevant.

4. The Library contains the legal authorities needed to complete the task and may also include some authorities that are not relevant. Any cases may be real, modified, or written solely for the purpose of this examination. If the cases appear familiar to you, do not assume that they are precisely the same as you have read before. Read them thoroughly, as if they all were new to you. You should assume that the cases were decided in the jurisdictions and on the dates shown. In citing cases from the Library, you may use abbreviations and omit page references.

5. Your response must be written in the answer book provided. In answering this performance test, you should concentrate on the materials in the File and Library. If you are taking the examination on a laptop computer, your jurisdiction will provide you with specific instructions. What you have learned in law school and elsewhere provides the general background for analyzing the problem; the File and Library provide the specific materials with which you must work.

6. Although there are no restrictions on how you apportion your time, you should be sure to allocate ample time (about 45 minutes) to reading and digesting the materials and to organizing your answer before you begin writing it. You may make notes anywhere in the test materials; blank pages are provided at the end of the booklet. You may not tear pages from the question booklet.

7. This performance test will be graded on your responsiveness to the instructions regarding the task you are to complete, which are given to you in the first memorandum in the File, and on the content, thoroughness, and organization of your response.

In re Mistover Acres LLC

FILE

LIBRARY

i

FILE

Palkovich, Van Every & Dooley
Attorneys at Law
3034 Sutton Avenue
Banford, Franklin 33518

To: Applicant
From: Lyle Palkovich
Re: Mistover Acres LLC
Date: July 24, 2007

We have been retained by Petra Flynn, one of three members of Mistover Acres LLC ("Mistover"), a Franklin limited liability company, to review a claim made against Mistover by Genesee Trout, Inc., for damage to its trout farm caused by the aerial crop dusting of a pesticide, MU-83, on Mistover's fields. Mistover is a well-respected grower and seller of apples, salad greens, and herbs.

We are representing Petra Flynn in her individual capacity. Mistover has its own legal counsel. Ms. Flynn has come to us because she is concerned about her potential personal liability for the harm claimed by the trout farm. She believes that Mistover's organization completely shields her from personal liability for Mistover's business-related activities, but she is understandably troubled by the demand letter from Genesee Trout's counsel. Another concern I have is whether the aerial crop dusting of MU-83 constituted an ultrahazardous activity, thereby raising the possibility of strict liability. The next meeting with Ms. Flynn on this matter is scheduled for July 31, 2007.

Please prepare an objective memorandum analyzing the following questions under Franklin law:

1) Can Ms. Flynn be held personally liable for the damage done by the aerial crop dusting?
2) Did the aerial crop dusting of MU-83 constitute an ultrahazardous activity?

You need not prepare a separate statement of facts, but in each part of the memorandum you should incorporate the relevant facts, analyze the applicable legal authorities, and explain how the facts and law affect your analysis. A carefully crafted subject heading should precede each discussion section. For the purpose of your analysis, assume that the aerial crop dusting caused the damage to the trout farm.

Client Interview Notes: Petra Flynn

July 17, 2007

Petra Flynn is one of three members of Mistover Acres LLC. The other two members are Petra's brother, Gilbert Flynn, and their cousin, Chip Kendall. They formed Mistover after Petra and Gil inherited two adjoining parcels of land in Sutton Township. Mistover grows apples, herbs, and unusual varieties of lettuce that have become very popular in gourmet restaurants. Under the terms of the Mistover Acres LLC Operating Agreement, Petra and Gil lease their land, about 60 acres, to the business. Petra and Gil do some work for Mistover, but as Chip has the expertise in agriculture, most of the decisions regarding planting are left to him. Petra supervises the marketing and sale of Mistover's produce.

Petra has come to the firm for advice regarding her potential personal liability for claims made by Genesee Trout, Inc., in a demand letter its attorneys sent to Mistover's office. She is concerned about Mistover being liable for such a large claim, as it has yet to turn a profit and Chip invested all the money he had in Mistover when they organized it five years ago. According to Petra, Chip "is essentially judgment proof," and Gil's financial situation has always been precarious. She fears that, because she has substantial assets of her own, any lawsuit by Genesee Trout will try to target her as a "deep-pocket" defendant.

Sutton Township is an area of rolling hills that has long been agricultural. In the 1990s, farmers experienced economic difficulties, but in recent years, small-scale, specialized producers like Mistover have been reviving the local economy. A number of these producers are devoted to organic agricultural practices. For example, across the road from Mistover is Haakon Farms, where the owner sells goat cheese made with the milk from her own herd. And, as noted in the demand letter, Genesee Trout's trout farm lies just east of Mistover.

According to Petra, the three members began Mistover to put into practice their belief that consumers deserved another option besides the bland fruits and vegetables grown by factory farms that dominate the selections in most supermarkets. Nonetheless, neither she nor Gil was particularly thrilled when Chip suggested growing new lettuce varieties. Mistover's heirloom apple varieties were selling well and the lettuce varieties could not be successfully raised in amounts needed for sale without the use of some chemical fertilizers and pesticides, which they generally try to avoid. Chip, however, persuaded them that these rare lettuces would soon be "must have" salad greens in the best restaurants, and that the price Mistover could charge would

2

soon generate enough income to allow it to expand into other vegetable crops. Chip also argued that, as one of the only operations offering a unique and locally grown lettuce variety, Mistover would earn a reputation for being an innovator in the gourmet produce market.

Mistover first grew lettuce two years ago and the crop did well. Last year, however, Chip discovered leaf slugs on the plants. If nothing had been done about the leaf slugs, they could have destroyed one-third of the crop. Chip proposed using a pesticide, but Petra expressed concerns about the marketing consequences, as they had always emphasized that Mistover's produce was locally grown with minimal chemicals. They researched pesticides together and ultimately selected MU-83, a new pesticide. Petra then ordered it last year through an agricultural supplier; MU-83 is not available to the general public. Chip walked through the fields with some of Mistover's seasonal help and sprayed the lettuce crop with MU-83. It was effective, but the labor costs of the pesticide application were high.

When Chip found the leaf slugs again this season, he determined that the slugs were more numerous than last year and that hand spraying would involve even higher labor costs. Before joining Mistover, when he lived in Columbia, Chip had worked one growing season using his small airplane to dust large corn and wheat fields with pesticides and herbicides. He and Petra decided to use aerial crop dusting, and Petra ordered more MU-83. The Franklin Environmental Code requires posting for aerial crop dusting, and Petra ensured that the proper notice was posted on the Sutton Township website, at the Town Hall, and at three other public places.

Chip sprayed the fields with MU-83 on March 28, 2007. Petra was at Mistover that afternoon and watched Chip take off in his airplane, circle the farm buildings, and then fly over the plants at a height of about 20 feet to apply the MU-83. She did not observe the yellow cloud described in the letter from Genesee Trout's attorneys, but does recall that there was a light breeze blowing from the west, which possibly could have carried MU-83 in the direction of the trout ponds. Two days later she and Chip walked through the fields and verified that the MU-83 had killed any visible leaf slugs.

The lettuce, Mistover's best crop yet, was picked and sold at a prime price. Until the letter from Genesee Trout's attorneys arrived, none of the LLC members had heard any complaints about the MU-83 aerial crop dusting or their farming activities in general. Petra will come in next week to discuss the situation.

3

FRENCH & ISENBERG, LLP
Attorneys at Law
222 Sheffield Ave
Centralia, Franklin 33530

July 17, 2007

Ms. Petra Flynn
Mistover Acres LLC
P.O. Box 572
Derby, Franklin 38440

Re: Genesee Trout, Inc.

Dear Ms. Flynn:

We represent Genesee Trout, Inc., the owner of the trout farm that abuts Mistover Acres on its eastern edge. On March 28, 2007, our client's employees observed a crop-dusting airplane flying over the fields of Mistover Acres, spraying a yellow-colored substance. They then observed a yellow cloud drifting over Genesee Trout's fish ponds. In the months since that date, a higher-than-expected percentage of our client's trout stock has died, and the number of successful egg hatchings has substantially declined. The water in the fish ponds has been tested and has been found to contain significant levels of the pesticide MU-83. The cost to clean the ponds and restock the trout will exceed $1 million. Genesee Trout is also concerned that MU-83 will leech into the local water supply.

The presence of MU-83 in the Genesee Trout fish ponds, the resulting decline in the trout stock and egg hatchings, and the potential damage to the water supply were caused by Mistover Acres LLC's aerial crop dusting on March 28, 2007.

Genesee Trout, Inc., is willing to settle its claims against Mistover Acres LLC. However, if a settlement cannot be reached, our client has instructed us to pursue legal action against Mistover Acres LLC and its members. If you are willing to discuss settlement, please respond to this letter within two weeks of its receipt.

Sincerely,

Walter French

Walter French

4

OPERATING AGREEMENT OF MISTOVER ACRES LLC

This OPERATING AGREEMENT is entered into by Petra Flynn, Gilbert Flynn, and Chip Kendall for the purpose of organizing a limited liability company pursuant to the Franklin Limited Liability Company Act, § 601 *et seq.*

1. **Name and Purpose**: The limited liability company shall be known as MISTOVER ACRES LLC (hereinafter "the LLC"). Its purpose is to grow and market apples and other produce for sale at farmers' markets and to restaurants and other commercial establishments.

2. **Members**: The members of the LLC are Petra Flynn, Gilbert Flynn, and Chip Kendall.

3. **Capital Contributions:** The capital contributions of the respective members shall be as follows:
   a. Chip Kendall: $50,000 (fifty thousand dollars).
   b. Petra Flynn: $10,000 (ten thousand dollars).
   c. Gilbert Flynn: $10,000 (ten thousand dollars).

4. **Lease of Agricultural Land**: On or before the date of filing of the Articles of Organization, leases will be entered into between the LLC and Petra Flynn, and the LLC and Gilbert Flynn, for the two adjoining 30-acre parcels on Schmidt Road, Derby, Franklin, identified as Tracts 37 and 38 of Sutton Township Certified Survey 2713. The LLC shall have the exclusive right to lease these parcels for as long as the LLC continues in existence or until such time as the members agree to terminate the leases.

5. **Management**: With respect to acquisition of capital assets by the LLC, or the addition of new members or employees of the LLC, the undersigned members shall in all cases act as a group, with a majority vote or consent of the members required to take action. Day-to-day decisions regarding planting and harvesting are delegated to Chip Kendall until the members agree otherwise. The marketing and sale of the LLC's produce shall be supervised by Petra Flynn.

6. **Sharing in Distributions and Profits**: For the first five (5) years of the LLC's existence, the profits, if any, will be reinvested into the LLC's operations. If any profit is realized in subsequent years, 50 percent (50%) will be reinvested into the LLC, and the remainder will be distributed in equal shares to the members.

7. **Accounting:** Members shall receive annual financial reports containing the LLC's balance sheet and a statement showing the net capital appreciation or depreciation.

8. **Applicable Law**: All questions concerning the construction, validity and interpretation of this agreement and the performance of the obligations imposed by this agreement shall be governed by the laws of the State of Franklin.

Dated: **February 15, 2002**

Petra Flynn

_____
Petra Flynn

Gilbert Flynn

_____
Gilbert Flynn

Chip Kendall

_____
Chip Kendall

USER'S GUIDE FOR MU-83 APPLICATION

Thank you for selecting an AgriShield, Inc., product to protect your crops! MU-83 is an effective pesticide for use on all crops, including those intended for human consumption. Studies by the University of Franklin Agricultural College have demonstrated that it is 98% successful in completely eradicating pests such as rootworm, boll weevils, and leaf slugs, when applied according to directions. It is suitable for application by hand, tractor-pulled spraying rig, or aerial dusting by airplane. Aerial dusting should occur at a distance no higher than 30 feet from the intended target area.

* * * *

As with all pesticides, persons applying MU-83 should use caution and be aware that pesticide "drift" (the movement of pesticide droplets or particles in the air from the targeted field to non-target areas) is always a risk of pesticide application. Drift and runoff may be toxic to aquatic organisms in neighboring areas. Drift will occur with every application. The amount of drift is subject to various controllable and uncontrollable factors, such as time of application, concentration, wind gusts, weather changes, and the physical characteristics of pesticide droplets or aerosols. Apply this product only in accordance with application instructions found on the label.

WARNING: Improper use or application of MU-83 may cause serious injury or death.

In re Mistover Acres LLC

PUBLIC NOTICE

In accordance with the Franklin Environmental Code, § 22(1),___Mistover Acres LLC___ hereby gives public notice that it will conduct aerial crop dusting of the following pesticide on the date indicated:

Pesticide:___MU-83_____

The pesticide application will occur on ___March 28, 2007___ on the following described property in Sutton Township:

> The two adjoining 30-acre parcels identified as Tracts 37 and 38 of Sutton Township Certified Survey 2713, according to the records of the Clerk and Recorder of Washington County, Franklin, and also known as Mistover Acres LLC, 200 W. Schmidt Rd.

For further information, contact: ____Petra Flynn_____

                                     _____200 W. Schmidt Road_____

                                     _____Derby, Franklin__33510_____

                                     _____(920) 555-1085_____

Dated this 25th day of _March_____, 2007

Mistover Acres LLC

by ___*Petra Flynn*_____

Petra Flynn, its authorized representative

LIBRARY

FRANKLIN LIMITED LIABILITY COMPANY ACT

§ 601 General Purposes.

(1) A limited liability company may be organized under this Act for any lawful purpose....

(2) Unless otherwise provided in an operating agreement, a limited liability company organized and existing under this Act has the same powers as an individual to do all things necessary and convenient to carry out its business, including but not limited to all of the following:

(a) Sue and be sued, complain and defend in its own name.

(b) Purchase, take, receive, lease, or otherwise acquire and own, hold, improve, use, and otherwise deal in or with real or personal property or any legal or equitable interest in real or personal property, wherever situated.

(c) Sell, convey, mortgage, lease, and otherwise dispose of all or any part of its property....

(d) Make contracts and guarantees; incur liabilities....

* * * *

(g) Elect or appoint managers, agents, and employees of the limited liability company, define their duties, and fix their compensation.

* * * *

§ 605 Liability of members.

(1) The debts, obligations, and liabilities of a limited liability company, whether arising in contract, tort, or otherwise, shall be solely the debts, obligations, and liabilities of the limited liability company.

(2) Except as otherwise provided in this Act or by written agreement of a member, a member of a limited liability company is not personally liable solely by reason of being a member of the limited liability company for any debt, obligation, or liability of the limited liability company, whether that liability or obligation arises in contract, tort, or otherwise, or for the acts or omissions of any other member, agent, or employee of the limited liability company.

(3) Nothing in this section shall be construed to affect the liability of a member of a limited liability company to third parties for the member's participation in tortious conduct.

(4) A member of a limited liability company is not a proper party to a proceeding by or against a limited liability company solely by reason of being a member of the limited liability company, except where the object of the proceeding is to enforce a member's right against or liability to the limited liability company or as otherwise provided in an operating agreement.

In re Mistover Acres LLC

Hodas v. Ice LLC

Franklin Court of Appeal (2004)

This is an action to recover damages for injuries sustained in a motor vehicle accident. The complaint alleged that on March 18, 2000, between 12:00 a.m. and 1:45 a.m., Tony Veit and Todd Hodas were patrons of the Firefly Bar in Groton, Franklin. The Firefly Bar is owned by Ice LLC. Defendants Duncan O'Malley, Joe Kaufman, and Victor Casellano are the only members of Ice LLC.

While at the Firefly Bar, Veit consumed large quantities of alcohol. Despite his being obviously intoxicated, the defendants and/or their employees continued to serve him. Veit and Hodas, both grossly intoxicated, left the Firefly in Veit's car. While speeding, Veit lost control of the vehicle and hit a tree. Veit died at the scene and Hodas was seriously injured.

Hodas claims that the defendants were negligent and reckless in their conduct by selling any alcohol to an obviously intoxicated person. O'Malley, Kaufman, and Casellano argue that they were entitled to summary judgment because liability cannot attach solely by virtue of the fact that they were members of Ice LLC, the entity that owned the bar. The trial court denied the summary judgment motion. We granted O'Malley, Kaufman, and Casellano leave to bring this interlocutory appeal.

DISCUSSION

It is undisputed that Ice LLC is a Franklin limited liability company organized under the Franklin Limited Liability Company Act (FLLCA), § 601 *et seq.* The original property lease agreement identifies Ice LLC as Lessee, acting through its members O'Malley and Kaufman. A liquor license application for the bar states that Casellano invested $80,000 in Ice LLC to be used for the purpose of renovating the building in Groton that houses the Firefly Bar. The Ice LLC operating agreement names the three as the sole members of the LLC.

A limited liability company, or "LLC," is a business entity that combines the attributes of a partnership for federal income tax purposes with the limited liability protections that a corporation provides to shareholders. Like a partnership, an LLC allows the owners, called members, to participate in the management of the business. LLCs are typically governed by operating agreements. The provisions pertaining to the liability of LLC members are found in § 605 of the FLLCA.

10

The FLLCA generally provides that a member of an LLC is not personally liable for acts or debts of the company solely by reason of being a member. Nevertheless, a member may be personally liable if the person participates in tortious conduct.

O'Malley and Kaufman contend that tort liability of an LLC member is limited to conduct committed *outside* the member role. We reject this approach as contravening the corporate and agency principles upon which the liability of LLC members is based. Nor does the language of the FLLCA support such a restriction. We recognize, however, that the "participation in tortious conduct" standard does not impose tort liability on a member for performing what is merely a general administrative duty. *See Lee v. Bayrd* (Franklin Ct. App. 1985) (no tort liability where corporate officer not shown to have authorized, directed, or participated in tortious act). There must be some participation; liability of individuals is derived from individual activities. This standard thus comports with the principle that members are not liable based only on their status.

O'Malley, Kaufman, and Casellano argue that this view of limited liability defeats the language of § 605(2) that bars tort liability predicated solely by reason of an individual's status as a member of the LLC.

We disagree. The phrase "solely by reason of" refers to liability based upon membership or management *status*. It does not immunize a member's *conduct*. It is not inconsistent to protect a member from vicarious liability (e.g., for the tortious acts of another LLC member or employee), while imposing liability when the member participates in a tort. In short, liability of LLC members is limited, but not to the extent claimed by O'Malley, Kaufman, and Casellano.

O'Malley and Kaufman

The complaint alleges that O'Malley and Kaufman failed to properly supervise and train their personnel and failed to monitor their patrons to ensure safety.

O'Malley and Kaufman both admitted at their depositions that they were at the bar on March 17, 2000, into the morning hours of the 18th, and that the place was very busy. Kaufman stated that he usually deals with the customers and personnel. O'Malley testified that on that night, he was "all over the place, making sure everyone was doing what they were supposed to, greeting customers and doing other 'PR' work." Neither defendant could affirm or deny whether he had personally served alcohol to Veit.

O'Malley and Kaufman would not be liable

11

solely because of their status as members of Ice LLC. But the FLLCA does not affect the liability of an LLC member who participates in tortious conduct, whether or not that conduct is on behalf of the LLC. *See* § 605(3). Given the participation of O'Malley and Kaufman in the operations of the business, there are material issues of fact which precluded the granting of summary judgment. *See Goff v. PureMilk LLC* (Franklin Ct. App. 1997) (summary judgment inappropriate where agreement required LLC's member/manager to provide human resources and consulting services to LLC and extent of member's/manager's participation in tortious conduct was unknown). A trial is necessary to develop the facts relating to allegations of O'Malley and Kaufman's participation in the alleged torts. For this reason, the court affirms the denial of summary judgment as to O'Malley and Kaufman.

Casellano

There was no evidence before the trial court that Casellano was at the Firefly Bar on March 17, 2000, or that he participated in the business operations at any point in time relevant to the allegations in the complaint. To support his claim for Casellano's liability, Hodas referred to the liquor license application that was signed and filed by Casellano, a trade name certificate recorded in the Groton Land Records listing Casellano as one of the persons involved in the business known as the Firefly Bar, and the operating agreement designating Casellano as a member of the LLC.

These documents clearly demonstrate that Casellano was a member of Ice LLC in March 2000. Nothing else has been presented as a basis for Casellano's liability. Hodas could not overcome the fact that his claim for liability is based solely upon Casellano's status as a member of the LLC. Section 605(2) of the FLLCA precludes liability based on membership status alone. Further, a member is not liable for the acts or omissions of any other member of the limited liability company. For this reason, the court reverses the denial of summary judgment as to Casellano.

Affirmed in part, reversed in part, and remanded for further proceedings.

12

Thurman v. Ellis

Franklin Court of Appeal (2003)

Defendant Gwen Ellis appeals from a judgment entered on a jury verdict awarding damages to plaintiff Adele Thurman in the amount of $50,000. The issue before us is whether the trial court erred in instructing the jury that breeders of pit bull dogs are strictly liable for any harm caused by their animals on the basis that raising pit bulls is an ultrahazardous activity.

Ellis has bred pit bulls for several years. Thurman was injured when, on a visit to Ellis's home, the mother of the current litter attacked her while she was holding a puppy. Thurman suffered deep wounds to her arm and hand before Ellis could restrain the dog. Although Thurman alleged three other counts in her complaint, only the claim for strict liability based on an ultrahazardous activity is before us on appeal.

Those who engage in ultrahazardous activities are, as a general rule, subject to strict liability for the harm caused to the innocent as a result of the activity. When determining whether an activity is ultrahazardous, we apply § 520 of the Restatement (Second) of Torts, which requires analysis of six factors: (1) existence of a high degree of risk of some harm to the person, land, or chattels of others; (2) likelihood that the resulting harm will be great; (3) inability to eliminate the risk by the exercise of reasonable care; (4) extent to which the activity is not a matter of common usage; (5) inappropriateness of the activity to the place where it is carried on; and (6) extent to which the activity's value to the community is outweighed by its dangerous attributes. *Sisson v. City of Bremerton* (Franklin Sup. Ct. 1975). This is a totality of the circumstances test. No one factor is determinative.

In Franklin, assessment of the § 520 factors has resulted in the imposition of strict liability for firework displays; rock blasting where injury occurred to property on an adjacent lot; emissions from chemical separation as part of weapons-grade plutonium production; and a common carrier's transportation of large quantities of gasoline. Under the same analysis of the factors in § 520, Franklin courts have held that the following activities are *not* ultrahazardous: household use of water, electricity, or gas; operation of oil and gas wells in rural areas; and ground damage caused by the crash landing of aircraft.

Sisson provides a detailed example of the court's reasoning when applying the § 520

13

factors. There, it was alleged that the city's demolition project, which caused the collapse of the retaining walls that protected the plaintiffs' homes, constituted an ultrahazardous activity rendering the city strictly liable for the damage. The court emphasized that the inability to eliminate the risk by the exercise of reasonable care would generally carry more weight than the other factors, but that this factor alone was not dispositive of whether an activity is ultrahazardous. Moreover, while the availability and relative costs, economic and otherwise, of alternative methods for conducting the activity are basic to the inquiry, the court stressed that an activity that was ultrahazardous in one context is not necessarily ultrahazardous for all occasions. Ultimately, the court held that the record was inadequate to determine whether the demolition project was ultrahazardous.

Fredricks v. Centralia Fire Dept. (Franklin Ct. App. 1999) explained that the value of an activity to the community will at times negate factors that would otherwise favor imposing strict liability. In *Fredricks*, it was claimed that the fire department had conducted an ultrahazardous activity in putting out a fire and that water used to put out the fire had spread toxic waste to adjoining properties, requiring costly cleanup. The court reasoned that, while firefighting presented a high degree of risk,

the value to the community far outweighed the inherent dangers of the activity. In addition, referring to the fifth factor, the court noted that there was no reasonable basis for the plaintiff's claim, as it "defied logic to argue that it is inappropriate to carry out firefighting at the site of a fire." *Id.*

Here, Ellis disputes the evidence of a high degree of risk of harm. She testified that, until the attack on Thurman, none of her dogs had behaved violently. Her expert, a nationally known breeder, opined that pit bulls are good-tempered, loyal animals, unless specifically trained to be aggressive. Thurman, however, presented the opinions of a veterinarian and an authority on pit bulls to show that years of breeding had created an aggressive breed that was easily provoked, especially if an animal thought its young were in danger.

While the precise degree of risk posed by pit bulls is uncertain, it is undisputed that because of the pit bull's powerful jaw structure, it is extremely difficult to open the dog's mouth once it bites someone or something. This practically ensures that anyone bitten by a pit bull will sustain a severe injury. In addition, the fact that Ellis was breeding pit bulls in her home in a residential neighborhood, in close proximity to young children, as opposed to a less populated area or at least a location with sufficient space for an outdoor dog kennel, leads us to conclude that the activity was being conducted in an inappropriate place. Ellis correctly points out that no city ordinance banned breeding dogs such as pit bulls within city limits. However, the fact that an activity is legal is not a defense to a claim that the activity is ultrahazardous. The first, second, and fifth factors support holding Ellis strictly liable for the harm caused by her dogs.

Turning to the fourth factor, we recognize that dog breeding in general is a common activity. While not as numerous as many breeds, pit bulls are not so rare that raising them should be considered uncommon. Nevertheless, we conclude that, with this breed, exercise of reasonable care is unlikely to eliminate the risk of severe injury, as pit bulls that have never bitten might, without warning, attack an individual perceived to be a threat and inflict grave injury. There was testimony from both parties' experts that preventive measures were possible, such as keeping muzzles on the adult dogs. But dogs cannot be muzzled all the time, and we are not persuaded that the availability of such measures overcomes the other factors favoring the conclusion that raising pit bulls in the circumstances identified here is an ultrahazardous activity. Finally, unlike the situation in *Fredricks*, the public benefit of the activity does not justify insulating the defendant from strict liability.

It is undisputed that the attack by Ellis's pit bull resulted in Thurman's injuries and therefore causation is not in doubt. Accordingly, we conclude that there is sufficient evidence to establish that by raising pit bulls in a residential neighborhood, Ellis engaged in an ultrahazardous activity. The trial court did not err in giving the ultrahazardous instruction.

Affirmed.

NOTES

POINT SHEET

DRAFTERS' POINT SHEET

In this performance test item, applicants' law firm represents Petra Flynn, one of the three members of Mistover Acres LLC ("Mistover"), a Franklin limited liability company. A limited liability company is a business entity that provides the liability protections of a corporation but has the attributes of a partnership for federal income tax purposes. Mistover grows and sells apples, salad greens, and other produce. Recently, Mistover received a demand letter from counsel for Genesee Trout, Inc., the corporate owner of a neighboring trout farm. The demand letter claims that a substantial amount of Genesee Trout's fish stock has died as a result of aerial pesticide spraying by Mistover. According to Genesee Trout's demand letter, it will cost upwards of $1 million to clean and restock the trout ponds, and Genesee Trout will bring suit against Mistover if a settlement cannot be agreed upon.

Mistover has its own legal counsel. Petra, however, is seeking legal advice in her individual capacity because she is concerned that the LLC business structure may not protect her from being held personally liable for the alleged harm to the trout farm. Unlike the other two members of Mistover (one of whom she describes as "judgment proof"), Petra has significant assets of her own and thus she fears that she could be an attractive "deep-pocket" defendant from Genesee Trout's perspective. Applicants' task is to write an objective memorandum evaluating Petra's potential liability for Genesee Trout's claim. In addition, applicants are asked to address whether Mistover's pesticide spraying constituted an ultrahazardous activity.

The File contains the memorandum from the supervising partner, notes from the client interview, a demand letter from counsel for Genesee Trout, the LLC operating agreement, an excerpt from the pesticide user's guide, and a copy of the public notice of pesticide application on Mistover's fields. The Library contains excerpts from the Franklin Limited Liability Company Act and two cases, one discussing the circumstances under which a member of an LLC is personally liable for tortious conduct involving the LLC and one describing the Franklin courts' approach to the ultrahazardous doctrine.

The following discussion covers all of the points the drafters intended to raise in the problem. Applicants need not cover them all to receive passing or even excellent grades. Grading decisions are entirely within the discretion of the user jurisdictions.

I.   Format and Overview

Applicants' work product should be objective in tone and resemble a legal memorandum such as an associate would write to a supervising partner. It should discuss the range of possibilities (i.e., on-the-one-hand, on-the-other-hand) and reach a reasoned conclusion on each of the issues presented. No separate statement of facts is expected, but it is anticipated that applicants will incorporate the relevant facts from the client interview, the operating agreement, etc., in their analysis. Applicants are instructed to use separate headings for each issue discussed. However, it is left to the jurisdictions to determine whether to credit, and by how much, the format of the answer.

Applicants are directed to focus on two issues:

(1) Can Petra be held personally liable for the damage done by the aerial crop dusting?

(2) Did the aerial crop dusting of MU-83 constitute an ultrahazardous activity?

Applicants should conclude that with respect to Petra Flynn's personal liability for Mistover's acts, reasonable arguments can be made both for and against finding her personally liable. On balance, however, it is more likely that her activities rise to the level of participation in tortious conduct, and therefore she cannot rely on Mistover's organization as a limited liability company to insulate her from personal liability for the damage claimed by Genesee Trout. Mistover's aerial spraying of the MU-83 pesticide, while a close call on some of the relevant factors, constitutes an ultrahazardous activity for which Mistover can be held strictly liable.

II.   *Discussion*

A.   Petra's Personal Liability for Damages Claimed by Genesee Trout

Applicants' first task is to analyze whether under Franklin law Mistover's organization as a limited liability company will insulate Petra from personal liability for the damage to the trout farm caused by the pesticide spraying. Applicants are expected to frame their discussion using the relevant provisions of the Franklin Limited Liability Company Act (FLLCA) and the standard for finding an LLC member liable in tort as explained in *Hodas v. Ice LLC* (Franklin Ct. App. 2004).

A limited liability company is often referred to as a "hybrid" form of business entity that offers the limited liability protection of a corporation with the tax advantages of a partnership. Like the LLC statutes enacted by most states, the FLLCA provides that "[t]he debts, obligations, and liabilities of a limited liability company, whether arising in contract, tort, or otherwise, shall be solely the debts, obligations, and liabilities of the limited liability company." FLLCA § 605(1). Further, unless otherwise specified in the statute, or by the written agreement of an LLC member, "a member of a limited liability company is not personally liable solely by reason of being a member of the limited liability company for any debt, obligation, or liability of the limited liability company, whether that liability or obligation arises in contract, tort, or otherwise, or for the acts or omissions of any other member, agent, or employee of the limited liability company." FLLCA § 605(2).

In *Hodas*, the Franklin Court of Appeal discussed the extent of protection against tort liability afforded to LLC members by the phrase in § 605(2) that "a member of a limited liability company is not personally liable solely by reason of being a member of the limited liability company . . . ." The court explained that imposition of personal liability on an LLC member is not limited to tortious conduct that is outside of the member role. On the other hand, tort liability will not be imposed on an LLC member for performing what are essentially administrative duties. Actual participation in the tortious conduct is required.

A thorough discussion of Petra's position as a member of Mistover Acres LLC would include these points:

- It is clear from the operating agreement and FLLCA § 605(1) that Petra has not agreed in writing to be personally liable for actions attributable to Mistover.

- However, Petra cannot claim that because she is a member of the LLC, she can never be personally liable for tortious acts. Under *Hodas*, the provision of the FLLCA stating that "a member of a limited liability company is not personally liable *solely by reason of being a member*" means that a member can be liable for tortious conduct, even when such conduct was performed as a member of and benefited the LLC.

- Thus, applicants must discuss the extent to which Petra participated in the pesticide spraying that damaged Genesee Trout's fish stock. While *Hodas* does not provide a comprehensive definition of the participation standard, it does state that no tort liability will be imposed for "performing what is merely a general administrative duty." The relevant facts are as follows:

  - Petra had ordered MU-83 the year before, and ordered more for the aerial application that Genesee Trout complained of.

- Together, she and Chip decided that the lettuce should be sprayed aerially, as opposed to manual pesticide application, to address the worsening leaf slug problem.
- She performed marketing and sales duties for the LLC.
- She posted the required notices that Mistover would be spraying pesticide on a particular date.
- She was at Mistover on the date of the spraying, and watched Chip fly his plane over the fields spraying the lettuce crop.
- Two days after the spraying, she and Chip walked through the fields to verify that the leaf slugs had been eradicated.
- Many of Petra's activities could be deemed essentially administrative in nature. Clearly her marketing and sales activities are not directly related to the tortious conduct. Even ordering the MU-83 and posting the pesticide spraying notices could be considered simply administrative. Similarly, walking through the fields after the spraying to verify that the MU-83 had worked does not meet the participation standard. At that point, the tortious activity had been completed.
- However, Petra appears to have participated equally with Chip in the decision to use an aerial pesticide application and the decision to use MU-83 as opposed to another pesticide. These facts, when combined with her being the LLC member who ordered the MU-83, strongly favor the conclusion that her actions exceeded those of a mere member of Mistover and that she was an actual participant in the alleged tortious conduct.
- Applicants who focus on Chip's liability as a basis for Petra's personal liability have missed the point. The FLLCA shields LLC members from liability for tortious conduct by other LLC members. Chip's potential liability is beyond the scope of this item.

Accordingly, it appears likely that, while there are a number of facts to support the argument that her actions were merely administrative in nature, Petra faces a substantial risk that her involvement in the decision to use MU-83 rises to the level of actual participation in tortious conduct. Therefore, the LLC business structure will not shield her from personal liability for the harm suffered by Genesee Trout.

B.   Ultrahazardous Activity

Applicants' second task is to determine whether the aerial spraying of the pesticide MU-83 constituted an ultrahazardous activity under Franklin law. If it is determined to be ultrahazardous, strict liability will attach. In other words, if Mistover's aerial pesticide spraying was ultrahazardous, Mistover (and Petra, as a result of her participation in the tortious conduct) will be held liable without Genesee Trout needing to prove negligence. For purposes of their analysis, applicants are instructed to assume that the pesticide spraying caused the alleged harm to Genesee Trout's fish stock.

Applicants should look to *Thurman v. Ellis* (Franklin Ct. App. 2003), which explains that when determining whether an activity is ultrahazardous, Franklin courts follow § 520 of the Restatement (Second) of Torts. Application of § 520 requires analysis of six factors:

(1) Existence of a high degree of risk of some harm to the person, land, or chattels of others;

(2) Likelihood that the resulting harm will be great;

(3) Inability to eliminate the risk by the exercise of reasonable care;

(4) Extent to which the activity is not a matter of common usage;

(5) Inappropriateness of the activity to the place where it is carried on; and

(6) Extent to which the activity's value to the community is outweighed by its dangerous attributes.

As demonstrated by the Restatement factors, the ultrahazardous activity doctrine emphasizes the dangerousness and inappropriateness of the activity. The policy underlying the doctrine reflects a goal to attribute costs to those who benefit from introducing an extraordinary risk of harm into the community by imposing strict liability on them.

In *Thurman*, the court emphasized that the test is one of the totality of the circumstances and no one factor is determinative, although some factors may carry substantially more weight than others. Further, the ultrahazardous label does not attach to a particular substance, such as the pesticide at issue here, in the abstract—it is the activity in which the substance is used that is examined under the § 520 criteria. Applicants should also recognize that Franklin courts do not limit the ultrahazardous category to those activities that are rarely conducted or unusual; the context in which an activity is performed can render it ultrahazardous. Thus activities that are ultrahazardous in one situation are "not necessarily ultrahazardous for all occasions." *Thurman*.

A discussion of whether the pesticide spraying will be considered an ultrahazardous activity should address the following points:

- **High degree of risk of harm**. The cases cited in *Thurman* and § 520 of the Restatement make it clear that harm from ultrahazardous activities is not limited to injuries to people, but also extends to property damage. The statements in the MU-83 User's Guide that "[pesticide] drift will occur with every application" and that pesticide "drift and runoff may be toxic to aquatic organisms" indicate that there is a substantial risk that pesticide will drift to a nontarget area and cause some harm.

- **Likelihood of great harm**. A plaintiff must show that the activity engaged in by the defendant was *likely* to produce *great* harm, not simply that the plaintiff suffered harm as an alleged result of the defendant's activities. In other words, the mere fact that a plaintiff suffered injury as a result of the defendant's actions does not establish that the activity at issue presented a likelihood of great harm. Here, the likelihood of harm from aerial spraying of MU-83 is unclear; it is not certain that harm to Genesee Trout was necessarily the likely result of applying MU-83 on a nearby field. The excerpt from the pesticide user's guide, however, includes an explicit warning that "Improper use or application of MU-83 may cause serious injury or death." This warning, and the warning about aquatic populations, combined with Genesee Trout's claim that the MU-83 killed its fish (evinced by the high levels of MU-83 found in the trout ponds) is probably sufficient to demonstrate a likelihood of great harm.

  - **Note:** Applicants may conflate factors (1) and (2). This should not be a basis for taking off points if applicants recognize the distinct concepts of the risk of harm and the seriousness or severity of any resulting harm.

- **Inability of reasonable care to eliminate risk**. Although no single factor is determinative, this factor is at the heart of an ultrahazardous assessment. Thus, in *Thurman*, the court states that this factor "would generally carry more weight than the other factors, but that this factor alone was not dispositive of whether an activity is ultrahazardous." The court's discussion includes a list of cases where the inherent dangerousness of the activities rendered them ultrahazardous: shooting fireworks, rock blasting, preparation of weapons-grade plutonium, and transportation of large amounts of gasoline. In all of these examples, even the exercise of reasonable care would not eliminate the risk of injury.

Here, the MU-83 User's Guide refers to "improper use" as presenting a risk of serious injury or death, thereby suggesting that, properly used, MU-83 does not pose a danger to humans, livestock, aquatic life, or crops. At the same time, the pesticide manual states that there is always a risk of "pesticide drift" in every application, depending upon various controllable and uncontrollable factors (temperature, wind gusts, etc.). The user's guide also states that MU-83 poses a danger to aquatic life. The implication is that even reasonable care cannot eliminate all risks, particularly those to aquatic life, inherent in MU-83 use. Applicants might reasonably conclude that the risks from aerial spraying of MU-83 are substantially greater than the risks associated with applying the pesticide by hand, and therefore it is an ultrahazardous activity under Franklin law.

- **Uncommon activity**. The facts that the township posts notices of pesticide spraying and that Chip has previous experience as a crop duster suggest that aerial pesticide application is not an uncommon activity, at least in an agricultural area. Further, crop dusting by airplane is listed in the user's guide as an acceptable method of applying MU-83. Franklin courts have declined to impose liability under an ultrahazardous theory for activities that are a common part of daily life. However, per *Thurman*, applicants should recognize that the legality of an activity (e.g., giving proper notice or compliance with other requirements) does not preclude an activity from being labeled ultrahazardous. Applicants should ultimately conclude that this factor weighs against finding the pesticide spraying to be ultrahazardous.

- **Inappropriateness of the activity where it is conducted**. In *Thurman*, the court held that the defendant's raising of pit bulls constituted an ultrahazardous activity, giving significant weight to the fact that she was breeding the animals in an inappropriate place—a residential neighborhood with many young children. In contrast, in *Fredricks v. Centralia Fire Department* (cited in *Thurman*), the court noted that the only logical place to engage in the dangerous activity of firefighting was at the site of a fire. The pesticide spraying at Mistover falls somewhere between these two extremes. As a farm that grows vegetables for sale and is located in an agricultural area, it seems entirely appropriate that Mistover uses pesticides to protect its crops. And, as noted above, aerial application of pesticides is lawful in the township, as long as the proper permits are obtained and posted. However, the fact that Mistover is close to several organic producers suggests that aerial pesticide spraying may not be appropriate because of the risk of drifting chemicals. This determination is a close call, and applicants can probably go either way on this factor. Better answers may even draw distinctions between ground application of the pesticide during the first year and aerial application of the pesticide during the second year.

- **Activity's value to the community**. Application of pesticides is a beneficial, and often necessary, activity to ensure production of food. Thus there is significant value to the community in the responsible use of pesticides. This weighs against the conclusion that the pesticide spraying is ultrahazardous and that strict liability should be imposed for any harm caused by the activity. On the other hand, in the interview, Petra mentions that the area surrounding Mistover is home to many small producers of organic crops; even Mistover Acres LLC was organized with the intention of raising crops with minimal chemicals. Thus, following *Thurman*'s observation that Franklin courts have refused to employ a narrow application of the ultrahazardous doctrine and that the context of the activity, and not just the activity itself, is a relevant consideration, applicants could conclude that the value to the community of aerial pesticide spraying is not so great as to overcome other factors favoring the conclusion that it is an ultrahazardous activity.

Considering the § 520 factors overall, this is a much closer case than the raising of pit bulls in *Thurman* because of the significant public benefit of protecting the food supply. (Indeed, the jurisdictions are split on whether spraying of herbicides/pesticides is ultrahazardous.) However, the inherent dangerousness of the activity (as described in the excerpt from the pesticide manual), the fact that even with reasonable care there is a risk of pesticide drift and potential harm to aquatic life, and the fact that the spraying was conducted in close proximity to farms devoted to organic agriculture suggest that it would be deemed ultrahazardous and strict liability for the harm caused would attach. Applicants who conclude that the pesticide spraying is not ultrahazardous can receive substantial credit (or even full credit) provided that their analysis is reasonably supported by the relevant facts and law.

Applicant Identification

In re Tamara Shea

**Read the directions on the back cover.
Do not break the seal until you are told to do so.**

NATIONAL CONFERENCE OF BAR EXAMINERS

INSTRUCTIONS

1. You will have 90 minutes to complete this session of the examination. This performance test is designed to evaluate your ability to handle a select number of legal authorities in the context of a factual problem involving a client.

2. The problem is set in the fictitious state of Franklin, in the fictitious Fifteenth Circuit of the United States. Columbia and Olympia are also fictitious states in the Fifteenth Circuit. In Franklin, the trial court of general jurisdiction is the District Court, the intermediate appellate court is the Court of Appeal, and the highest court is the Supreme Court.

3. You will have two kinds of materials with which to work: a File and a Library. The first document in the File is a memorandum containing the instructions for the task you are to complete. The other documents in the File contain factual information about your case and may also include some facts that are not relevant.

4. The Library contains the legal authorities needed to complete the task and may also include some authorities that are not relevant. Any cases may be real, modified, or written solely for the purpose of this examination. If the cases appear familiar to you, do not assume that they are precisely the same as you have read before. Read them thoroughly, as if they all were new to you. You should assume that the cases were decided in the jurisdictions and on the dates shown. In citing cases from the Library, you may use abbreviations and omit page references.

5. Your response must be written in the answer book provided. In answering this performance test, you should concentrate on the materials provided. What you have learned in law school and elsewhere provides the general background for analyzing the problem; the File and Library provide the specific materials with which you must work.

6. Although there are no restrictions on how you apportion your time, you should be sure to allocate ample time (about 45 minutes) to reading and digesting the materials and to organizing your answer before you begin writing it. You may make notes anywhere in the test materials; blank pages are provided at the end of the booklet. You may not tear pages from the question booklet.

7. This performance test will be graded on your responsiveness to the instructions regarding the task you are to complete, which are given to you in the first memorandum in the File, and on the content thoroughness, and organization of your response.

In re Tamara Shea

FILE

LIBRARY

POINT SHEET

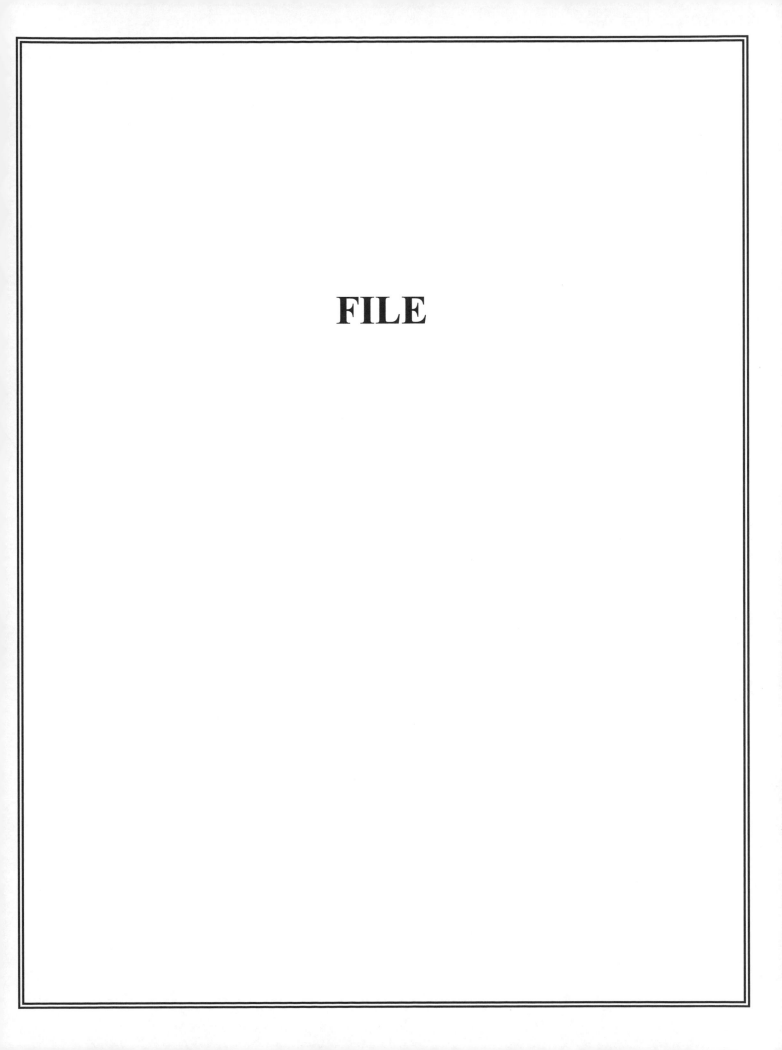

FILE

Allender, Levine & Chu LLP
Attorneys at Law
3020 Hayden Square, Suite 700
Victoria, Franklin 33117
(608)555-9412

MEMORANDUM

TO:	Applicant
FROM:	Laura Levine
DATE:	February 27, 2007
RE:	Tamara Shea

Our client Tamara Shea, a real estate broker, seeks legal advice concerning her entitlement to payment for services rendered in connection with a real estate transaction. When the property was first listed for sale, Shea and the seller, Ann Remick, entered into a written "listing agreement," which is a contract between a real estate broker and a property owner setting forth the terms of the broker's services, the rights and duties of the parties, and the broker's right to compensation. Typically, the seller pays the broker a commission, expressed as a percentage of the agreed-upon sale price, when the property is sold with the broker's assistance.

Remick sold the property a few weeks ago. Shea believes that the purchaser, Dan Anderson, convinced Remick to sell the property to him directly at a reduced price, thereby avoiding payment of Shea's commission. To date, Shea has not received any compensation in connection with the sale of the property. I want to know what legal recourse she may have.

Please draft a memorandum analyzing the following:

(1)   Whether Shea can maintain a breach of contract claim against Remick; and

(2)   Whether Shea can maintain a claim for interference with contractual relations and/or interference with prospective economic advantage against Anderson.

You need not include a separate statement of facts, but in each part of your memorandum be sure to incorporate the relevant facts, analyze the applicable legal authorities, and explain how the facts and law affect your analysis. Another associate is researching whether Shea can recover under the doctrine of promissory estoppel, so you need not address that issue.

In re Tamara Shea

Levine: I'm glad we could meet on such short notice. In your phone message, you mentioned something about a real estate deal that fell through. What's going on?

Shea: Well, I'm pretty upset—I've been cheated out of a commission.

Levine: Why don't you start at the beginning and walk me through what happened?

Shea: Okay. In early November, I was approached by Ann Remick, who owned a 20-acre undeveloped parcel of land in the Briarwood Township in Cleveland County. Remick told me she had been referred to me by a friend and said that she wanted my assistance in selling the property. After I met with her and inspected the property, we signed a 60-day listing agreement setting forth the terms of our relationship as broker and client.

Levine: I'm familiar with the Briarwood area. It's really beautiful country out there, but a little off the beaten track. Did you bring a copy of the listing agreement with you?

Shea: Yes. As you'll see, the agreement clearly states that I was to be paid a 10 percent commission if I found a buyer for the property during the listing period.

Levine: What happened after you put the property on the market?

Shea: I was confident the property would sell within a couple of months, because properties of that size in Briarwood are hard to come by. It was just a matter of finding the right buyer, someone seeking country living less than two hours outside of town. I did everything from listing the property in local newspapers and on the Multiple Listing Service, to circulating flyers to other real estate agents and showing the property to potential buyers. Before the listing agreement expired, I'd already received inquiries from more than a dozen people and had shown the property to three individuals who expressed serious interest in it. Because none of these prospects had panned out, and because more than one potential buyer had expressed concern about the listing price, Remick agreed in writing to reduce her asking price from $225,000 to $200,000. She seemed very motivated to sell and I could tell she was getting frustrated, even after I told her that the holiday season was historically a slow time for real estate sales. Nevertheless, I was certain that we'd be receiving at least one offer within the next several days, based on the efforts I'd made to market the property, the price reduction, and my discussions with potential buyers.

Levine: I'm somewhat familiar with the Multiple Listing Service, but can you tell me a little more about it?

2

Shea: Sure. The Multiple Listing Service, or MLS, maintains a computer database of all the property listings in a particular area. It's available to real estate brokers as well as the general public, who can access MLS listings online. This is a copy of the MLS listing for the Remick property.

Levine: Thanks. You mentioned earlier that the property has been sold. What happened?

Shea: On January 10, I got a call from a guy named Dan Anderson. He said he'd seen the MLS listing for the property and he wanted to schedule a tour as soon as possible. I knew that my listing agreement with Remick had expired. Although I wasn't worried at the time about Remick agreeing to extend the agreement, I felt I could not show the property without her express authority, so I tried to contact her to see how she wanted to handle the situation.

Levine: Were you able to reach her?

Shea: Not directly. I left her a voicemail message indicating that Anderson was interested in seeing the property and that I wanted to show it to him, but that because our listing agreement had expired, I needed to know how she wanted to proceed. She left me a reply voicemail stating she was out of town due to a family emergency and wasn't sure how long she'd be gone. She said she would extend the listing agreement as soon as she got back in town and that I should go ahead and continue showing the property in the meantime. I sent her a confirmation letter for her signature that she never returned. Here's a copy of what I sent.

Levine: Thanks. By the way, other than the listing agreement and the letter you sent Remick, were there any other written communications between the two of you?

Shea: Only Remick's written authorization to reduce the price.

Levine: Did you ever end up showing the property to Anderson?

Shea: Yes, we met as planned the morning of January 13, 2007. When he saw the land, he was really excited and said it was exactly what he was looking for. He wanted to submit an offer that day, so I helped him put one together and he signed it in my office.

Levine: What were the terms of the offer?

Shea: Anderson offered to buy the property for $185,000. I told him I didn't think Remick would accept the offer, because she had already reduced her asking price from $225,000 to $200,000, and that the reduced asking price—which worked out to only $10,000 an acre—was already at the lower end of the market. Anderson said he couldn't go any higher than $185,000. I should point out that if Remick had accepted Anderson's

3

$185,000 offer, I would have received a commission of $18,500 and Remick would have netted $166,500 from the sale before her closing costs. Anyway, that evening, I left Remick a voicemail message informing her of the offer. I also faxed the offer to her so she'd have it when she got back in town.

Levine: Did she accept the offer?

Shea: No. She called a few days later to say Anderson's offer was too low and that she wasn't interested in making a counteroffer or considering any other offers because she had decided not to sell the property after all. When I called Anderson to deliver the bad news, he didn't act surprised or seem particularly disappointed. Then I learned that Remick went ahead and sold the property directly to Anderson, and now she's refusing to pay my commission!

Levine: I can understand your concerns, and I agree that this doesn't pass the smell test. How did you find out about the sale, anyway?

Shea: About a week ago, a broker friend of mine heard that the property had sold. He remembered that I'd been involved with the property, and he called to congratulate me on the sale. I was blown away when I found out what had happened. I did some checking and confirmed that the sale closed on February 2, and the property sold for $180,000. Since then, I've tried to reach Anderson and Remick. Anderson hasn't returned my calls. Remick finally called back the other night after business hours and left a message stating that Anderson had told her that realtors couldn't be trusted because all we wanted were quick sales to get our commissions with as little work as possible. Remick said Anderson also told her that if she dealt directly with him she wouldn't owe me any commission. When I heard this, I decided I needed a lawyer and called you for advice.

Levine: Did you and Anderson ever discuss the subject of your commission?

Shea: As a matter of fact, we did. When we were putting together his offer, he asked who would be responsible for paying my commission if his offer were accepted. I explained that because I had a listing agreement with Remick and she was the seller, she would be responsible for the commission, as long as he didn't default prior to the closing. He wanted to know what my commission would be. I told him that it was customary for brokers to receive 10 percent of the agreed-upon purchase price where, as here, the sale involved unimproved land. At the time, I thought the conversation was a little odd, but now I think I know why he was asking all those questions about my commission!

4

Levine: I can understand why you're so upset. Let me look into this. I should be able to get back to you within the next couple of days.

Shea: That would be great. Thanks for your help.

LISTING AGREEMENT

This Listing Agreement (Agreement) is entered into between Ann Remick (Seller) and Tamara Shea (Broker) and concerns the following property (Property):

> The parcel consisting of 20 acres located in the Briarwood Township of Cleveland County, Franklin, and legally described by the Deed dated September 5, 1987, and recorded in the Cleveland County Records, in Record Book 725 at page 317, and Plat Book 50 at page 72.

In consideration of the mutual promises contained herein, Seller gives Broker the exclusive right to sell the Property at the listing price of two hundred twenty-five thousand dollars ($225,000) cash or such other terms and conditions as Seller may agree to in writing.

The period of this Agreement shall be sixty (60) days, from the date hereof up to and including January 8, 2007.

Broker agrees to use reasonable efforts to procure a ready, willing, and able buyer for the Property in accordance with the terms and conditions of this Agreement. Broker is granted the sole authority to undertake any one or more of the following actions: advertise the Property; post "For Sale" signs on the Property; . . . and disclose, print, or publish information that is obtained during the listing period to prospective buyers and other brokers.

Seller will pay Broker a brokerage commission of 10 percent of the agreed-upon sale price if, prior to the expiration of this Agreement, Broker procures a buyer ready, willing, and able to purchase the property, in accordance with the price, terms, and conditions of this Agreement, or on such other price, terms, and conditions as shall be acceptable to Seller.

Seller agrees to refer all inquiries and offers made for the purchase of the Property to Broker, to cooperate with Broker in every reasonable way, and to maintain and insure the Property.

*   *   *   *

Seller represents that she is the owner of the Property, and that the information contained in this Agreement is true and accurate. Receipt of a copy of this Agreement is hereby acknowledged. This Agreement shall be interpreted in accordance with the laws of the State of Franklin.

This Agreement can be extended, cancelled, or revoked only if Seller and Broker agree in writing.

IN WITNESS WHEREOF, the parties have executed this Agreement as of the date set forth below.

Seller: _____   Date: _____ November 10, 2006
       Ann Remick

Broker: _____   Date: _____ November 10, 2006
       Tamara Shea, Shea Realty

Shea Realty

Victoria's Premier Real Estate Company
420 Tenth Street
Victoria, FR 33117
333.555.0602
www.SheaRealty.com

14014 Memorial Crossing
Lakewood Park, Franklin 33017

January 10, 2007

Ms. Ann Remick
5632 Birdie Lane
Diamond Springs, Franklin 33017

Re: Briarwood Parcel

Dear Ann:

This will confirm that our Listing Agreement dated November 10, 2006, is extended for a period of 30 days, effective as of January 9, 2007, through and including February 7, 2007.

I look forward to continuing to assist you in selling your Briarwood property. Please countersign and return this letter to me at your earliest convenience.

Sincerely,

Tamara Shea
Licensed Real Estate Broker

I hereby consent to the Listing Agreement extension set forth above.

Seller: _____   Date: _____
Ann Remick

6

In re Tamara Shea

Shea Realty

MLS# 07046619

No Photo
Available

Contact: Tamara at Shea Realty
Tamara@SheaRealty.com
(333) 555-0602

Location, Location, Location!!! A new listing available exclusively from Shea Realty! If you're looking for that special setting off the beaten path, don't miss out on this rare 20-acre tract of undeveloped land in the Briarwood Township, Cleveland County. Very private location at the end of a rural county road with Victoria Creek running through the property. Close to the Carmel Hills with magnificent views to the east. Lots of wooded acreage with abundant wildlife, including mule deer, whitetails, and turkeys. Also contains a small crop of alfalfa. Accessible to town. Power is available.

OFFER FOR THE PURCHASE OF REAL PROPERTY

To: Ann Remick, Seller

The undersigned hereby offers One Hundred Eighty-Five Thousand Dollars ($185,000) for the purchase of the following real estate:

A 20-acre parcel located in the Briarwood Township of Cleveland County, Franklin, and legally described by the Deed dated September 5, 1987, and recorded in the Cleveland County Records, in Record Book 725 at page 317, and Plat Book 50 at page 72.

This offer to purchase is contingent on the following terms:

1. An earnest money deposit of five thousand dollars ($5,000) as part of the purchase price shall be paid to Seller upon acceptance of this offer and placed in escrow pending execution of a deed, real estate contract, or other conveyance, with the remaining balance of $180,000 to be paid by cash, cashier's check, or certified check at closing.

2. Taxes, insurance, and other applicable expenses shall be prorated as of the closing date.

3. Seller shall deliver the property free and clear of all liens, restrictions, and encumbrances and shall furnish a policy of title insurance. Title shall be conveyed by warranty deed.

If purchaser defaults following acceptance of this offer, the earnest money deposit shall be forfeited and applied to payment of the broker's commission and any expenses incurred, with the balance paid to seller.

This offer is withdrawn if not accepted within 10 days.

_____   January 13, 2007_____
Dan Anderson   Date
219 South Figueroa
Lakewood Park, Franklin 33020

ACCEPTANCE

I accept the above offer for the purchase of the described real property.

_____   _____
Ann Remick, Seller   Date

8

In re Tamara Shea

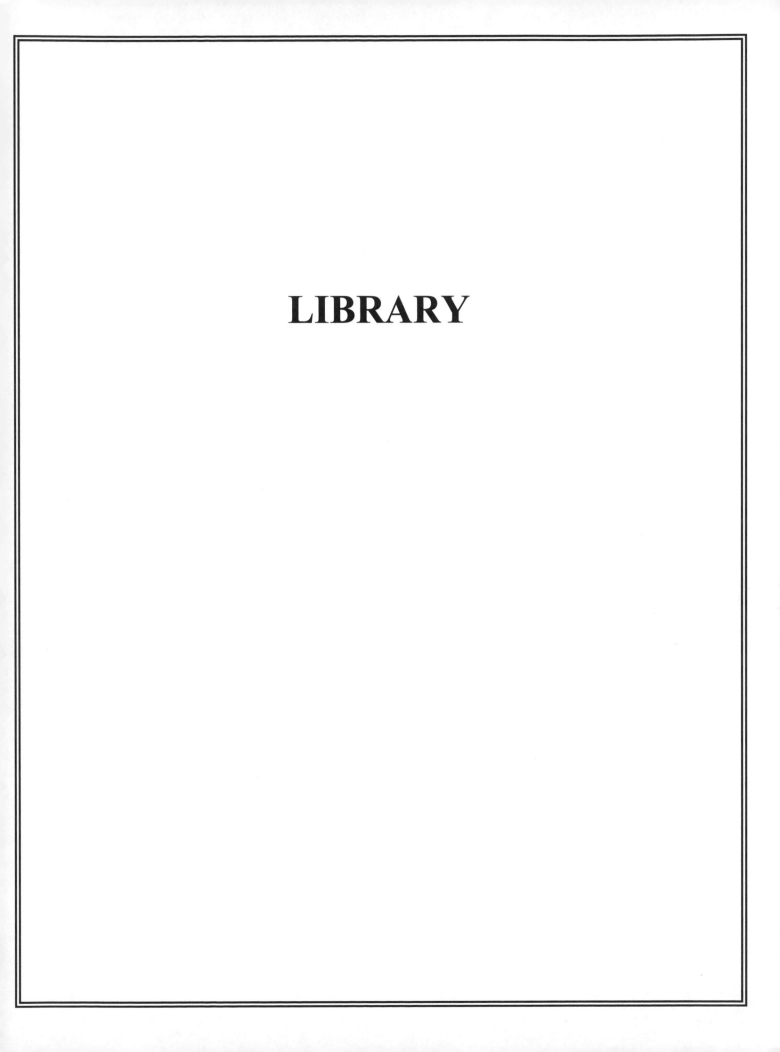

LIBRARY

§ 1500. Agreements required to be in writing.

The following agreements are unenforceable, unless they, or some note or memorandum thereof, are in writing and subscribed by the party to be charged:

(a) An agreement that by its terms is not to be performed within a year from the making thereof;

(b) A special promise to answer for the debt, default, or miscarriage of another;

(c) An agreement for the leasing of real property for a longer period than one year, or for the sale of real property or of an interest therein;

(d) An agreement that authorizes or employs a broker, for compensation or a commission:

    1. To procure a purchaser or seller of real estate; or

    2. To procure a lessee or lessor of real estate where the lease is for longer than one year; or

(e) An agreement that by its terms is not to be performed during the lifetime of the promisor.

Mather v. Bowen
Franklin Court of Appeal (1997)

This is an action to recover a broker's commission allegedly due plaintiff Karen Mather for her services in procuring defendant Crown Research Corporation (CRC) as a tenant for defendant William Bowen's commercial real property.

Mather's complaint alleged the following: Mather is a licensed real estate broker and Bowen is the owner of the property. In June 1995, Mather attended an open house conducted by Bowen at the property site for the purpose of soliciting real estate brokers to procure tenants for the property on a 10-year lease. At the open house, Bowen distributed an offering brochure stating that brokers and prospective tenants would be registered and including a schedule of brokers' commissions.

Mather further alleged that in December 1995, she advised Bowen by telephone that she wished to bring a prospective tenant, defendant CRC, to view the property. In the phone call, Bowen acknowledged that Mather would be entitled to a broker's commission if and when CRC leased the premises. Mather then brought a CRC representative to view the property and completed Bowen's client-broker registration form, identifying herself as the broker and CRC as the prospective lessee, with Bowen signing the form identifying himself as lessor. Two weeks later, CRC submitted a written lease offer that identified Mather as broker and CRC as prospective

lessee, and which further provided that "Lessor agrees to pay all commissions due Broker arising out of or in connection with Lessee's offer to lease." Bowen rejected the lease offer. However, in March 1996, Bowen and CRC executed a written lease for the property at a lower cost, without Mather's knowledge.

After finding out about the lease and receiving no commission, Mather brought this action against Bowen and CRC. Mather's first cause of action was directed against Bowen for breach of contract, and alleged that the brochure and client-broker registration form collectively constituted a written agreement under which Bowen owed Mather a commission. Mather's second cause of action alleged that CRC interfered with her economic and contractual relationship with Bowen. The defendants' motions to dismiss the complaint were granted without allowing Mather leave to amend her complaint.

The function of a motion to dismiss is to test the sufficiency of a plaintiff's pleading by raising questions of law. The allegations in the complaint must be regarded as true and are to be liberally construed. On appeal, the court is not concerned with a party's possible difficulty or inability in *proving* the allegations of the complaint, but only that the party *may* be entitled to some relief. We apply these principles in reviewing the complaint.

1. The writings satisfy the statute of frauds and support the claim against Bowen for breach of contract.

The Franklin statute of frauds provides that an agreement to pay a commission to a real estate broker to procure a buyer or seller of real property, or to procure a lessee or lessor of property for a period of more than a year, must be in writing. Franklin Civil Code § 1500(d). The purpose of the statute of frauds is to protect real estate sellers and purchasers from false claims by brokers for commissions. As such, § 1500(d) is designed to protect consumers, and is strictly enforced.

For a writing to satisfy the statute of frauds, it need not contain all the terms of the contract. The principal requirements for a broker to satisfy the statute of frauds are: (1) the writing shows the authority of the broker to act for the party to be charged, and (2) the writing is subscribed (signed) by or on behalf of the party to be charged. When these requirements are met, the other terms, including the amount of the commission, and even the agreement to pay the commission, may be shown by extrinsic evidence. Such evidence may also show the circumstances that attended the writing's making, or explain ambiguities on the writing's face. Finally, where a plaintiff relies on multiple writings, the court must determine whether the writings as a whole constitute an enforceable agreement.

Bowen maintains the writings are insufficient because they do not show on their face the fact of Mather's employment as Bowen's real estate broker. We disagree. The brochure and registration form appear to be related to each other. Both were prepared by Bowen, and he signed the registration form. The registration form containing the reference to broker commissions did not appear in a vacuum, but supplemented the initial brochure, which set forth the amount of commission to be paid and further provided that "brokers will be protected." Moreover, Bowen's signature on the registration form is sufficient to satisfy the subscription requirement as to this set of writings.

Together, these documents show that Bowen, in writing, actively solicited and engaged the cooperation of real estate brokers *en masse* in an effort to lease the property, with assurances that the brokers would be protected and compensated. Relying on these written representations, Mather brought CRC as a prospective tenant, and registered herself and CRC on Bowen's registration form, in accordance with Bowen's advertised procedure, with Bowen himself subscribing the document. As no other conceivable purpose could be served by Bowen's having Mather register CRC as a prospective tenant, the writings warrant the inference that Bowen authorized Mather to procure CRC as a tenant for the property.[1] Therefore, Mather properly alleged a cause of action against Bowen for breach of contract.

---

[1] Because the writings satisfy the statute of frauds, evidence of the December 1995 telephone conversation between Bowen and Mather (in which Bowen allegedly confirmed that Mather would receive a commission if CRC leased the property) may be admitted to explain any ambiguity in the registration form's purpose or function, as well as to show the circumstances that attended its making.

Bowen's reliance on *Phillip v. Carter Industries* (Franklin Ct. App. 1991) is misplaced. There, the broker sued his client for breach of contract, alleging that an exchange of letters between the broker and client showed that the client had retained the broker to act on its behalf and had agreed to pay the broker's commission. However, the only writings that related to the broker's commission were *from the broker to the client,* not from the client to the broker. Thus, the writings did not satisfy the statute of frauds, as they were not subscribed by the party to be charged.

2. Mather's interference claims against CRC also withstand a motion to dismiss.

Mather pleaded one cause of action against CRC, labeling it "interference with economic advantage and contract." As such, Mather inartfully combined two distinct torts, interference with prospective economic advantage and interference with contractual relations, into one claim. Although these two torts are closely related and share many of the same elements, liability for interference with contractual relations requires an *existing valid and enforceable* contract. In contrast, a cause of action for interference with prospective economic advantage necessarily assumes that a contract has not yet been formulated (e.g., where the relationship is based on pending negotiations) or that the contract involved is unenforceable (e.g., due to lack of consideration or violation of the statute of frauds). The two torts, however, involve basically the same conduct on the part of the tortfeasor. In one case, the interference takes place when a valid contract is already in existence, in the other, when either a contract likely would have been consummated but for the conduct of the tortfeasor or where the plaintiff would otherwise have received an economic benefit but for the defendant's interference.

We note initially that even though these two torts are distinct, some plaintiffs may be able to state causes of action for both torts. Thus, a plaintiff who believes that she has a contract but who recognizes that the trier of fact might conclude otherwise, might bring claims for both torts so that, in the event of a finding of no contract, the plaintiff might prevail on a claim for interference with prospective economic advantage. Where the exact nature of the facts is in doubt, or where the exact legal nature of plaintiff's rights and defendant's liability depends on facts not known by the plaintiff, the pleading may properly state alternative theories in separate, inconsistent causes of action. However, where there is no existing enforceable contract for whatever reason, only a claim for interference with prospective economic advantage may be maintained.

We conclude that Mather pleaded both theories in the alternative, and will consider each claim against CRC in turn. The elements of the tort of interference with prospective economic advantage are: (1) an economic relationship between the plaintiff and a third party containing the probability of future economic benefit to the plaintiff, (2) the defendant's knowledge of the existence of the relationship, (3) intentional *and* improper acts on the part of the defendant designed to disrupt the relationship, (4) actual disruption of the relationship, and (5) economic harm to the

12

plaintiff proximately caused by the defendant's acts.

As stated above, the tort of interference with prospective economic advantage is not dependent on compliance with the statute of frauds. The wrong complained of in this cause of action is that CRC interfered in Mather's advantageous relationship with Bowen. Specifically, Mather alleged that she had an economic relationship with Bowen containing the probability of future economic benefit (i.e., payment of her broker's commission); that CRC had knowledge of the relationship, as evidenced by the commission provision contained in CRC's lease offer; that CRC intentionally excluded Mather from the lease negotiations, knowing and intending that such conduct would disrupt the relationship between Mather and Bowen; that CRC secured the lease at a lower price than it would have if Mather's commission had been paid; and that Mather was therefore damaged in an amount at least equal to the commission. These allegations are sufficient to state a cause of action for interference with prospective economic advantage. *See, e.g., Howard v. Youngman* (Franklin Ct. App. 1985) (defendant real estate broker's economic interest in getting a higher commission if seller sold home to a different buyer did not give broker legal right to interfere with ongoing negotiations for sale of home).

Turning to Mather's second claim against CRC, to state a cause of action for interference with contractual relations, a plaintiff must allege: (1) a valid and enforceable contract between the plaintiff and a third party, (2) the defendant's knowledge of the existence of the contractual relationship, (3) intentional *and* improper acts on the part of the defendant designed to disrupt the relationship, (4) actual disruption of the relationship, (5) economic harm to the plaintiff proximately caused by the defendant's acts.

CRC moved to dismiss this cause of action solely on the ground that there was no valid and existing contract between Mather and Bowen. Because the brochure and registration form were sufficient to satisfy the statute of frauds, we hold that Mather properly pleaded a claim for interference with contractual relations against CRC.

Accordingly, the trial court's judgment of dismissal is reversed and the case is remanded for further proceedings.

Downey & Co. v. Sierra Growers
Franklin Court of Appeal (2000)

Plaintiff Downey & Co. (Downey) appeals from the trial court's judgment dismissing its action against defendant Sierra Growers (Sierra). The facts stated in Downey's complaint reveal that commencing in 1990, Downey entered into a series of contracts with Margaret Livingston, the sole proprietor of Villa D'Oro Olive Oil Company, an olive oil processing plant located in Butte County, Franklin. The Downey-Livingston contracts, which are incorporated into the complaint, provided for the sale of certain olive products to Downey.

Following execution of the contracts, a legal dispute arose between Downey and Livingston. As a result, in September 1993, Livingston advised Downey in writing that she intended to rescind and cancel the contracts on grounds of material breach and fraudulent misrepresentation by Downey. Downey filed an action in Cleveland County seeking declaratory and related relief against Livingston. While the Cleveland County action was pending, Livingston sold the Villa D'Oro processing plant to Sierra. Thereupon, Downey brought the present action against Sierra, purporting to state causes of action on the dual tort theories of interference with contractual relations and interference with prospective economic advantage. The district court granted Sierra's motion to dismiss the complaint and entered judgment against Downey. We affirm.

The gist of Downey's grievance is that, by buying the processing plant from Livingston, Sierra improperly interfered with and induced the breach of the Downey-Livingston contracts and also interfered with Downey's prospective economic advantage. It is well established that one who intentionally and improperly interferes with the contractual relations between the plaintiff and a third party is liable to the plaintiff for the harm caused thereby. It is likewise settled that the elements of the torts of interference with contractual relations and interference with prospective economic advantage are identical except that the former requires the existence of a legally binding agreement. Both torts require a showing of the defendant's knowledge of the existence of the plaintiff's relationship with a third party, intentional and improper acts by the defendant designed to disrupt the relationship, actual disruption of the relationship, and resulting economic harm to the plaintiff.

When tested against the foregoing standards, the challenged causes of action are facially deficient. Downey's complaint alleges that Sierra acquired knowledge of the Downey-Livingston contracts the day *after* it purchased the processing plant from Livingston. It is elementary that interference with contractual relations and interference with prospective economic advantage are intentional torts. The interference is intentional if the actor desires to bring it about or if he knows that the interference is certain or substantially certain to occur as a result of his action. Intent may be established by inference as well as by direct proof. In addition, a plaintiff must show

14

either that the defendant had actual knowledge of the existence of the relationship or knowledge of facts and circumstances that would lead a reasonable person to believe in the existence of the relationship and plaintiff's interest in it. If the defendant had no knowledge of the existence of the relationship or if his actions were not intended to interfere with the relationship, he cannot be held liable even if an actual breach results from his acts.

Downey's complaint not only fails to allege that Sierra intentionally interfered with Downey's relationship with Livingston, but also fails to allege that at the time of purchasing the plant Sierra was even aware of the existence of the Downey-Livingston contracts, rendering Downey's claims against Sierra fatally defective. Liability will not be imposed for unforeseeable or unknown harm, since a plaintiff must prove that the defendant knew that the consequences were substantially certain to occur.

Similarly, Downey has failed to allege that Sierra's conduct was improper. Impropriety can be established by showing the defendant's bad motive or bad conduct. Absent such motive or conduct, a defendant's acts will not be deemed improper. Downey's novel proposition that Sierra acted improperly by failing to rescind or cancel its contract to purchase the plant after learning about the Downey-Livingston contracts is supported by neither reason nor law. While the law rightly prohibits an intentional interference with contractual rights or economic relations existing between others, there is no equivalent duty to rescind a contract lawfully entered into on the ground that it might offend the legal rights of others. To the contrary, no impropriety exists where, as here, the defendant's conduct consists of something that it had an absolute right to do. As such, this case stands in stark contrast to those cases finding the defendant's actions improper.

A plaintiff seeking to hold a defendant liable for improperly inducing another to breach a contract must allege that the contract would otherwise have been performed and that it was breached by reason of the defendant's conduct. Here, performance of the Downey-Livingston contracts had been abandoned by Livingston several months prior to Sierra's acquisition of the plant. Under these circumstances, proximate causation, a vital element of both causes of action, was lacking as a matter of law. Thus, Downey failed to allege a valid cause of action under either tort.

Affirmed.

NOTES

POINT SHEET

In re Tamara Shea

DRAFTERS' POINT SHEET

In this performance test item, the client, Tamara Shea, is a real estate broker who handled the listing for a 20-acre undeveloped parcel owned by seller Ann Remick. Shea and Remick entered into a 60-day listing agreement under which Remick retained Shea to serve as her broker and agreed to list the property at $225,000. Pursuant to the express terms of the agreement, Shea was to be paid a commission of 10 percent of the purchase price if she procured a buyer for the property. Shortly after the listing agreement lapsed, Shea was contacted by Dan Anderson, a potential buyer. Shea then contacted Remick, who confirmed, in a telephone message, her intention to extend the listing agreement, and instructed Shea to show the property. Shea showed Anderson the property and he made an offer on it. Remick, however, rejected the offer, claiming it was too low. Shea subsequently discovered that following expiration of the listing agreement, Remick sold the property directly to Anderson for $180,000 ($5,000 less than Anderson's previous offer and $20,000 less than the reduced listing price of $200,000). Remick is now refusing to pay Shea any commission on the sale, claiming that she need not compensate Shea because she sold the property directly to Anderson. Shea seeks advice from applicants' firm on whether she has any legal recourse against Remick and/or Anderson.

Applicants' task is to draft an objective memo to the supervising attorney analyzing whether Shea can maintain claims against Remick for breach of contract and against Anderson for interference with contractual relations and/or interference with prospective economic advantage.

The File contains the task memorandum, a transcript of an interview between the supervising attorney and Shea, the listing agreement, a letter from Shea confirming the extension of the listing agreement, the property's MLS listing, and Anderson's initial offer to purchase the property for $185,000. The Library contains the Franklin statute of frauds and two cases.

The following discussion covers all of the points the drafters intended to raise in the problem. Applicants need not cover them all to receive passing or even excellent grades. Grading is entirely within the discretion of the user jurisdictions.

I.   Format and Overview

Applicants' work product should resemble a memorandum from one attorney to another. They are told that the discussion of each issue in the memorandum should set out the relevant facts, analyze the legal authorities, and explain how the facts and law affect their analyses.

- Applicants are instructed that they need not write a separate statement of facts, but must use the facts in the File to support their analyses.
- Better applicants will use headings to identify the issues.
  - The headings set forth below are examples only and are not to be taken by graders as the prescribed headings.
- Applicants must first determine whether Shea can maintain a claim for breach of contract against Remick.
  - Because commission agreements between real estate brokers and clients are subject to the statute of frauds (Franklin Civil Code § 1500(d)), applicants must analyze whether the communications between Shea and Remick satisfy the statute of frauds.
- Applicants should note that the listing agreement had expired and conclude that Remick's oral consent to extend the agreement is not enforceable.
  - Moreover, Shea's confirming letter dated January 10, 2007, does not cure the deficiency, as it was not signed (subscribed) by Remick.
- Consequently, Shea cannot maintain a claim against Remick for breach of contract.
- To state a claim for interference with contractual relations against Anderson, there must be an existing valid and enforceable contract between Shea and Remick. This threshold issue is dispositive. Because there is no contract between Shea and Remick, Shea cannot maintain a cause of action against Anderson for interference with contractual relations.
- Applicants should reach the opposite conclusion regarding a claim for interference with prospective economic advantage against Anderson.
  - The facts show that Shea and Remick had an existing economic relationship, that Anderson knew of their relationship, that he intentionally contacted Remick for the improper purpose of eliminating Shea's commission so that he could buy the property at a lower price, that Anderson actually disrupted Shea's relationship with Remick by so doing, and that Shea lost a prospective economic advantage—the commission she would have earned but for Anderson's acts.

II.   Detailed Analysis

A.   Shea Cannot Maintain a Breach of Contract Claim Against Remick Because the Communications Between Them Do Not Satisfy the Franklin Statute of Frauds.

The Franklin statute of frauds requires that an agreement to pay a broker a commission for procuring a buyer for real property must be in writing to be enforceable. Fr. Civil Code § 1500(d)1.

- For a writing to satisfy the statute of frauds in a real estate brokerage situation, it must meet two requirements: (1) it must show the authority of the broker to act for the party to be charged, and (2) it must be subscribed (signed) by or on behalf of the party to be charged. *Mather v. Bowen.*

- Where, as here, the plaintiff relies on multiple writings to satisfy the statute of frauds, the court must examine the writings to determine whether, as a whole, they constitute an enforceable contract. *Id.*

- As a preliminary matter, applicants should discuss the initial contractual relationship between Shea and Remick, which forms the backdrop for analysis of their relationship at the time Shea showed the property to Anderson.

  - The initial 60-day listing agreement (in effect from November 10, 2006, through January 8, 2007) was valid under the statute of frauds because Remick signed it and it showed that she had retained Shea to serve as her broker.

- Shea showed the property to Anderson on January 13 and assisted him in preparing an offer to purchase. These events occurred *after* the listing agreement had expired on January 9, but within the period that would have been covered by the letter confirming Remick's oral consent to extend the listing, had she signed it as Shea requested. Anderson's purchase of the property was also within this attempted extension (the sale closed on February 2, 2007). Thus, if Shea could establish that she had an existing listing agreement when she showed the property to Anderson, she would be able to state a claim for breach of contract against Remick. However, there would have to be an additional writing signed by Remick to show a continued contractual relationship following expiration of the listing agreement.

- No such writing exists. Shea's January 10, 2007, letter to Remick confirming receipt of Remick's voicemail message and attempting to extend the listing agreement through February 7, 2007, does not comply with the statute of frauds. Although the writing purports to show Shea's authority to act for Remick, the letter is not "subscribed" (signed) by or on behalf of the party to be charged (Remick). *See Phillip v. Carter Ind.* (cited in *Mather*) (writings from broker to client did not satisfy statute of frauds where client was party to be charged).

- Because the statute of frauds has not been complied with, extrinsic evidence (such as the phone message from Remick authorizing Shea to continue serving as her broker) is not admissible to show the circumstances surrounding the letter. *Mather*.

- Thus, unlike the plaintiff in *Mather*, who was able to demonstrate that a series of writings collectively established an existing valid and enforceable contract between the broker and her client and could then introduce extrinsic evidence to establish the circumstances surrounding the agreement and to resolve ambiguities, Shea cannot satisfy the statute of frauds.

- Applicants who discuss in depth how the doctrine of promissory estoppel could be asserted to circumvent the requirements of the statute of frauds are not following the directions in the task memorandum, which explicitly instructs them that another associate is researching that issue, so they need not address it.

B. **Shea *Cannot* Maintain a Claim for Interference with Contractual Relations Against Anderson Because She Did Not Have an Existing Valid and Enforceable Contract With Remick at the Time Her Claim Arose.**

A claim for interference with contractual relations requires: (1) a valid existing contract between the plaintiff and a third party, (2) knowledge by the defendant of the existence of the contractual relationship, (3) intentional and improper acts on the part of the defendant designed to disrupt the relationship, (4) actual disruption of the relationship, and (5) damages to the plaintiff proximately caused by the acts of the defendant. *Mather*.

- As discussed above, Shea cannot maintain a breach of contract action against Remick for violation of the listing agreement because it was not validly extended by Shea's letter of January 10, 2007, or any other writing. Thus, at the time of Anderson's actions, there was no existing contractual relationship between Shea and Remick. It follows, then, that Shea is precluded from bringing a claim against Anderson for interference with contractual relations.

- There is no need to discuss the additional elements of this tort since the threshold requirement cannot be satisfied.

  - Better applicants should begin and end an analysis of the contract interference claim by referencing their conclusion that Shea has no potential contract action against Remick, since this threshold inquiry determines whether the claim is even available. Applicants who analyze the remaining requirements for a contract interference claim will simply be duplicating the analysis they will have to set out on the potential claim for interference with prospective economic advantage, as the remaining elements of both torts are virtually identical.

NOTE: It is up to the user jurisdictions to determine whether such duplicative analysis constitutes a basis for making grading distinctions.

- On a related note, *Mather* indicates that in some cases a plaintiff may state alternative claims under both interference tort theories where the exact nature of the facts is in doubt or where the exact legal nature of the plaintiff's rights and the defendant's liabilities depends on facts not known by the plaintiff. However, *Mather* also cautions that "where there is no existing enforceable contract for whatever reason, only a claim for interference with prospective economic advantage may be maintained."

  - Here it is clear from the client interview that there are no additional writings between Shea and Remick that could affect the analysis of whether they had an existing valid and enforceable contract. Moreover, the statute of frauds is a consumer protection device to be strictly enforced. *Mather*. Consequently, answers stating that the tort claims should be pled in the alternative may be considered less responsive to the call of the question and therefore may provide a basis to make grading distinctions.

C. Shea *Can* Maintain a Claim for Interference with Prospective Economic Advantage Against Anderson.

The tort of interference with prospective economic advantage is closely related to the tort of interference with contractual relations in that they involve basically the same conduct on the part of the tortfeasor. However, the former assumes that a contract has not yet been formed (e.g., where the relationship is based on pending negotiations), or that a contract is unenforceable (e.g., lack of consideration or violation of the statute of frauds). By contrast, the latter requires an existing valid and enforceable contract. *See Mather*; and Sections II A & B, above.

- The tort of intentional interference with prospective economic advantage is not dependent on the existence of a contract; thus, there is no need for applicants to discuss compliance with the statute of frauds. The necessary elements are: (1) an economic relationship between the plaintiff and a third party containing the probability of future economic benefit to the plaintiff, (2) the defendant's knowledge of the existence of the relationship, (3) intentional *and* improper acts on the part of the defendant designed to disrupt the relationship, (4) actual disruption of the relationship, and (5) economic harm to the plaintiff proximately caused by the acts of the defendant. *Mather.*

- Here, the facts and case law show that these elements can be met, at least for purposes of proceeding with a claim under this theory.

  - Better applicants may cite to the standard articulated in *Mather* for the necessary pleading requirements and may recognize that the primary concern at this stage is whether such a claim can be asserted, not whether it can be proven; in other words, whether Shea *may* be entitled to some relief. ("The allegations in the complaint must be regarded as true and are to be liberally construed." *Mather*.)

(1) The existence of a protected economic relationship:

- The facts in the File indicate that Shea and Remick had an economic relationship with the probability of future economic benefit to Shea, in that they had previously entered into a listing agreement which, by all indications, would have been extended but for Anderson's interference. Pursuant to this arrangement, Shea was to receive 10 percent of the purchase price of Remick's property, which clearly constitutes an economic benefit to Shea.

- Although one could argue that there was no guarantee that Shea would find a buyer for the property and thus earn her commission, the facts suggest a likely sale. According to the interview transcript, Shea had received more than a dozen inquiries concerning the property and had shown the property to several potential buyers. Indeed, Anderson himself initially offered to buy the property for $185,000—$5,000 more than the eventual sale price.

(2) The defendant's knowledge of that relationship:

- A plaintiff must show that the defendant had either actual knowledge of the existence of the relationship between the plaintiff and the third party, or knowledge of such facts and circumstances that would lead a reasonable person to believe in the existence of the relationship and the plaintiff's interest in it. If the defendant had no knowledge of the existence of the relationship, there will be no liability even if an actual breach results from the defendant's acts, because liability will not be imposed for unforeseeable or unknown harm. *Downey & Co. v. Sierra Growers.*

- Anderson knew about Shea and Remick's economic relationship.

- Not only did he specifically ask about Shea's commission while she helped him prepare an offer, his own written offer made reference to the commission, stating that in the event of default, "the earnest money deposit shall be forfeited and applied to *payment of the broker's commission* and any expenses incurred . . . ." (Emphasis added)

- Anderson's knowledge can also be inferred from the MLS listing and from the fact that he contacted Shea to view the property and enlisted her help in preparing his initial offer, thereby evidencing his understanding that Shea was the broker handling the listing.

- The facts here parallel those in *Mather*, where the defendant's written lease offer referred to the plaintiff's commission. This is not a situation where the defendant first learned of the existence of the underlying relationship between the plaintiff and the third party after the defendant had engaged in the alleged tortious acts, as was the case in *Downey*. As such, *Downey* is distinguishable.

(3) The defendant's intentional and improper acts:

- *(a) Intentional:* The interference with another's prospective economic advantage is intentional if the actor desires to bring it about or if he knows that the interference is certain or substantially certain to occur as a result of his action. *Downey*.

  - Because interference with prospective economic advantage is an intentional tort, an action will lie only if the defendant *purposely* interfered with the plaintiff's economic relationship with a third party. *Id.*

  - Intent may be established by inference as well as by direct proof. *Id.*

  - Here, the facts and inferences to be drawn conclusively demonstrate the purposefulness of Anderson's acts. After questioning Shea about the amount of her commission, Anderson approached Remick to engineer a deal behind Shea's back, knowing full well that Shea was the listing broker for the property and that she was supposed to receive a 10 percent commission if her efforts found a buyer, thus evidencing an intent to achieve precisely the result that followed (i.e., sale of the property at a reduced price, cutting out Shea's commission).

- *(b) Improper:* Typically, the wrongfulness of a defendant's act may be shown by demonstrating bad motive or bad conduct. Absent a motive or purpose to injure the plaintiff, or to appropriate an economic advantage belonging to the plaintiff, or some other aggravating circumstance, a defendant's acts will not be deemed tortious. *Downey*.

- Every reasonable inference to be drawn from the facts suggests that Anderson's interference was improper. He took advantage of Shea's efforts in marketing the property, made disparaging comments about real estate brokers to Remick, and also told Remick that if she dealt directly with him, she wouldn't owe Shea a commission. In this way, Anderson persuaded Remick to exclude Shea from the negotiations and induced Remick to accept a lower price. Shea was thus deprived of the commission to which she would otherwise have been entitled. Such conduct has been found improper in similar circumstances and held to be tortious. *See Mather*; *Howard v. Youngman* (cited in *Mather*) (broker's personal interest in obtaining higher commission did not give him legal right to interfere with ongoing negotiations for sale of home).

(4) Actual disruption of the relationship:
- To maintain a claim for interference with prospective economic advantage, a plaintiff must demonstrate that the prospective relationship with the third party would have come to fruition but for the defendant's wrongful acts—in other words, that the defendant's acts were the proximate cause of the plaintiff's injuries. *Downey*.

- Although it is unclear from the File exactly when Remick was contacted by Anderson, it can be inferred that this occurred sometime after Anderson submitted his initial offer of $185,000 and before Remick declined the offer. Prior to that point, Remick appeared willing to extend the listing agreement. She also appeared motivated to sell the property, having reduced the price and reconfirmed with Shea that she wanted to sell. Remick's sudden disinterest in making a counteroffer and Anderson's apparent lack of surprise or disappointment upon learning that his offer had been rejected suggest that Remick and Anderson were already negotiating at that point. This inference is bolstered by the fact that Remick's outright rejection of Anderson's $185,000 offer was quickly followed by her sale of the property to him for $180,000.

- This is not a situation where the disputed relationship had been abandoned and discontinued months prior to the defendant's alleged interference, as was the case in *Downey* (in which the olive oil plant owner had notified the plaintiff of her intent to rescind the contract months before the defendant bought the plant, the latter action having given rise to the plaintiff's unsuccessful claims for tortious interference with contractual relations and interference with prospective economic advantage). Here, Anderson's interference was likely the direct cause of Remick's change in position.

- Nor was this a situation where the alleged prospective economic relationship was too speculative to support the interference claim; that is, Anderson could not successfully assert that Shea would have been unable to sell the property at the higher price that included her commission. On the contrary, the listing at a higher price that *included* Shea's commission had generated substantial interest to date (including Anderson's own initial offer of $185,000).

(5) Economic harm to the plaintiff proximately caused by the defendant's acts:

- Shea suffered economic harm as a result of Anderson's actions.

- Shea's 10 percent commission ($20,000 had the property sold for $200,000, $18,500 had Remick accepted Anderson's initial $185,000 offer) is itself an undeniable economic benefit. Thus, there is a nexus between Anderson's acts and Shea's damages. While it is not a *certainty* that the property would have sold for $185,000 or more, there is evidence to support such a conclusion.

- In *Mather*, the court upheld a claim for interference with prospective economic advantage on facts substantially similar to those presented here. In *Mather*, the measure of the plaintiff's loss was the commission she would have received but for the defendant's wrongful actions.

- Thus, a court would likely conclude that Shea can maintain a claim against Anderson for interference with prospective economic advantage.

Applicant Identification

Glickman v. Phoenix Cycles, Inc.

Read the directions on the back cover.
Do not break the seal until you are told to do so.

NATIONAL CONFERENCE OF BAR EXAMINERS

INSTRUCTIONS

1. You will have 90 minutes to complete this session of the examination. This performance test is designed to evaluate your ability to handle a select number of legal authorities in the context of a factual problem involving a client.

2. The problem is set in the fictitious state of Franklin, in the fictitious Fifteenth Circuit of the United States. Columbia and Olympia are also fictitious states in the Fifteenth Circuit. In Franklin, the trial court of general jurisdiction is the District Court, the intermediate appellate court is the Court of Appeal, and the highest court is the Supreme Court.

3. You will have two kinds of materials with which to work: a File and a Library. The first document in the File is a memorandum containing the instructions for the task you are to complete. The other documents in the File contain factual information about your case and may also include some facts that are not relevant.

4. The Library contains the legal authorities needed to complete the task and may also include some authorities that are not relevant. Any cases may be real, modified, or written solely for the purpose of this examination. If the cases appear familiar to you, do not assume that they are precisely the same as you have read before. Read them thoroughly, as if they all were new to you. You should assume that the cases were decided in the jurisdictions and on the dates shown. In citing cases from the Library, you may use abbreviations and omit page references.

5. Your response must be written in the answer book provided. In answering this performance test, you should concentrate on the materials provided. What you have learned in law school and elsewhere provides the general background for analyzing the problem; the File and Library provide the specific materials with which you must work.

6. Although there are no restrictions on how you apportion your time, you should be sure to allocate ample time (about 45 minutes) to reading and digesting the materials and to organizing your answer before you begin writing it. You may make notes anywhere in the test materials; blank pages are provided at the end of the booklet. You may not tear pages from the question booklet.

7. This performance test will be graded on your responsiveness to the instructions regarding the task you are to complete, which are given to you in the first memorandum in the File, and on the content thoroughness, and organization of your response.

i

Glickman v. Phoenix Cycles, Inc.

Glickman v. Phoenix Cycles, Inc.

FILE

LIBRARY

POINT SHEET

iv

FILE

Anderson, Simmons & Bayrd, LLP
Attorneys at Law
2000 Highland Avenue
Lawton, Franklin 33623

Memorandum

To: Applicant
From: Michael Simmons
Date: February 27, 2007
Re: *George Glickman v. Phoenix Cycles, Inc.*

Our client, George Glickman, believes that he was wrongfully demoted by his employer, Phoenix Cycles, Inc., after he took leave from work under the federal Family and Medical Leave Act (FMLA). Before his FMLA leave, Glickman was *Vice President* of Bicycle Marketing; when he returned to work, he was given the position of *Coordinator* of Bicycle Marketing.

Ideally, Glickman would like to get his former job back without going to court. However, if the matter cannot be resolved short of litigation, he wants us to pursue whatever relief he can get.

After interviewing Glickman and getting his approval, I called Phoenix's general counsel, Regina Snow, and told her that we have been retained by Glickman regarding this employment matter. Snow asserted that Phoenix fully complied with the FMLA by granting Glickman's leave request. Snow acknowledged that there had been some changes to his employment, but claimed that none of the changes in his position was substantial. In any event, she said that Phoenix had legitimate business reasons for making the changes. She also asserted that the FMLA permits an employer not to reinstate an executive like Glickman to his former position.

Please draft a letter to Snow to persuade her that Phoenix has violated Glickman's FMLA rights, and refute her assertions to the contrary. In addition, you should argue that if Glickman is not restored to his former position (or its equivalent), and the matter is litigated, Phoenix will be responsible for all potential relief available under the FMLA, which you should identify and explain. Be sure to present the law and the facts in the light most favorable to Glickman's position. However, contrary authority should be explained and distinguished. Because Snow is familiar with the situation, your letter need not include a separate fact section; however, because FMLA cases are very fact-dependent, be sure to explain how the facts fit into the relevant legal standard.

1

Attorney: George, good to see you! I gather from your message that you'd like to talk about some issues with your position at Phoenix Cycles.

Glickman: My *former* position. I've been demoted.

Attorney: I'm sorry to hear that. Tell me what happened. Let's start with your history at Phoenix Cycles.

Glickman: I knew John Pearsall from competitive cycling in college. He owned a bike shop and hired me as a bike mechanic. Two years later John patented his bike frame modification and started manufacturing his own bikes under the name Phoenix Cycles.

Attorney: I didn't know the company had started as such a small outfit. Tell me more about how Phoenix is organized.

Glickman: For the last few years, Phoenix has had about 80 employees, all here at the company headquarters in Lawton, Franklin. I was one of six division vice presidents—my area was bicycle marketing. The marketing of helmets, clothing, etc., was headed by Sue Cowen in the Bicycle Accessories Division. There are four other divisions: Engineering, Production, Legal, and Accounting. At the top is the Executive Board, composed of John Pearsall, his wife, the comptroller, and two finance people.

Attorney: How did you become a vice president at Phoenix Cycles?

Glickman: I started out as a bike mechanic 15 years ago, but I really enjoyed sales, too, especially putting together sales campaigns and contributing ideas about how we could broaden our customer base. When we began to manufacture our own bikes, I continued to work in marketing. I even started working on an MBA by taking some night courses. Eventually, I became Vice President of Marketing for the Bicycle Division.

Attorney: What did that job entail?

Glickman: I was in charge of a number of marketing projects: supervising market research, monitoring Phoenix Cycles retailers, and developing new product ideas and presenting them to Engineering. I also coordinated product reviews, dealer education seminars, and industry trade shows. I had two marketing assistants working with me as well as support staff.

2

Attorney:	Okay, when did problems develop?
Glickman:	Approximately four months ago when I started having migraines. On November 15, 2006, the day before my appointment with a neurologist, I was at my desk when I got an excruciating headache and passed out. When I came to in the hospital, I was told that I'd had a stroke. My left arm and the left side of my face were numb. I spent the next five weeks recovering.
Attorney:	But I must say, you look fine now.
Glickman:	Yeah, I was amazingly lucky. I feel pretty good and I'm back to my usual activities, including biking.
Attorney:	Were there repercussions at Phoenix after your stroke?
Glickman:	At first everyone seemed really supportive. John helped me find a top physical therapist, and I was looking forward to returning to work.
Attorney:	So, what changed?
Glickman:	You know how everything always has to happen at once? My wife Lauren and I had been on a list to adopt a baby for two years. Well, in the second week of December, I was getting ready to return to work when we were notified that a baby girl was available for adoption immediately. We were told that we had a week to prepare for her.

Right away I called John at Phoenix and told him that, although I'd planned to return to work in a week, I needed another four weeks to be home to help Lauren with the baby. John seemed happy for us, but I could tell he was disappointed that I needed more time off. He suggested that I let Lauren manage the baby.

Initially, John offered to extend my leave for two more weeks. When I insisted on four weeks, he agreed, but he noted that the work was really piling up. John pointed out that my absence would create stress at the company. In the weeks before my stroke, I'd been leading a new project—a line of retro-styled bikes that were my idea. Engineering had created a prototype, and I was overseeing its testing and the marketing campaign. The project was on hold while I was recuperating, and I knew that John was anxious to get the final design to Production.

John's whole life is Phoenix Cycles, and I think he just couldn't comprehend why I would want to be gone during this time. Even though I was really excited about the new bike line, my family was my top priority.

Attorney: What was the atmosphere like when you returned to work at Phoenix?

Glickman: I was gone a total of nine weeks—five weeks for the stroke and four weeks with the baby. My recovery was 100 percent but I wasn't willing to work 70–hour weeks any more because I wanted to be with the baby. Life's too short. Anyway, shortly after I returned to work, on January 18, I learned that a marketing assistant and a member of my support staff had been transferred to the Accessories Division.

Attorney: Did John tell you why?

Glickman: John told me that while I'd been on leave, he'd discovered that my division was overstaffed, and so he'd ordered the transfers. He also said that he was making several changes that our management consultants, Hutchison Consulting, had recommended, including combining the bicycle and accessories marketing divisions for increased profitability. He said that my salary and benefits wouldn't change, but I would no longer be Vice President of Bicycle Marketing. Instead, I would be Coordinator of Bicycle Marketing, and would report to Sue Cowen, who had been promoted to Marketing Director of the new combined division. Sue's very capable, but I'd been at Phoenix a lot longer, and I know the industry better. If anyone had the ability to lead the unified marketing division, it was me.

Attorney: What are your job responsibilities now as Coordinator of Bicycle Marketing?

Glickman: I have the same salary but I am no longer a vice president. I've lost my support staff and I have to report to Sue Cowen, my former peer. Sue is overseeing all the marketing plans that I used to make alone.

Attorney: What's happened to the retro bike line?

Glickman: John said that he'd had to "put in several days on the project to cover the bases" when I was on leave and so he was "letting the chips fall where they may." After all the work I did, Sue's now in charge of the retro bike line and it is likely that she will receive the $25,000 bonus that John promised me months ago.

Attorney: Why do you think you were demoted?

Glickman: I'm not entirely sure, but the more I think about it, I'm certain that John is mad because I took time off for the baby. It just doesn't make sense to have Sue in

4

charge of all marketing without more help. In fact, she confided to me that she was stressed by her added duties. And I don't believe that John was being up front with me when he said that he was just implementing the changes recommended by the management consultants—that report was completed over eighteen months ago and this is the first time I've heard of any of Hutchison's suggestions being followed. And on top of that, I wasn't even given a chance to interview for the new marketing position that Sue was given.

   Ideally, I'd like to get my old job back. I love the company and the work that I used to do. If I can't get my job back, I think I'm entitled to damages or something for being demoted without cause.

Attorney: Did Phoenix Cycles give you any information about your rights and benefits when you began your leave, either at the time of your stroke or with the baby?

Glickman: They sent me a letter about reinstatement when John approved the last four weeks of leave. I'll get that to you tomorrow along with a copy of the Hutchison Consulting report and an article from the *Franklin Business News* about the bike I designed.

Attorney: I think that you have a claim under the federal Family and Medical Leave Act. I happen to know the general counsel at Phoenix. I'd like to talk to her about your potential claim under the FMLA. Is that okay?

Glickman: Yes, anything to help me get my old job back.

PHOENIX CYCLES GEARING UP NEW PRODUCT LINE

LAWTON, FRANKLIN – Phoenix Cycles, Inc., announced today that it will soon begin production of its latest bicycling innovation, the Retro RoadMaster. Phoenix, a relative newcomer to the biking world, is now widely recognized as one of the industry's premier manufacturers, having built a reputation for cutting-edge design backed by superior technology and a true commitment to quality. A locally owned company, Phoenix now sells bicycles and accessories nationwide and in over 30 countries. The Retro RoadMaster is expected to make its first appearance at the Franklin Bike Expo this summer, and the bikes will be shipped to Phoenix's worldwide dealers a few months later.

"Everyone at Phoenix is really thrilled with our creation of 'The Retro,'" enthused John Pearsall, Phoenix's founder and CEO. "This line embodies our passion for bicycling and our continuing desire to improve performance while giving us the chance to celebrate some of the design features that made classic bikes of the 1960s and '70s so special." Pearsall added that the engineering division at Phoenix had done outstanding work in developing the new bicycles, but "the real credit for initiating this project goes to George Glickman, one of our marketing executives. He really has a talent for knowing what will appeal to our customers, and his contribution to creating 'The Retro' has been invaluable. Unfortunately, George is on leave due to a sudden illness, but I'm looking forward to his full recovery and I'm counting on him to be a significant part of the product launch for this new model."

When asked about rumors that Phoenix might become a publicly traded company, Pearsall denied that such a move was in the works. "Our current organization has enabled us to become one of the leaders of the industry. Being a privately held company allows me to put my employees and our bicycles first, without worrying about how the numbers will spin for Wall Street."

Phoenix has received many design awards, including "Best Racing Cycle of the Year" from Cycling World magazine. The company also sponsors the Tour de Franklin, a bicycle race that attracts world-class athletes.

6

Phoenix Cycles, Inc.
Your Ride to the Future of Bicycling!
2300 LeMond Parkway
Lawton, Franklin 33623

December 19, 2006

Mr. George Glickman
2842 Trevayne Court
Lawton, Franklin 33606

Re: Request for additional FMLA leave

Dear George:

I have approved your request, arising from the adoption of your new daughter, for four weeks' Family and Medical Leave Act (FMLA) leave from your position as Vice President of Bicycle Marketing at Phoenix Cycles, Inc., effective from December 19, 2006, through January 15, 2007. This leave is in addition to the five weeks of FMLA leave you used for your illness.

Unfortunately, we cannot guarantee that restoration to your pre-leave position will be available at the end of the four weeks. You are part of the highest-paid 10 percent of Phoenix Cycles' salaried employees; thus, you are a "highly compensated employee" under the FMLA and employment restoration is not required under the FMLA for such employees. *See* 29 U.S.C. § 2614(b). If we determine that restoration after your leave is not feasible, we will telephone you at that time to discuss the matter.

Please direct any other questions regarding your benefits to Jill Carr in our Human Resources Department.

Yours truly,

John Pearsall, CEO

cc: Jill Carr, HR Dept.

Hutchison Consulting, LLC

Organizational Analysis Prepared for Phoenix Cycles, Inc.
Executive Summary
June 15, 2005

Objective

To evaluate the organizational structure at Phoenix Cycles, Inc., identify areas in need of streamlining, increase cost effectiveness, improve communication, and enhance teamwork, so that Phoenix Cycles can meet the evermore competitive demands of the bicycling marketplace.

Process

Our assessment consisted of four phases: review of Phoenix's financials for the last four quarters; interviews with key managers; observation of corporate culture; and firm-wide employee surveys.

Preliminary Conclusions

Phoenix has done tremendous work in maintaining its focus on manufacturing a high-quality product despite the pressures caused by rapid growth in the last few years. Our concern is that Phoenix's past performance may encourage complacency—something that no company can afford in today's global economy. However, small changes in organization can have a huge impact. The following recommendations are intended to help Phoenix differentiate between operations that are critical to success and those that are expendable.

Recommendations

- Create collaborative relationships with suppliers to avoid their problems becoming Phoenix's problems.
- Invest in state-of-the-art inventory tracking to make Phoenix a more responsive organization.
- Schedule annual corporate retreats to facilitate communication and foster strong working relationships between divisions and individual managers.
- Although Phoenix's profits are above average for the industry, and its six divisions currently operate at or below budget targets, the present scheme of two marketing divisions poses significant risks of unnecessary duplicative efforts. One centralized marketing division could maximize communication between the Bicycle and Accessories groups, thereby ensuring that Phoenix projects a consistent brand image across product lines. Such a restructuring would first require that Phoenix identify a manager with the experience and creativity to lead the new division.
- Reallocate all support staff positions in Marketing, Legal, and Accounting. With such a redesign, Phoenix's corporate work could be done with an 8 percent smaller workforce.
- Consider redefining the functions and composition of the Executive Board

Glickman v. Phoenix Cycles, Inc.

LIBRARY

§ 2612. Leave requirement

(a) In general.

    (1)   Entitlement to leave. An eligible employee shall be entitled to a total of 12 workweeks of leave during any 12-month period for one or more of the following:

        (A) Because of the birth of a son or daughter of the employee and in order to care for such son or daughter.

        (B) Because of the placement of a son or daughter with the employee for adoption or foster care.

*   *   *   *

        (D) Because of a serious health condition that makes the employee unable to perform the functions of the position of such employee.

*   *   *   *

§ 2614. Employment and benefits protection

(a) Restoration to position.

    (1)   In general. Except as provided in subsection (b), any eligible employee who takes leave under this Act . . . shall be entitled, on return from such leave—

        (A) to be restored by the employer to the position of employment held by the employee when the leave commenced; or

        (B) to be restored to an equivalent position with equivalent employment benefits, pay, and other terms and conditions of employment.

    (2)   Loss of benefits. The taking of leave . . . shall not result in the loss of any employment benefit accrued prior to the date on which the leave commenced.

    (3)   Limitations. Nothing in this section shall be construed to entitle any restored employee to–

        (A) the accrual of any seniority or employment benefits during any period of leave; or

        (B) any right, benefit, or position of employment other than any right, benefit, or position to which the employee would have been entitled had the employee not taken the leave.

*   *   *   *

(b) Exemption concerning certain highly compensated employees.

    (1)   Denial of restoration. An employer may deny restoration under subsection (a) to any eligible employee . . . if—

        (A) such denial is necessary to prevent substantial and grievous economic injury to the operations of the employer; [and]

        (B) the employer notifies the employee of the intent of the employer to deny restoration on such basis at the time the employer determines that such injury would occur . . . .

*   *   *   *

    (2)   Affected employees. An eligible employee described in paragraph (1) is a salaried eligible employee who is among the highest paid 10 percent of the employees employed by the employer. . . .

§ 2615. Prohibited acts

(a) Interference with rights.

(1) Exercise of rights. It shall be unlawful for any employer to interfere with, restrain, or deny the exercise of or the attempt to exercise, any right provided under this Act.

* * * *

§ 2617. Enforcement

(a) Civil action by employees.

(1) Liability. Any employer who violates this Act shall be liable to any eligible employee affected [for damages equal to the amount of]—

(i) any wages, salary, employment benefits, or other compensation denied or lost to such employee by reason of the violation; [and]

* * * *

(iii) an additional amount as liquidated damages equal to the sum of the amount described in clause (i) . . . and . . . such equitable relief as may be appropriate, including employment, reinstatement, and promotion.

* * * *

Ridley v. Santacroce General Hospital

United States Court of Appeals (15th Cir. 2001)

At issue is whether Santacroce General Hospital (SGH) violated the Family and Medical Leave Act (FMLA), 29 U.S.C. § 2601 *et seq.*, when it failed to restore Lena Ridley to her former position upon her return from maternity leave and later terminated her employment. The district court granted summary judgment to SGH, and Ridley appeals.

Ridley worked full time as nursing supervisor of SGH's surgical unit. In March 1996, Ridley began 12 weeks of paid FMLA leave for her son's birth. When she returned to work, her salary and benefits were unchanged but she was now scheduled for the evening shift every two weeks. Pre-leave, Ridley worked days only. Further, her duties as nursing supervisor had now been split between two other nurses. When she complained about the evening shifts and reduction in responsibilities, SGH offered to transfer her to pediatrics or to a per diem home health nurse position. Ridley declined the transfer to pediatrics, as there was no guarantee of a day shift and it was not a supervisory position. She also rejected the home health nurse job, because while her hourly wage would be higher, her health insurance costs would increase.

One month after her return from leave, SGH notified Ridley that, due to falling patient admissions, staffing levels were being cut and Ridley's surgical unit position was being eliminated. SGH informed Ridley that at this time the only nursing position available was for a home health nurse. For a second time, Ridley refused this option and her position at SGH was terminated. A month after her job at SGH ended, she found work at Valley View Medical Center.

Ridley filed this action alleging that SGH violated her rights under the FMLA. She is seeking reinstatement to her position as nursing supervisor of the surgical unit or its equivalent, and damages for lost wages and benefits.

The district court held that SGH had complied with the FMLA and that Ridley had not brought forth evidence to dispute SGH's claim that the changes in her position and its subsequent elimination were caused by anything other than legitimate business reasons.

The FMLA entitles an eligible employee to up to 12 weeks of leave for the birth of a child. To make out a prima facie claim for a violation of FMLA rights, a plaintiff must establish that (1) she was entitled to FMLA leave; (2) she suffered an adverse employment decision; and (3) there was a causal connection between the employee's FMLA leave and the adverse employment action. An employer who interferes with FMLA rights is liable for damages and/or appropriate equitable relief. *See* 29 U.S.C. § 2617(a)(1). The amount of lost wages or other monetary losses may be doubled (the additional portion called "liquidated

11

damages") unless the employer can prove that the violation was in good faith and that it reasonably believed that the act or omission did not violate the FMLA. While there is a strong presumption in favor of liquidated damages, the FMLA does not authorize punitive damages.

Ridley's eligibility for FMLA leave is not disputed. At issue are whether SGH restored Ridley to her pre-leave employment (or its equivalent) and whether any changes to her position were due to legitimate business reasons.

An equivalent position is one that is equal or substantially similar in the conditions of employment. *See* § 2614(a)(1)(B). The factfinder considers whether the duties and essential functions of the new position are materially different from the pre-leave position. If the undisputed facts show that, as a matter of law, the employer offered the employee an equivalent position upon her return, summary judgment in favor of the employer is appropriate.

To be equivalent, an employee's new position must be virtually identical to the employee's former position in terms of pay, benefits, and working conditions, including privileges, perquisites, and status. It must involve the same or substantially similar duties and responsibilities, which must entail substantially equivalent skill, effort, responsibility, and authority. It must also have similar opportunities for promotion and salary increase. For example, there was no FMLA violation in *Mills v. Telco, Inc.* (15th Cir. 1998) where the employee

returning from FMLA leave was given a new position not involving statewide travel as in her pre-leave auditing position, but rather auditing from a central office. Apart from the travel, the nature of the work and the pay and benefits remained the same.

That Ridley was not restored to her pre-leave position is not seriously questioned. While SGH argues that Ridley's salary remained the same, SGH concedes that eliminating her duties as a supervisor rendered her a manager in name only. The terms of her employment also changed when, after her leave, Ridley was scheduled for evening shifts. These changes, notably removing her managerial duties, were not *de minimis*, but, in contrast to the facts in *Mills*, affected the essential functions of Ridley's pre-leave employment. Nor were the other jobs SGH offered Ridley equivalent in status and duties to her previous position.

SGH asserts that the changes in Ridley's employment were necessitated by legitimate business reasons. The FMLA does not give an employee an absolute right to reinstatement. It does not confer "any right, benefit, or position of employment other than any right, benefit, or position to which the employee would have been entitled had the employee not taken the leave." 29 U.S.C. § 2614(a)(3)(B). Thus, if, as SGH claims here, Ridley's employment was already slated for reduced hours or termination for legitimate business reasons, it has not violated the Act because the adverse employment action was not causally connected to the employee's taking FMLA leave. *See, e.g., Floyd v. Cullen Mfg.* (15th

12

Cir. 1995) (no violation of FMLA where one month after returning from leave, employee was fired for excessive tardiness and insubordination). Alternatively, an employer is not required to reinstate an employee who has exceeded the amount of leave permitted under the statute.

Here, SGH relied on testimony from its human resources manager, Ann Levine, who stated that SGH's accounting office projected lower patient admissions for the second half of 1996 and that such projections required the staff reduction in Ridley's unit. Levine noted that Ridley was not the most senior nurse in her unit and that SGH had been working on staff restructuring prior to Ridley's leave.

SGH, however, does not dispute the fact that Ridley was the only surgical staff member in six years to take a full 12 weeks of maternity leave. Nor does it dispute that hers was the only nursing position eliminated among all of SGH's medical departments. SGH also concedes that six months after Ridley's termination, the surgical unit resumed previous staffing levels.

The relatively brief interval between Ridley's return from leave and her termination is problematic, as is the fact that she was the only member of the surgical unit to use the full amount of maternity leave in several years. Most telling, SGH does not dispute that it returned to full staffing levels a few months after it eliminated Ridley's position. Thus, summary judgment in favor of SGH on

Ridley's FMLA claims was improper as there is a genuine issue of material fact regarding whether SGH's actions were the result of a legitimate business decision and not in response to Ridley's having taken 12 weeks of FMLA leave.

Reversed and remanded.

13

Jones v. Oakton School District

United States Court of Appeals (15th Cir. 2004)

This case arises from plaintiff Greg Jones's use of Family and Medical Leave Act (FMLA) leave. Jones, an employee of the defendant Oakton School District, appeals from the lower court's ruling that the district could lawfully refuse to reinstate him under the FMLA.

Jones worked for the district as principal of Taft Elementary School. In March 2002, Jones requested, and was granted, 12 weeks of FMLA leave for back surgery. This meant that Jones would be absent during budget planning for the next school year as well as during the preparation period for a new test required by Franklin law, the Elementary Skills Assessment. Eligibility for certain educational grants depended upon how Taft students performed on the assessment.

Concerned that Jones would be unavailable during this time, the district hired Anne Rios to take over as principal at Taft. Rios, an experienced school administrator, would not fill the position on a temporary basis, so the district hired her as a permanent replacement for Jones. Further, because Taft had had substantial staff turnover in the preceding two years, the district decided that a permanent replacement was preferable to an interim principal.

In late May, Jones asked to return to work, but the district refused to dismiss Rios. Nor did it offer Jones employment as principal of another school, as all such positions were filled. Jones then commenced this action against the district.

Jones's right to take 12 weeks of FMLA leave for his serious medical condition is not contested. The question is whether the district may deny restoration to Jones under the FMLA's exception for highly compensated employees, 29 U.S.C. § 2614(b). If an employer can show that reinstatement of the employee would result in "substantial and grievous economic injury," the FMLA permits an employer to elect not to reinstate that employee. We note that the requisite economic injury is not that caused by the employee's *absence*, but the injury that will result from *restoring* the employee to his prior position or its equivalent. It is not disputed here that Jones received the required notice under § 2614(b)(1)(B).

Jones argues that the district failed to meet the "substantial and grievous" standard as a matter of law. We disagree.

There is no precise test that identifies the extent of economic injury that an employer must show to take advantage of the FMLA's key employee exception. The pertinent regulation defines "substantial and grievous economic injury" as follows:

> If the reinstatement of a "key employee" threatens the economic viability of the employer, that would constitute "substantial and grievous economic injury." A lesser injury which causes substantial, long-term

14

economic injury would also be sufficient. Minor inconveniences and costs that the employer would experience in the normal course of doing business would certainly not constitute "substantial and grievous economic injury." 29 C.F.R. § 825.218(c).

When assessing economic impact, the employer may consider the cost of reinstating the employee to an equivalent position if hiring a permanent replacement for the employee on leave was unavoidable. *Id.*

Here, the district had no reasonable alternative but to hire a permanent re-placement for Jones. Restoring Jones to his prior position would require the district to breach its employment contract with Rios. Further, we are satisfied that placing Jones in a position equivalent to school principal would create substantial economic hardship.

Jones is among the highest paid 10 percent of the district's salaried employees. The district provided ample evidence that there were no funds available to pay for another position. Indeed, part of the budget planning that occurred during Jones's leave involved selecting programs to cut in the face of declining tax revenue and increasing enrollments. Because of the district's financial constraints, restoring Jones after contracting with Rios would create more than a minor inconvenience—the added stress of his salary would force cuts in other areas and the repercussions would be felt for years to come. As a public entity, the district cannot raise its prices to make up for the shortfall. We conclude that, as a matter of law, the district met the threshold for "substantial and grievous economic injury," and that therefore Jones's FMLA rights were not violated.

Affirmed.

NOTES

POINT SHEET

Glickman v. Phoenix Cycles, Inc.

DRAFTERS' POINT SHEET

In this performance test item applicants' law firm represents George Glickman, who was demoted from his vice president position at Phoenix Cycles, Inc. Glickman recently returned to work after taking nine weeks' leave to recover from a stroke and to care for his newly adopted baby daughter. It appears that his demotion is connected to his leave from work; if so, Phoenix's actions violate Glickman's rights under the Family and Medical Leave Act (FMLA), 29 U.S.C. § 2601 *et seq.*, specifically, the right to be restored to pre-leave employment or an equivalent position. The supervising partner has already spoken to Phoenix's in-house counsel, Regina Snow, in an attempt to resolve Glickman's claims without resorting to litigation. Applicants' task is to draft a follow-up letter to Ms. Snow persuasively setting forth the basis for Glickman's claim under the FMLA and explaining why none of the exceptions in the Act applies. The letter should discuss the specific FMLA provisions that Phoenix has violated and demonstrate that Glickman has a right to relief under the statute. In addition, applicants are to respond to the potential defenses raised by Phoenix's in-house counsel in her conversation with the managing partner.

The File consists of the task memo describing the assignment, the transcript of the client interview, a newspaper article about Phoenix's new bike design, a letter to Glickman regarding his FMLA leave, and a management consulting firm's report on Phoenix.

The Library contains provisions of the FMLA that may or may not be relevant and two cases from the United States Court of Appeals for the Fifteenth Circuit.

The following discussion covers all of the points the drafters intended to raise in the problem. Applicants need not cover them all to receive passing or even excellent grades. Grading decisions are entirely within the discretion of the user jurisdictions.

I.   **Overview and Format**

Applicants' work product should resemble legal correspondence (including citations to the relevant legal authority) and be persuasive in tone. Because this is a fact-intensive item and the analysis will require applicants to apply the facts to the legal standards, no separate statement of facts is necessary, and applicants are so informed in the task memorandum. (However, some applicants may begin with an introductory paragraph briefly describing the nature of the matter and noting that this is a follow-up letter to the previous telephone conversation between the supervising partner and Phoenix's in-house counsel.)

There are four issues that applicants should identify and discuss:

- Whether Phoenix restored Glickman to the same or an equivalent position upon his return from FMLA leave.

- Assuming Glickman was demoted, whether Phoenix acted in furtherance of legitimate business reasons in failing to restore Glickman to the same or equivalent position.

- Whether Phoenix properly denied Glickman reinstatement based on the "key employee" exemption under the FMLA.

- What potential remedies Glickman would be entitled to under the FMLA.

These headings are suggestions only. Likewise, applicants need not discuss these issues in any particular order, although some forms of organization may be more persuasive to opposing counsel than others. It is left to the user jurisdictions to decide whether the organization of applicants' papers is a basis for grading distinctions. All issues require applicants to examine the facts of the case in light of the relevant FMLA provisions and case law.

II.   Argument: Phoenix Violated Glickman's FMLA Rights.

The FMLA entitles eligible employees to take up to 12 weeks of leave from work for a serious medical condition, or for the birth or adoption of a child. 29 U.S.C. § 2612(a)(1). Upon returning from FMLA leave, an employee is entitled to his or her pre-leave position or its equivalent. It is unlawful "for any employer to interfere with, restrain, or deny the exercise of or the attempt to exercise, any right provided under this Act." § 2615. Employees may pursue a private right of action against an employer who interferes with the rights conferred by the statute. *See* § 2617. Employers violate the FMLA when they deny an employee the benefits provided by the statute (e.g., deny requests for leave, refuse to return employee to pre-leave employment) or when they take negative action against an employee who has taken FMLA leave (e.g., demotion, termination).

As an employee claiming that his employer has violated the FMLA, Glickman has the initial burden to establish a prima facie case that his leave from work is protected by the statute.

Ridley v. Santacroce Gen. Hosp. (15th Cir. 2001). A plaintiff must establish (1) that she was entitled to FMLA leave; (2) that she suffered an adverse employment decision; and (3) that there was a causal connection between the employee's FMLA leave and the adverse employment action. *Id.*

Although it appears that Phoenix does not challenge the first component, that Glickman had the right to take FMLA leave, thorough applicants may briefly note the basis for Glickman's entitlement to leave:

- Both Glickman's stroke (a serious medical condition) and the adoption of his child are valid reasons for FMLA leave. 29 U.S.C. § 2612(a)(1)(B) & (D).

- The length of his leave, a total of nine weeks, is well within the 12 weeks allowed by the FMLA. 29 U.S.C. § 2612(a)(1).

A. Phoenix Did Not Restore Glickman to His Pre-Leave Employment or Its Equivalent.

To establish that Phoenix denied Glickman the rights accorded by the FMLA, applicants should argue that Glickman was not restored to his pre-leave position or its equivalent, referencing the applicable FMLA section and the court's discussion in *Ridley*. Such a discussion should include the following points:

- Employees returning from FMLA leave are entitled to restoration of their previous position or to an equivalent position. 29 U.S.C. § 2614(a).

- "Equivalent position" is defined by the FMLA as employment with equivalent benefits, pay, and "other terms and conditions of employment." 29 U.S.C. § 2614(a)(1)(B).

- An equivalent position "must be virtually identical to the employee's former position in terms of pay, benefits, and working conditions, including privileges, perquisites, and status. It must involve the same or substantially similar duties and responsibilities, which must entail substantially equivalent skill, effort, responsibility, and authority. It must also have similar opportunities for promotion and salary increase." *Ridley.*

- Thus the focus in the "equivalent position" inquiry is "whether the duties and essential functions of the new position are materially different from the pre-leave position." *Id.* In *Ridley*, the combination of changing the plaintiff's work hours and greatly decreasing her job responsibilities rendered her employment materially different from her pre-FMLA leave position.

- However, *de minimis* changes to employment will not contravene the FMLA. *See Mills v. Telco, Inc.* (15th Cir. 1998) (no FMLA violation where post-leave employment differed from pre-leave position only in that employee now worked from central office and no longer traveled to branch offices) (cited in *Ridley*).

- Applicants should compare Glickman's pre- and post-leave employment, noting the changes in his responsibilities and status.

- Before taking FMLA leave, Glickman was Vice President of Bicycle Marketing, one of six division heads working under the guidance of Phoenix's CEO and Executive Board. He had two marketing assistants and support staff working for him. His duties included supervising market research, monitoring retailers, developing new product concepts and presenting them to Engineering, coordinating product reviews, overseeing dealer education, and preparing for industry trade shows.

- After returning from nine weeks of FMLA leave, Glickman's job title was changed to Coordinator of Bicycle Marketing, although his salary and benefits remained the same. Other changes to his employment included:

  - Glickman supervised fewer people; two of his marketing assistants were transferred to another division.

  - Glickman now reports to Sue Cowen, his former counterpart in Bicycle Accessories, who was promoted over him to run the new consolidated marketing division.

- Glickman said that after returning to work, "Sue is overseeing all the marketing plans that I used to make alone."

- Although Glickman initiated the idea for the Retro bike line, Sue Cowen is now in charge of that project and will likely receive the $25,000 bonus for it that John Pearsall, Phoenix's CEO, promised Glickman.

- Glickman has effectively been demoted, in that there is now a new layer of management between his position and the Executive Board.

- Analogizing to *Ridley*, applicants should argue that Phoenix failed to restore Glickman to a position that was equivalent to his pre-leave employment as Vice

President of Bicycle Marketing. Glickman's responsibilities and status within the company were reduced substantially; thus the changes are not *de minimis* but in fact deprive Glickman of his right to job restoration under the FMLA.

B.   Phoenix Did Not Have Legitimate Business Reasons for Failing to Restore Glickman to Pre-leave Employment or Its Equivalent.

The third element of establishing a violation of FMLA rights is that the plaintiff employee must demonstrate a nexus between the adverse employment action and taking FMLA leave. *Ridley.* Applicants should recognize that under § 2614 the right to job reinstatement under the FMLA is not absolute, and employees taking leave are not entitled to "any right, benefit, or position of employment other than any right, benefit, or position to which the employee would have been entitled had the employee not taken the leave." In *Ridley*, the court noted that the FMLA is not violated if the employee's position "was already slated for reduced hours or termination for legitimate business reasons."

When viewed overall, the facts suggest that Glickman's demotion was very likely a negative response to his taking FMLA leave (particularly the additional four weeks to care for his newly adopted daughter) rather than the result of legitimate business reasons. Facts supporting this allegation include:

- As in *Ridley*, the temporal proximity between taking FMLA leave and the negative employment action supports an inference that the employer's action is not simply the result of a business decision. Glickman learned that his bicycle-marketing division was being subsumed into a larger marketing department only three days after returning from leave.

- Nothing was communicated to Glickman during his leave to indicate that such changes were imminent or even under consideration.

- Glickman was not afforded an opportunity to apply for the position that was ultimately handed to Sue Cowen.

- Such substantial changes in company structure on such short notice would seem inconsistent with a planned, deliberate reorganization.

- John Pearsall tried to dissuade Glickman from taking four weeks' leave for the adoption of Glickman's daughter.

- Pearsall told Glickman that he'd had to put in time on the Retro bike project because Glickman was on leave—a possible reason for Pearsall's resenting the extra four weeks for the adoption. Indeed, Pearsall remarked to Glickman that he was "letting the chips fall where they may."

- This statement is in stark contrast to the *Franklin Business News* article about Phoenix, dated November 24, 2006, just before Glickman requested additional FMLA leave for the adoption, in which Pearsall praises Glickman's contributions to the new bike line and his performance as a marketing executive.

- Also in the news article, John Pearsall denies that an IPO is in the works and observes that, "Our current organization has enabled us to become one of the leaders of the industry." This remark underscores the last-minute character of the changes in Glickman's position.

- Statements in the Hutchison Consulting report conclude that the company is profitable with its current (i.e., pre-FMLA leave) organization.

- According to Glickman's comments at the client interview, Sue Cowen is feeling stressed with all the added responsibilities of her promotion to Marketing Director. In his interview, Glickman suggests that he was better qualified for the new Marketing Director position.

Nevertheless, there is some support for Phoenix to assert that legitimate business reasons justify the changes in Glickman's employment:

- The Hutchison Consulting report expressly recommends consolidating the marketing divisions, stating that "the present scheme of two marketing divisions poses significant risks of unnecessary duplicative efforts."

  - However, the Hutchison report was completed approximately 18 months ago and the changes in Glickman's employment were the first he'd heard of any of the consultant's recommendations being implemented.

- It is only Glickman's opinion that he was better qualified to head the new division.

- Glickman indicates that, because of his new family responsibilities, he is no longer willing to work the long hours that he did before taking FMLA leave. Phoenix may argue that Glickman is not available to carry the workload of having sole responsibility for bicycle and accessories marketing.

C. Phoenix Cannot Deny Glickman Reinstatement Based on the FMLA's "Key Employee" Exemption.

According to the task memorandum, Phoenix intends to deny any FMLA claim by Glickman on the basis that "the FMLA permits an employer not to reinstate an executive like Glickman to his former position." Thus, applicants should address and refute application of the FMLA's "key employee" exemption.

Under 29 U.S.C. § 2614(b), employers may deny job restoration to "certain highly compensated employees." This exemption applies to salaried employees that are among the highest-paid 10 percent of the employer's workforce. § 2614(b)(2). Such workers are also known as "key employees." *See Jones v. Oakton School District* (15th Cir. 2004).

To successfully use the "key employee" exemption an employer must show that

1. denying restoration was necessary in order "to prevent substantial and grievous economic injury to the operations of the employer," and

2. upon determining that such an injury would occur, the employer notified the affected employee that he or she would not be restored to pre-FMLA leave employment.

Jones provides guidance as to what constitutes "substantial and grievous economic injury." The FMLA does not require job restoration when doing so "threatens the economic viability of the employer." *Id.* A lesser harm, but one that causes "substantial, long-term economic injury," may be sufficient for an employer to deny job restoration without running afoul of the FMLA. Minor inconveniences and costs imposed on the employer, however, do not meet the "substantial and grievous" standard. *Id.*

When discussing whether Phoenix could rely on the FMLA's key employee exemption as justification for not restoring Glickman to his pre-leave employment, pertinent facts are:

- Phoenix informed Glickman, when granting the additional four weeks of leave, that he is among the highest-paid 10 percent of Phoenix employees, and that restoration to his pre-leave position was not guaranteed.

- However, the letter indicates that Phoenix has not yet determined whether Glickman's job will be available at the end of his leave—"If we determine that restoration after your leave is not feasible, we will telephone you at that time to discuss the matter." It is unclear when Phoenix made that determination and/or explicitly conveyed such information to Glickman. Presumably, the conversation in which Pearsall told

Glickman that Phoenix was implementing the management consultant's recommendations constituted the required notice.

- The fact that Phoenix did not notify Glickman of its intention to invoke the highly
  compensated employee exemption until he requested the additional leave to care
  for his new daughter casts further doubt on whether the change in Glickman's
  position was the result of a legitimate business reason. (*See* section B, *infra*).

- Applicants should focus on whether Phoenix could prevail on a claim that restoring
  Glickman would cause substantial and grievous economic harm.

  - Upon returning to work, Glickman's salary and benefits were the same; only his
    job description and title changed. The inference is that continuing to employ
    Glickman in a position equivalent to his pre-leave position would not cause
    Phoenix significant financial hardship.

  - Unlike the situation in *Jones*, Phoenix did not have to hire a permanent
    replacement (or even a temporary replacement) while Glickman was on FMLA
    leave, despite the fact that Pearsall took on some of his responsibilities during that
    time.

- The notification to Glickman that he was considered a "key employee" came only
  when he requested four weeks leave to care for his daughter—not when he first took
  FMLA leave to recuperate from his stroke.

Note: In *Jones*, the court emphasized that the pertinent harm is not that caused by the
employee *taking* leave, but the harm resulting from *restoring* the employee to the pre-leave
position. Thus, applicants who focus on Pearsall's comments to Glickman that he (Pearsall) had
worked hard to "cover the bases" while Glickman was on leave (indicating that Glickman's
absence from the company during the production of the Retro RoadMaster created a hardship)
have missed the point on the question of whether Glickman may be denied job restoration
because of his key employee status.

D.   Potential Damages and Other Relief

Section 2617 of the FMLA provides that an employer who violates an employee's rights
under the statute is liable for damages equal to wages, salary, benefits, and/or other
compensation lost by the employee because of the employer's actions. The FMLA also allows
for double damages: an employee can recover liquidated damages equal to the award of lost

wages or other compensation. There is a presumption in favor of such damages, but the court has discretion to deny an award of liquidated damages if the employer can show it had a good faith belief that its actions were not in violation of the FMLA. *See Ridley*. Finally, a wronged employee may receive "such equitable relief as may be appropriate, including employment, reinstatement, and promotion." § 2617(a)(1)(iii).

Thus, the letter to Phoenix's counsel should state that if Glickman is forced to sue, he will seek damages in the amount of other compensation lost since he was demoted, liquidated damages, and a return to his pre-leave position at the company.

- Because Glickman's current position as Coordinator of Bicycle Marketing is not equivalent to his pre-leave employment as Vice President of Bicycle Marketing, a court may award equitable relief in the form of reinstatement.

- Although Glickman's salary and benefits have not changed, it appears likely that he will lose out on a $25,000 bonus that he would have received had he not taken FMLA leave.

  - The lost bonus would qualify as "other compensation" under the FMLA, as it is not part of his normal wages or salary.

- Given the description of Pearsall's comments when Glickman requested four weeks' additional leave to care for his new daughter, it is doubtful that Phoenix could successfully argue that it had a good faith belief that its failure to reinstate Glickman to his pre-leave employment was consistent with its obligations under the FMLA.

- Thus it is likely that a court would award another $25,000 in liquidated damages.

The key point is that applicants recognize that Glickman's remedies are not restricted to compensatory monetary damages; the FMLA explicitly allows plaintiffs to receive double damages and reinstatement as forms of relief.